# Voice Over!
## Seiyu Academy

Vol.11
Story & Art by
**Maki Minami**

**Vol.11**

| | |
|---|---|
| Chapter 59 | 3 |
| Chapter 60 | 35 |
| Chapter 61 | 65 |
| Chapter 62 | 95 |
| Chapter 63 | 125 |
| Chapter 64 | 155 |
| Bonus Pages | 187 |

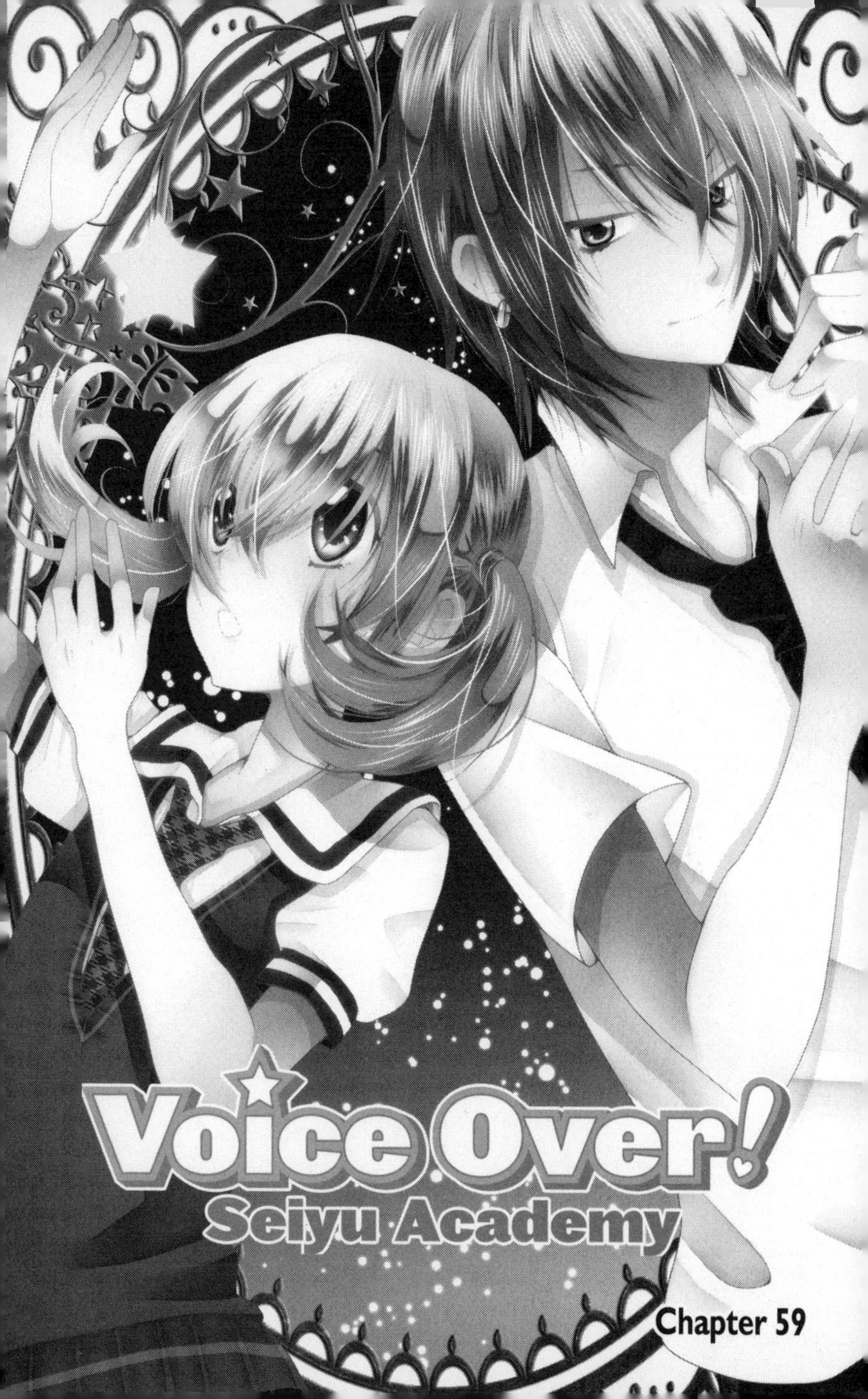
Voice Over!
Seiyu Academy
Chapter 59

VOICE OVER!

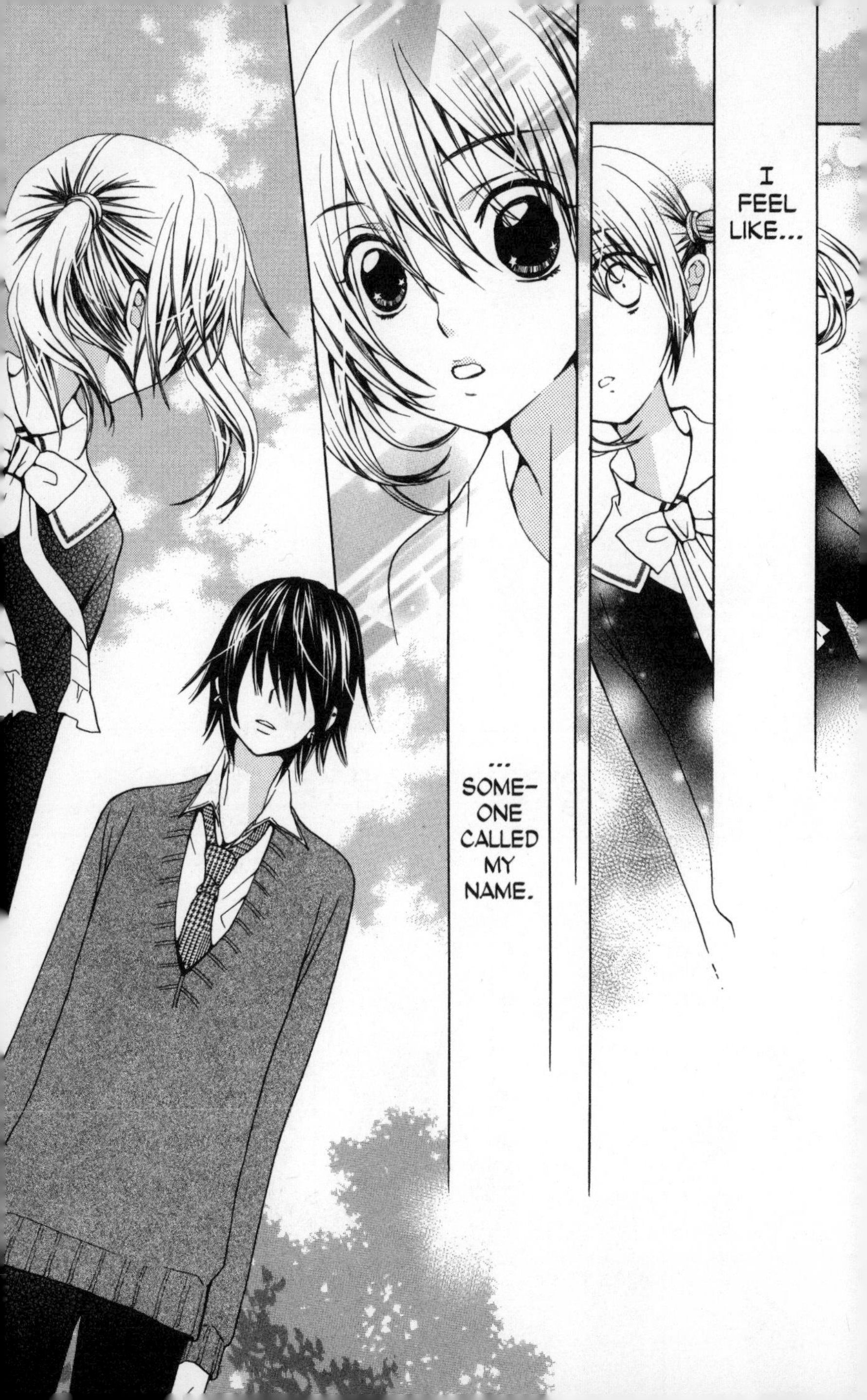
I FEEL LIKE...
...SOME-ONE CALLED MY NAME.

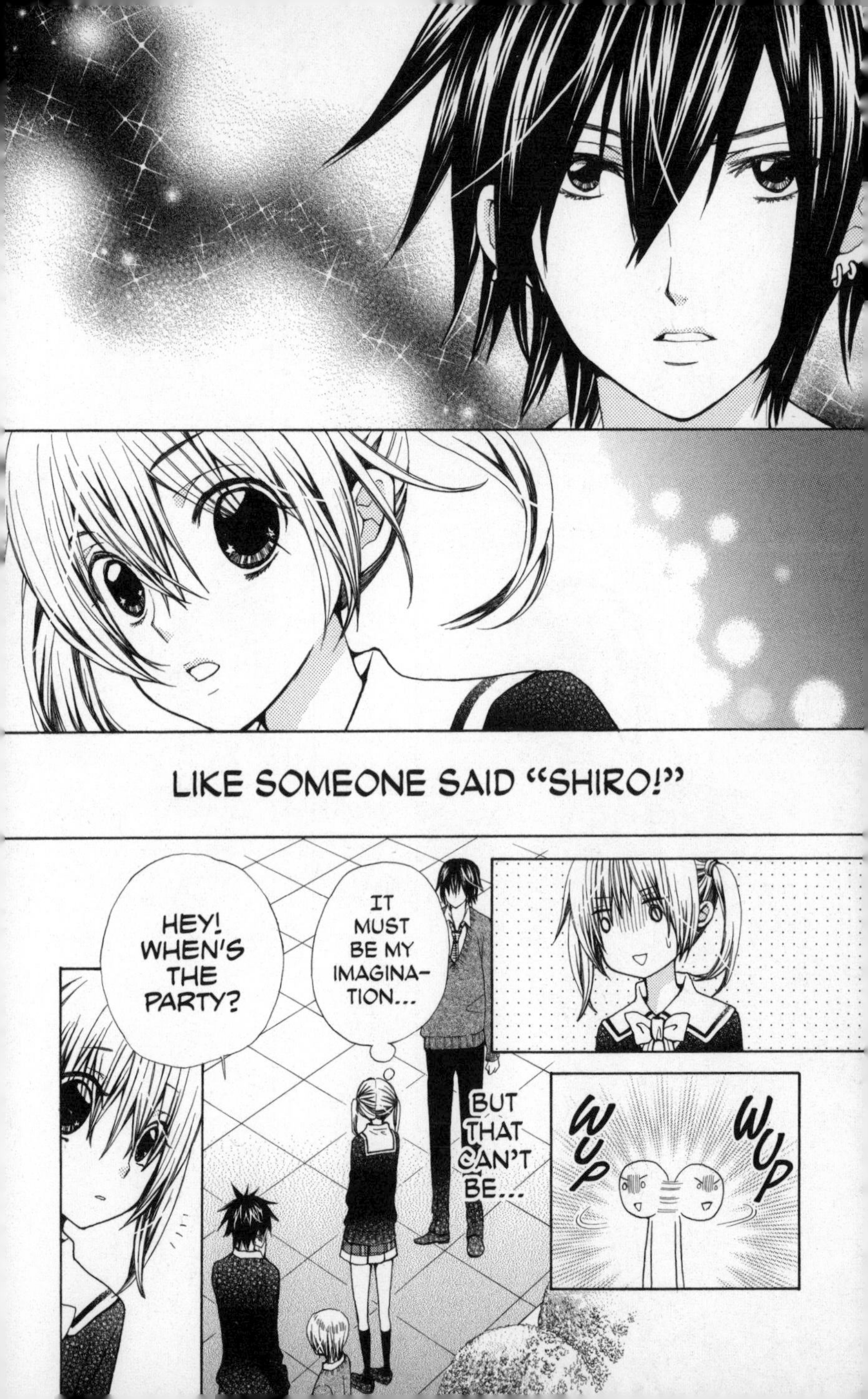

LIKE SOMEONE SAID "SHIRO!"
WUP WUP
IT MUST BE MY IMAGINATION...
BUT THAT CAN'T BE...
HEY! WHEN'S THE PARTY?

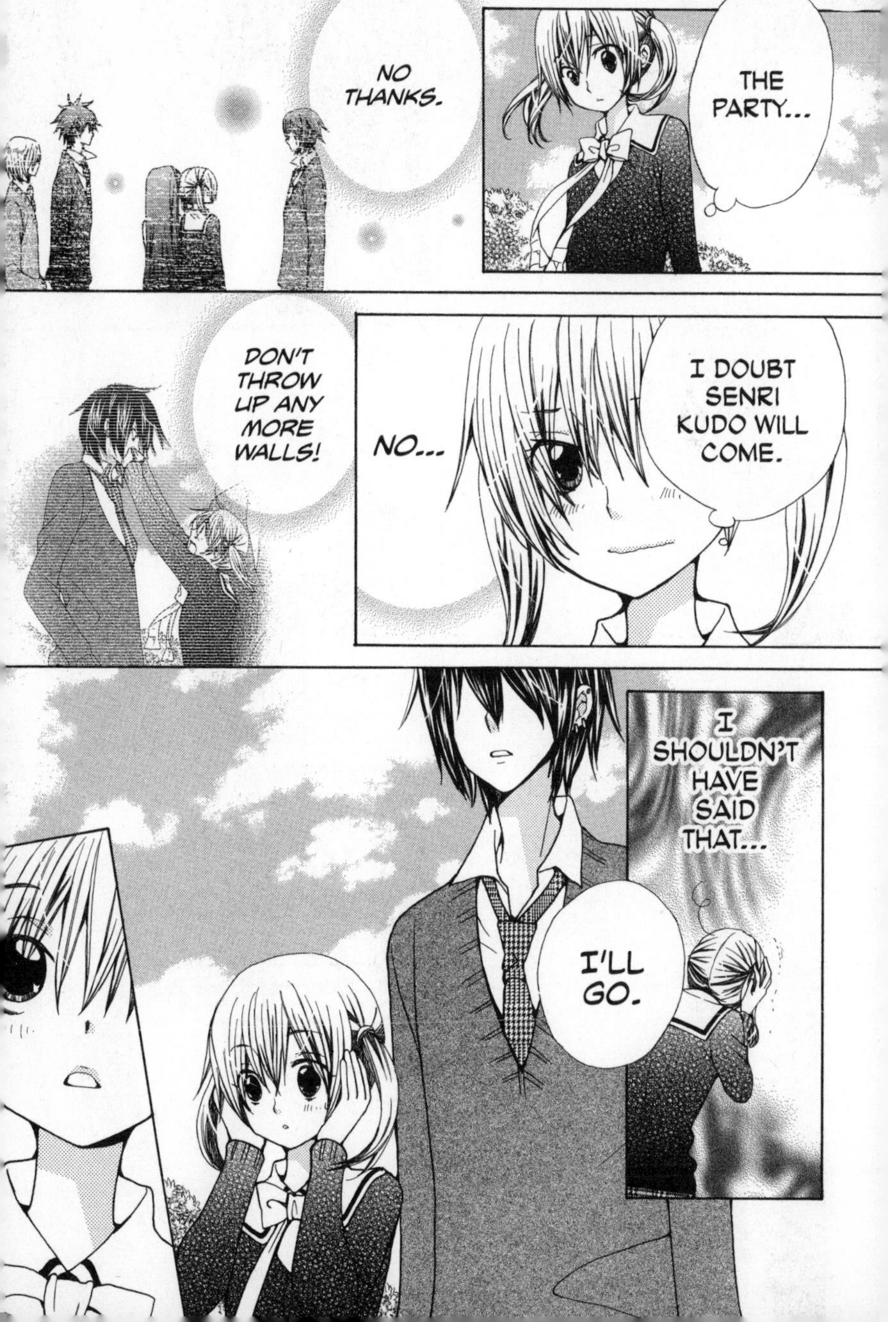
THE PARTY...
NO THANKS.
I DOUBT SENRI KUDO WILL COME.
NO...
DON'T THROW UP ANY MORE WALLS!
I SHOULDN'T HAVE SAID THAT...
I'LL GO.

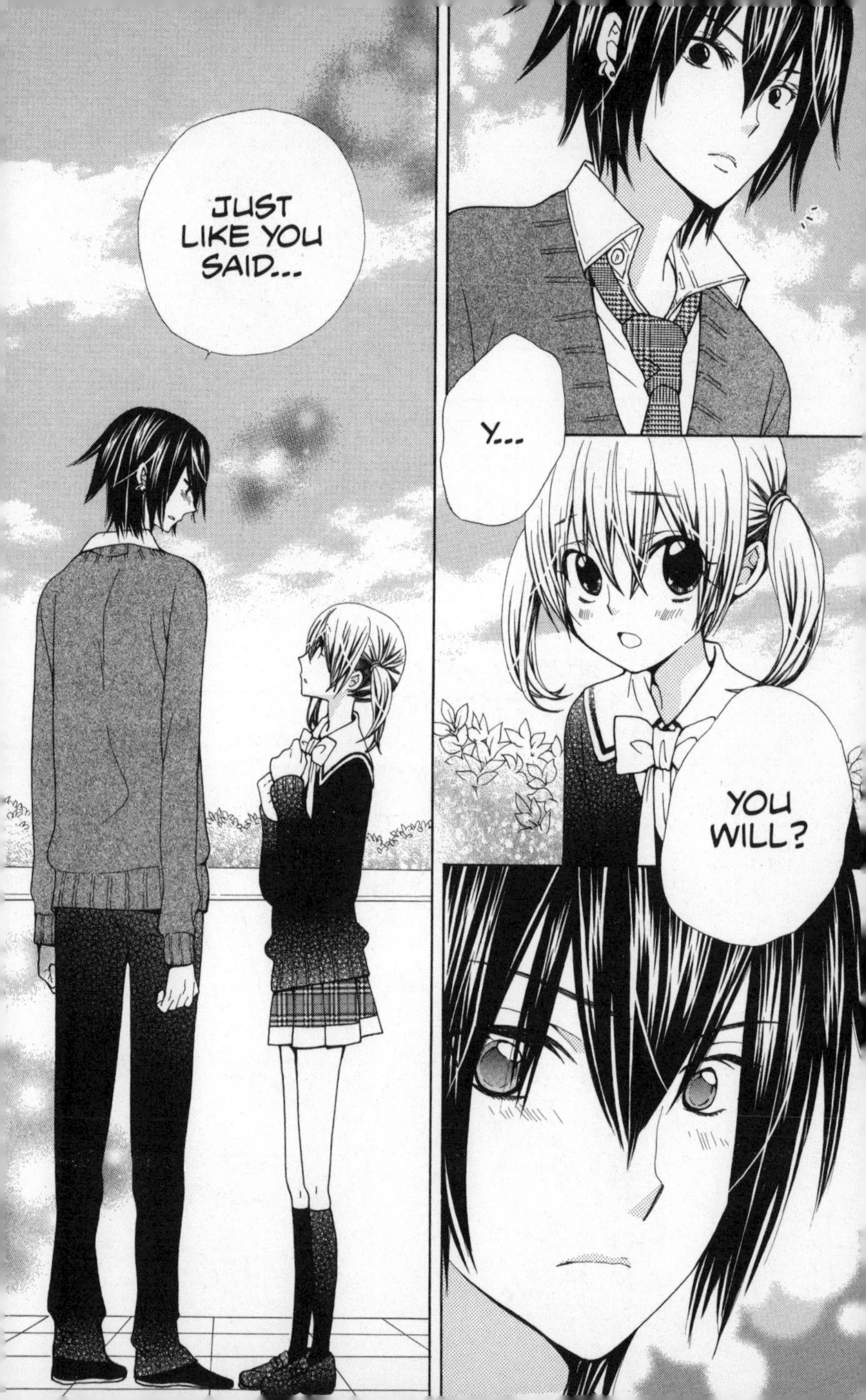
Y...
YOU WILL?
JUST LIKE YOU SAID...

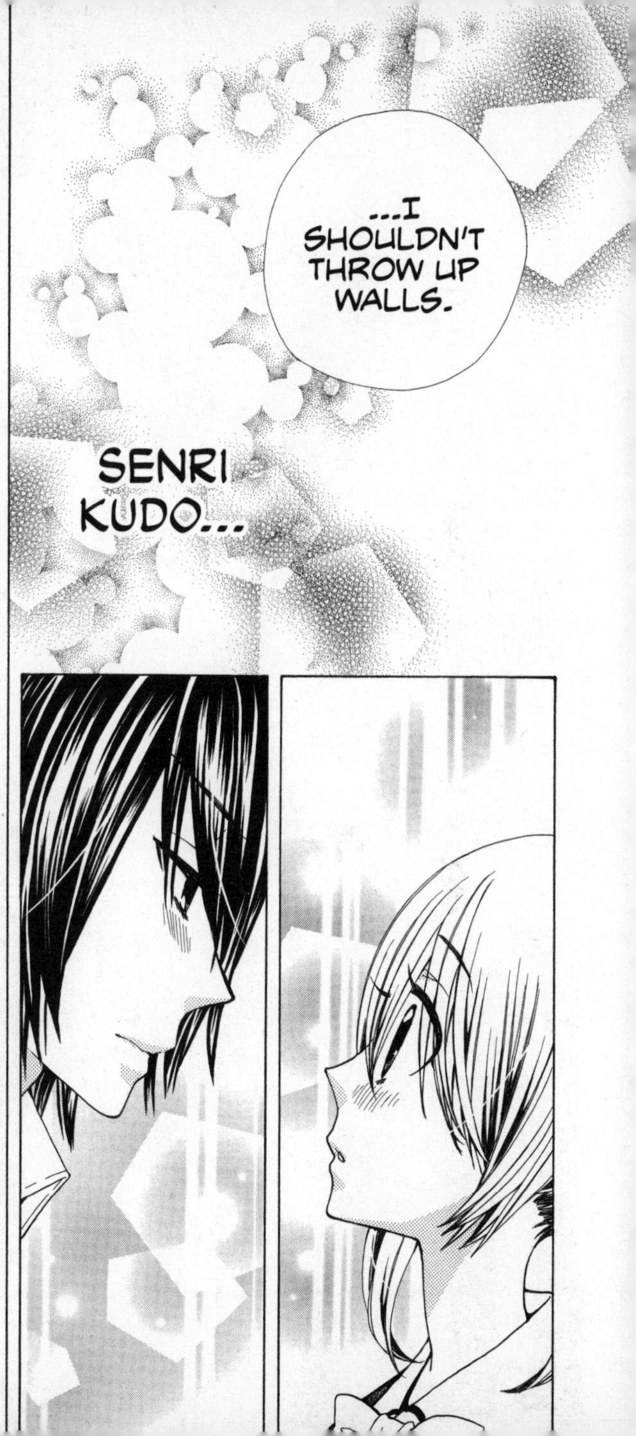
...I SHOULDN'T THROW UP WALLS.
SENRI KUDO...

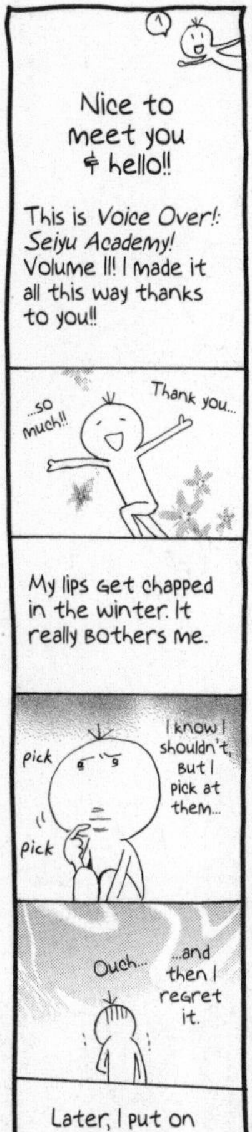
Nice to meet you & hello!!
This is Voice Over!: Seiyu Academy! Volume 11! I made it all this way thanks to you!!
Thank you...
...so much!!
My lips get chapped in the winter. It really bothers me.
I know I shouldn't, but I pick at them...
pick
pick
Ouch...
...and then I regret it.
Later, I put on lip balm.
* See Vol. 5 Sidebar.
Then in the spring...
Hay fever?
It's not allergies
smirk
smirk
That sneeze...

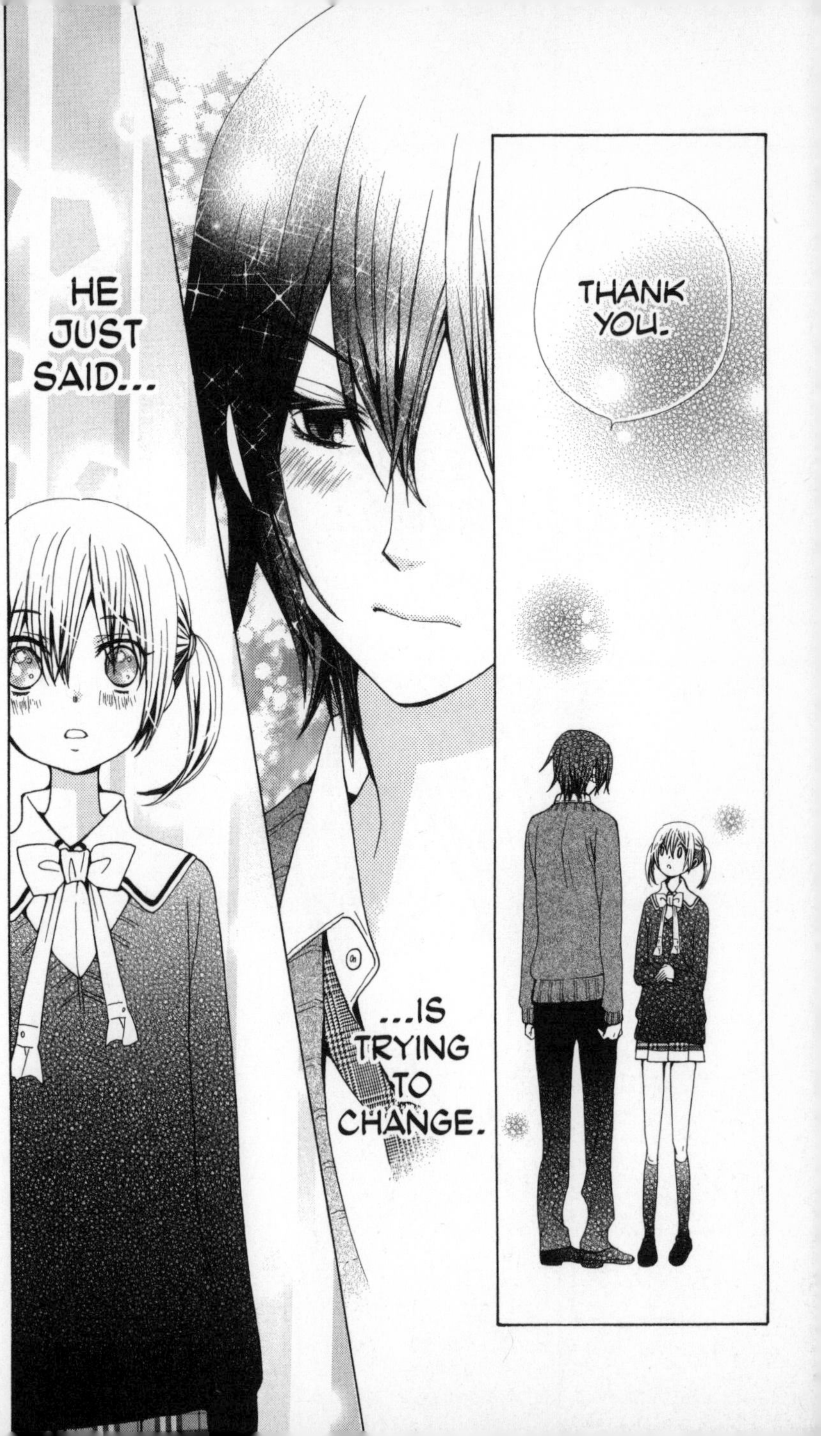
THANK YOU.
HE JUST SAID...
...IS TRYING TO CHANGE.

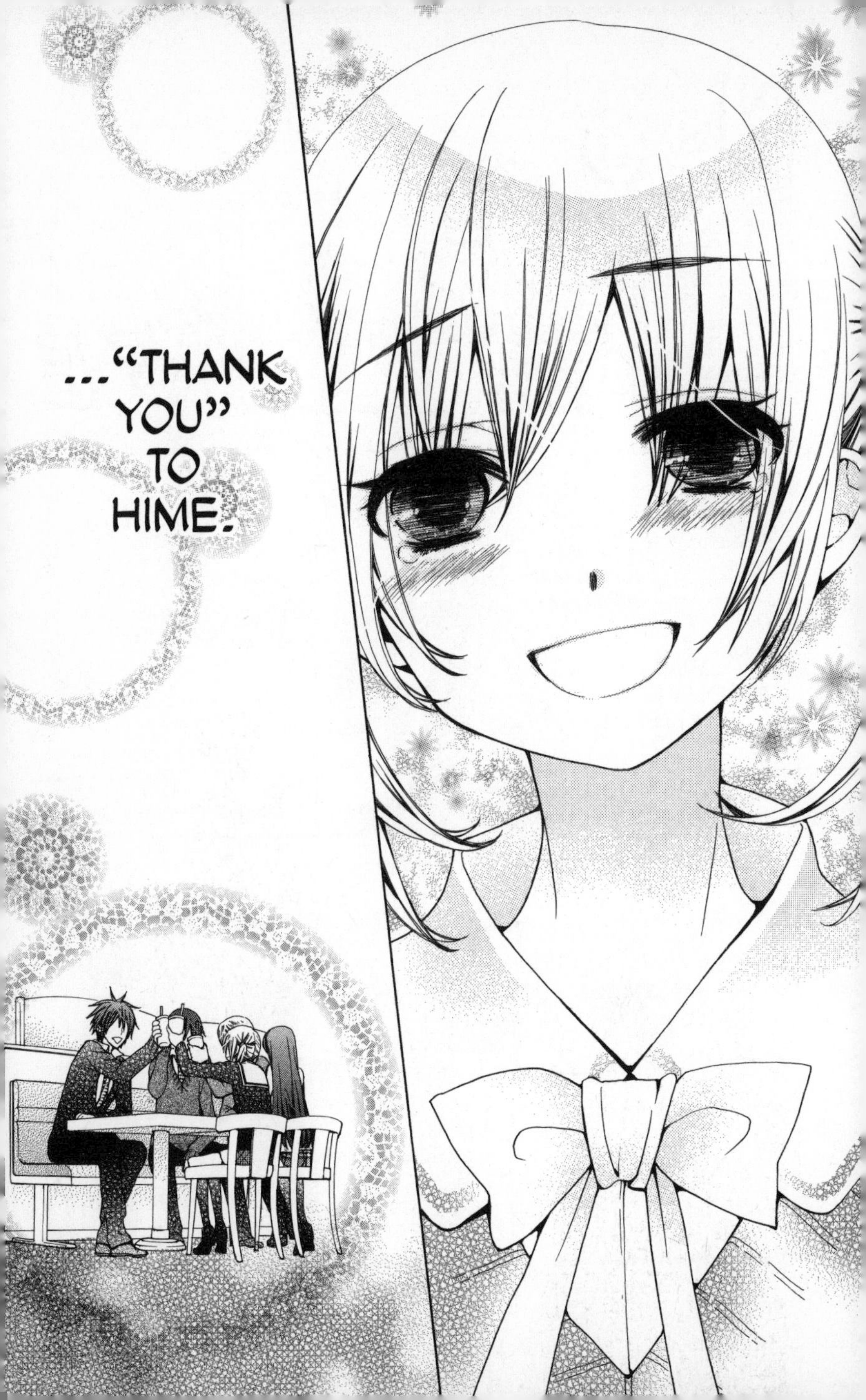
..."THANK YOU" TO HIME.

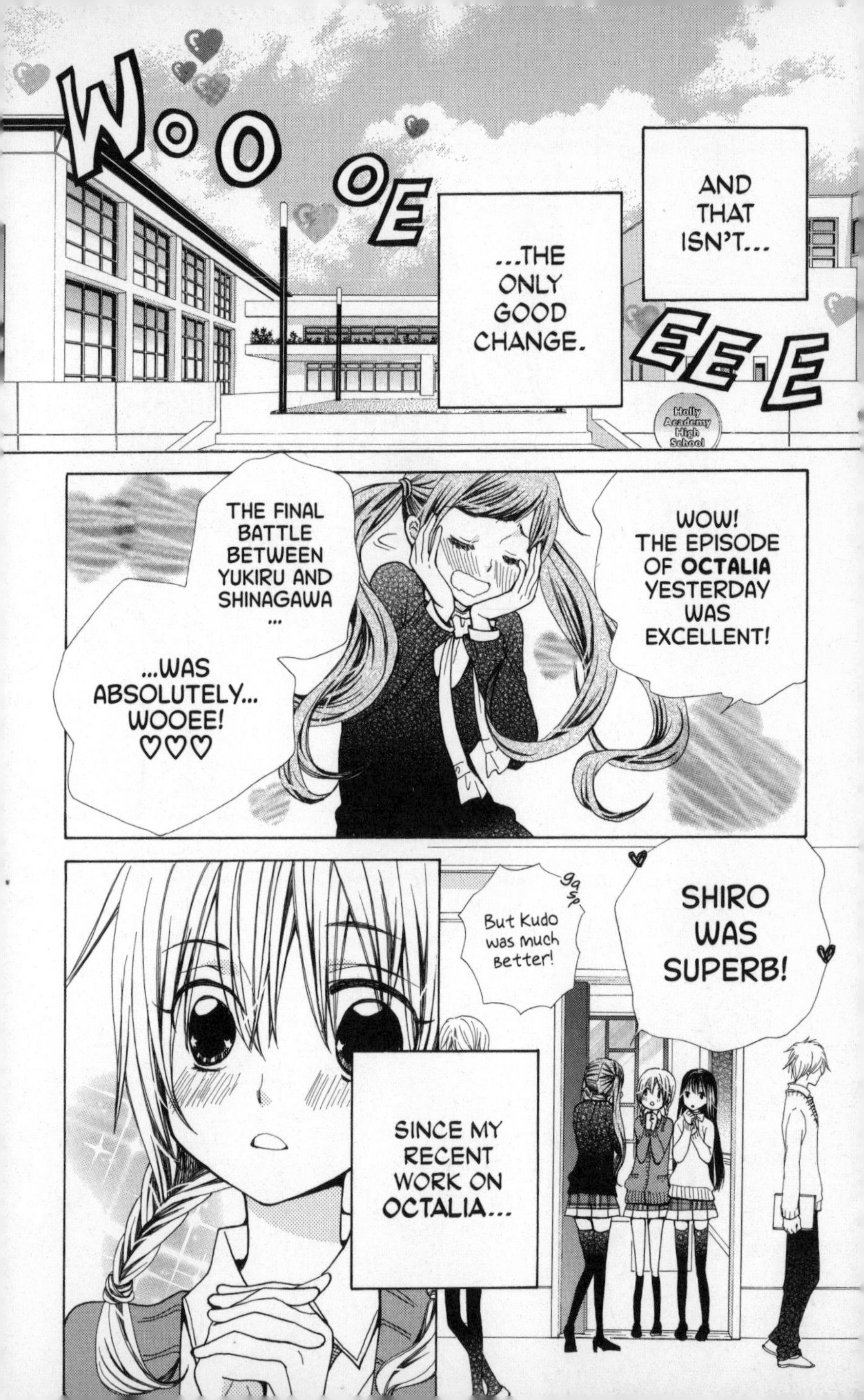
AND THAT ISN'T...
...THE ONLY GOOD CHANGE.
WOOOEEEE
Holly Academy High School
WOW! THE EPISODE OF OCTALIA YESTERDAY WAS EXCELLENT!
THE FINAL BATTLE BETWEEN YUKIRU AND SHINAGAWA...
...WAS ABSOLUTELY... WOOEE! ♡♡♡
SHIRO WAS SUPERB!
gasp
But Kudo was much better!
SINCE MY RECENT WORK ON OCTALIA...

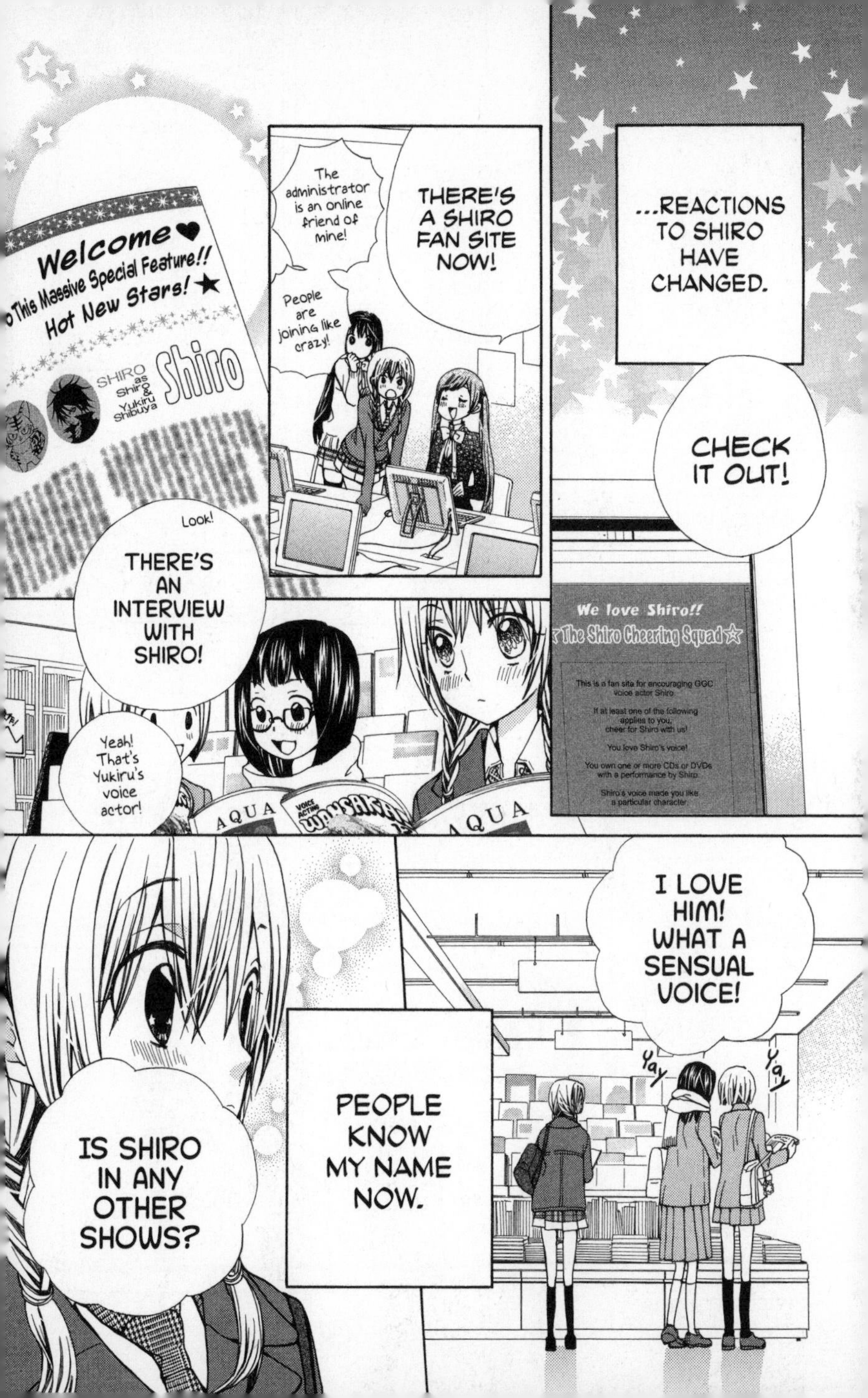

...REACTIONS TO SHIRO HAVE CHANGED.
CHECK IT OUT!
We love Shiro!!
☆The Shiro Cheering Squad☆
This is a fan site for encouraging GGC voice actor Shiro.
If at least one of the following applies to you, cheer for Shiro with us!
You love Shiro's voice!
You own one or more CDs or DVDs with a performance by Shiro.
Shiro's voice made you like a particular character.
THERE'S A SHIRO FAN SITE NOW!
The administrator is an online friend of mine!
People are joining like crazy!
Welcome♥
o This Massive Special Feature!!
Hot New Stars!★
SHIRO as Shiro & Yukiru Shibuya
Shiro
Look!
THERE'S AN INTERVIEW WITH SHIRO!
Yeah! That's Yukiru's voice actor!
AQUA
VOICE ACTING
AQUA
I LOVE HIM! WHAT A SENSUAL VOICE!
Yay
Yay
PEOPLE KNOW MY NAME NOW.
IS SHIRO IN ANY OTHER SHOWS?

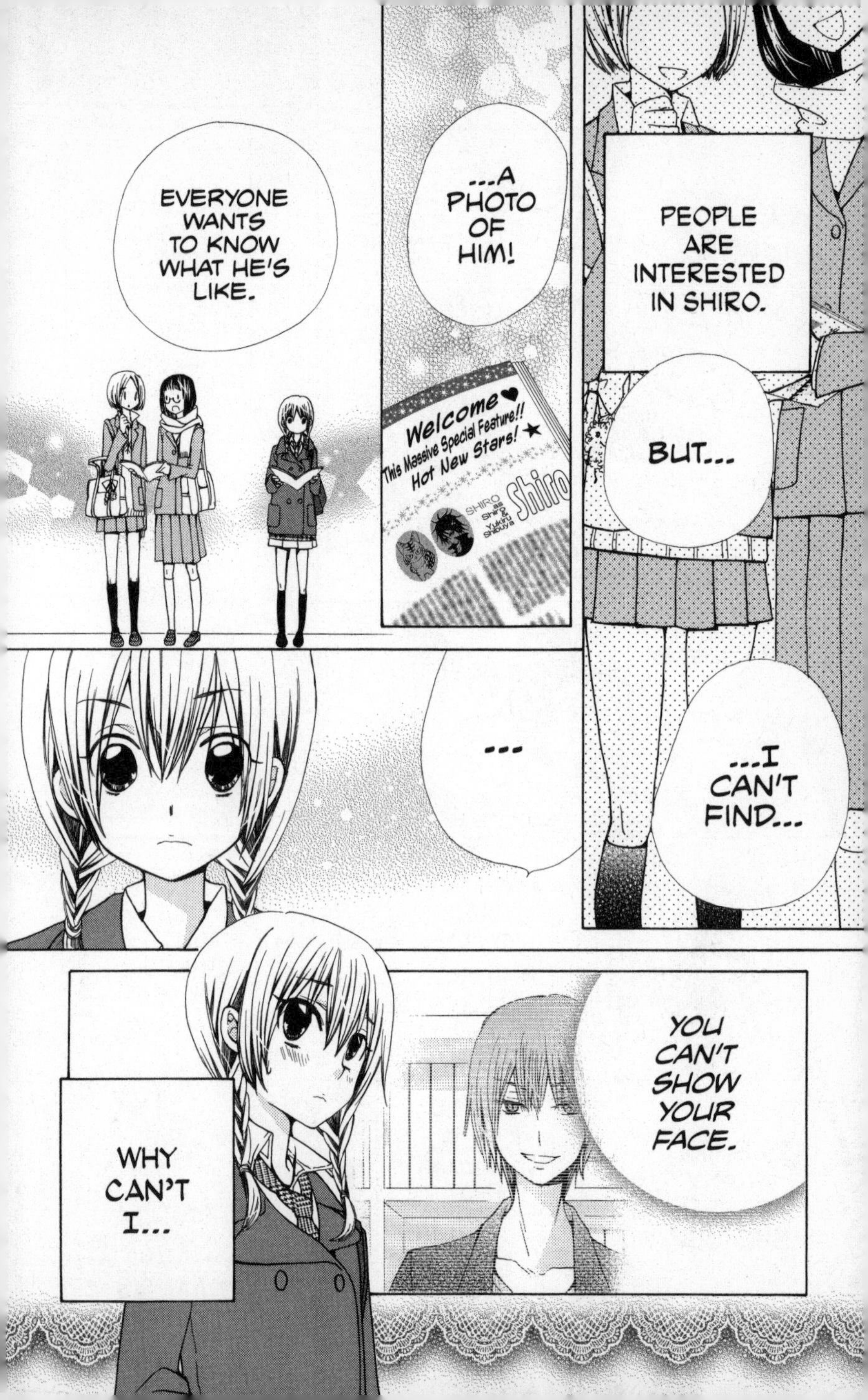
PEOPLE ARE INTERESTED IN SHIRO.
BUT...
...I CAN'T FIND...
...A PHOTO OF HIM!
Welcome♥
This Massive Special Feature!!
Hot New Stars!★
Shiro
EVERYONE WANTS TO KNOW WHAT HE'S LIKE.
...
YOU CAN'T SHOW YOUR FACE.
WHY CAN'T I...

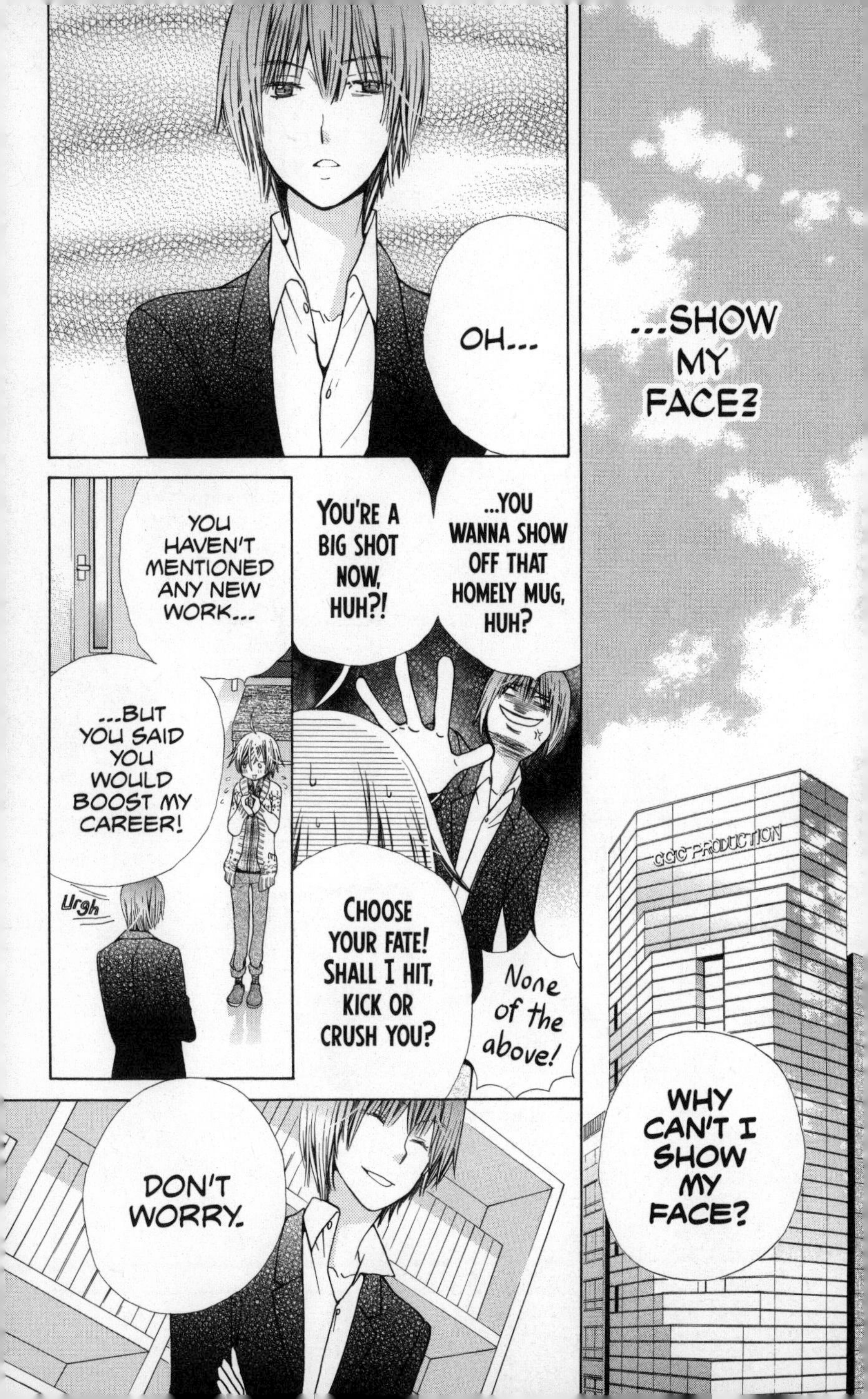
...SHOW MY FACE?
GGC PRODUCTION
WHY CAN'T I SHOW MY FACE?
OH...
...YOU WANNA SHOW OFF THAT HOMELY MUG, HUH?
YOU'RE A BIG SHOT NOW, HUH?!
CHOOSE YOUR FATE! SHALL I HIT, KICK OR CRUSH YOU?
None of the above!
YOU HAVEN'T MENTIONED ANY NEW WORK...
...BUT YOU SAID YOU WOULD BOOST MY CAREER!
Urgh
DON'T WORRY.

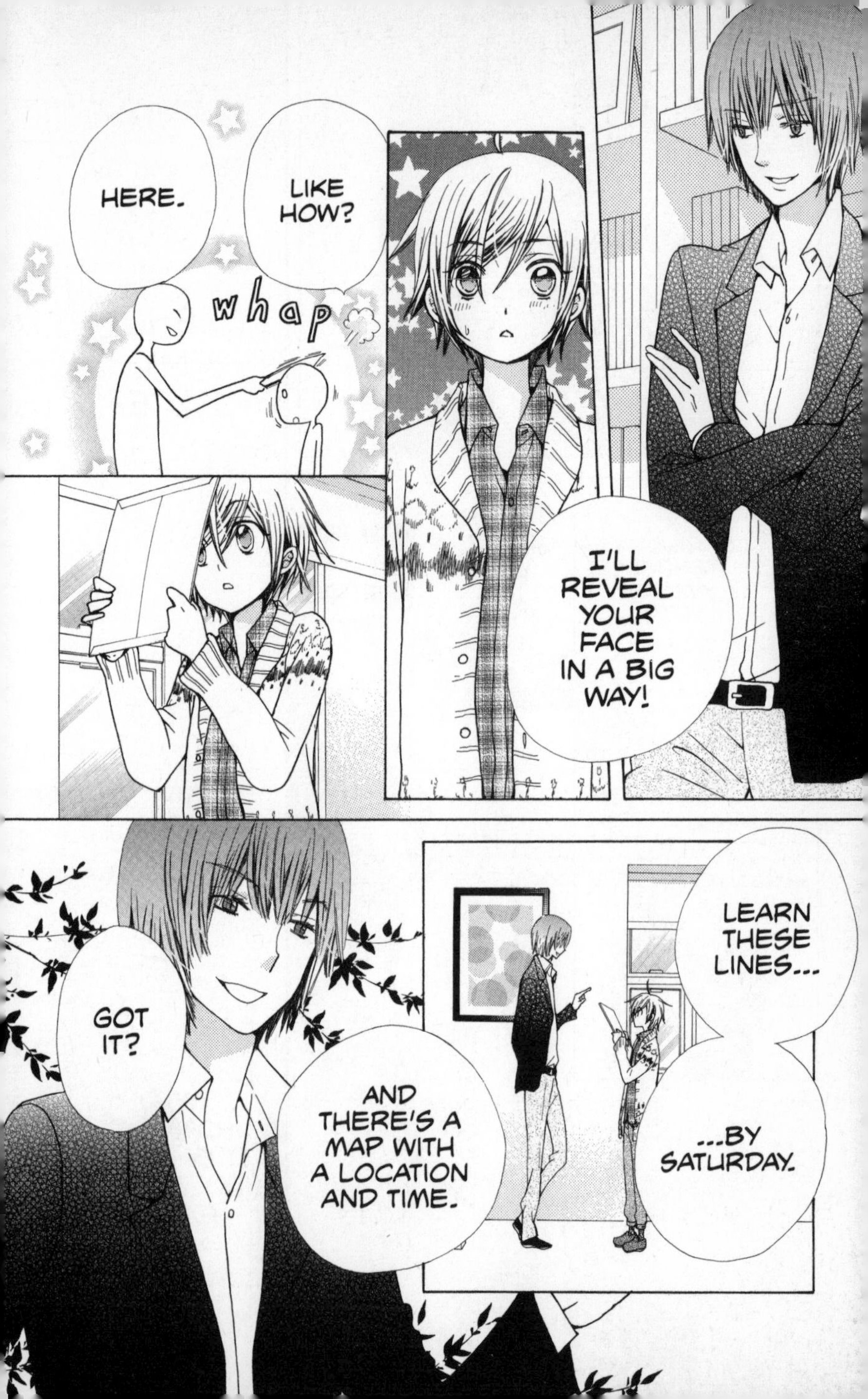
I'LL REVEAL YOUR FACE IN A BIG WAY!
LIKE HOW?
HERE.
whap
LEARN THESE LINES...
...BY SATURDAY.
AND THERE'S A MAP WITH A LOCATION AND TIME.
GOT IT?

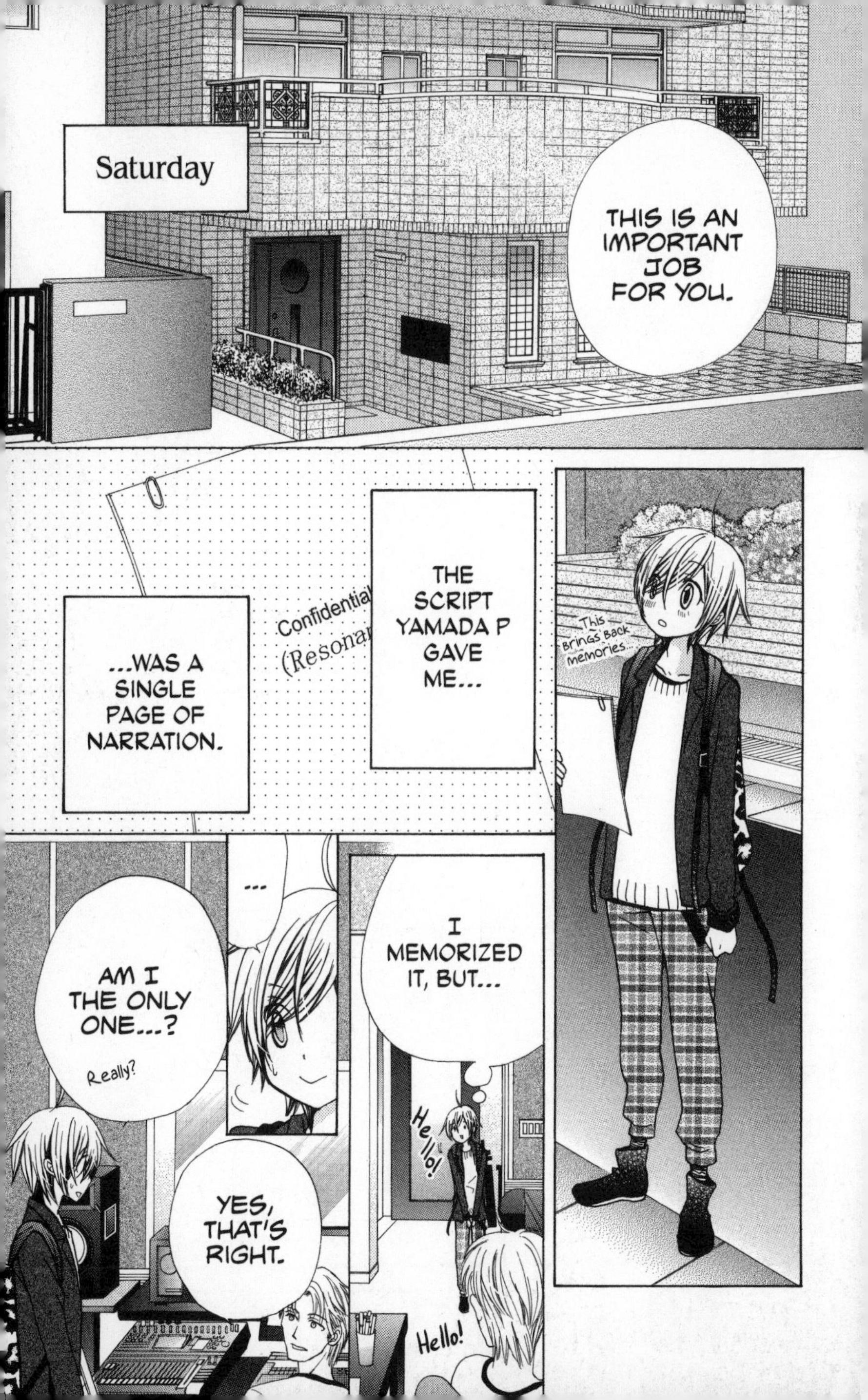
THIS IS AN IMPORTANT JOB FOR YOU.
Saturday
This brings back memories...
THE SCRIPT YAMADA P GAVE ME...
Confidential
(Resonar
...WAS A SINGLE PAGE OF NARRATION.
I MEMORIZED IT, BUT...
Hello!
Hello!
...
AM I THE ONLY ONE...?
Really?
YES, THAT'S RIGHT.

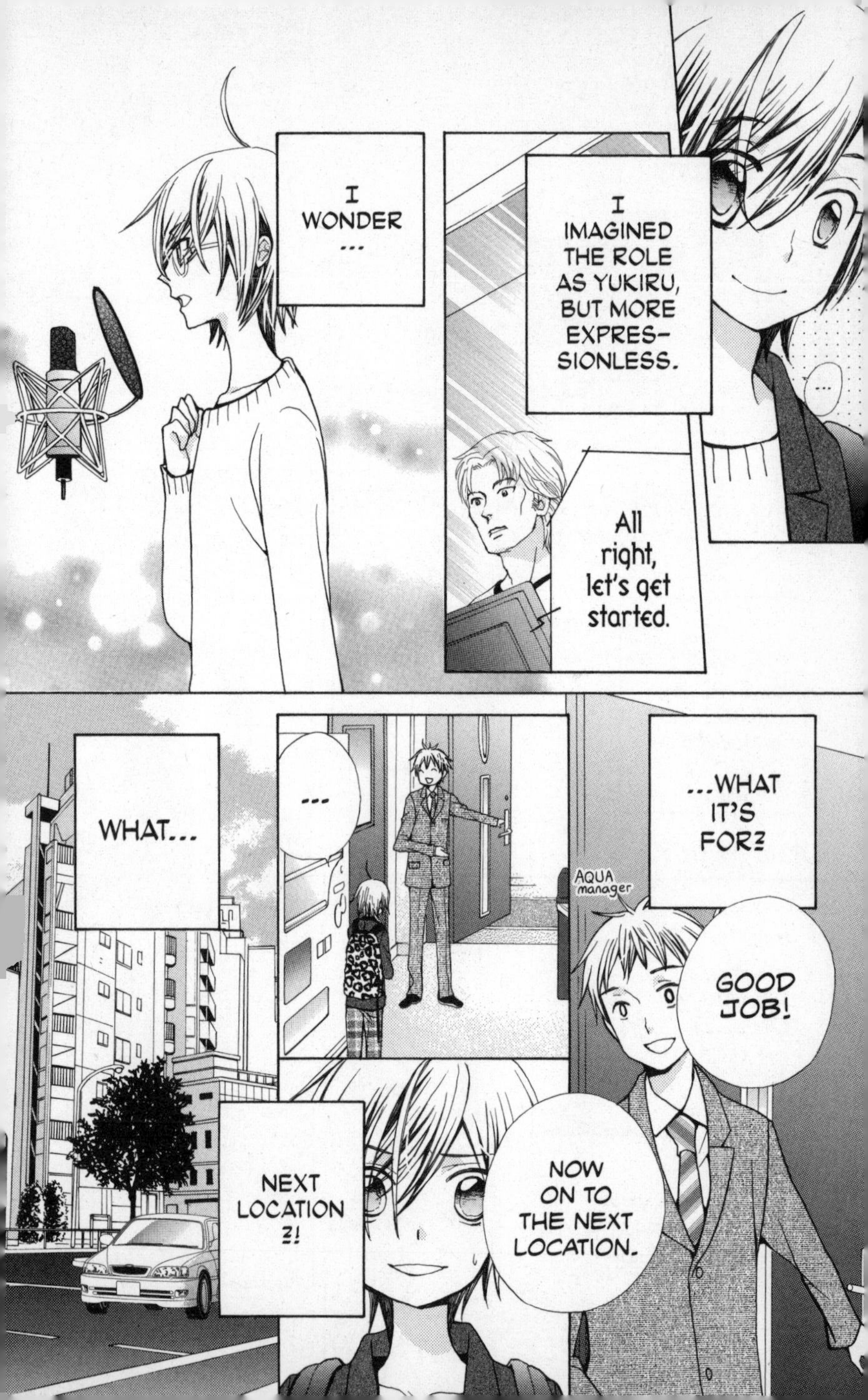

...
I IMAGINED THE ROLE AS YUKIRU, BUT MORE EXPRES-SIONLESS.
All right, let's get started.
I WONDER ...
...WHAT IT'S FOR?
AQUA manager
GOOD JOB!
...
NOW ON TO THE NEXT LOCATION.
NEXT LOCATION ?!
WHAT...

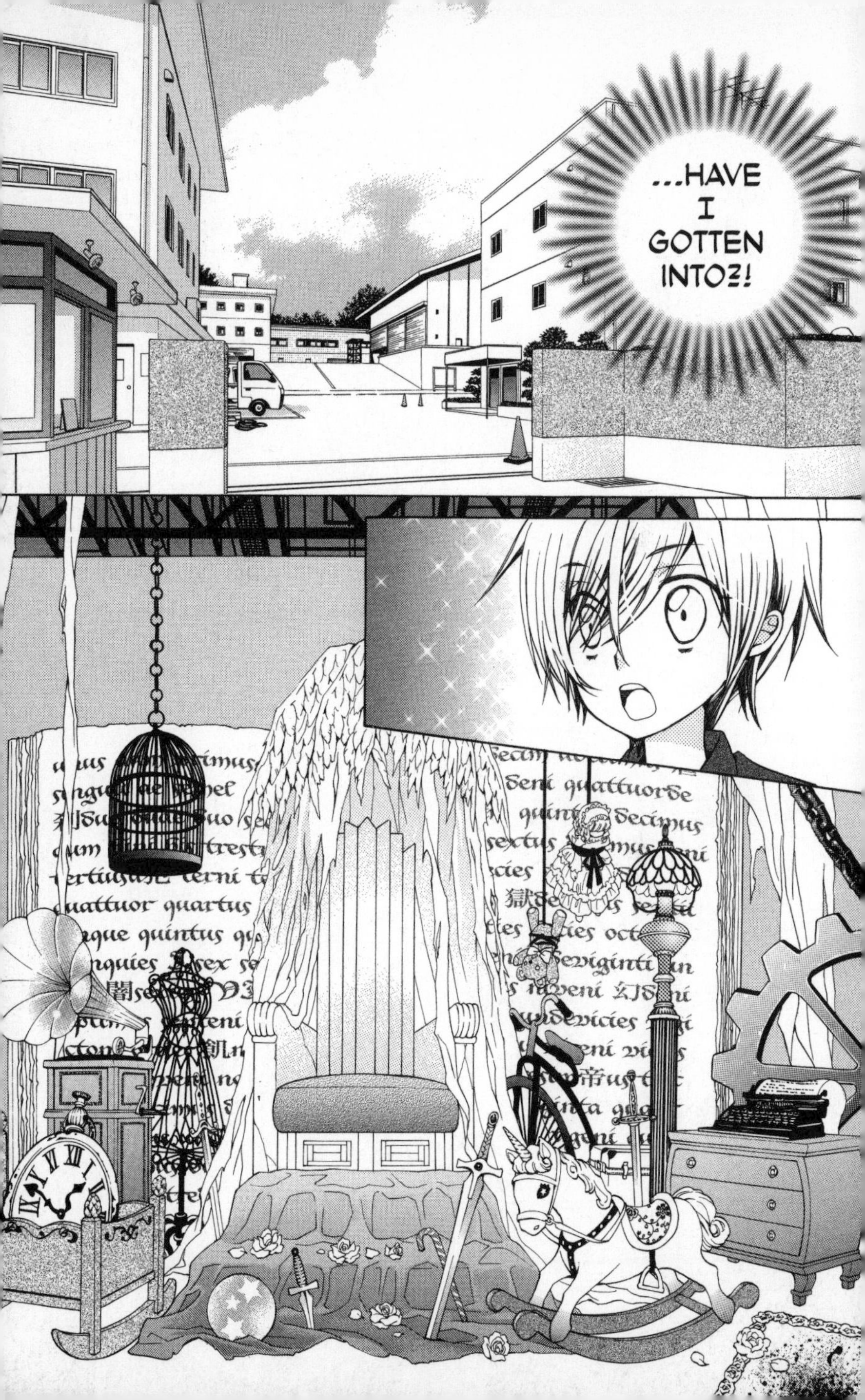
...HAVE I GOTTEN INTO?!

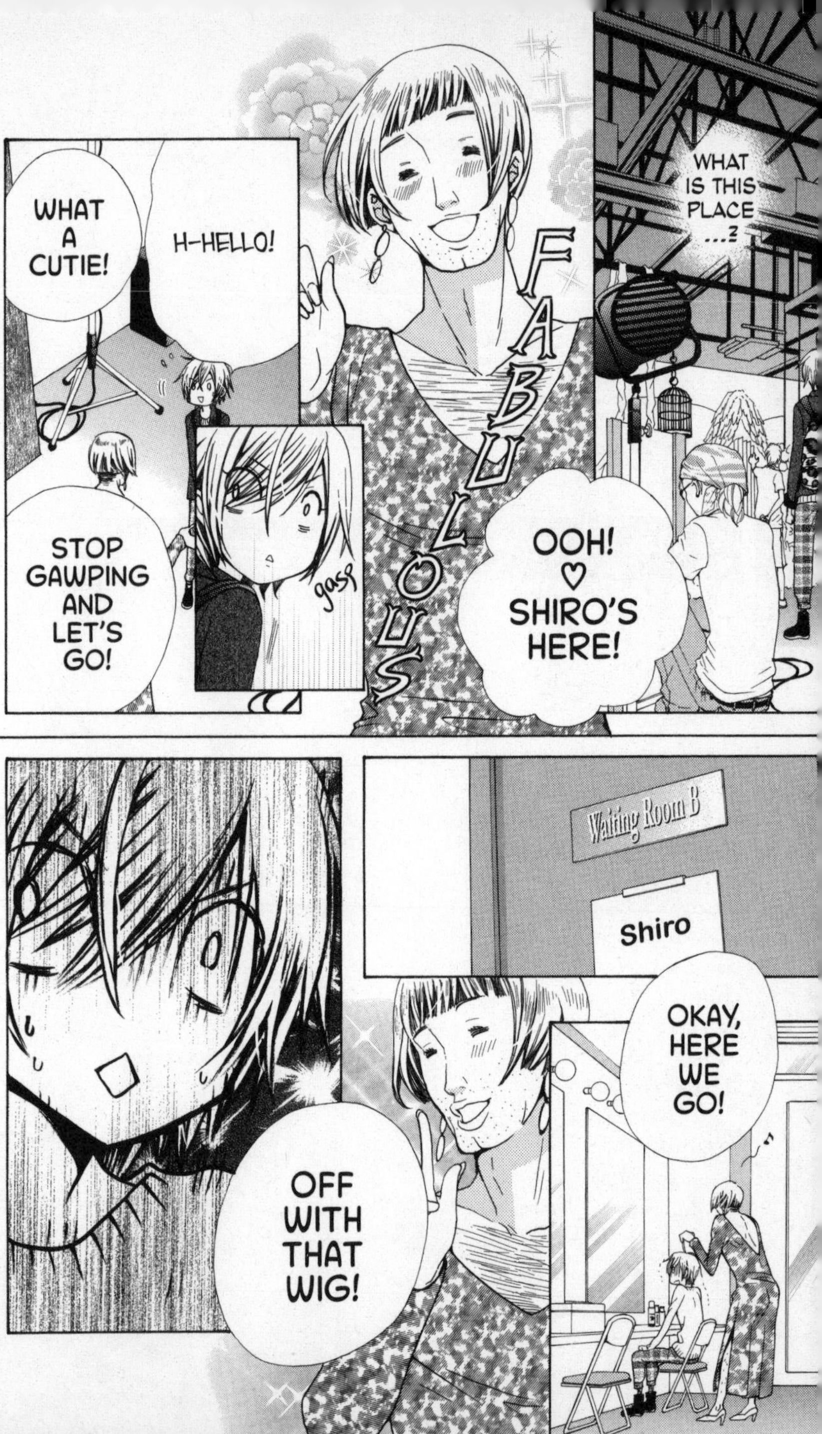
WHAT IS THIS PLACE ...?
FABULOUS
OOH! ♡ SHIRO'S HERE!
H-HELLO!
WHAT A CUTIE!
gasp
STOP GAWPING AND LET'S GO!
Waiting Room B
Shiro
OKAY, HERE WE GO!
OFF WITH THAT WIG!

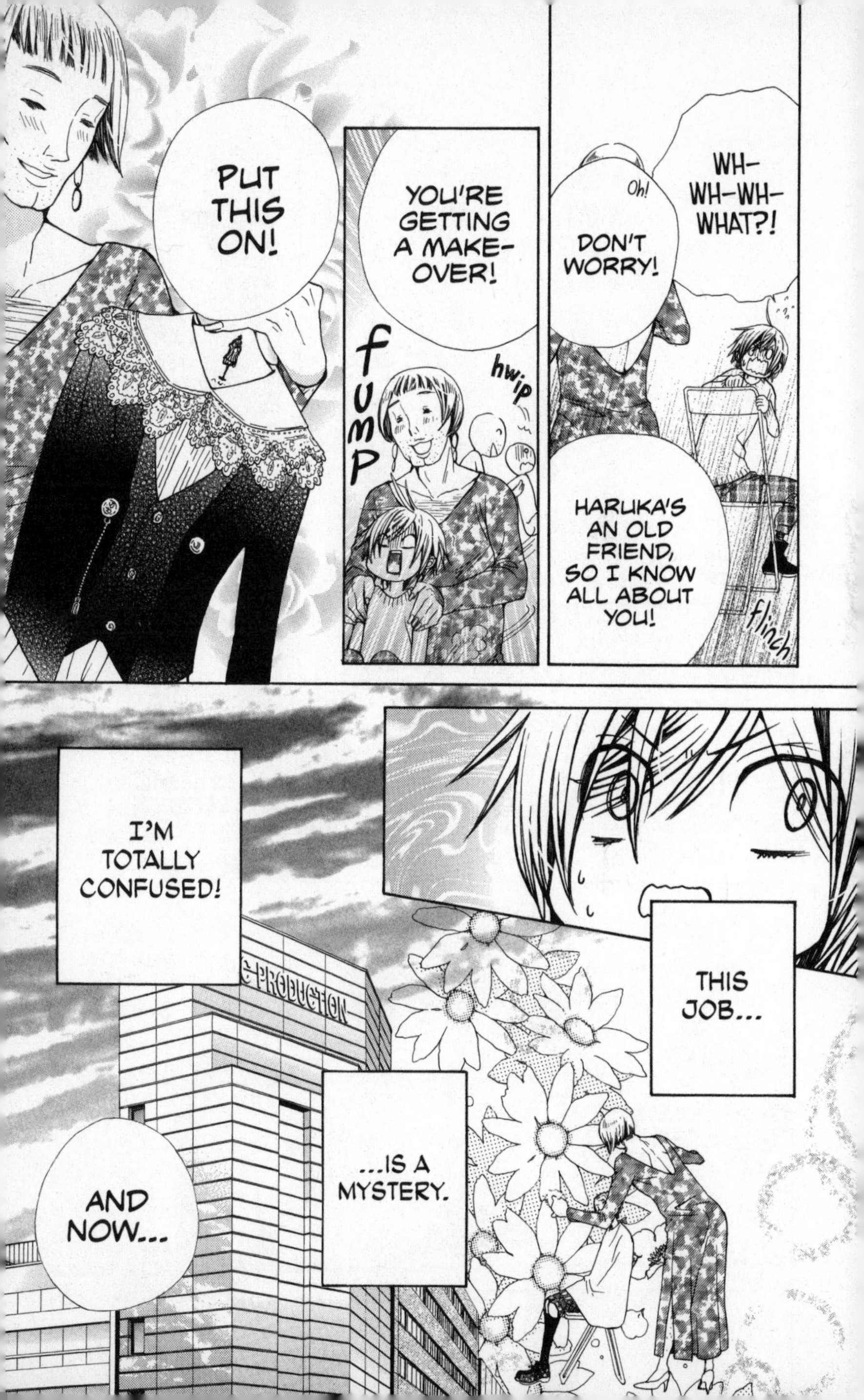
WH-WH-WH-WHAT?!
Oh!
DON'T WORRY!
HARUKA'S AN OLD FRIEND, SO I KNOW ALL ABOUT YOU!
flinch
YOU'RE GETTING A MAKE-OVER!
hwip
FUMP
PUT THIS ON!
THIS JOB...
...IS A MYSTERY.
I'M TOTALLY CONFUSED!
PRODUCTION
AND NOW...

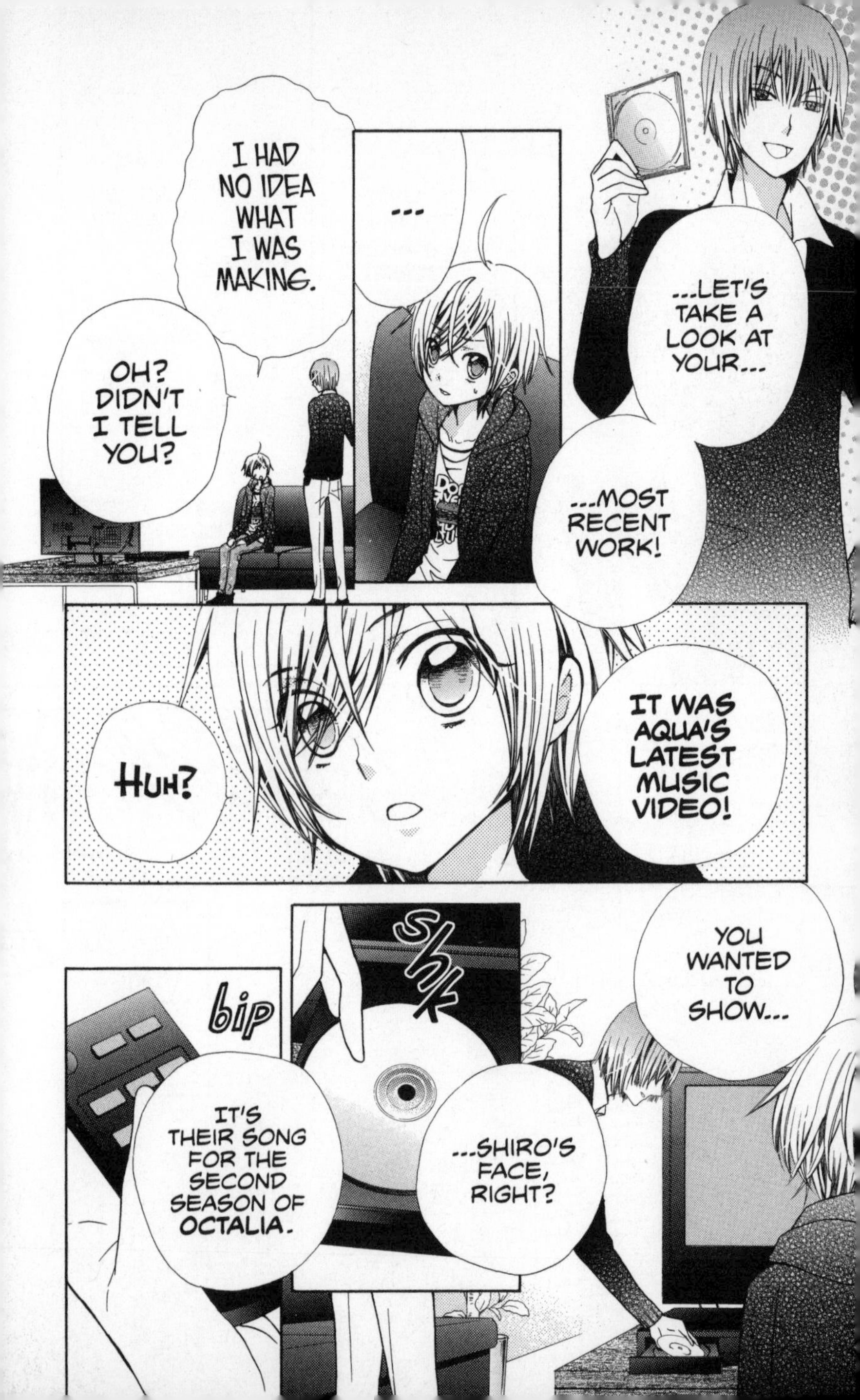
...LET'S TAKE A LOOK AT YOUR...
...MOST RECENT WORK!
...
I HAD NO IDEA WHAT I WAS MAKING.
OH? DIDN'T I TELL YOU?
IT WAS AQUA'S LATEST MUSIC VIDEO!
HUH?
YOU WANTED TO SHOW...
...SHIRO'S FACE, RIGHT?
SHK
bip
IT'S THEIR SONG FOR THE SECOND SEASON OF OCTALIA.

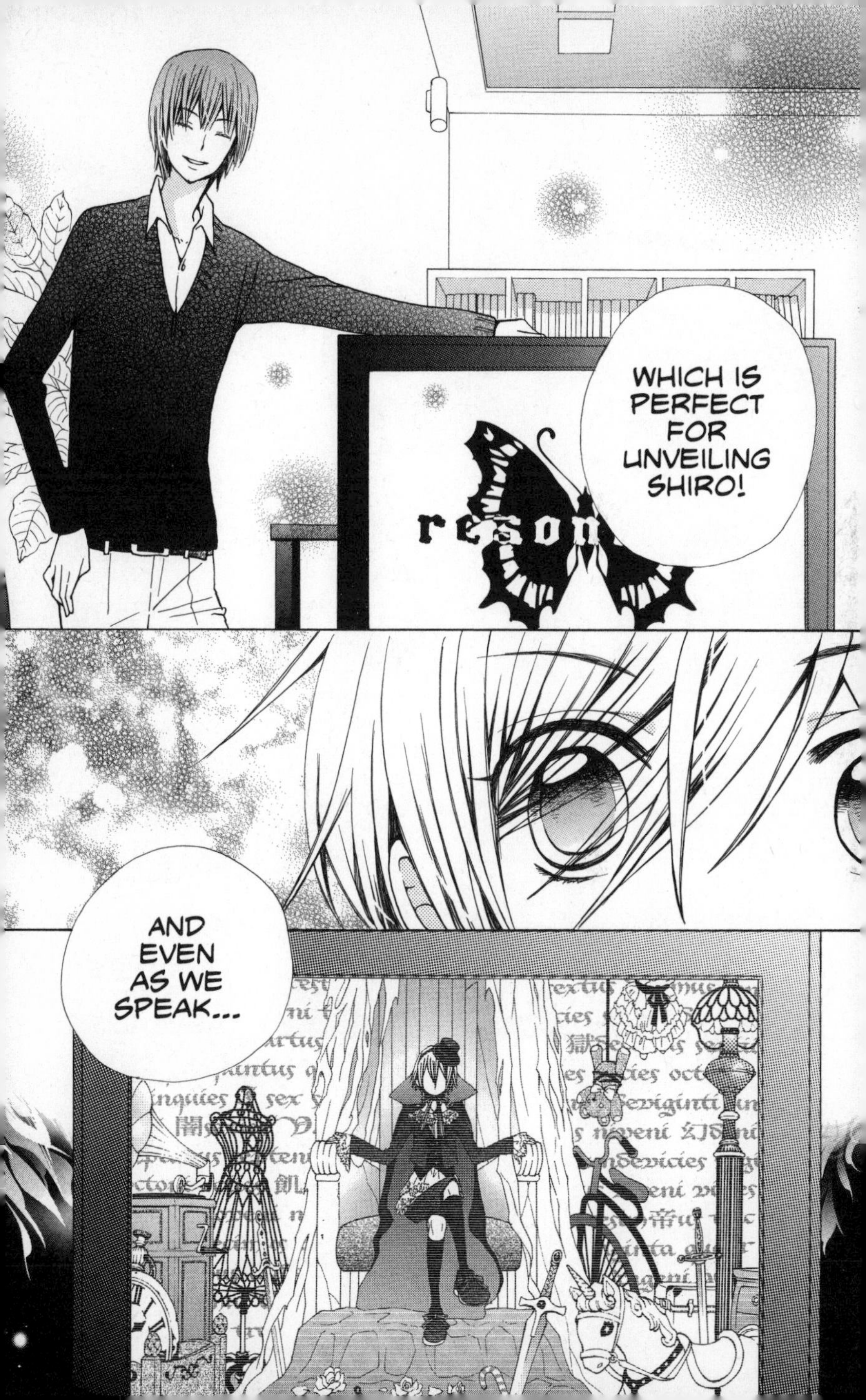
WHICH IS PERFECT FOR UNVEILING SHIRO!
reson
AND EVEN AS WE SPEAK...

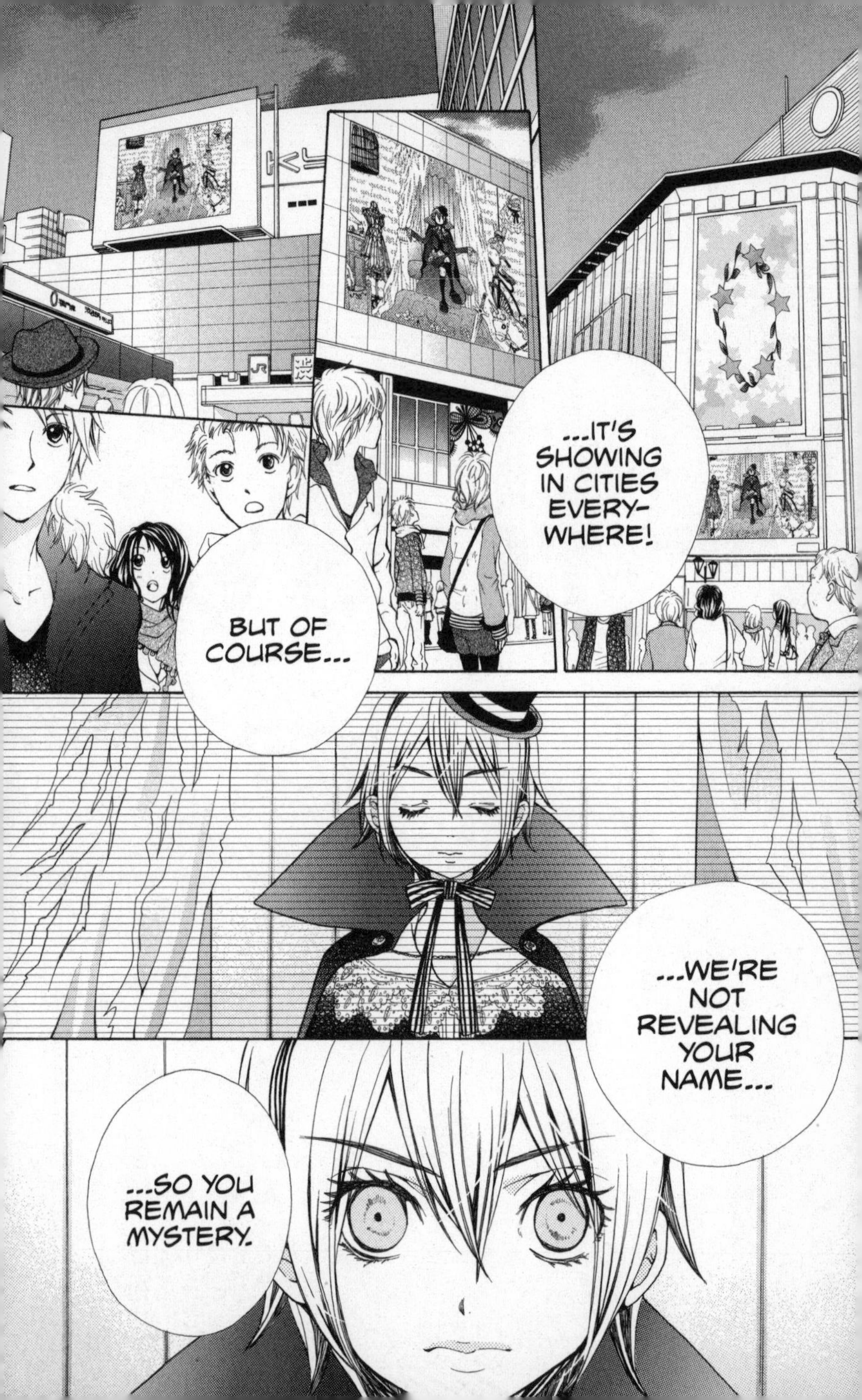
...IT'S SHOWING IN CITIES EVERY-WHERE!
BUT OF COURSE...
...WE'RE NOT REVEALING YOUR NAME...
...SO YOU REMAIN A MYSTERY.

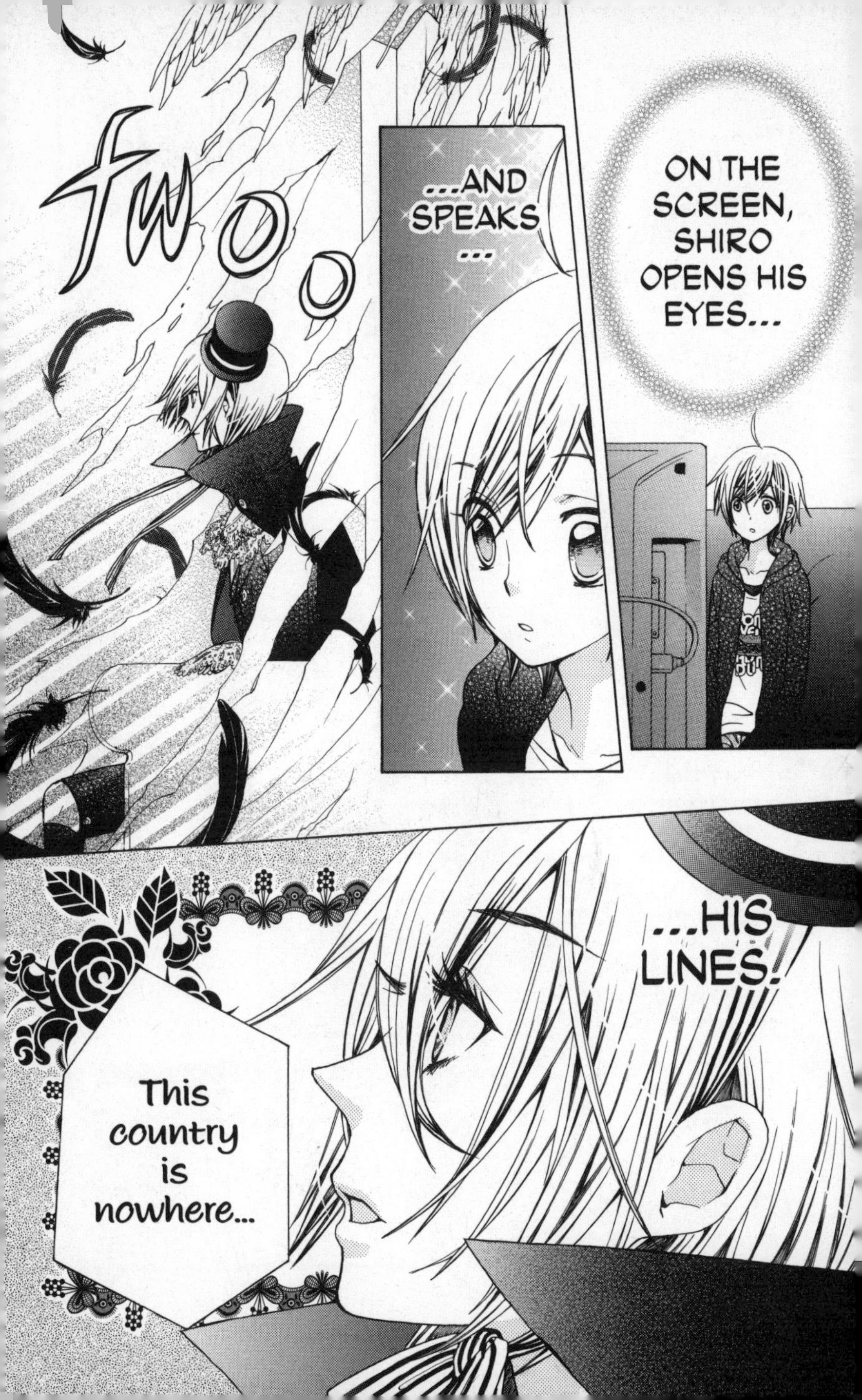
ON THE SCREEN, SHIRO OPENS HIS EYES...
...AND SPEAKS...
fwoo
...HIS LINES.
This country is nowhere...

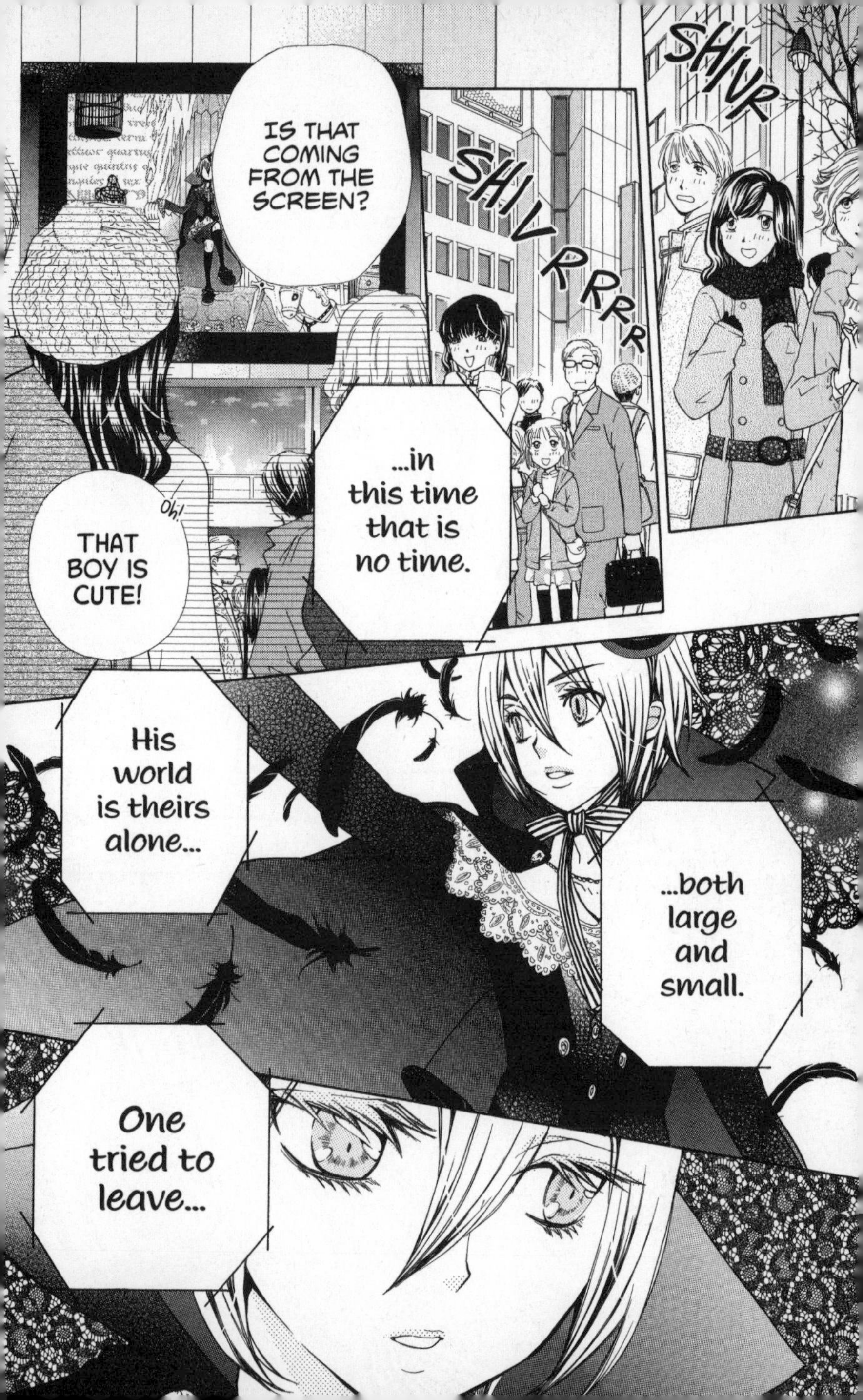
SHIVR
SHIVRRRR
...in this time that is no time.
IS THAT COMING FROM THE SCREEN?
Oh!
THAT BOY IS CUTE!
His world is theirs alone...
...both large and small.
One tried to leave...

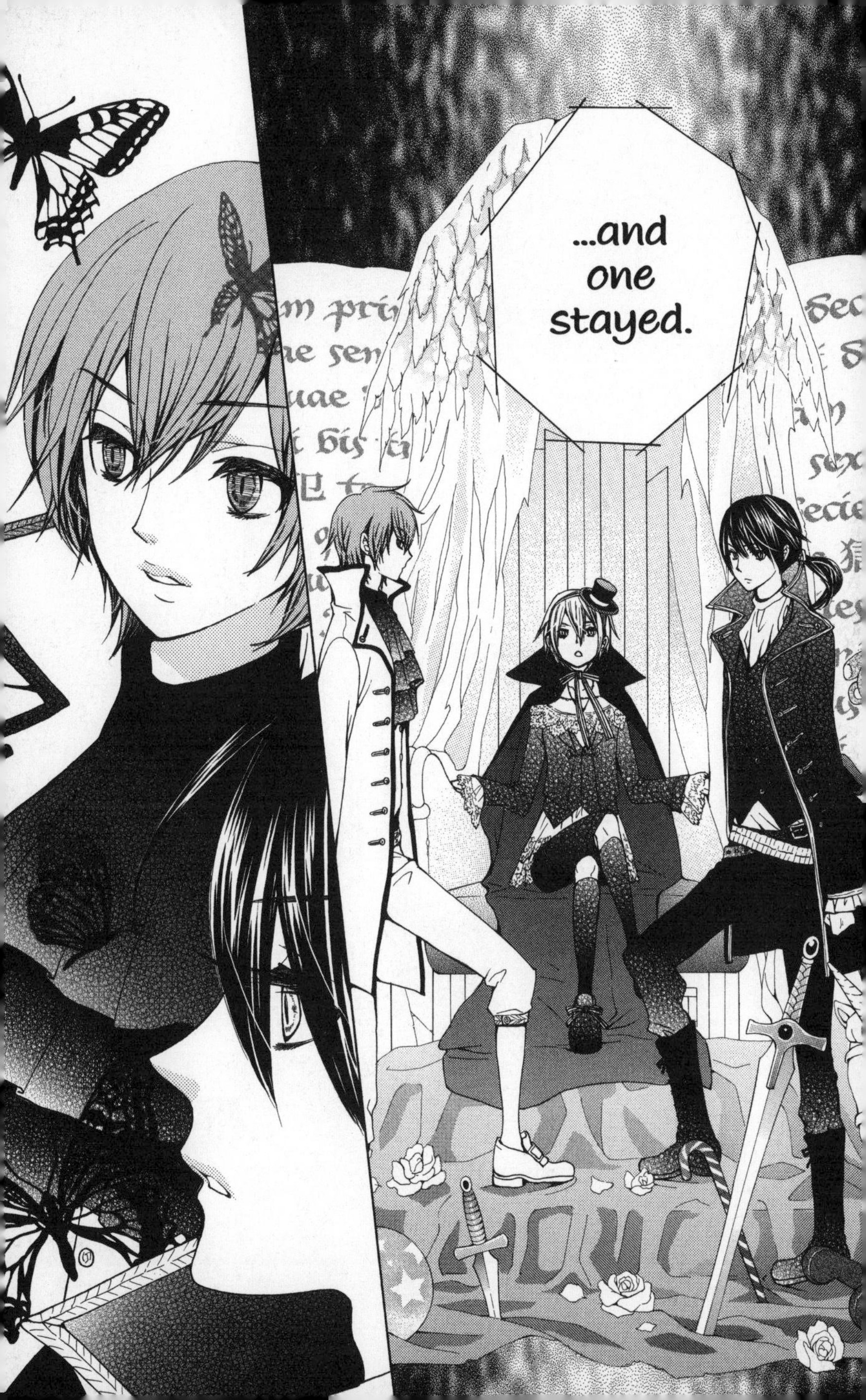
...and one stayed.

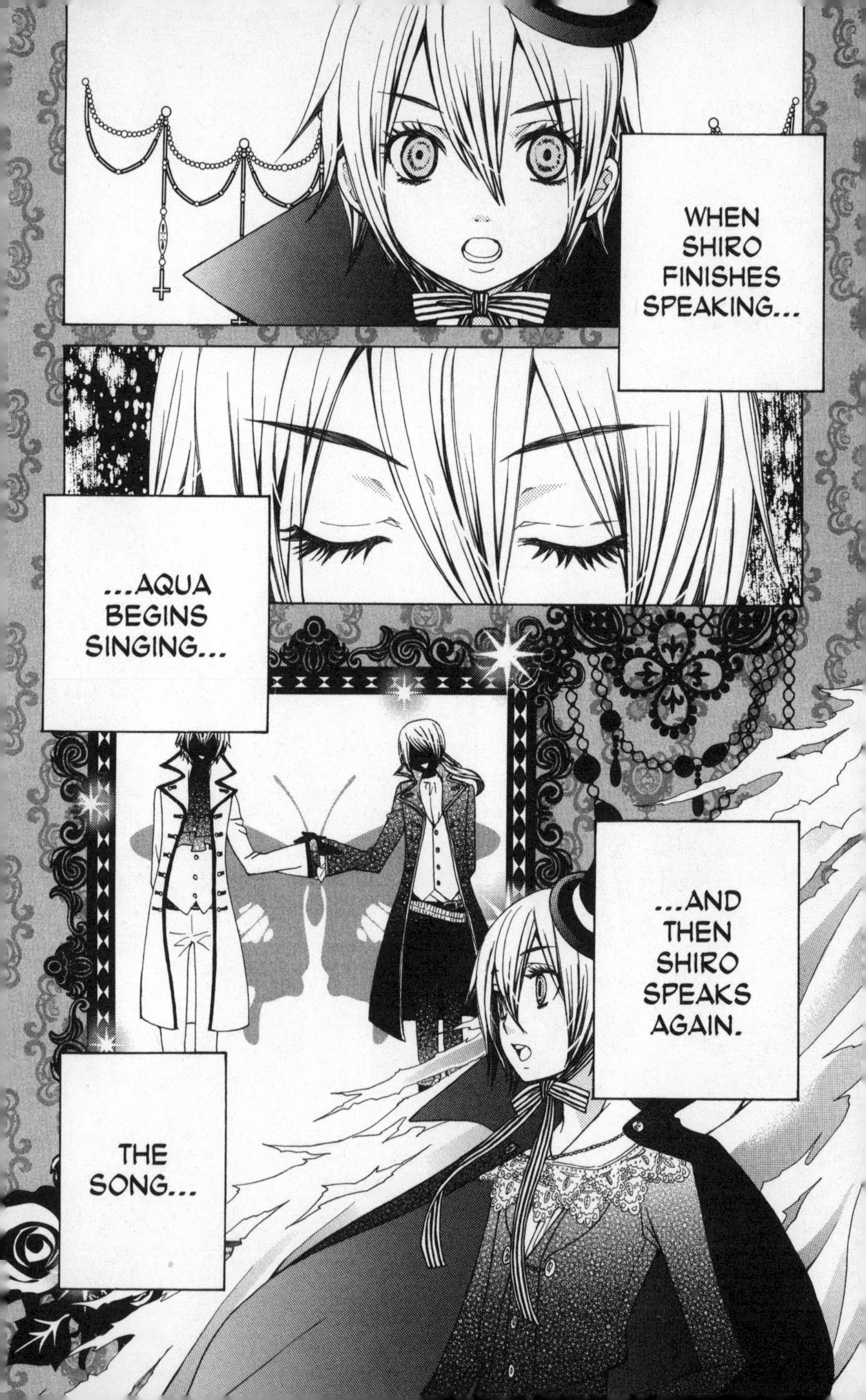
WHEN SHIRO FINISHES SPEAKING...
...AQUA BEGINS SINGING...
...AND THEN SHIRO SPEAKS AGAIN.
THE SONG...

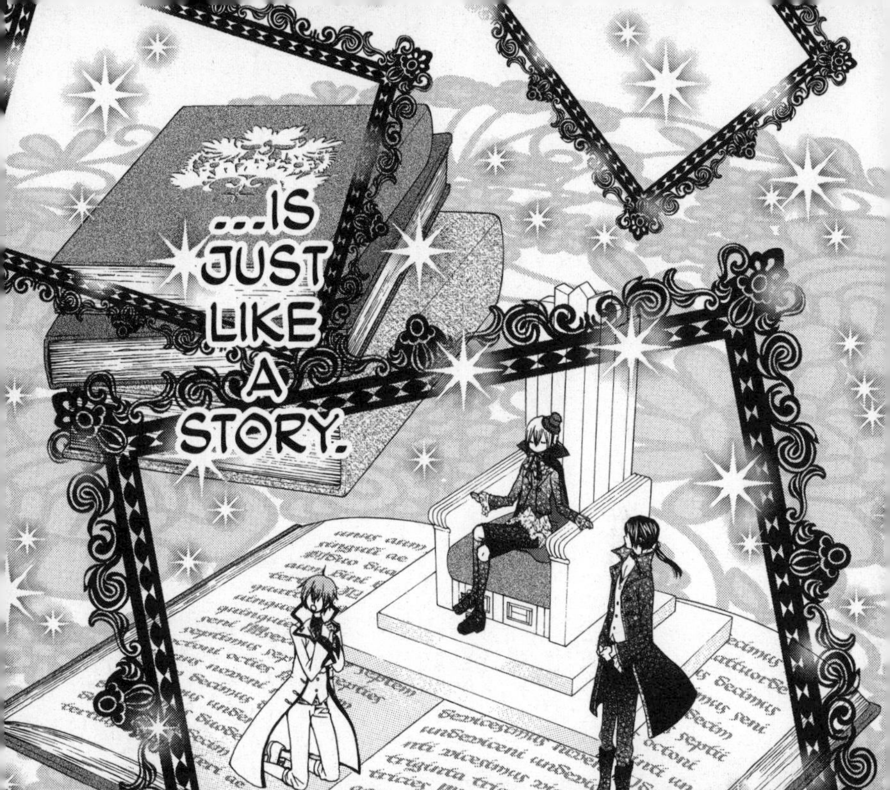
...IS JUST LIKE A STORY.

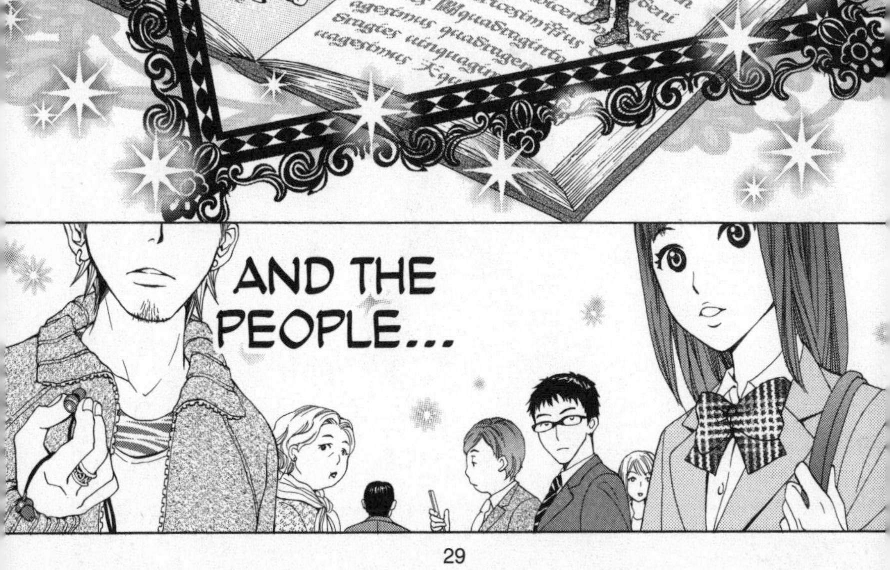
AND THE PEOPLE...

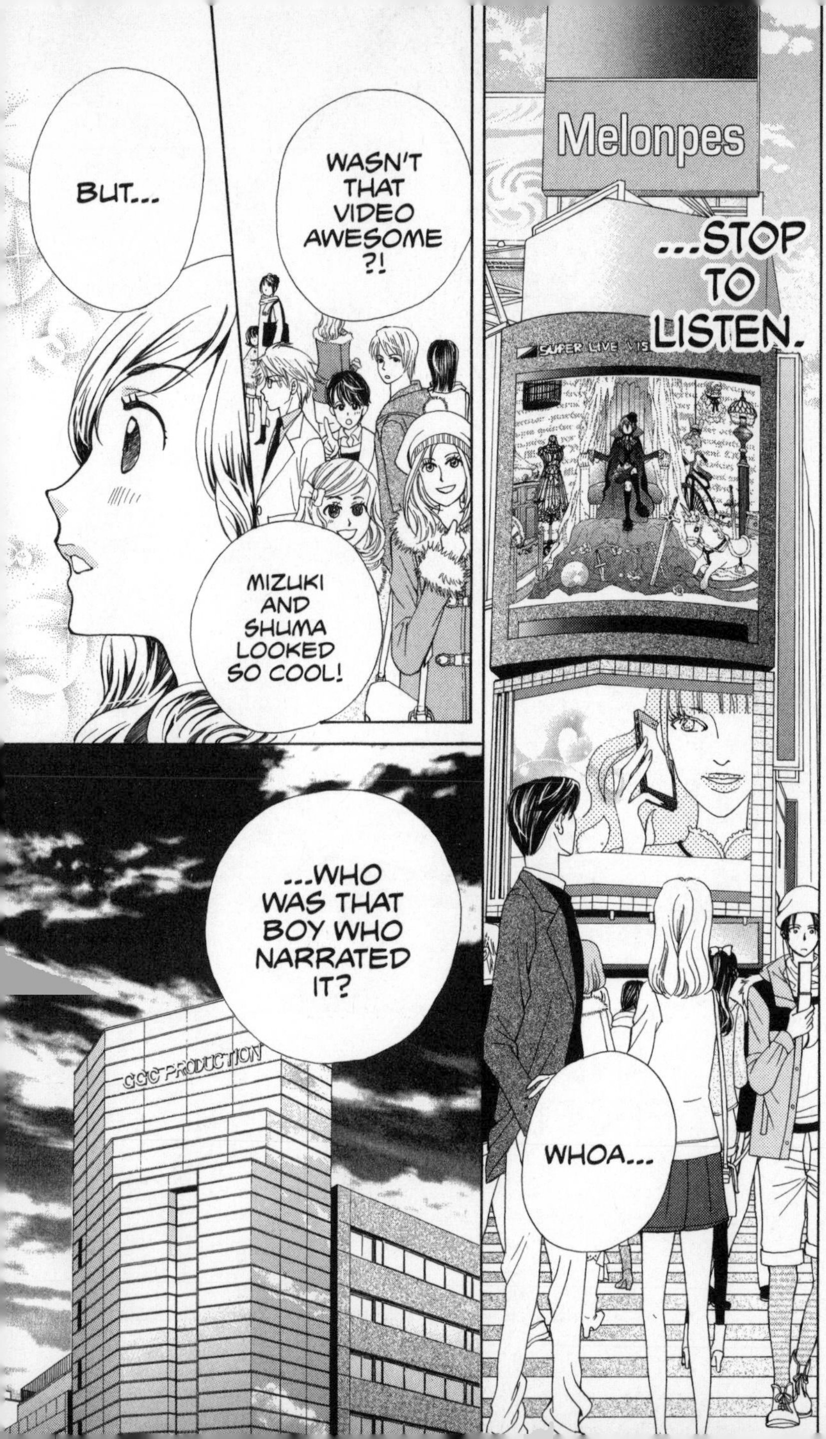
Melonpes
...STOP TO LISTEN.
WHOA...
WASN'T THAT VIDEO AWESOME?!
MIZUKI AND SHUMA LOOKED SO COOL!
BUT...
...WHO WAS THAT BOY WHO NARRATED IT?
GGC PRODUCTION

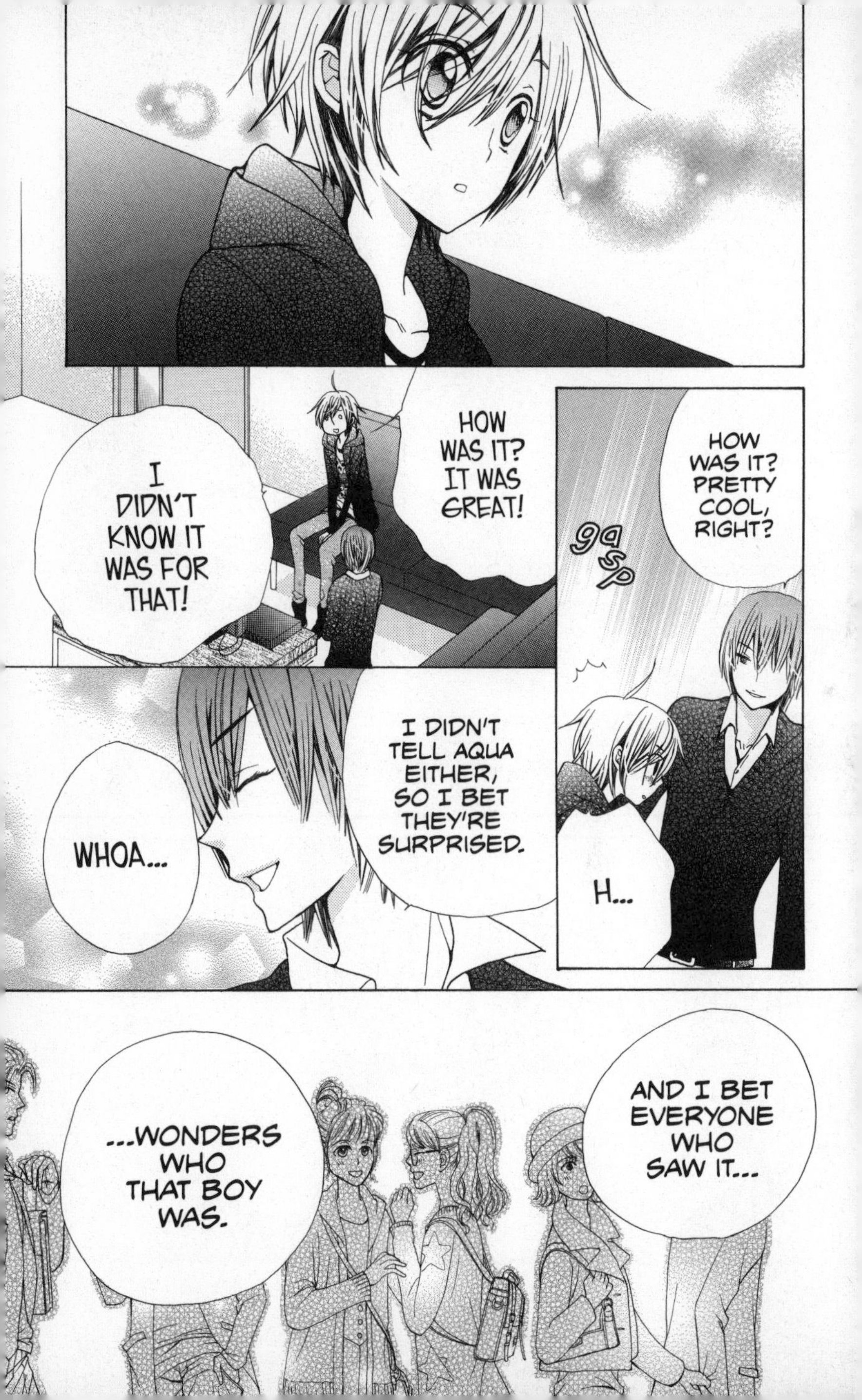
HOW WAS IT? PRETTY COOL, RIGHT?
gasp
H...
HOW WAS IT? IT WAS GREAT!
I DIDN'T KNOW IT WAS FOR THAT!
I DIDN'T TELL AQUA EITHER, SO I BET THEY'RE SURPRISED.
WHOA...
AND I BET EVERYONE WHO SAW IT...
...WONDERS WHO THAT BOY WAS.

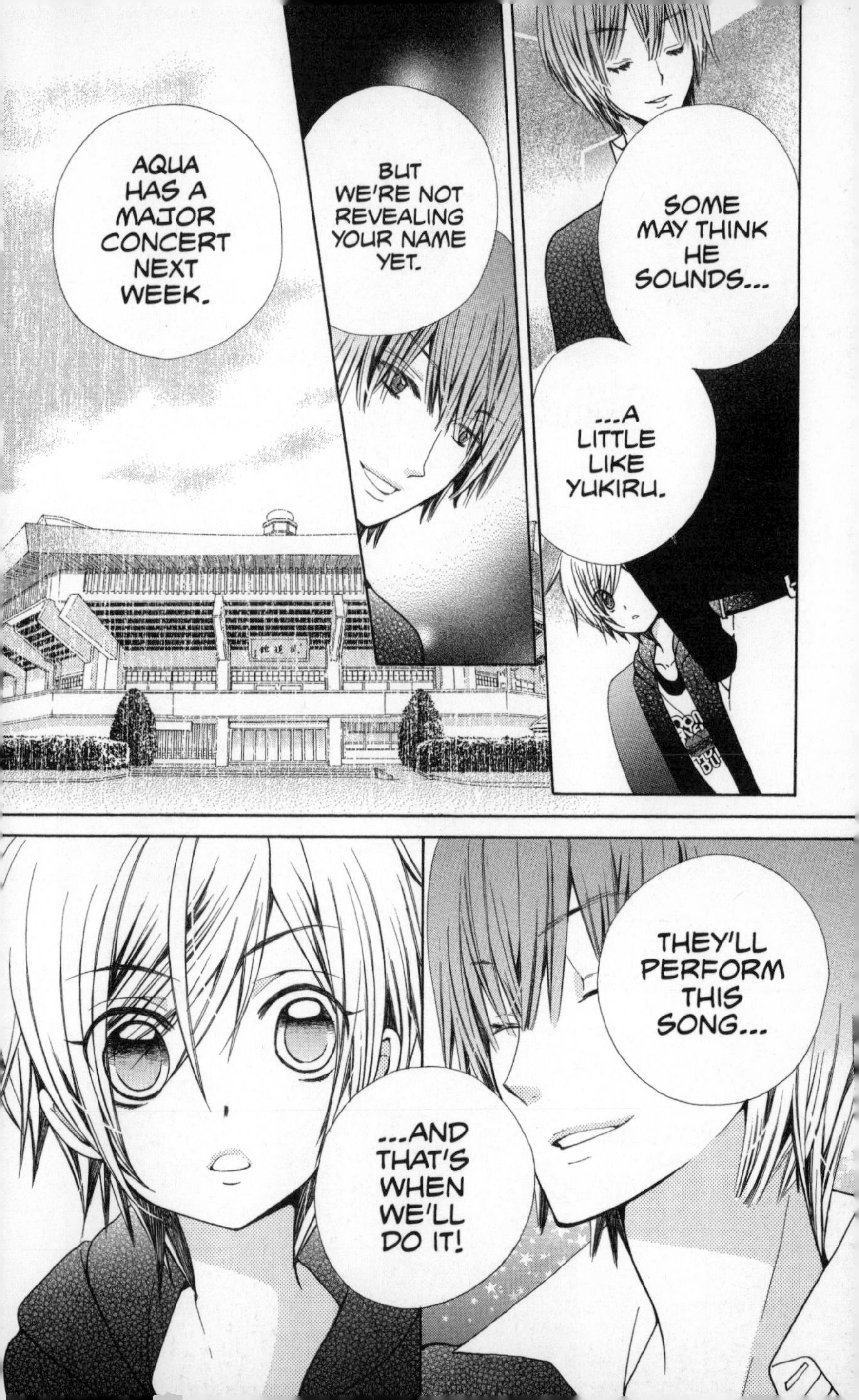
SOME MAY THINK HE SOUNDS...
...A LITTLE LIKE YUKIRU.
BUT WE'RE NOT REVEALING YOUR NAME YET.
AQUA HAS A MAJOR CONCERT NEXT WEEK.
THEY'LL PERFORM THIS SONG...
...AND THAT'S WHEN WE'LL DO IT!

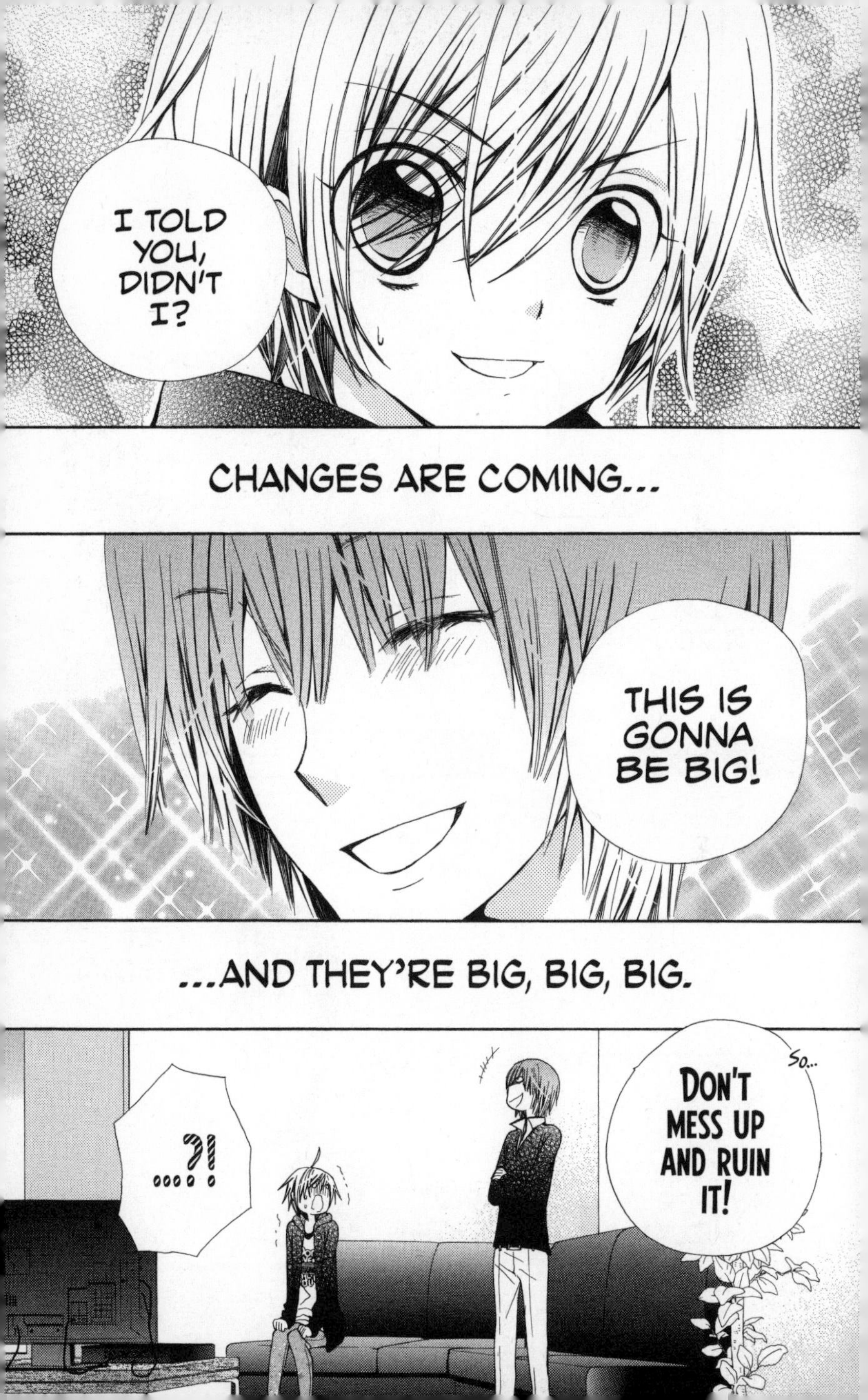
I TOLD YOU, DIDN'T I?
CHANGES ARE COMING...
THIS IS GONNA BE BIG!
...AND THEY'RE BIG, BIG, BIG.
So...
DON'T MESS UP AND RUIN IT!
...?!

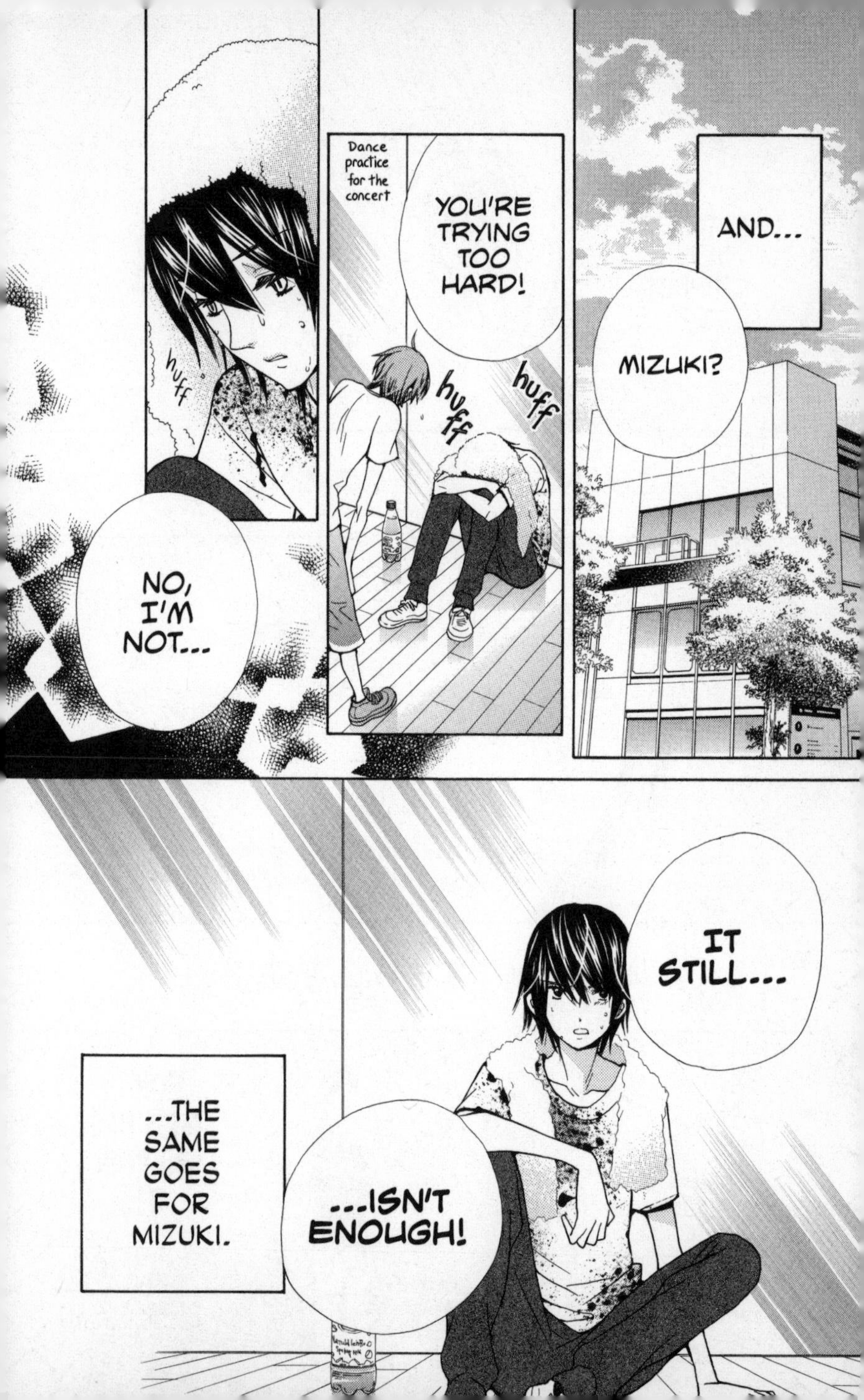
AND...
MIZUKI?
Dance practice for the concert
YOU'RE TRYING TOO HARD!
huff
huff
huff
NO, I'M NOT...
IT STILL...
...ISN'T ENOUGH!
...THE SAME GOES FOR MIZUKI.

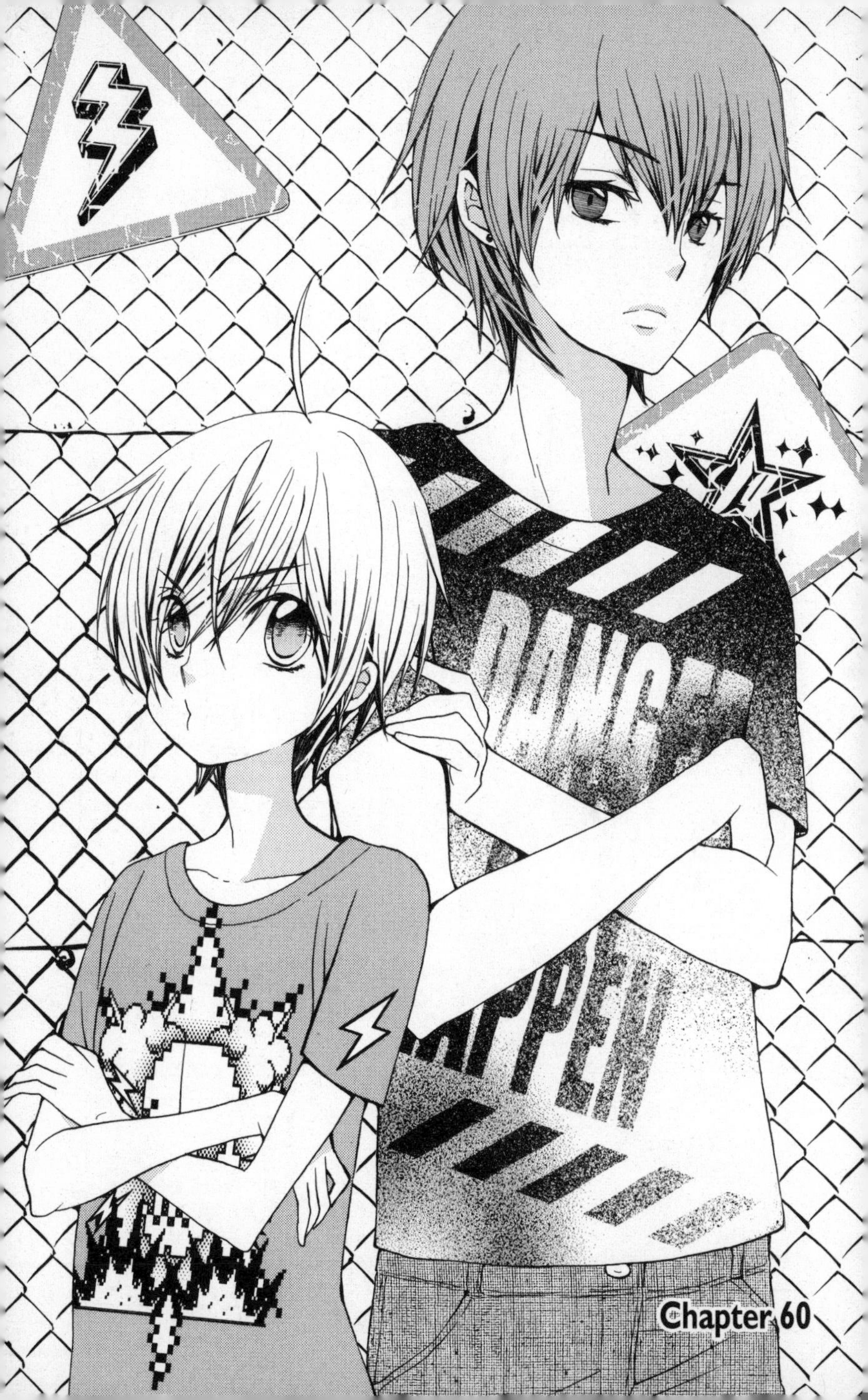

# Chapter 60

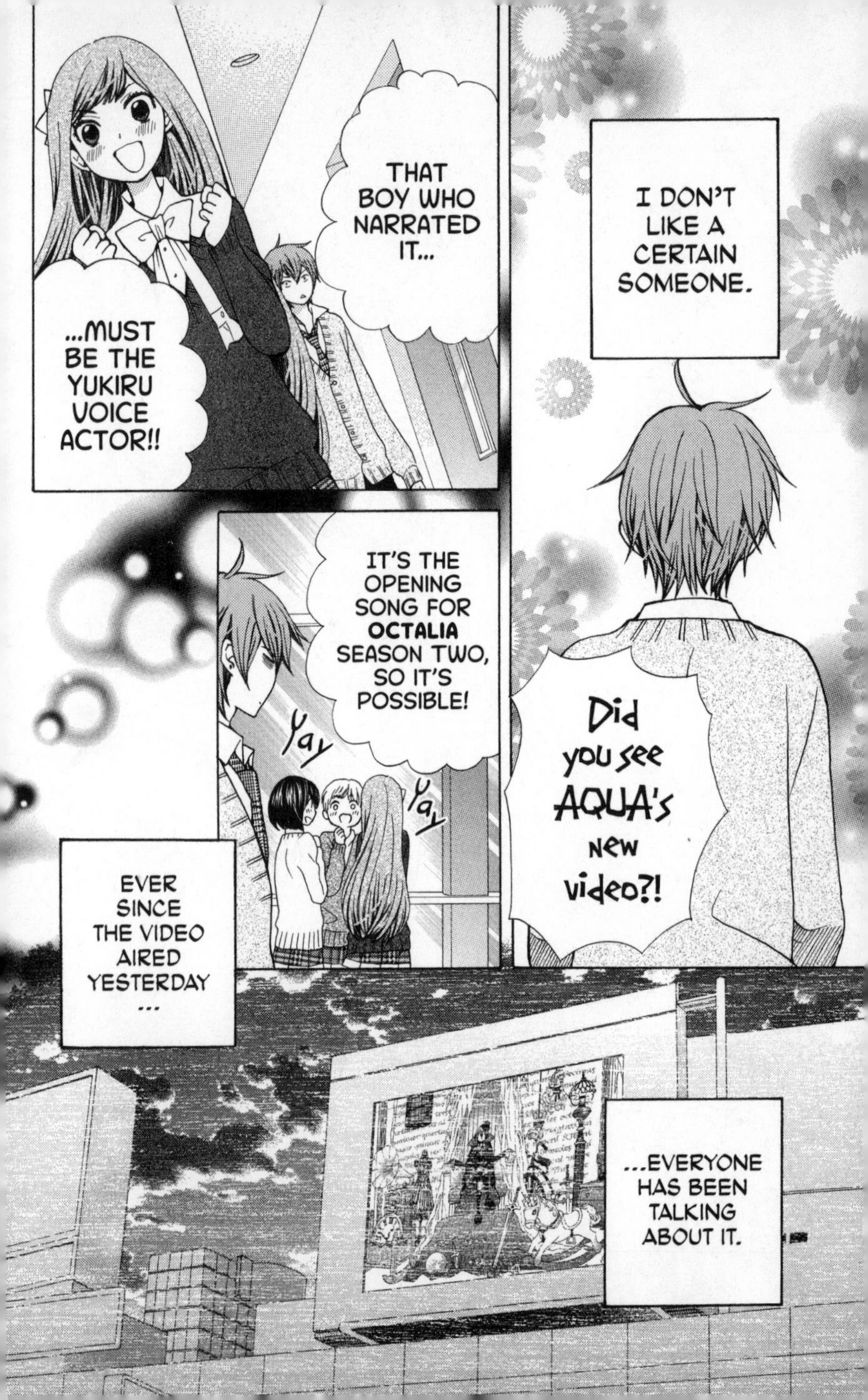
I DON'T LIKE A CERTAIN SOMEONE.
Did you see AQUA's new video?!
THAT BOY WHO NARRATED IT...
...MUST BE THE YUKIRU VOICE ACTOR!!
IT'S THE OPENING SONG FOR OCTALIA SEASON TWO, SO IT'S POSSIBLE!
Yay
Yay
EVER SINCE THE VIDEO AIRED YESTERDAY...
...EVERYONE HAS BEEN TALKING ABOUT IT.

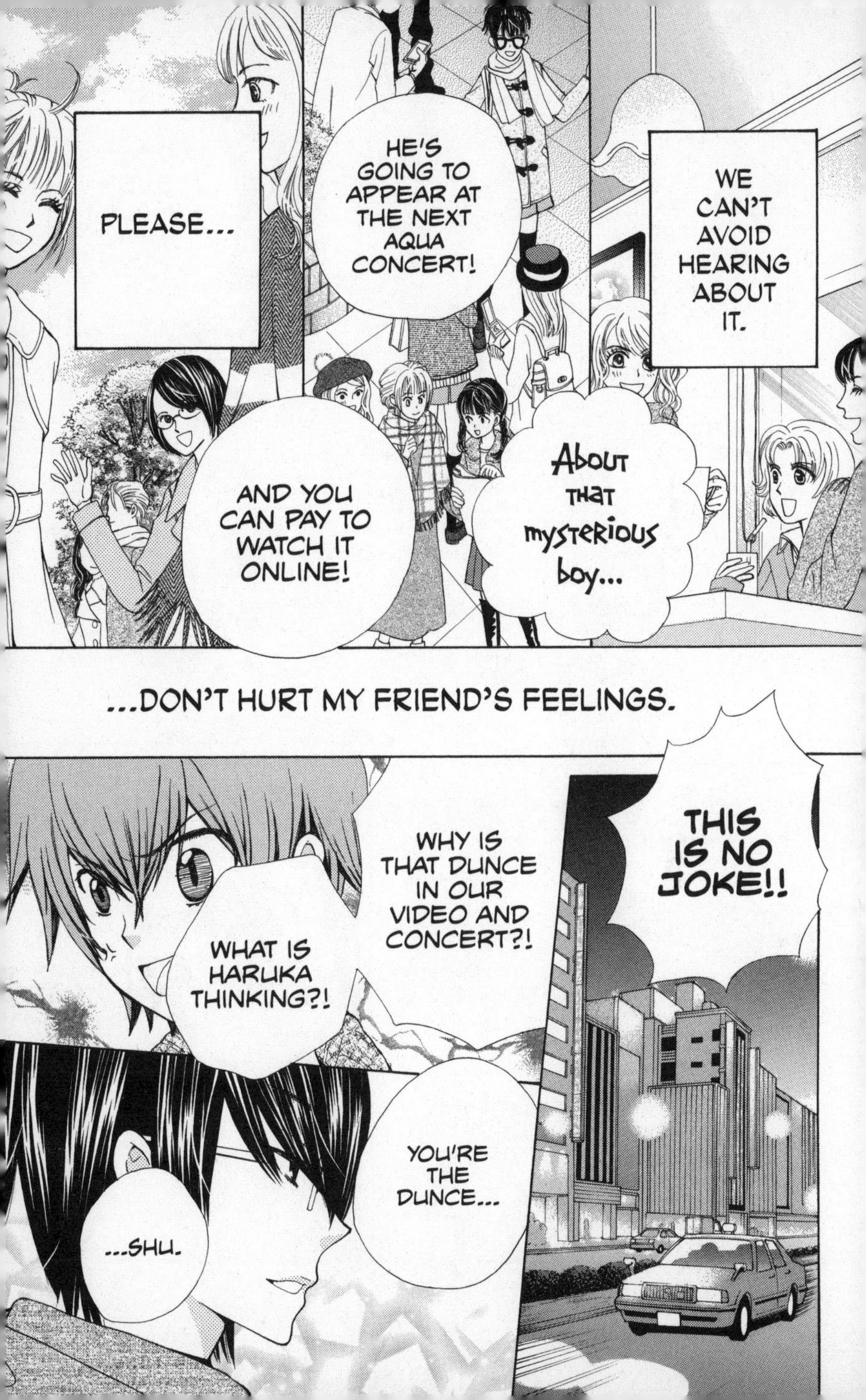
WE CAN'T AVOID HEARING ABOUT IT.
About that mysterious boy...
HE'S GOING TO APPEAR AT THE NEXT AQUA CONCERT!
AND YOU CAN PAY TO WATCH IT ONLINE!
PLEASE...
...DON'T HURT MY FRIEND'S FEELINGS.
THIS IS NO JOKE!!
WHY IS THAT DUNCE IN OUR VIDEO AND CONCERT?!
WHAT IS HARUKA THINKING?!
YOU'RE THE DUNCE...
...SHU.

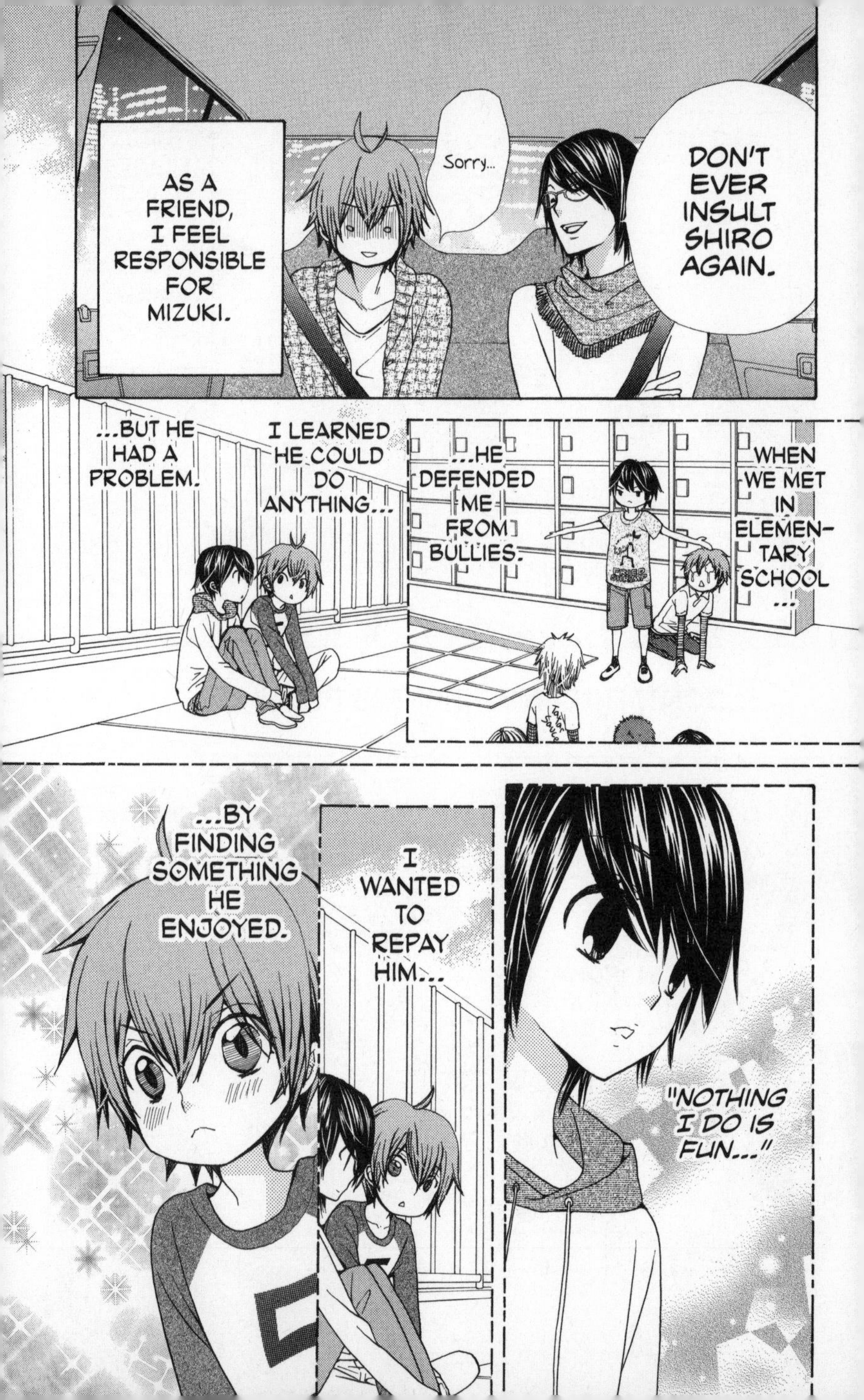
DON'T EVER INSULT SHIRO AGAIN.
Sorry...
AS A FRIEND, I FEEL RESPONSIBLE FOR MIZUKI.
WHEN WE MET IN ELEMENTARY SCHOOL...
...HE DEFENDED ME FROM BULLIES.
I LEARNED HE COULD DO ANYTHING...
...BUT HE HAD A PROBLEM.
"NOTHING I DO IS FUN..."
I WANTED TO REPAY HIM...
...BY FINDING SOMETHING HE ENJOYED.

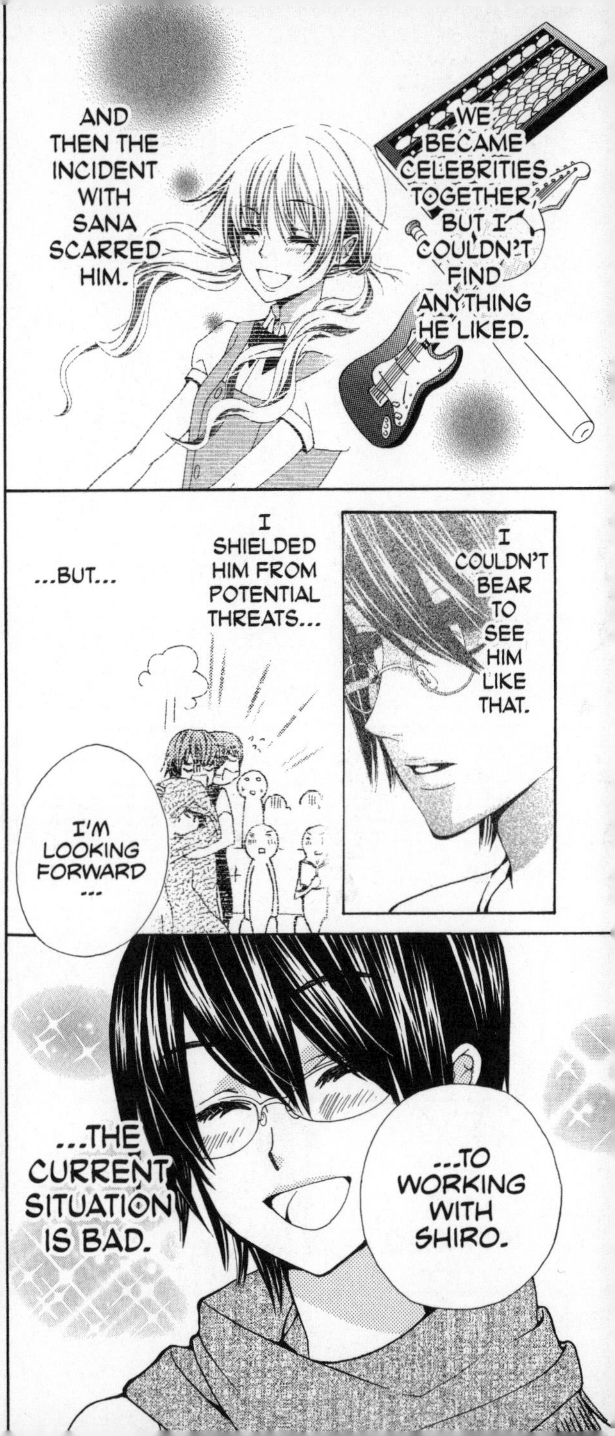
WE BECAME CELEBRITIES TOGETHER, BUT I COULDN'T FIND ANYTHING HE LIKED.
AND THEN THE INCIDENT WITH SANA SCARRED HIM.
I COULDN'T BEAR TO SEE HIM LIKE THAT.
I SHIELDED HIM FROM POTENTIAL THREATS...
...BUT...
I'M LOOKING FORWARD...
...TO WORKING WITH SHIRO.
...THE CURRENT SITUATION IS BAD.

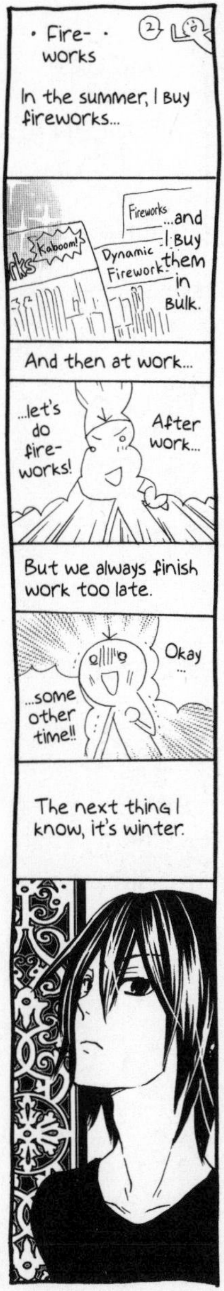
· Fire-works ·
②
In the summer, I buy fireworks...
Fireworks
Kaboom!
Dynamic Firework
...and I buy them in bulk.
And then at work...
After work...
...let's do fire-works!
But we always finish work too late.
Okay...
...some other time!!
The next thing I know, it's winter.

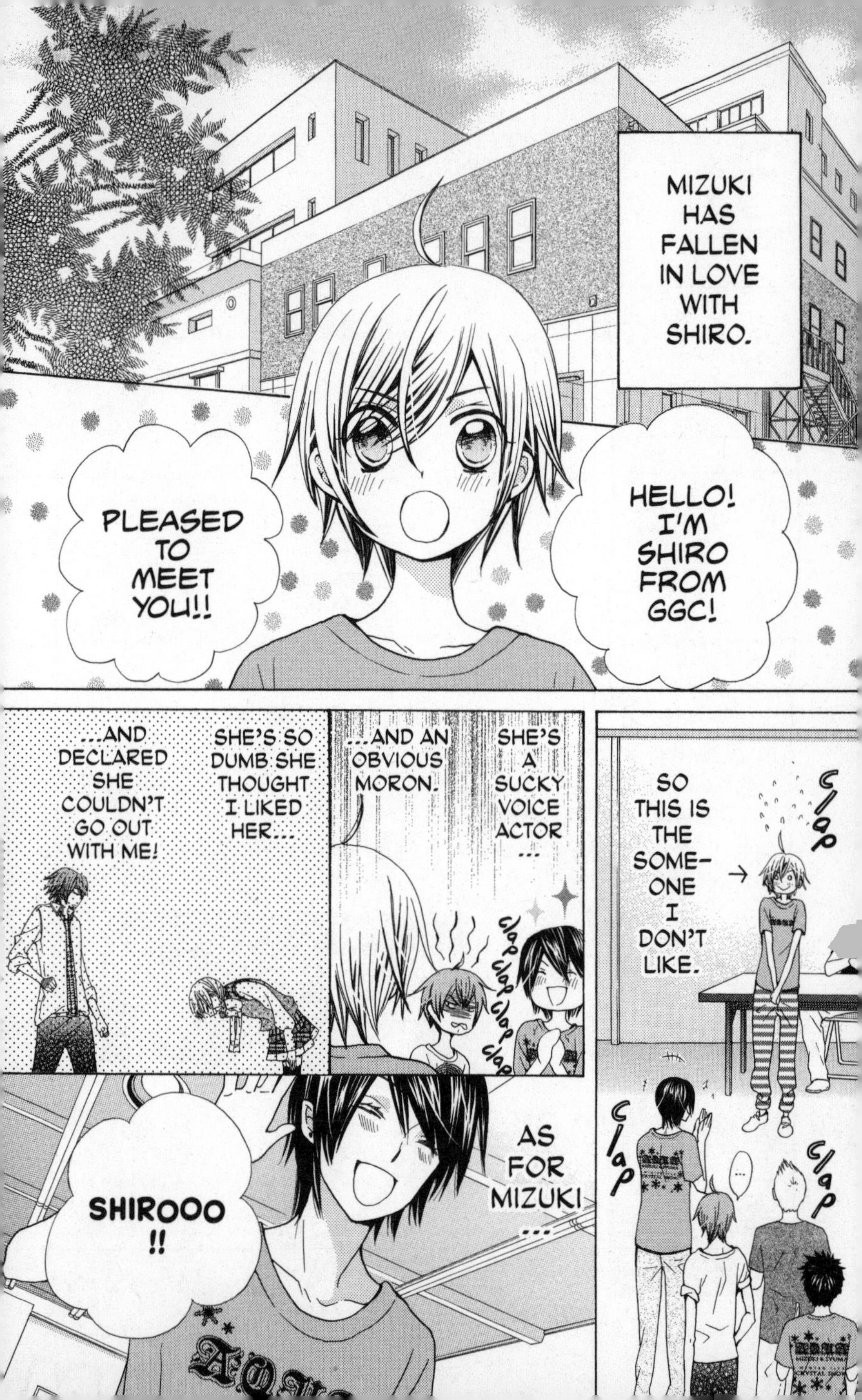
MIZUKI HAS FALLEN IN LOVE WITH SHIRO.
HELLO! I'M SHIRO FROM GGC!
PLEASED TO MEET YOU!!
SO THIS IS THE SOME-ONE I DON'T LIKE.
clap
clap
clap
...
SHE'S A SUCKY VOICE ACTOR ...
...AND AN OBVIOUS MORON.
clap clap clap clap clap
SHE'S SO DUMB SHE THOUGHT I LIKED HER...
...AND DECLARED SHE COULDN'T GO OUT WITH ME!
AS FOR MIZUKI ...
SHIROOO !!

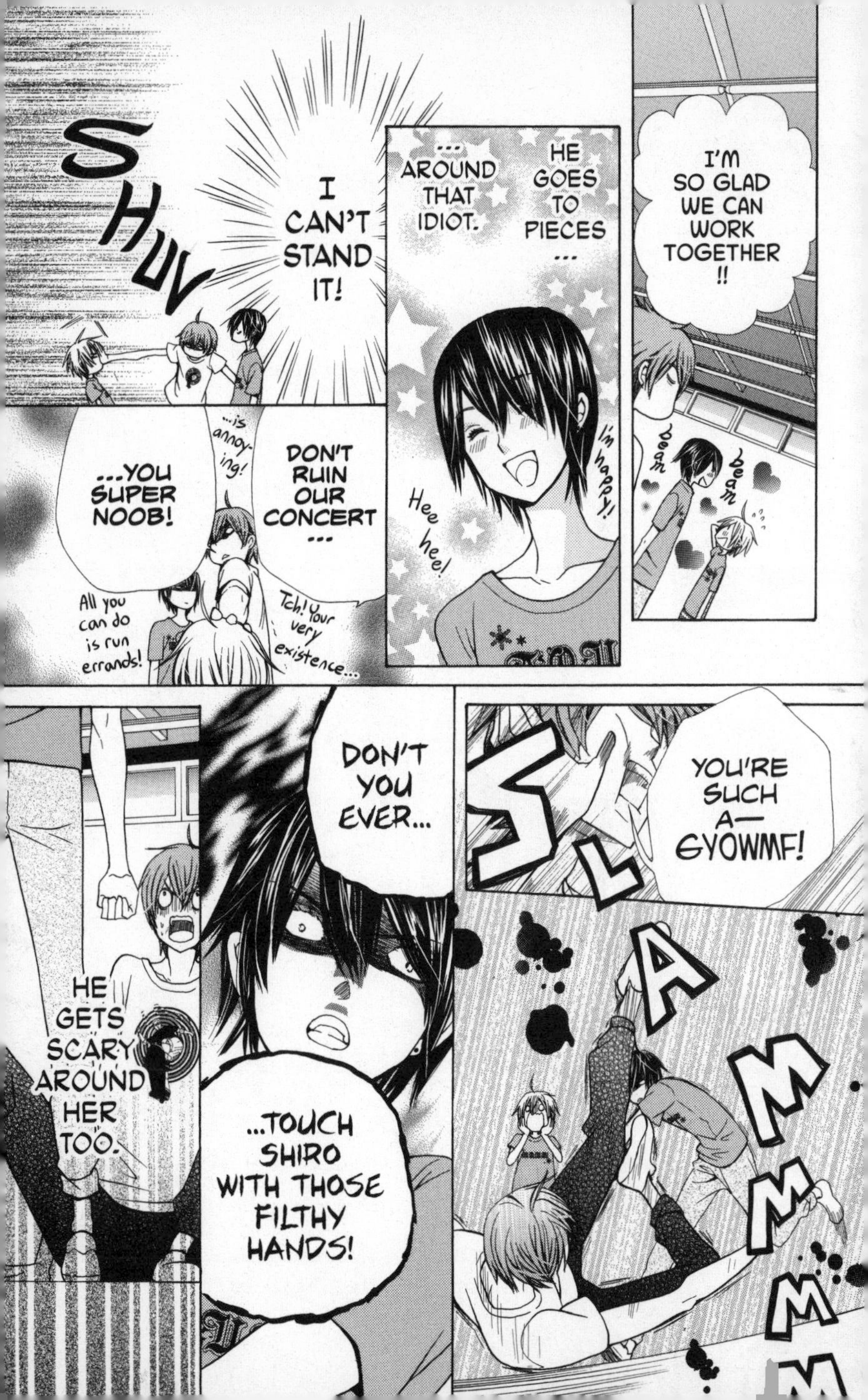
I'M SO GLAD WE CAN WORK TOGETHER!!
beam
beam
HE GOES TO PIECES...
...AROUND THAT IDIOT.
I'm happy!
Hee hee!
I CAN'T STAND IT!
SHUV
DON'T RUIN OUR CONCERT...
...YOU SUPER NOOB!
Tch! Your very existence...
...is annoying!
All you can do is run errands!
YOU'RE SUCH A—GYOWMF!
SLAMMMM
DON'T YOU EVER...
...TOUCH SHIRO WITH THOSE FILTHY HANDS!
HE GETS SCARY AROUND HER TOO.

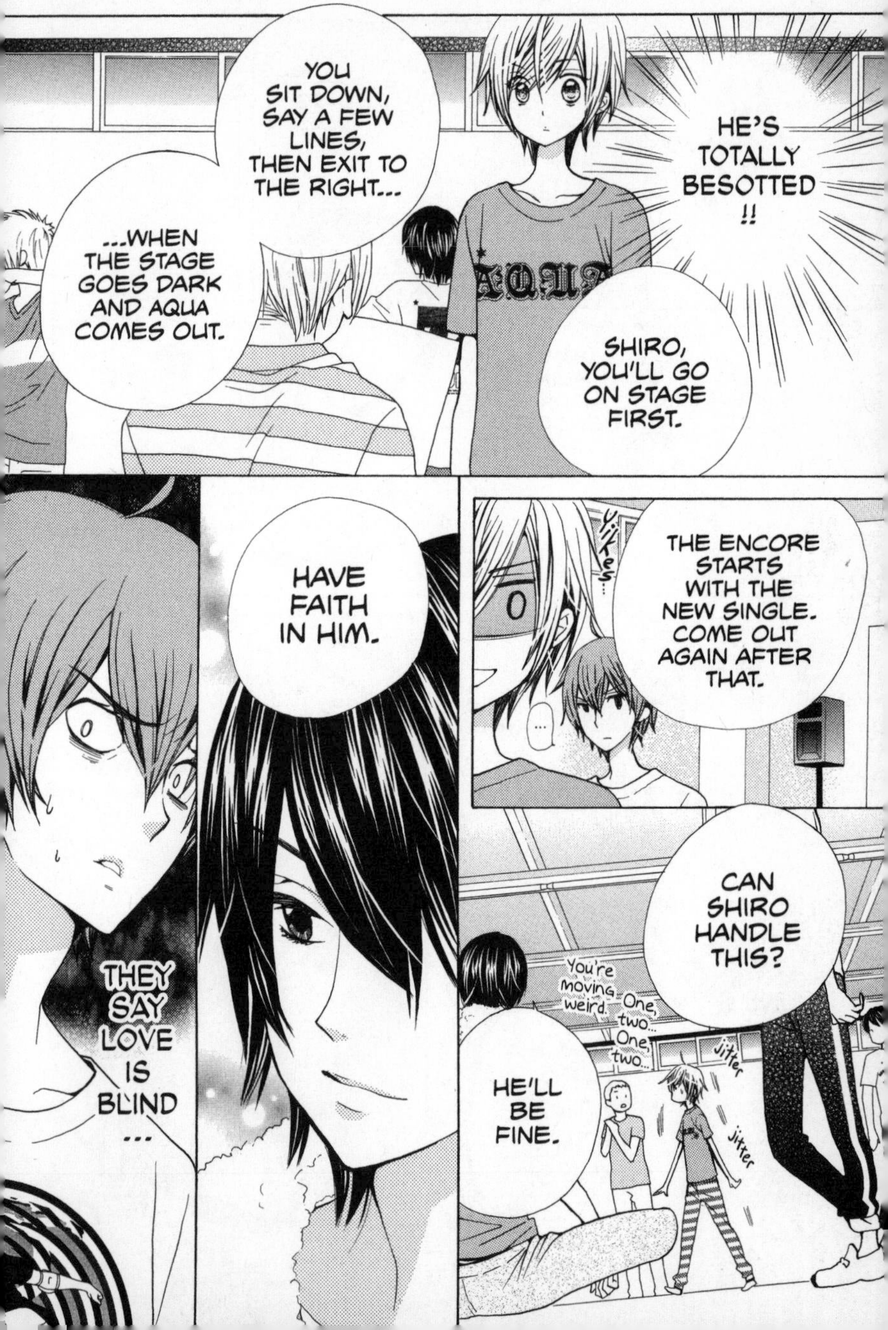
HE'S TOTALLY BESOTTED !!
SHIRO, YOU'LL GO ON STAGE FIRST.
YOU SIT DOWN, SAY A FEW LINES, THEN EXIT TO THE RIGHT...
...WHEN THE STAGE GOES DARK AND AQUA COMES OUT.
AQUA
Yikes...
THE ENCORE STARTS WITH THE NEW SINGLE. COME OUT AGAIN AFTER THAT.
...
CAN SHIRO HANDLE THIS?
jitter
jitter
One, two... One, two...
You're moving weird.
HE'LL BE FINE.
HAVE FAITH IN HIM.
THEY SAY LOVE IS BLIND ...

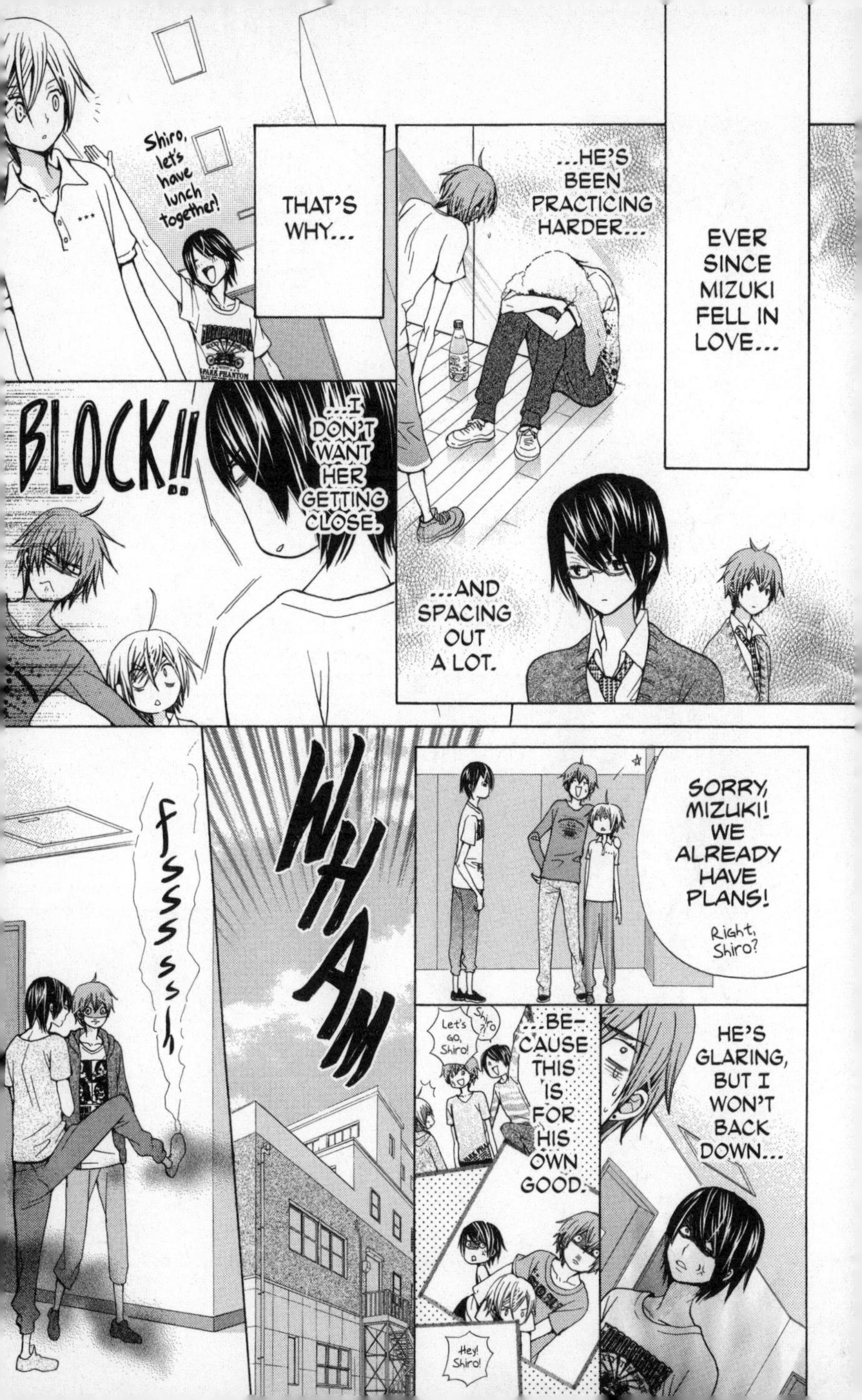
EVER SINCE MIZUKI FELL IN LOVE...
...HE'S BEEN PRACTICING HARDER...
...AND SPACING OUT A LOT.
THAT'S WHY...
Shiro, let's have lunch together!
...I DON'T WANT HER GETTING CLOSE.
BLOCK!!
SORRY, MIZUKI! WE ALREADY HAVE PLANS!
Right, Shiro?
HE'S GLARING, BUT I WON'T BACK DOWN...
...BE-CAUSE THIS IS FOR HIS OWN GOOD.
Shiro?!
Let's go, Shiro!
Hey! Shiro!
WHAM
fsssss

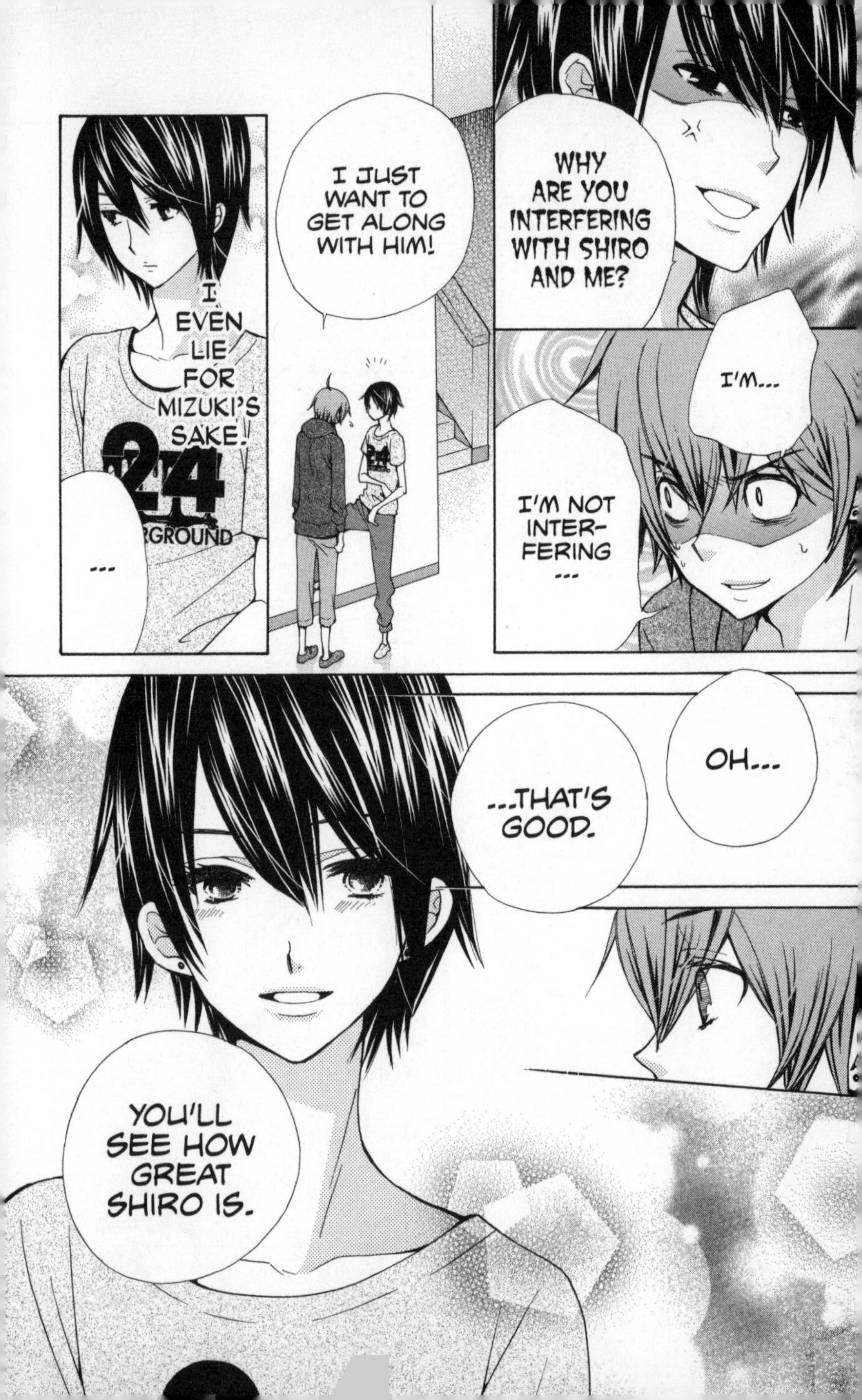
WHY ARE YOU INTERFERING WITH SHIRO AND ME?
I'M...
I'M NOT INTERFERING...
I JUST WANT TO GET ALONG WITH HIM!
I EVEN LIE FOR MIZUKI'S SAKE!
...
OH...
...THAT'S GOOD.
YOU'LL SEE HOW GREAT SHIRO IS.

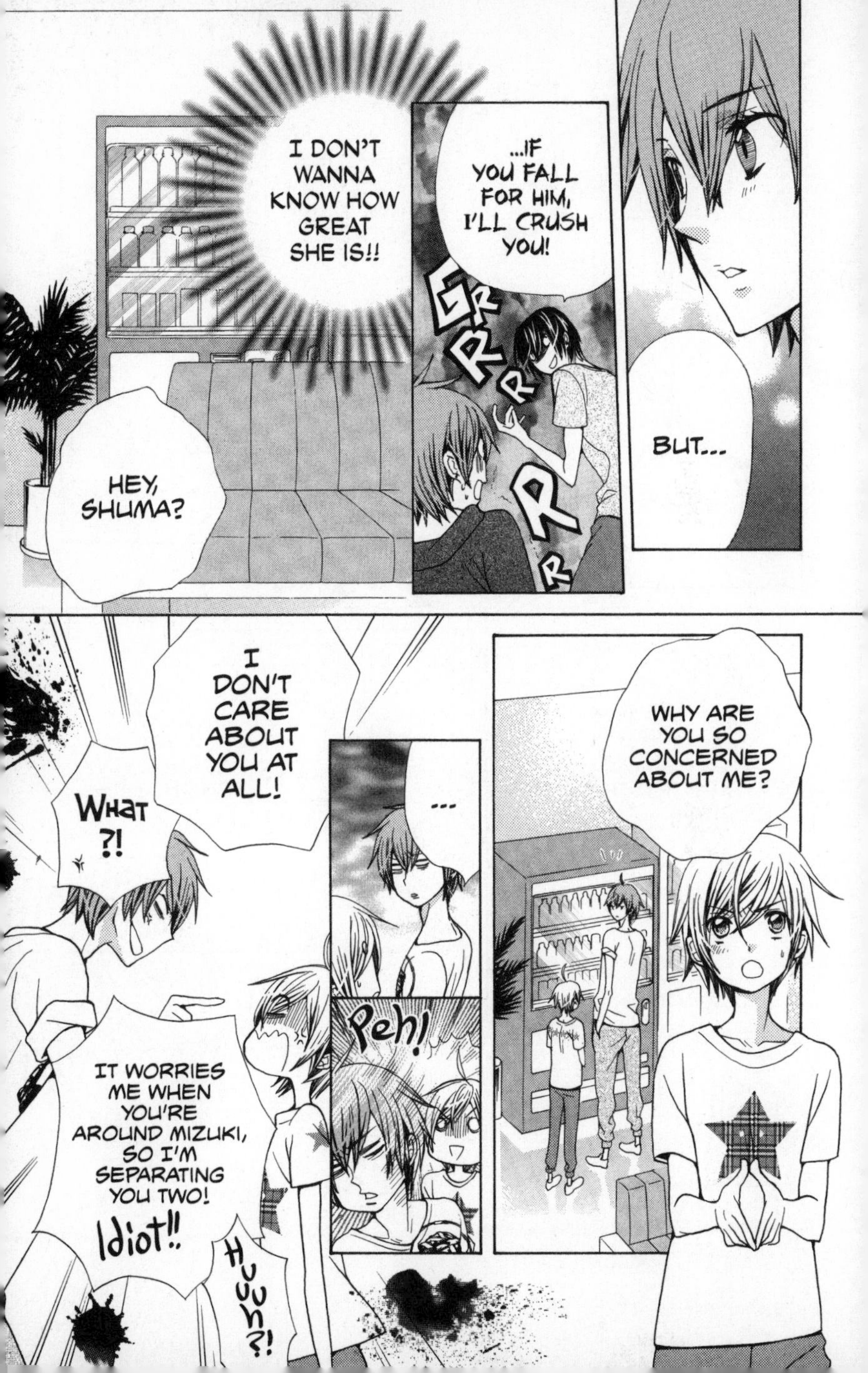
BUT...
...IF YOU FALL FOR HIM, I'LL CRUSH YOU!
GRRRRR
I DON'T WANNA KNOW HOW GREAT SHE IS!!
HEY, SHUMA?
WHY ARE YOU SO CONCERNED ABOUT ME?
...
Peh!
I DON'T CARE ABOUT YOU AT ALL!
WHAT?!
IT WORRIES ME WHEN YOU'RE AROUND MIZUKI, SO I'M SEPARATING YOU TWO!
Idiot!!
Huuun?!

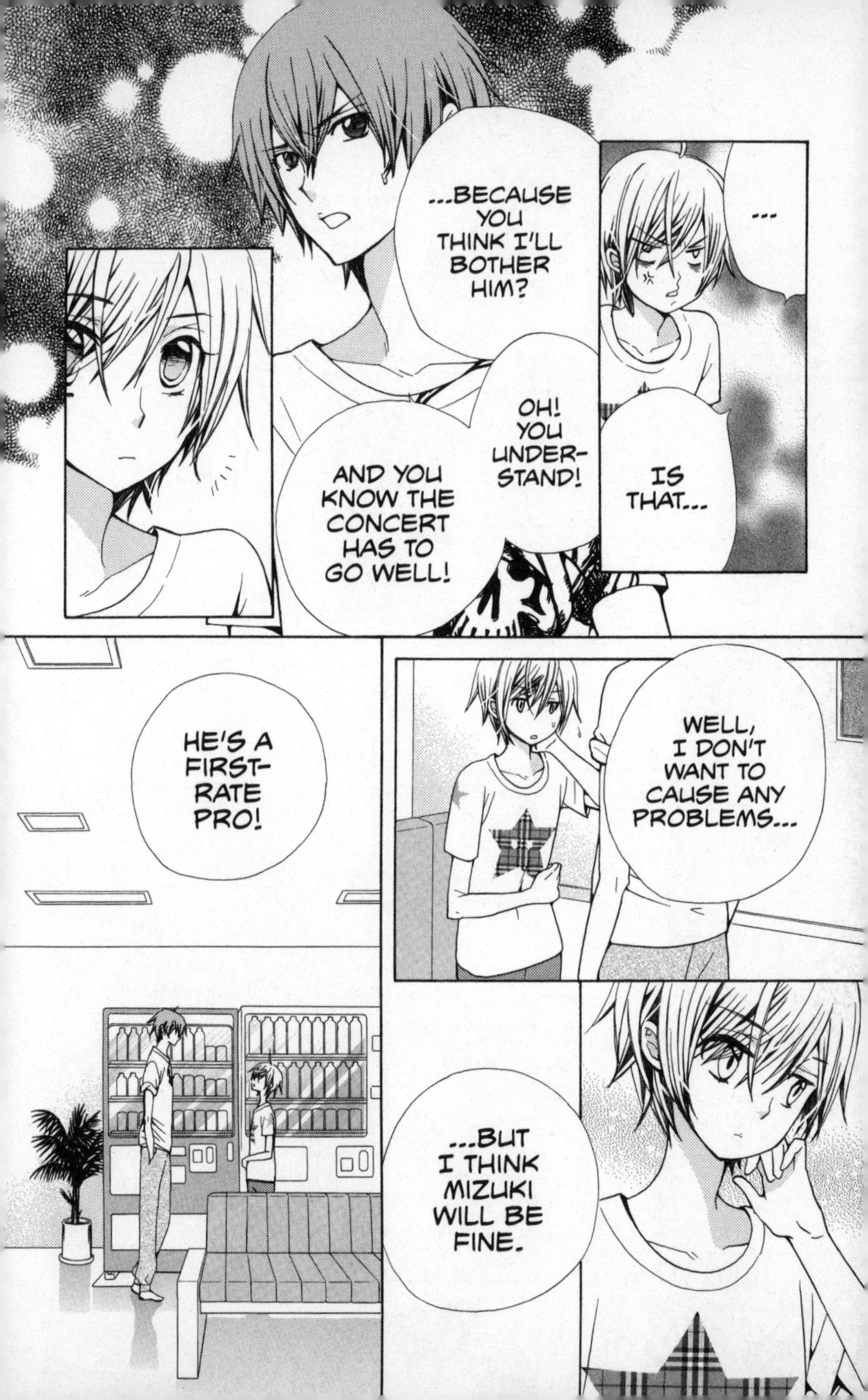
...
IS THAT...
...BECAUSE YOU THINK I'LL BOTHER HIM?
OH! YOU UNDER-STAND!
AND YOU KNOW THE CONCERT HAS TO GO WELL!
WELL, I DON'T WANT TO CAUSE ANY PROBLEMS...
HE'S A FIRST-RATE PRO!
...BUT I THINK MIZUKI WILL BE FINE.

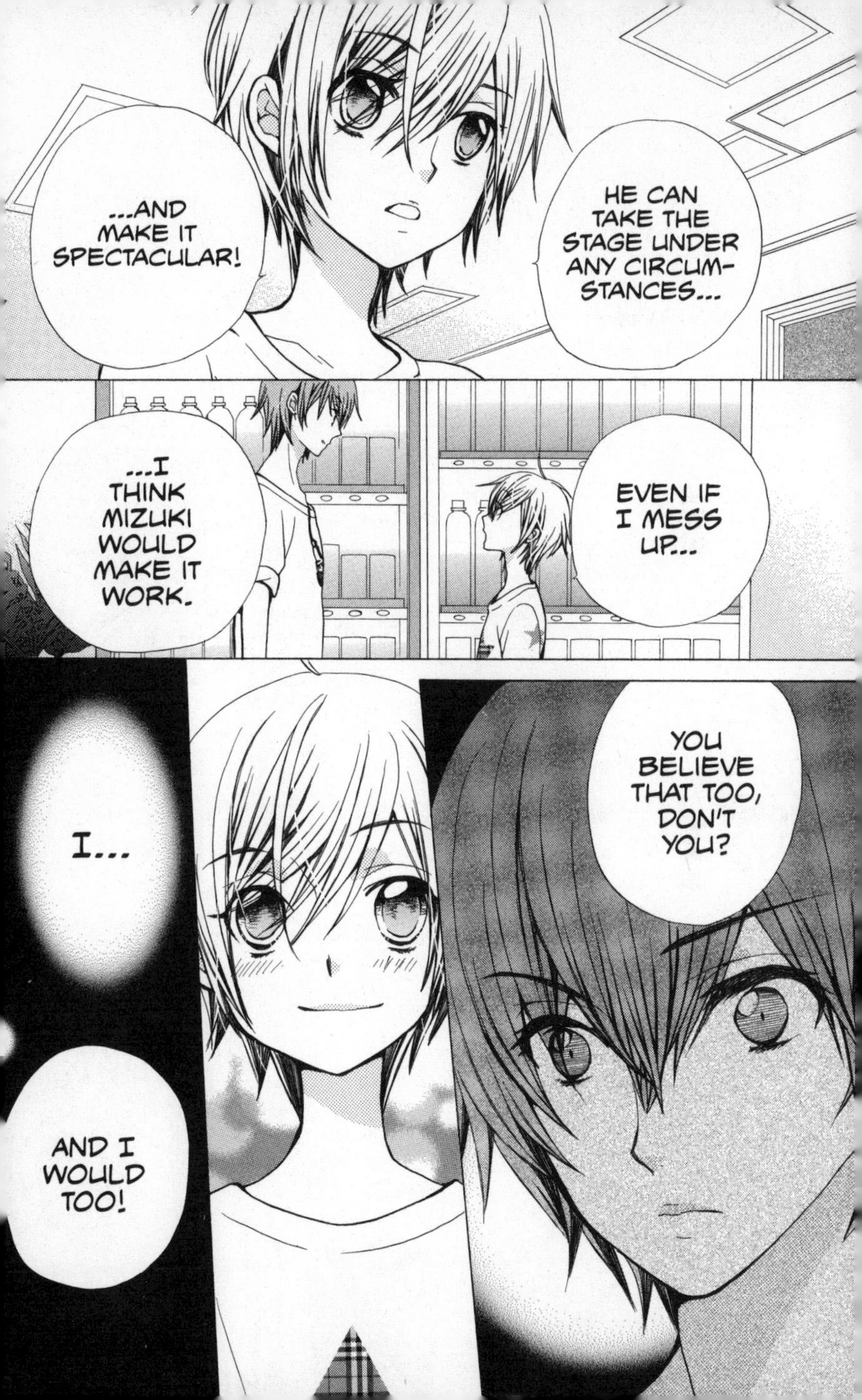
HE CAN TAKE THE STAGE UNDER ANY CIRCUM-STANCES...
...AND MAKE IT SPECTACULAR!
EVEN IF I MESS UP...
...I THINK MIZUKI WOULD MAKE IT WORK.
YOU BELIEVE THAT TOO, DON'T YOU?
I...
AND I WOULD TOO!

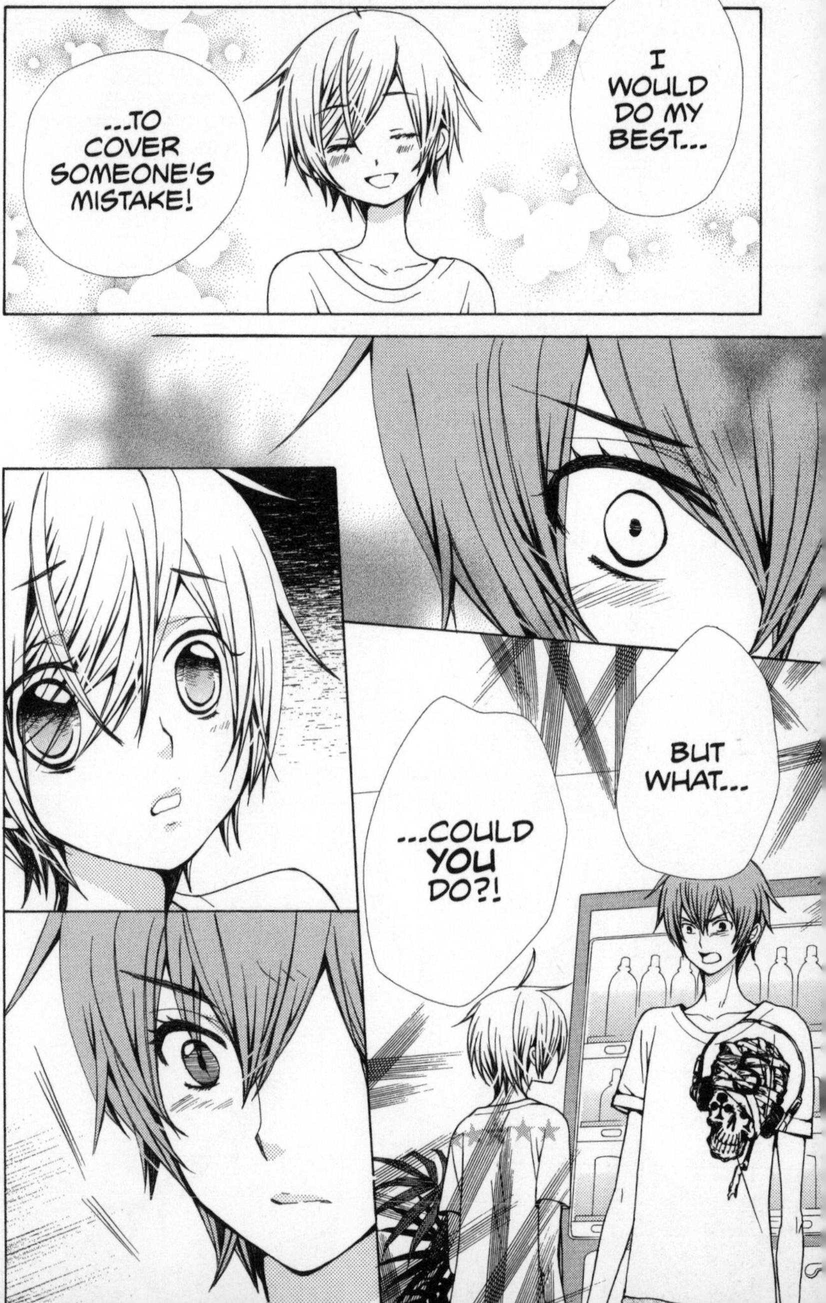
I WOULD DO MY BEST...
...TO COVER SOMEONE'S MISTAKE!
BUT WHAT...
...COULD YOU DO?!

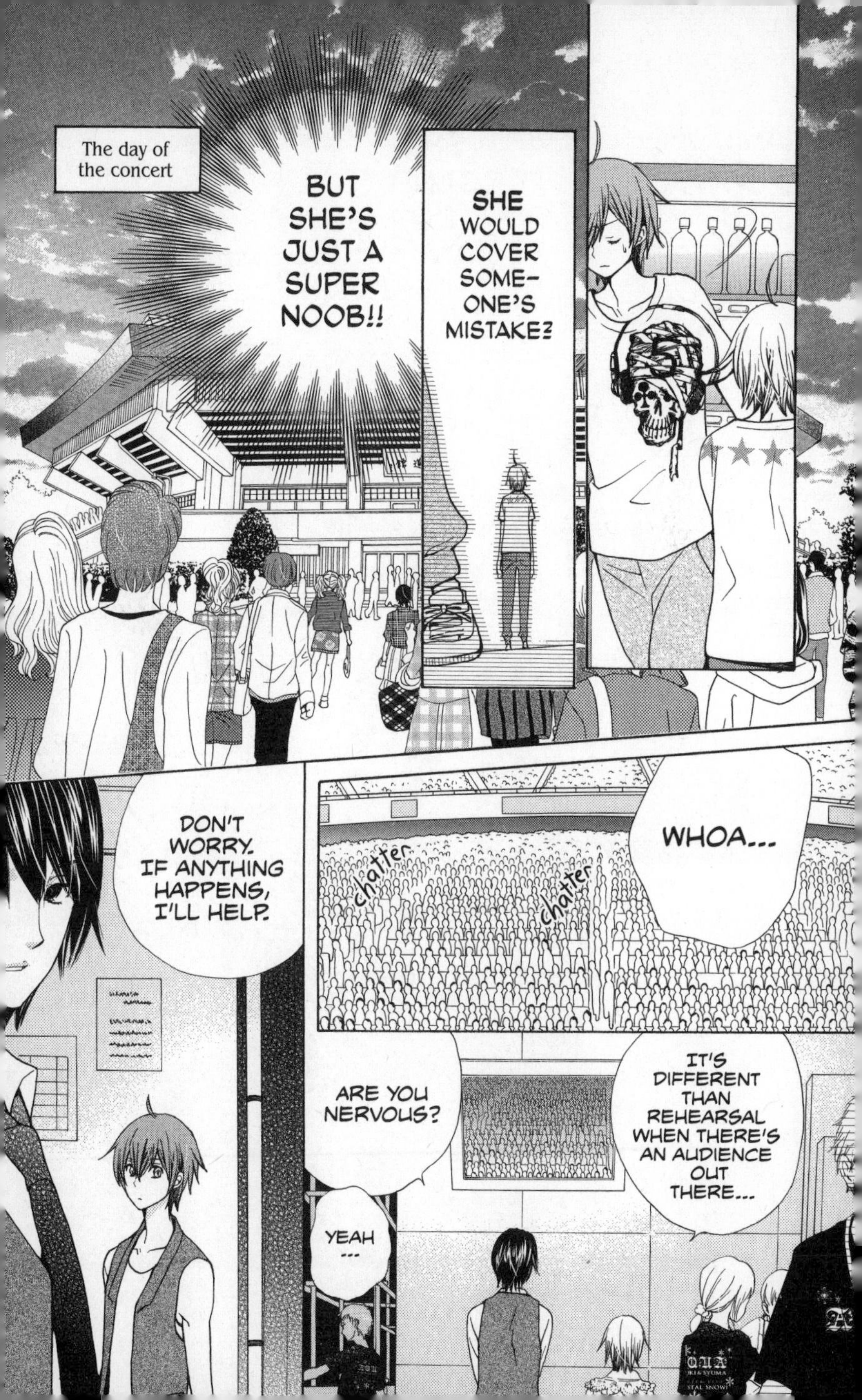
SHE WOULD COVER SOME-ONE'S MISTAKE?
BUT SHE'S JUST A SUPER NOOB!!
The day of the concert
WHOA...
chatter
chatter
IT'S DIFFERENT THAN REHEARSAL WHEN THERE'S AN AUDIENCE OUT THERE...
ARE YOU NERVOUS?
YEAH...
DON'T WORRY. IF ANYTHING HAPPENS, I'LL HELP.

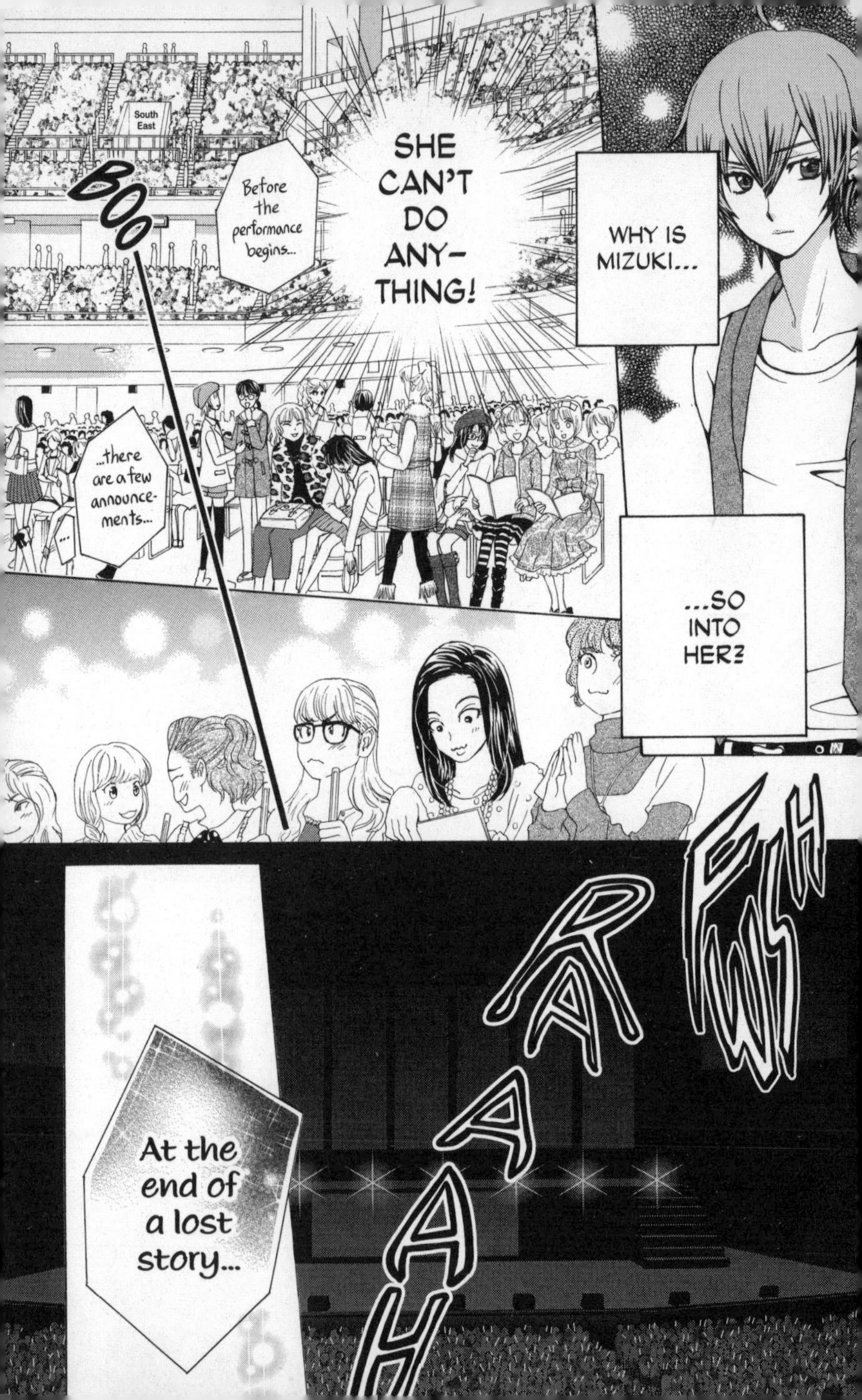
WHY IS MIZUKI...
...SO INTO HER?
SHE CAN'T DO ANY-THING!
Before the performance begins...
South East
BOO
...there are a few announce-ments...
...
FWISH
RAAAH
At the end of a lost story...

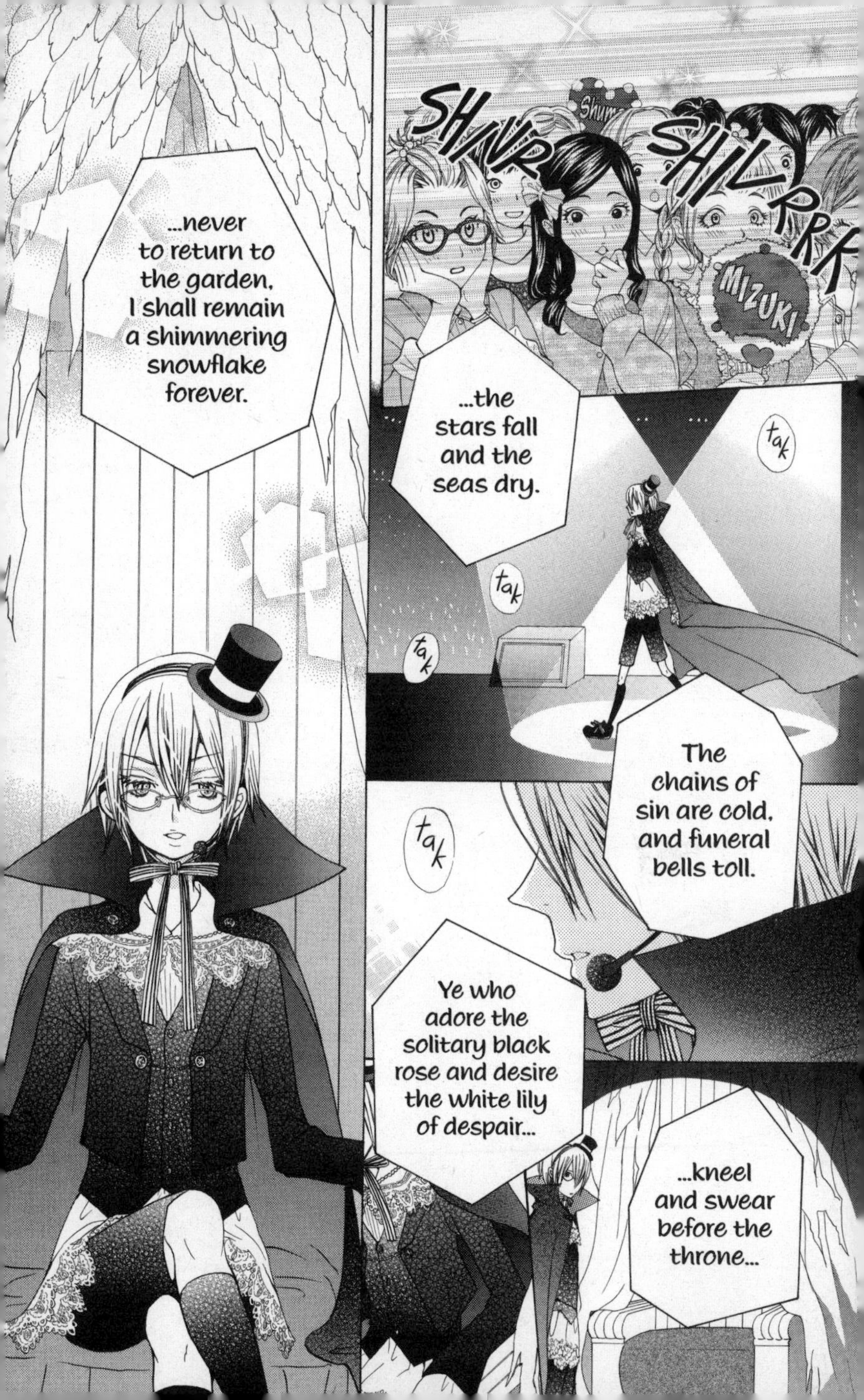
SHILRRRK
MIZUKI
Shum
SHWR
...the stars fall and the seas dry.
tak
tak
tak
The chains of sin are cold, and funeral bells toll.
tak
Ye who adore the solitary black rose and desire the white lily of despair...
...kneel and swear before the throne...
...never to return to the garden, I shall remain a shimmering snowflake forever.

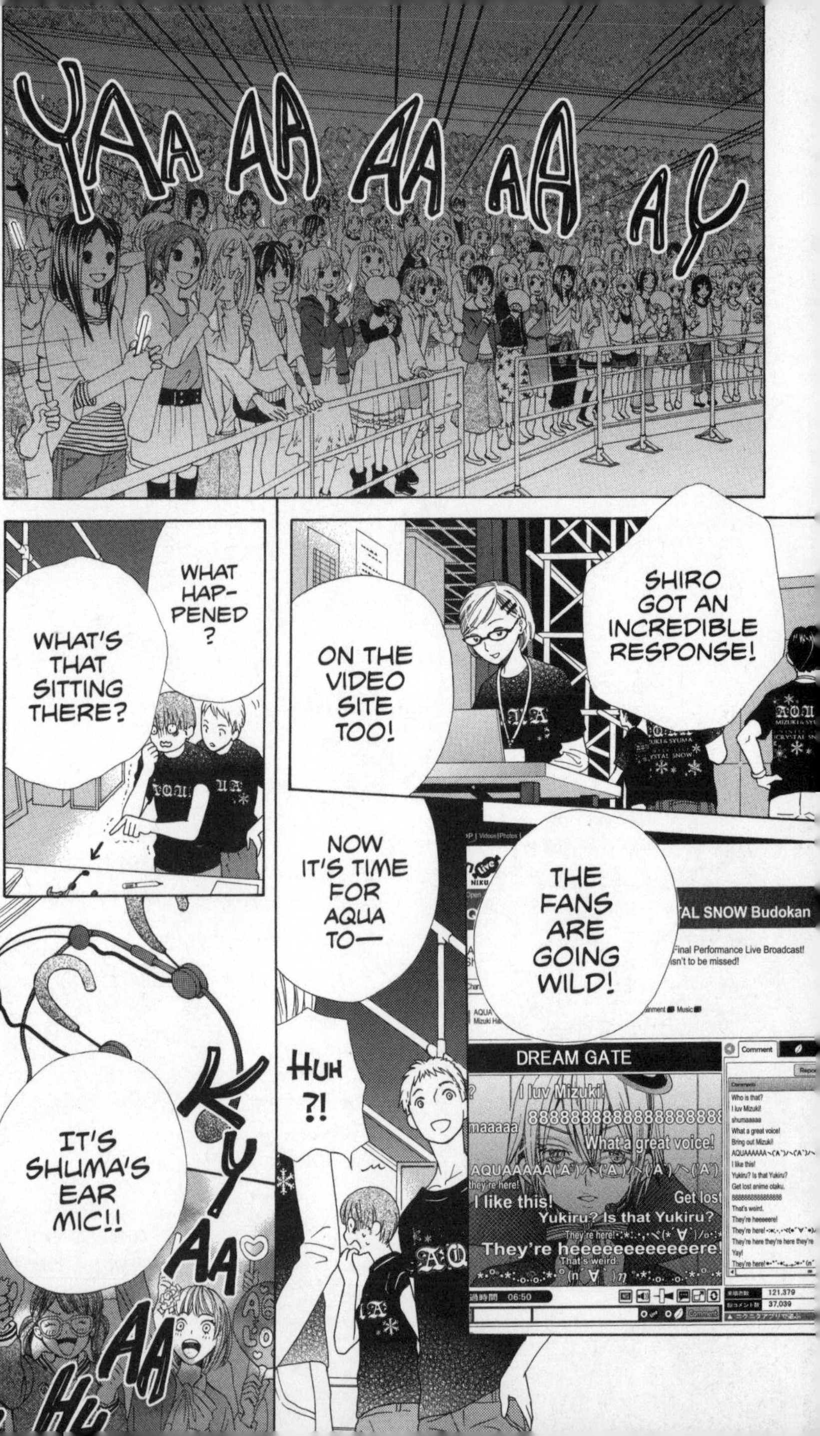
YAAAAAAAAAAY
SHIRO GOT AN INCREDIBLE RESPONSE!
ON THE VIDEO SITE TOO!
WHAT HAPPENED?
WHAT'S THAT SITTING THERE?
THE FANS ARE GOING WILD!
TAL SNOW Budokan
Final Performance Live Broadcast!
isn't to be missed!
DREAM GATE
Comment
I luv Mizuki!
What a great voice!
I like this!
Get lost
Yukiru? Is that Yukiru?
They're heeeeeeeeeeeere!
That's weird.
Who is that?
I luv Mizuki!
What a great voice!
Bring out Mizuki!
I like this!
Yukiru? Is that Yukiru?
Get lost anime otaku.
That's weird.
They're heeeeere!
They're here they're here they're
Yay!
06:50
121,379
37,039
NOW IT'S TIME FOR AQUA TO—
HUH ?!
IT'S SHUMA'S EAR MIC!!
KYAAAAAA
HU

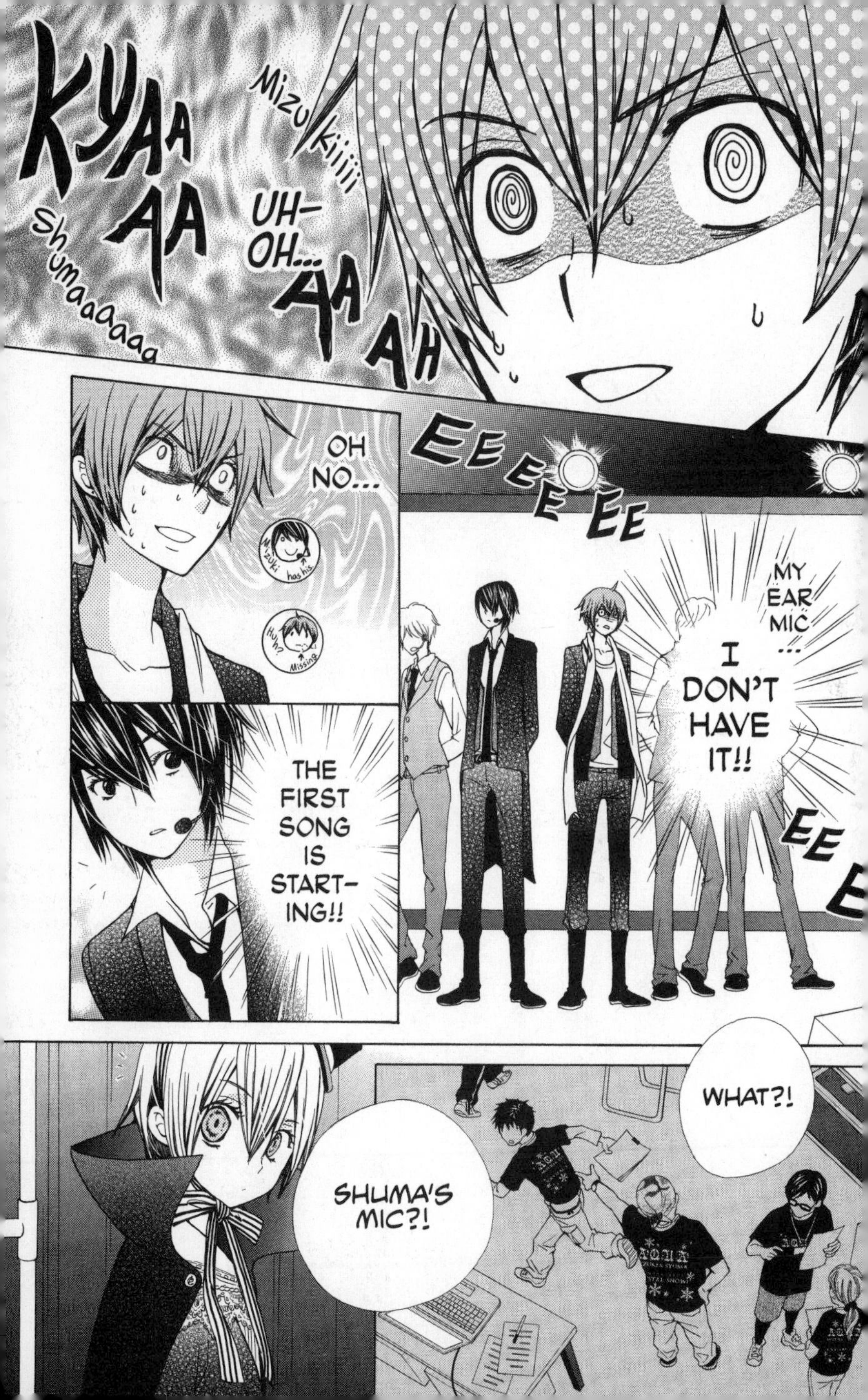
UH-OH...
Mizukiiiiii
KYAAAAAAAH
Shumaaaaaaa
EEEEEEEEE
MY EAR MIC...
I DON'T HAVE IT!!
OH NO...
Mizuki has his.
Huh?
Missing
THE FIRST SONG IS STARTING!!
WHAT?!
SHUMA'S MIC?!

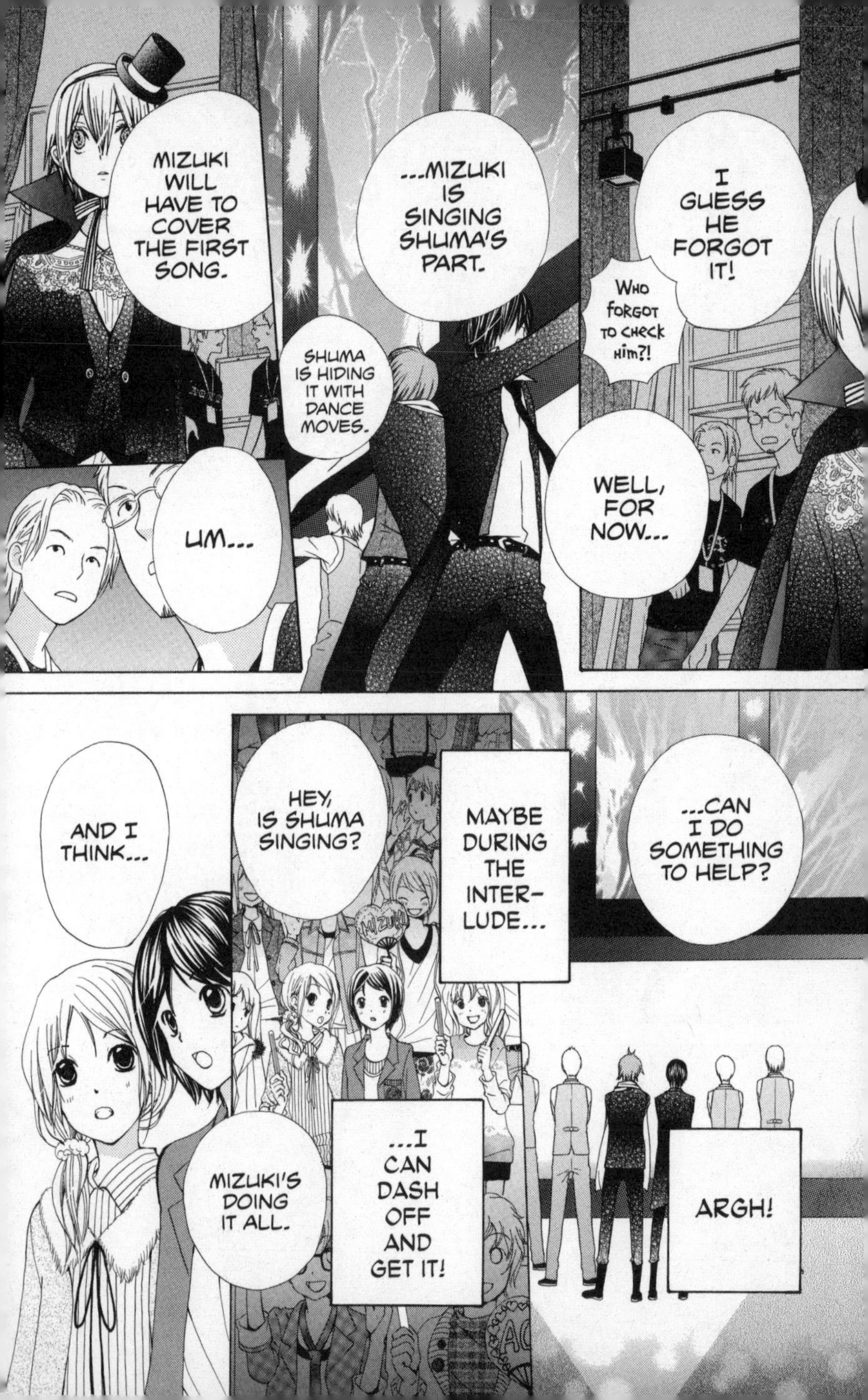
I GUESS HE FORGOT IT!
WHO FORGOT TO CHECK HIM?!
WELL, FOR NOW...
...MIZUKI IS SINGING SHUMA'S PART.
SHUMA IS HIDING IT WITH DANCE MOVES.
MIZUKI WILL HAVE TO COVER THE FIRST SONG.
UM...
...CAN I DO SOMETHING TO HELP?
ARGH!
MAYBE DURING THE INTERLUDE...
...I CAN DASH OFF AND GET IT!
HEY, IS SHUMA SINGING?
MIZUKI'S DOING IT ALL.
AND I THINK...

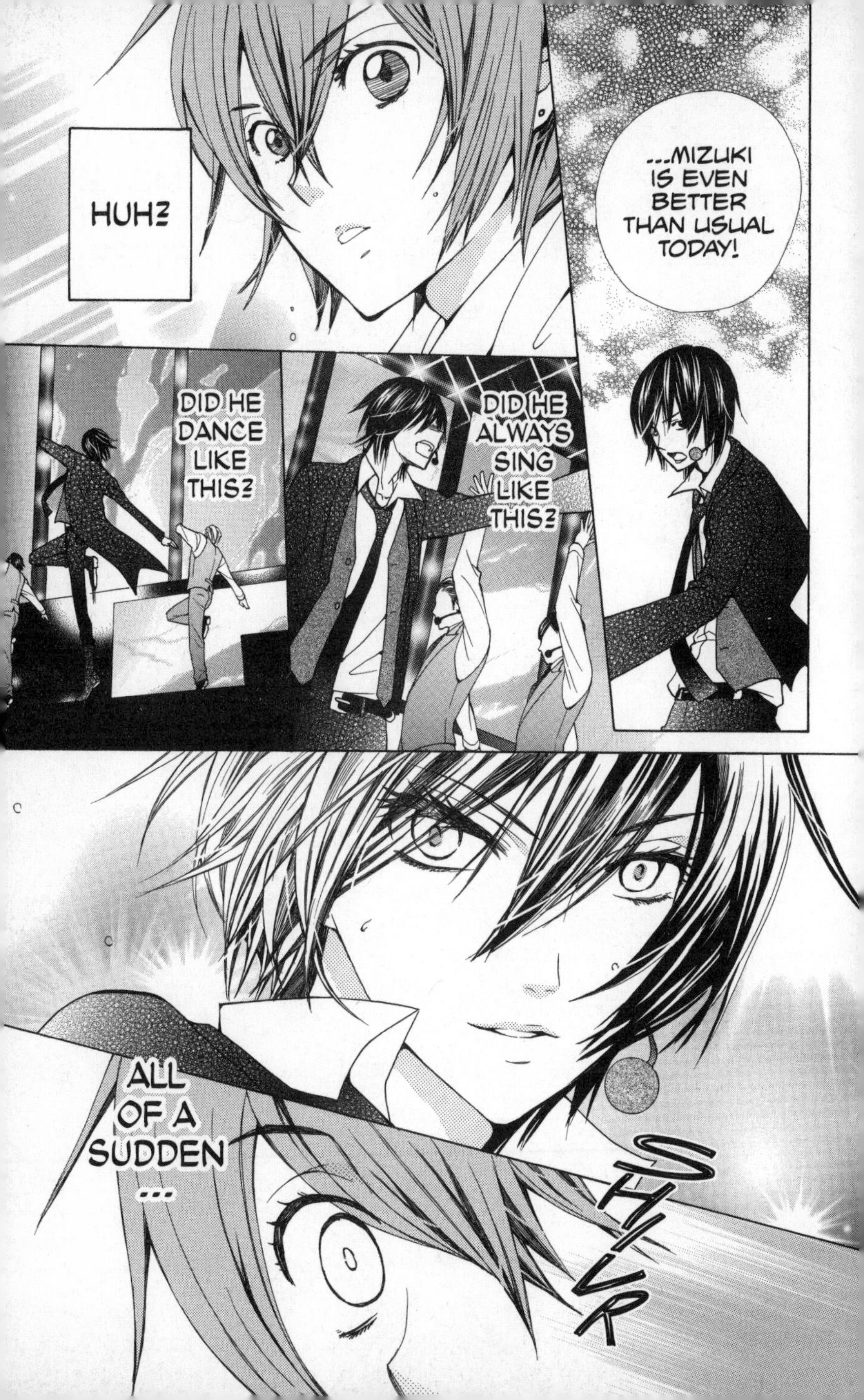
...MIZUKI IS EVEN BETTER THAN USUAL TODAY!
HUH?
DID HE ALWAYS SING LIKE THIS?
DID HE DANCE LIKE THIS?
SHIVR
ALL OF A SUDDEN ...

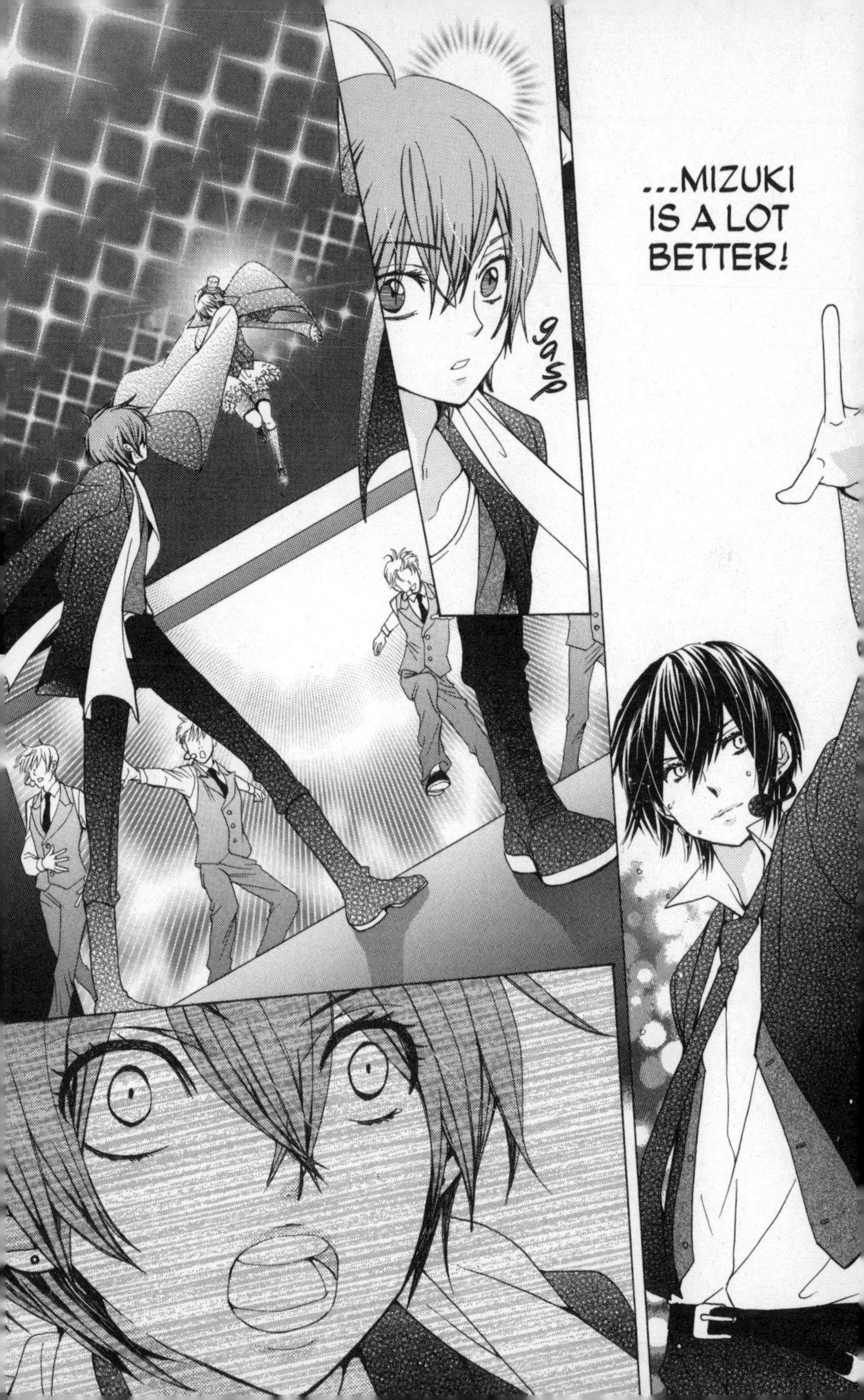
...MIZUKI IS A LOT BETTER!
gasp

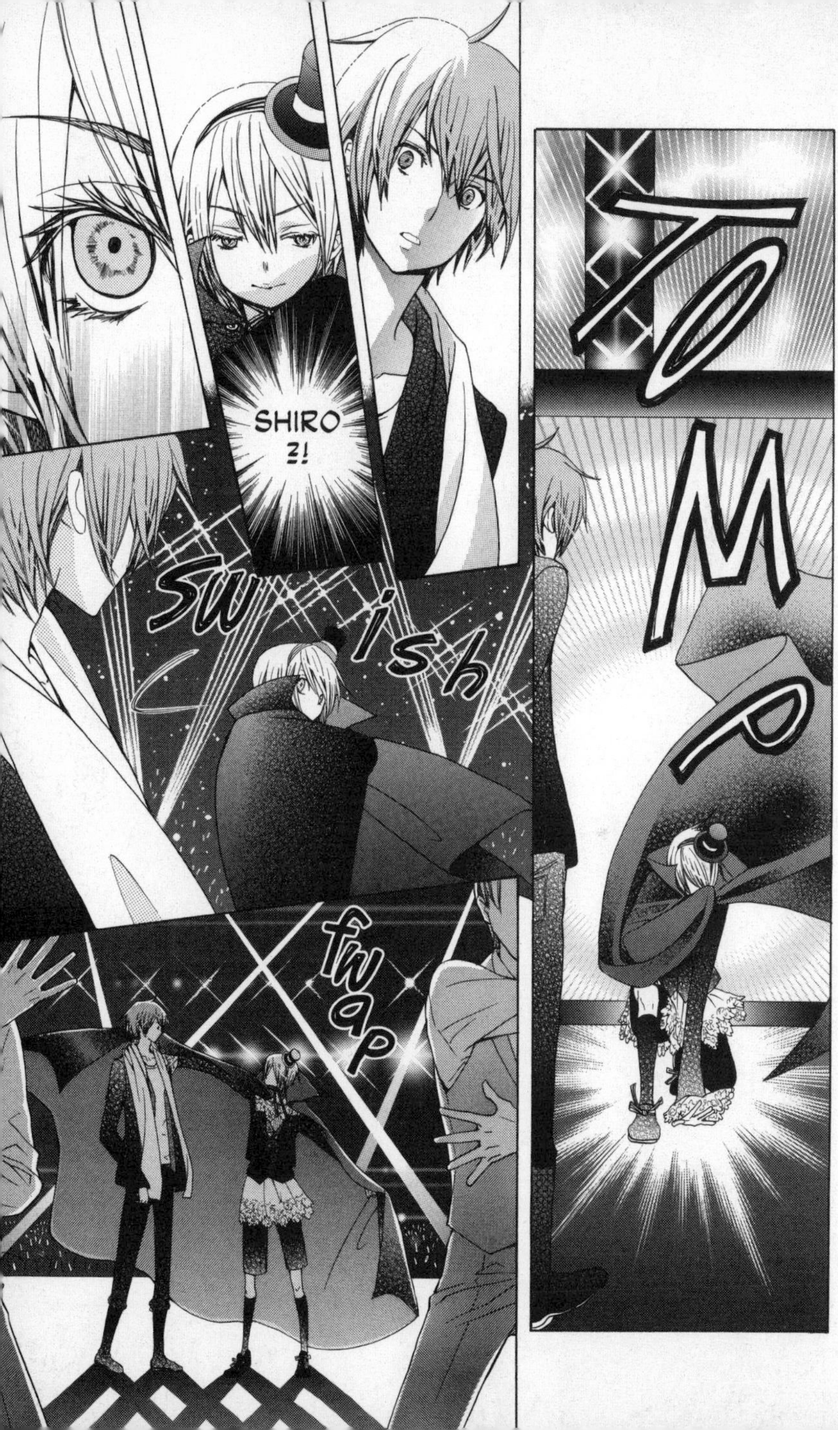

SHIRO?!
TOMP
Swish
fwap

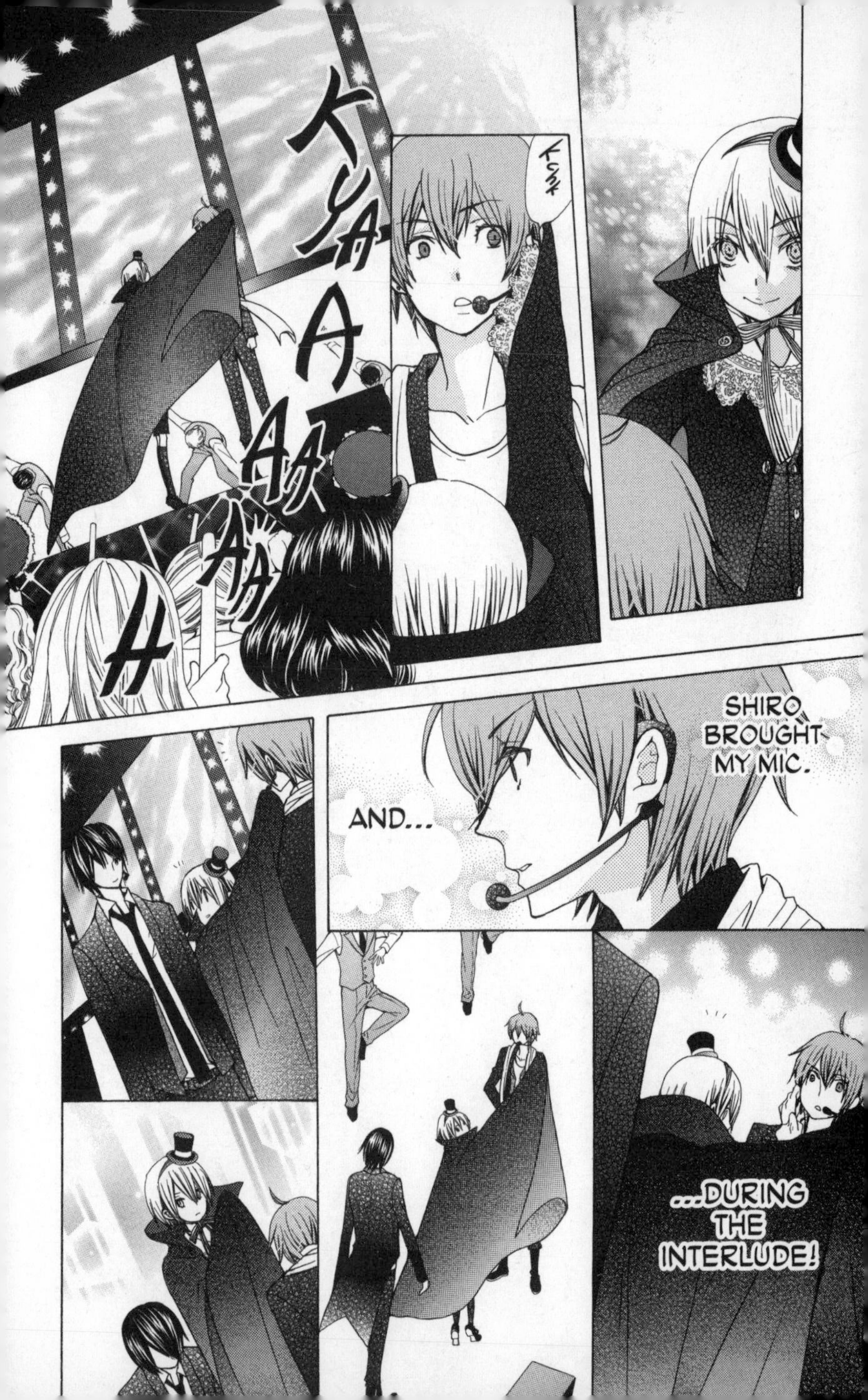
KUNK
KYAAAAAAH
SHIRO BROUGHT MY MIC.
AND...
...DURING THE INTERLUDE!

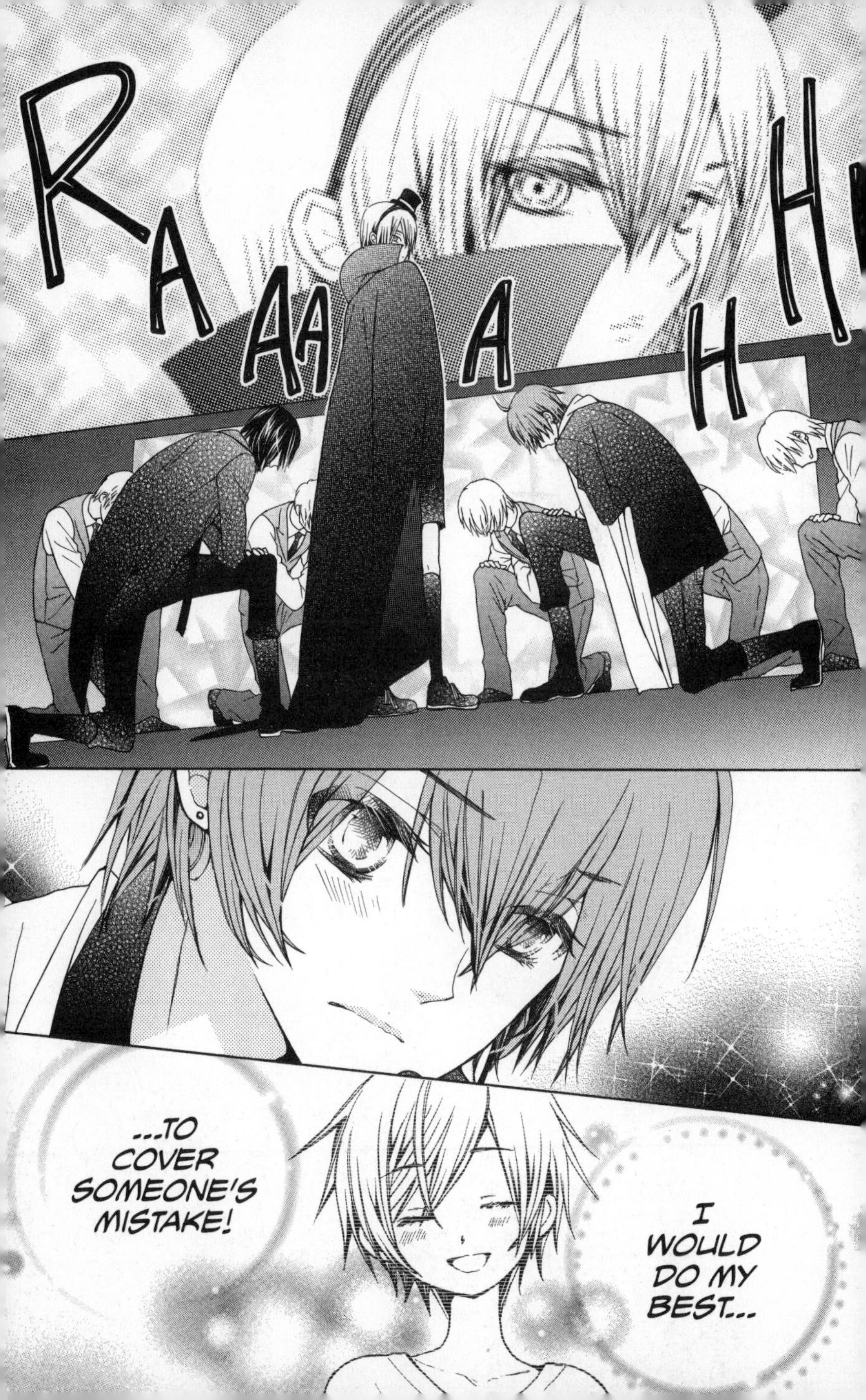
RAAAAHHH
I WOULD DO MY BEST...
...TO COVER SOMEONE'S MISTAKE!

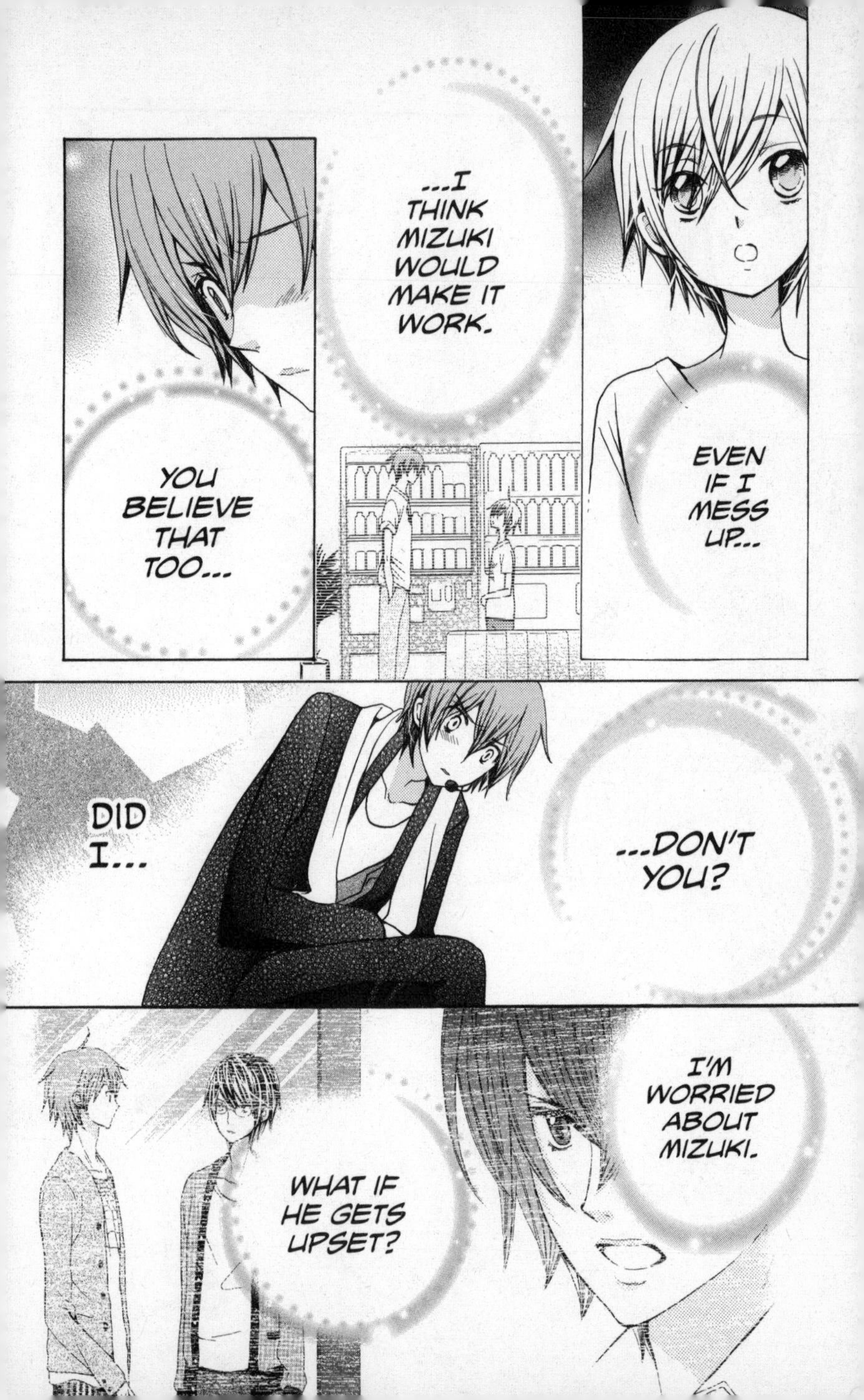
EVEN IF I MESS UP...
...I THINK MIZUKI WOULD MAKE IT WORK.
YOU BELIEVE THAT TOO...
...DON'T YOU?
DID I...
I'M WORRIED ABOUT MIZUKI.
WHAT IF HE GETS UPSET?

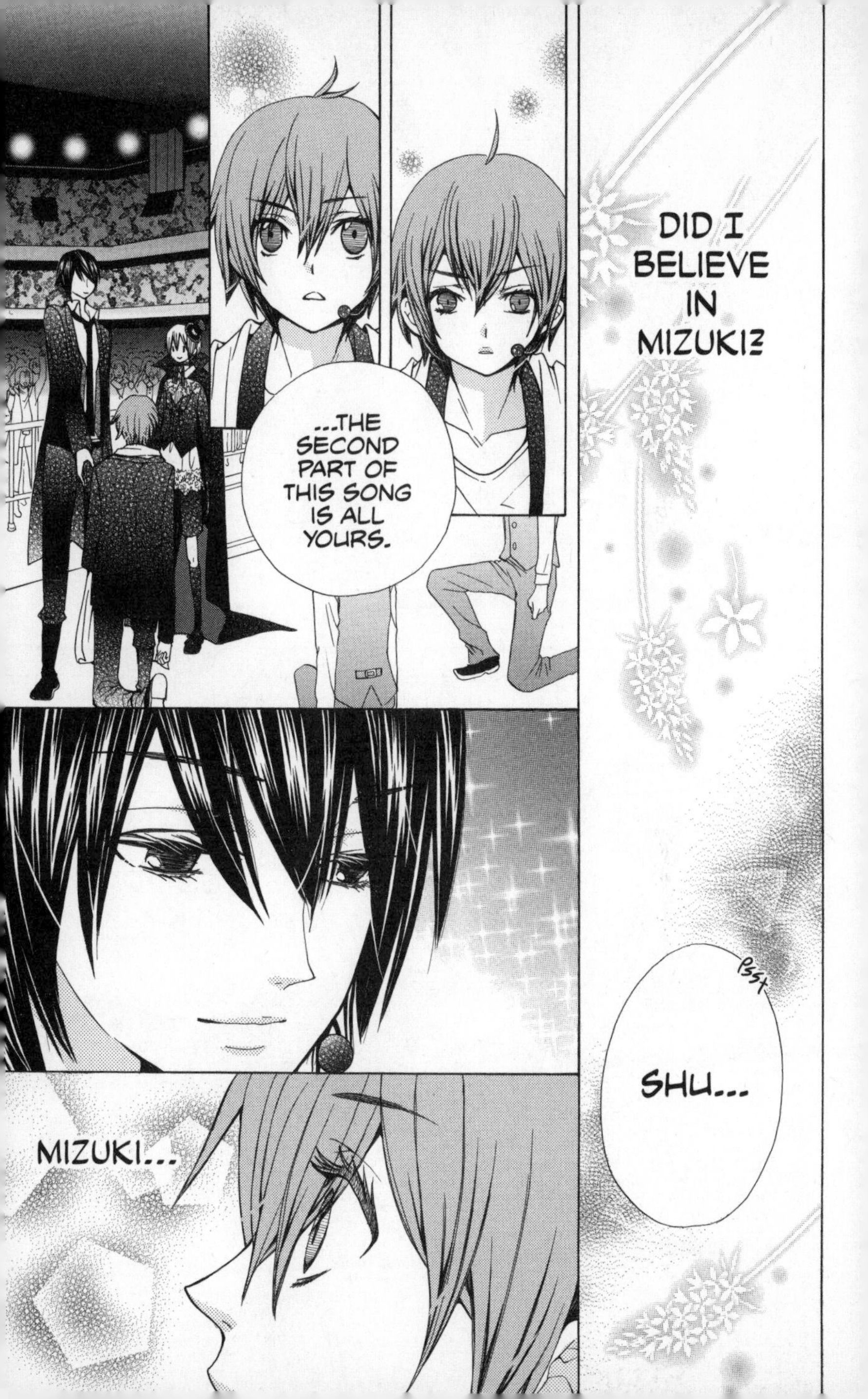
DID I BELIEVE IN MIZUKI?
Psst
SHU...
...THE SECOND PART OF THIS SONG IS ALL YOURS.
MIZUKI...

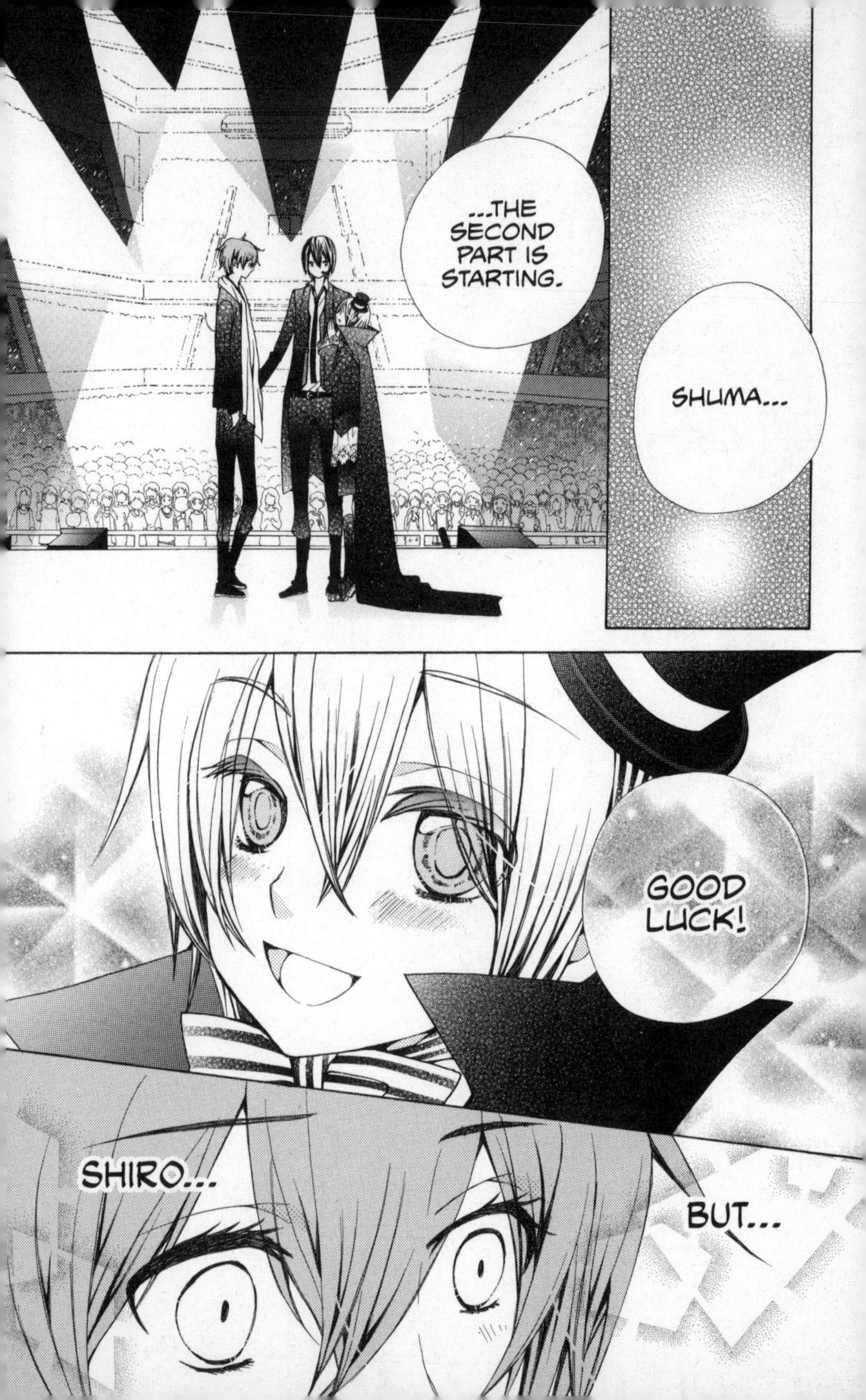
SHUMA...
...THE SECOND PART IS STARTING.
GOOD LUCK!
SHIRO...
BUT...

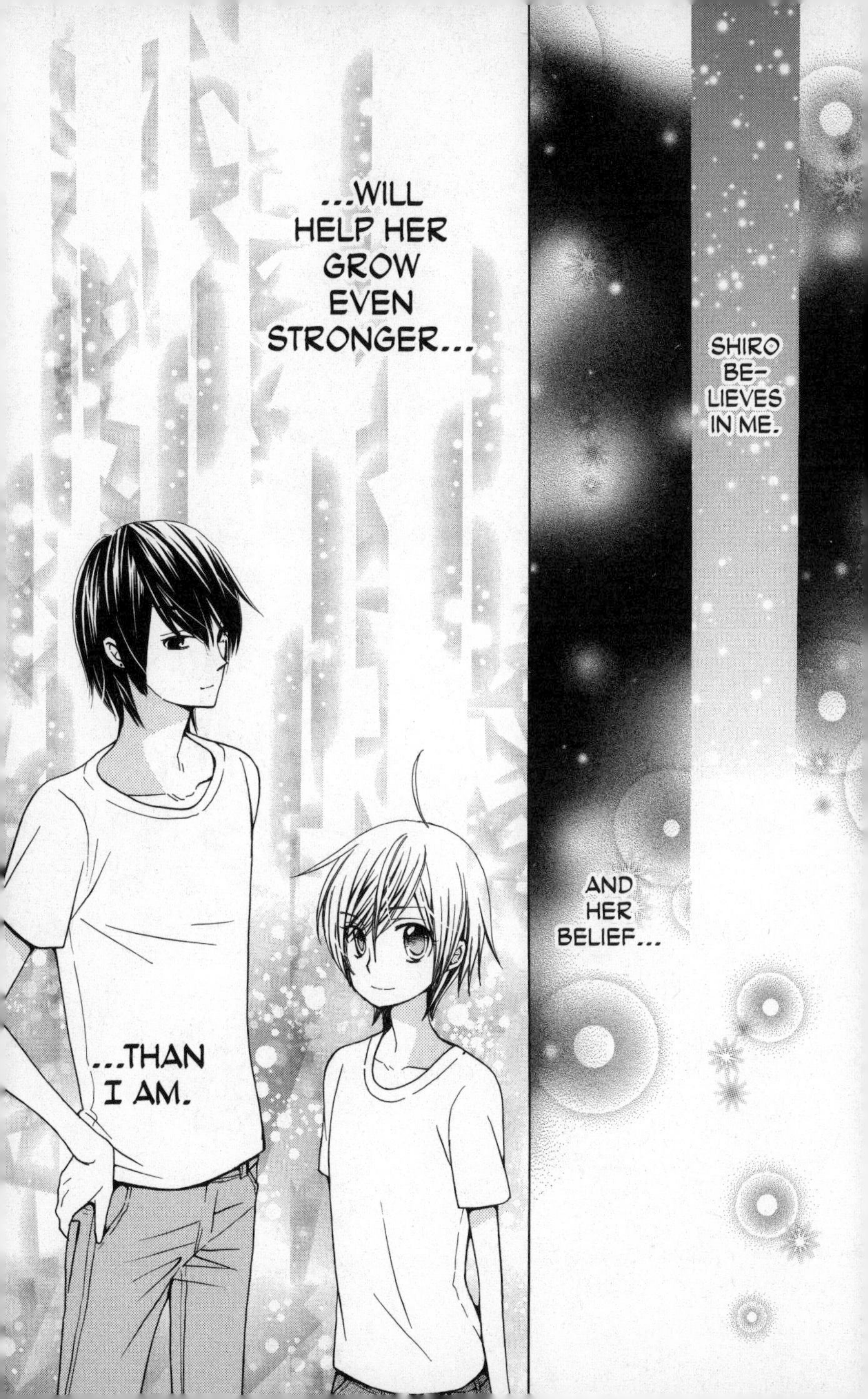
SHIRO BE-LIEVES IN ME.
AND HER BELIEF...
...WILL HELP HER GROW EVEN STRONGER...
...THAN I AM.

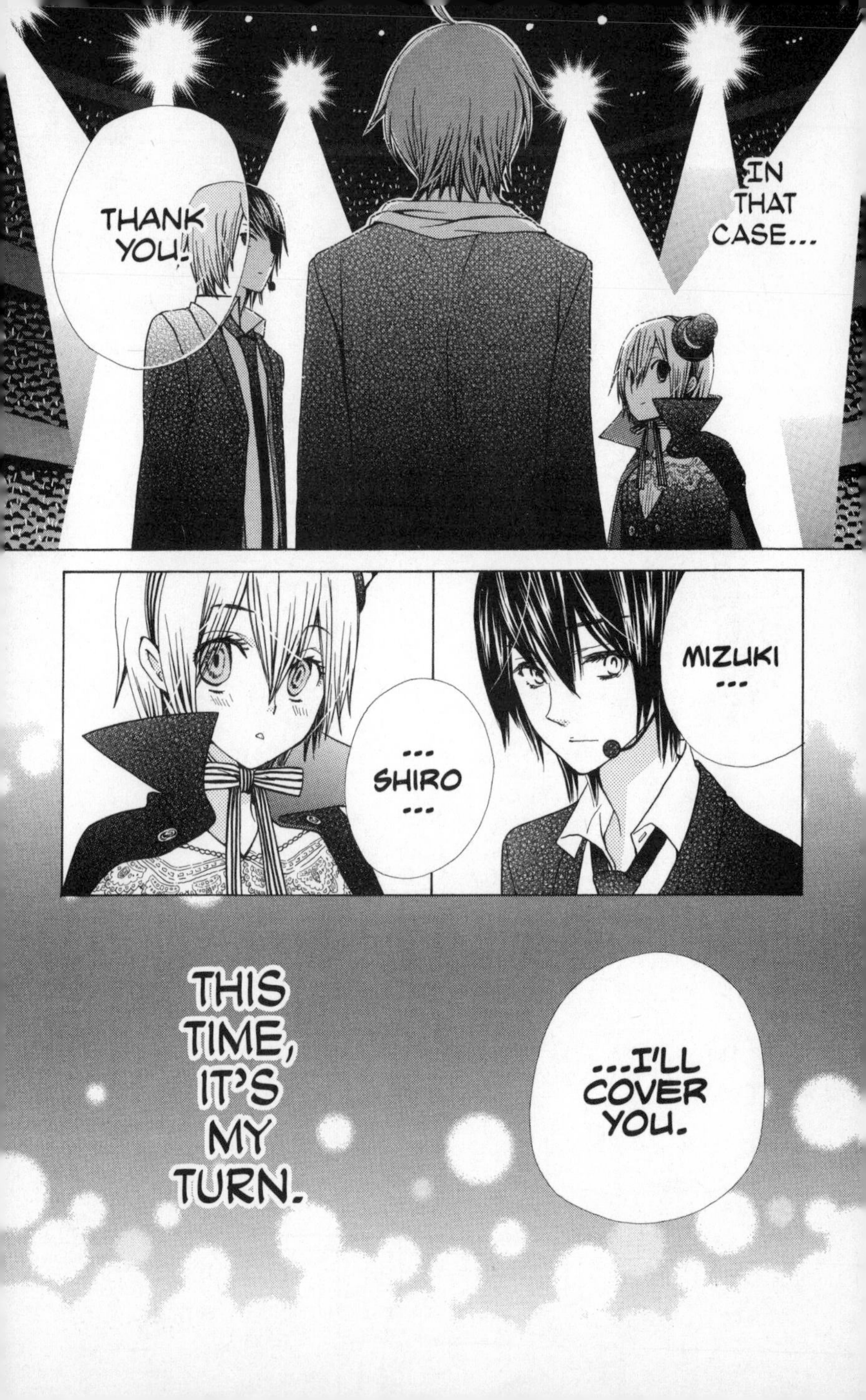
IN THAT CASE...
THANK YOU!
MIZUKI...
...SHIRO...
...I'LL COVER YOU.
THIS TIME, IT'S MY TURN.

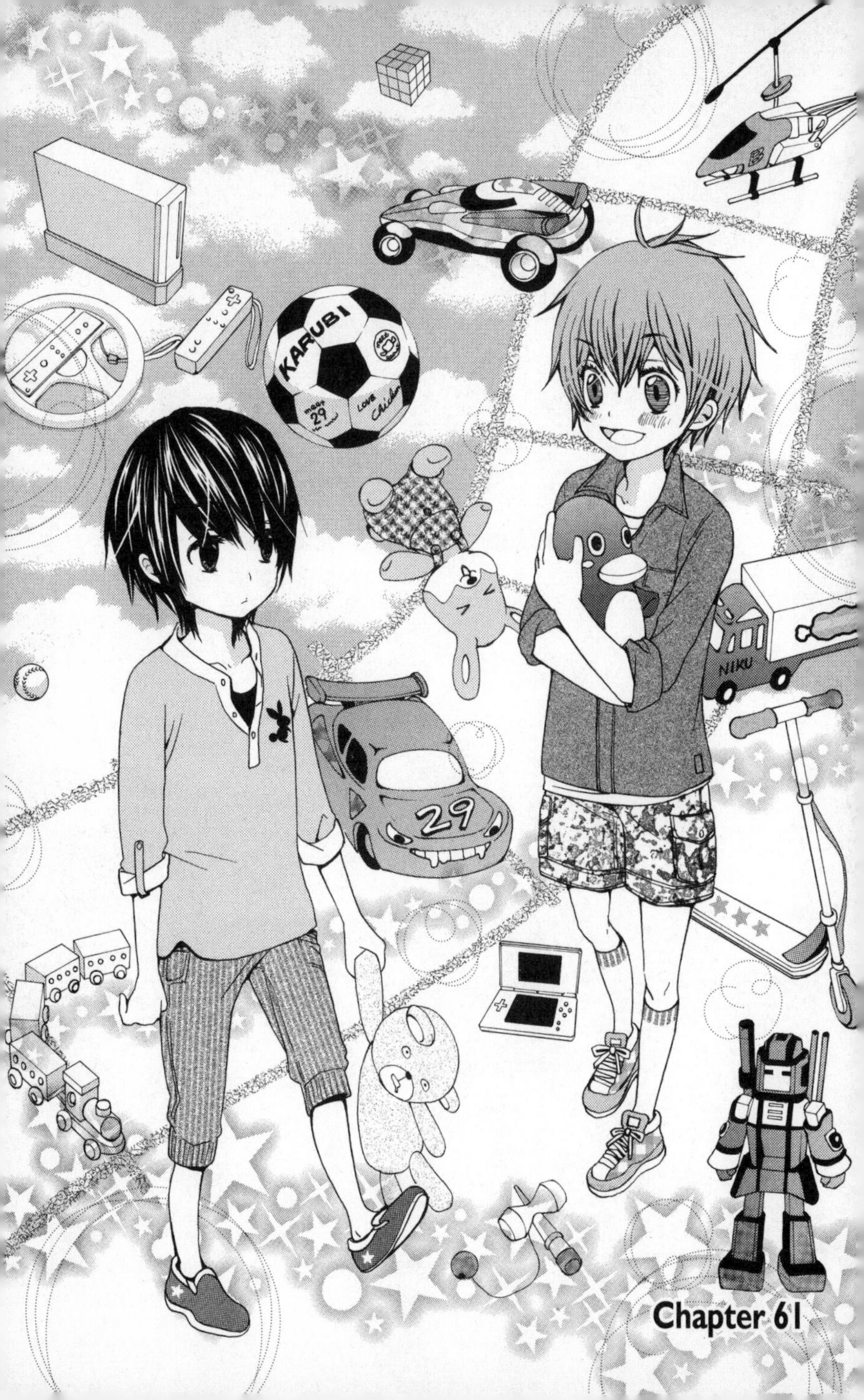
KARUBI
29
LOVE
NIKU
29

# Chapter 61

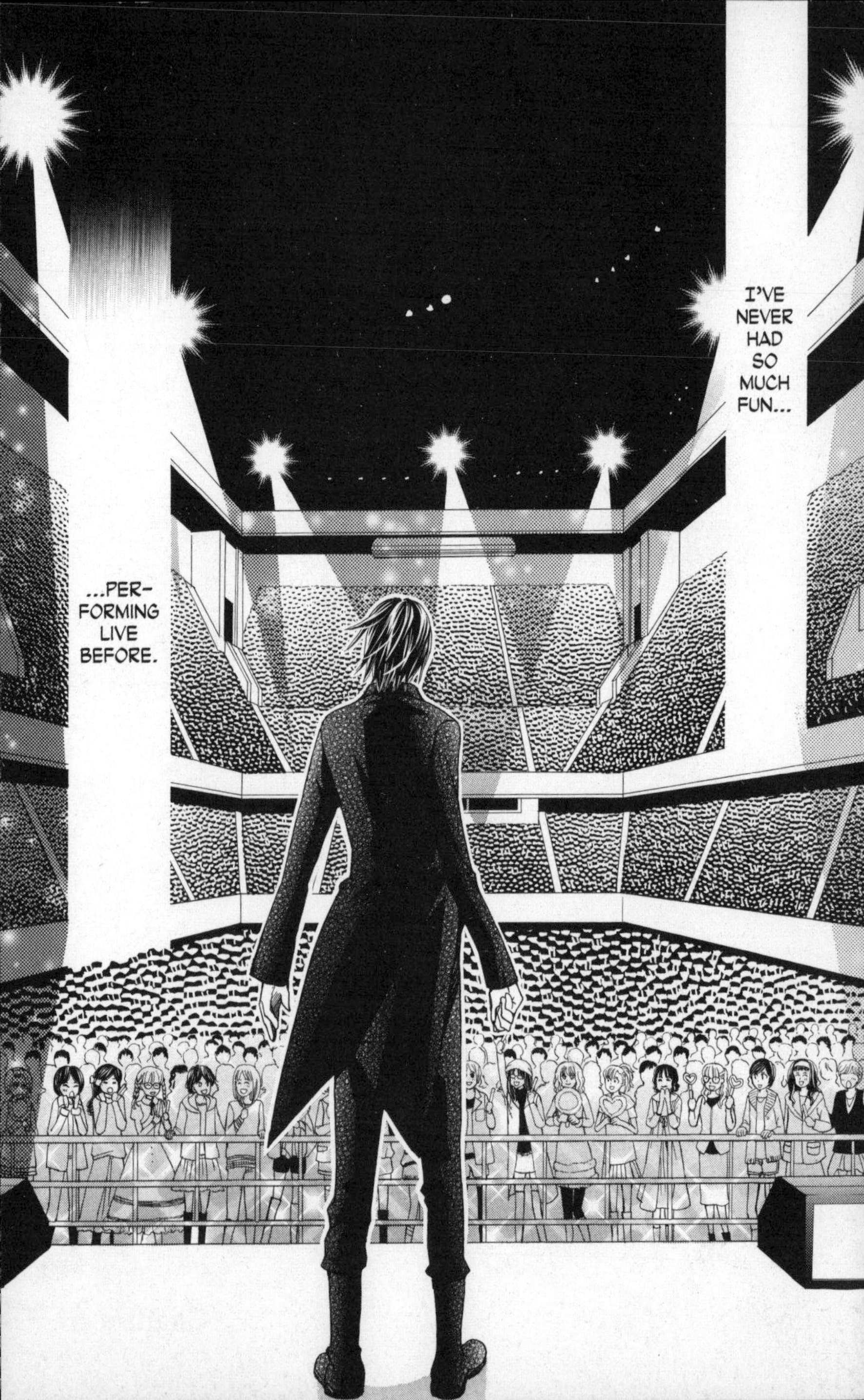
I'VE NEVER HAD SO MUCH FUN...
...PER-FORMING LIVE BEFORE.

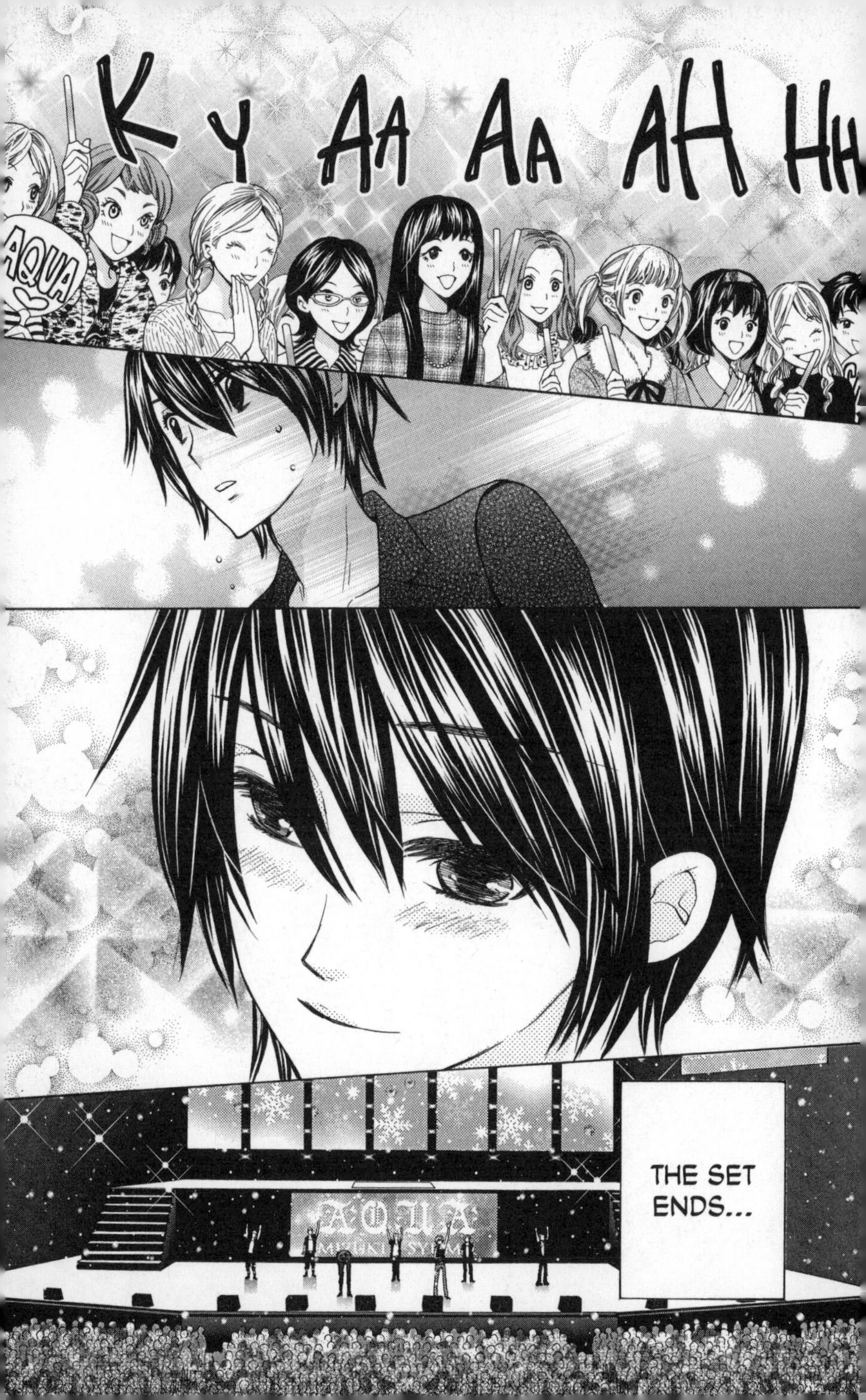
KYAAAAAHHH
AQUA
THE SET ENDS...

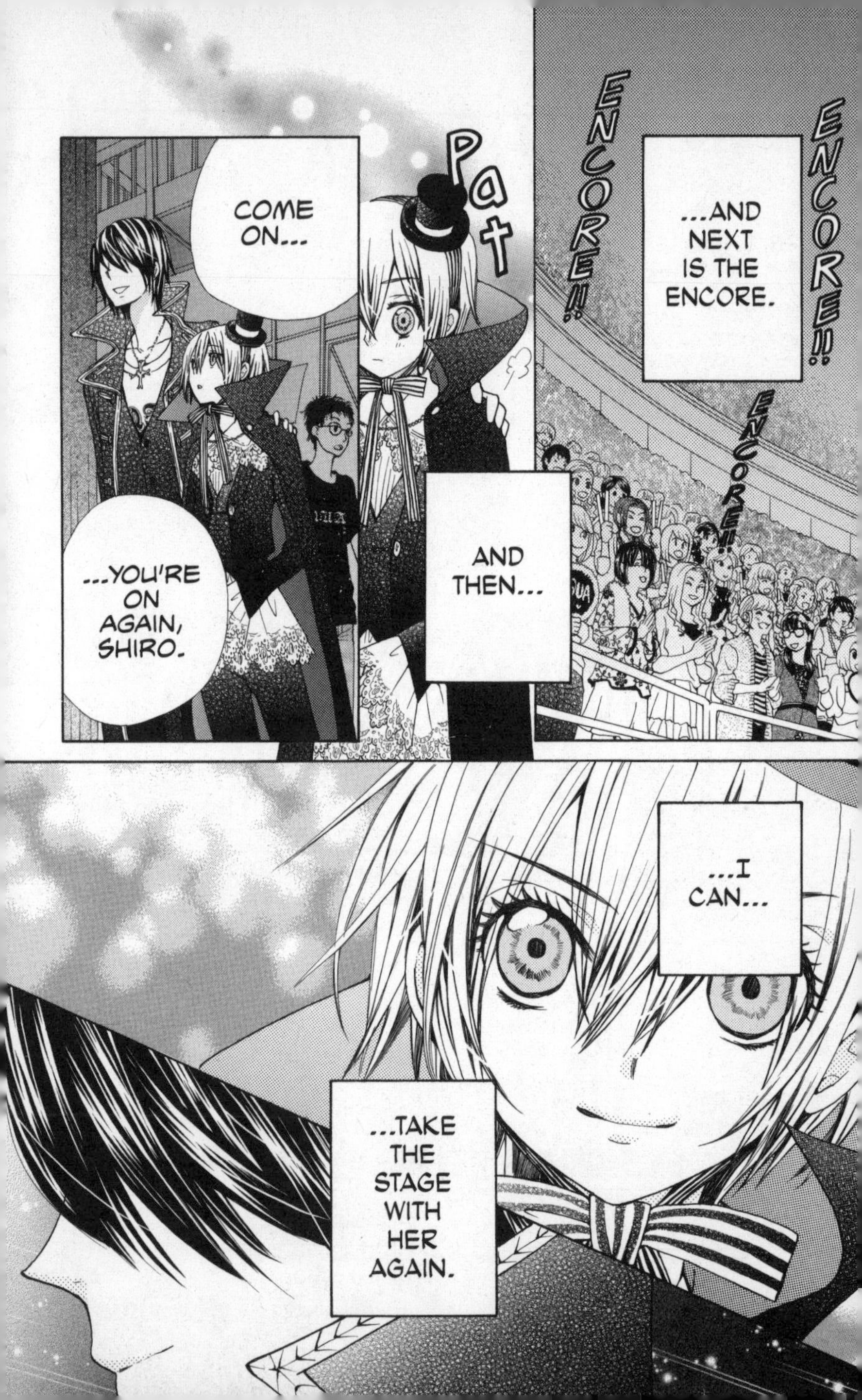
ENCORE!!
...AND NEXT IS THE ENCORE.
ENCORE!!
ENCORE!!
Pat
AND THEN...
COME ON...
...YOU'RE ON AGAIN, SHIRO.
...I CAN...
...TAKE THE STAGE WITH HER AGAIN.

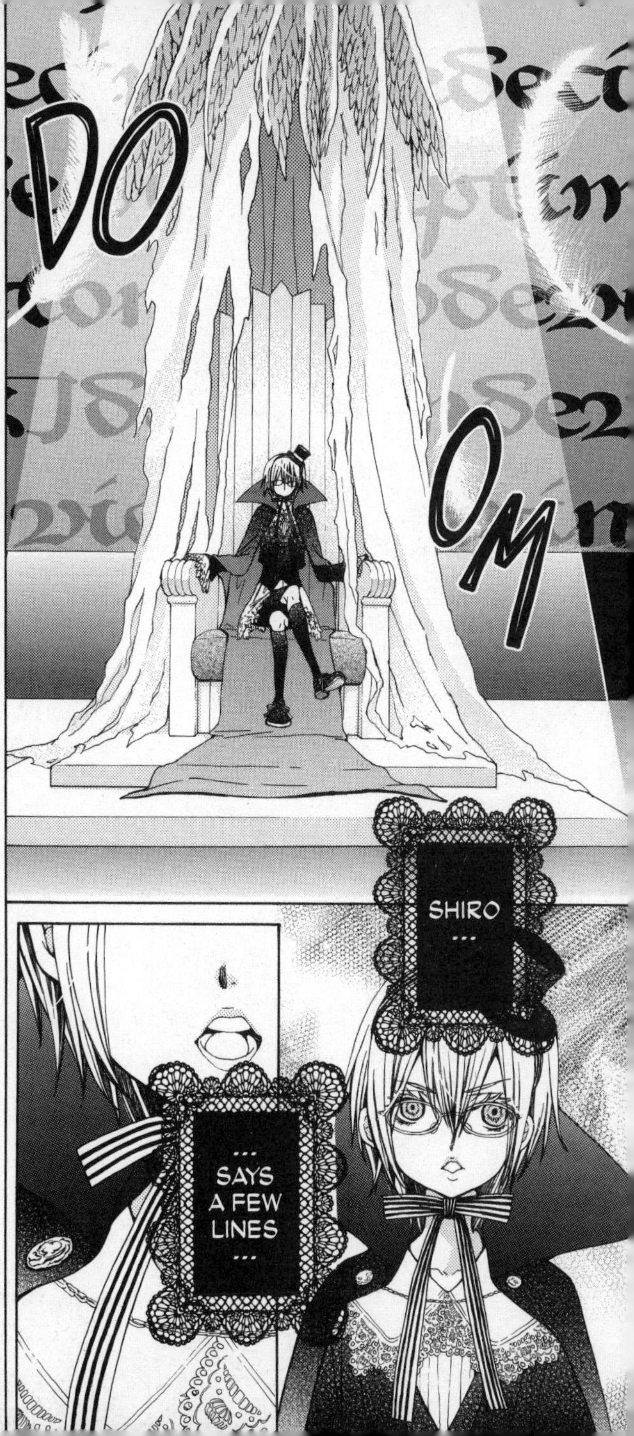
DO
OM
SHIRO ...
... SAYS A FEW LINES ...

· Printer ·③

One of my assistants put cute eyes on the printer at our studio.

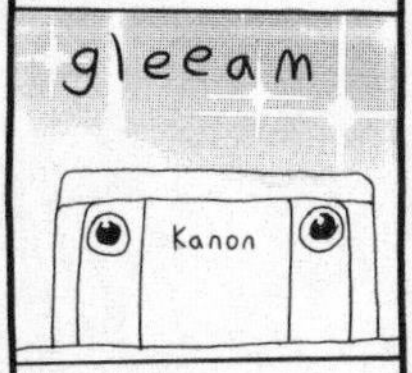
gleeam
Kanon

They're made of regular copy paper, so as time passes, they're getting worn out.

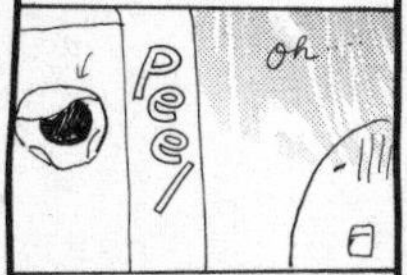
Peel
oh...

It's practically crying out, "I'm so tired..."

Then it broke down one day and we had to send it for repairs.

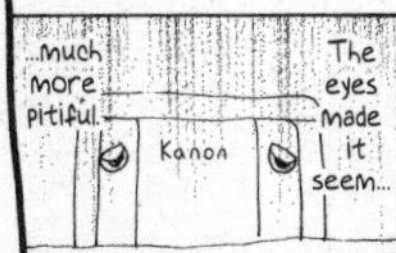
The eyes made it seem...
...much more pitiful.
Kanon

After packing and sending it, I realized something...

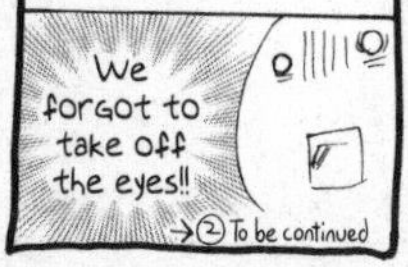
We forgot to take off the eyes!!

→② To be continued

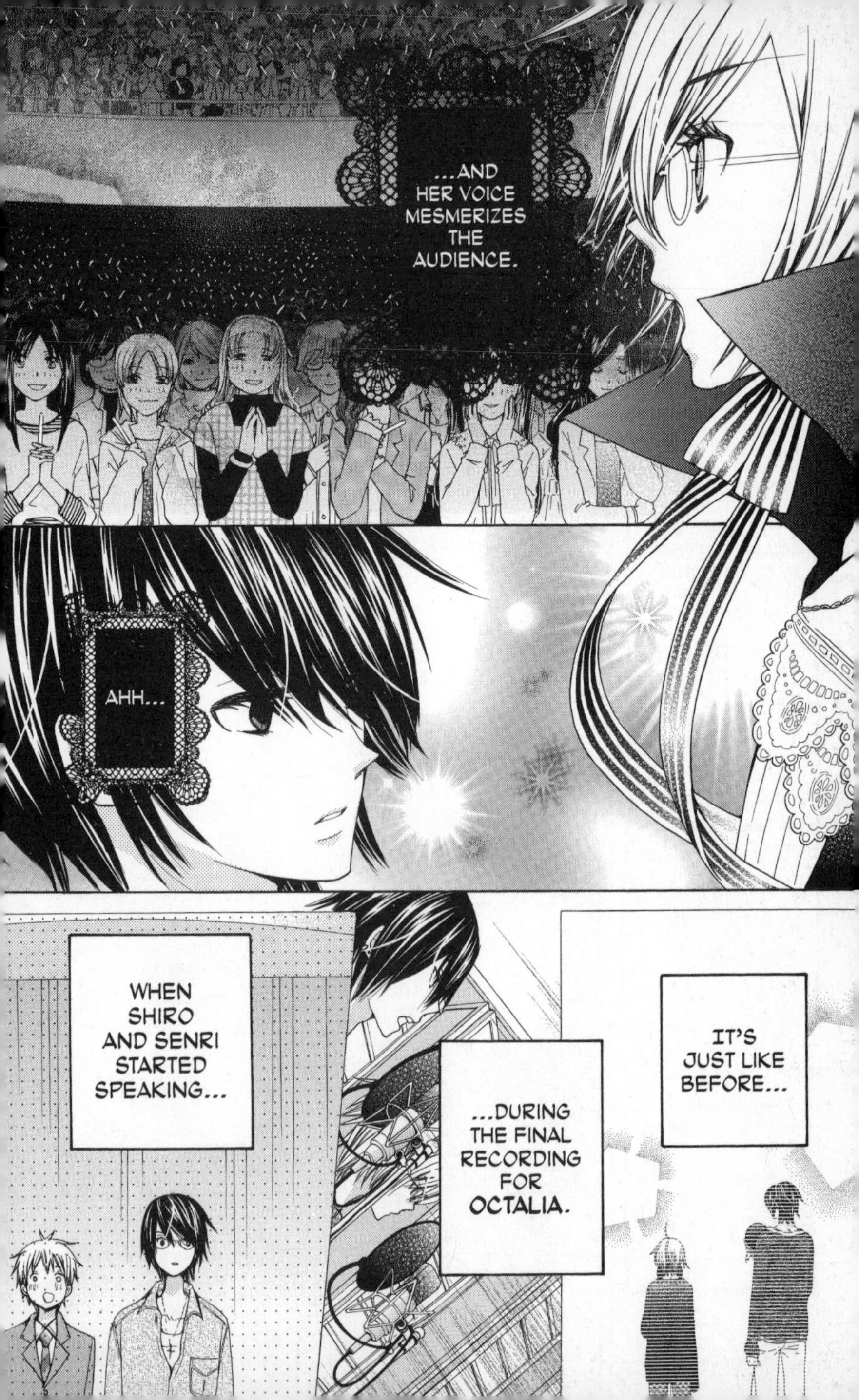
...AND HER VOICE MESMERIZES THE AUDIENCE.
AHH...
IT'S JUST LIKE BEFORE...
WHEN SHIRO AND SENRI STARTED SPEAKING...
...DURING THE FINAL RECORDING FOR OCTALIA.

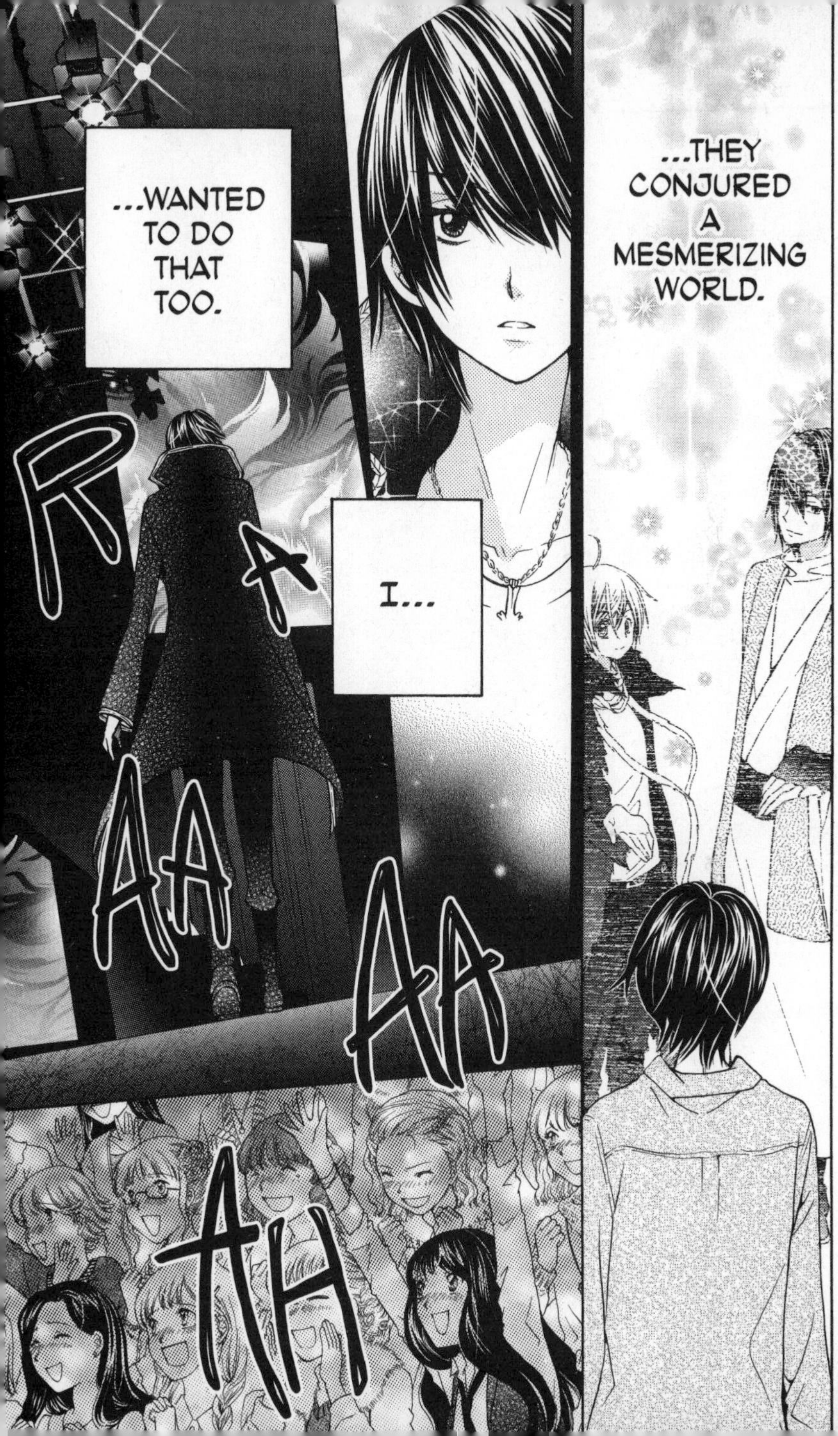
...THEY CONJURED A MESMERIZING WORLD.
I...
...WANTED TO DO THAT TOO.
RAAAAAAH

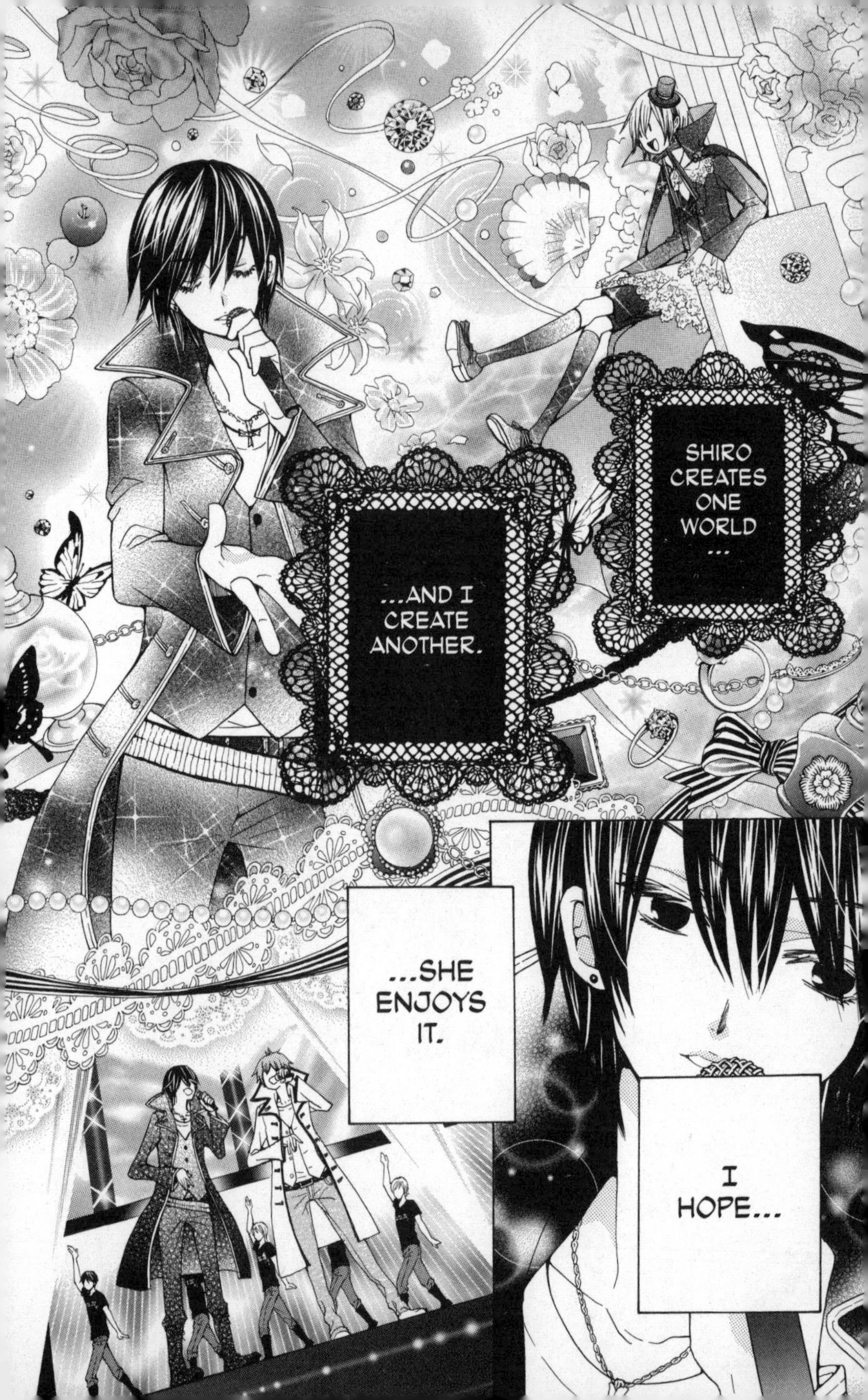
SHIRO CREATES ONE WORLD ...
...AND I CREATE ANOTHER.
I HOPE...
...SHE ENJOYS IT.

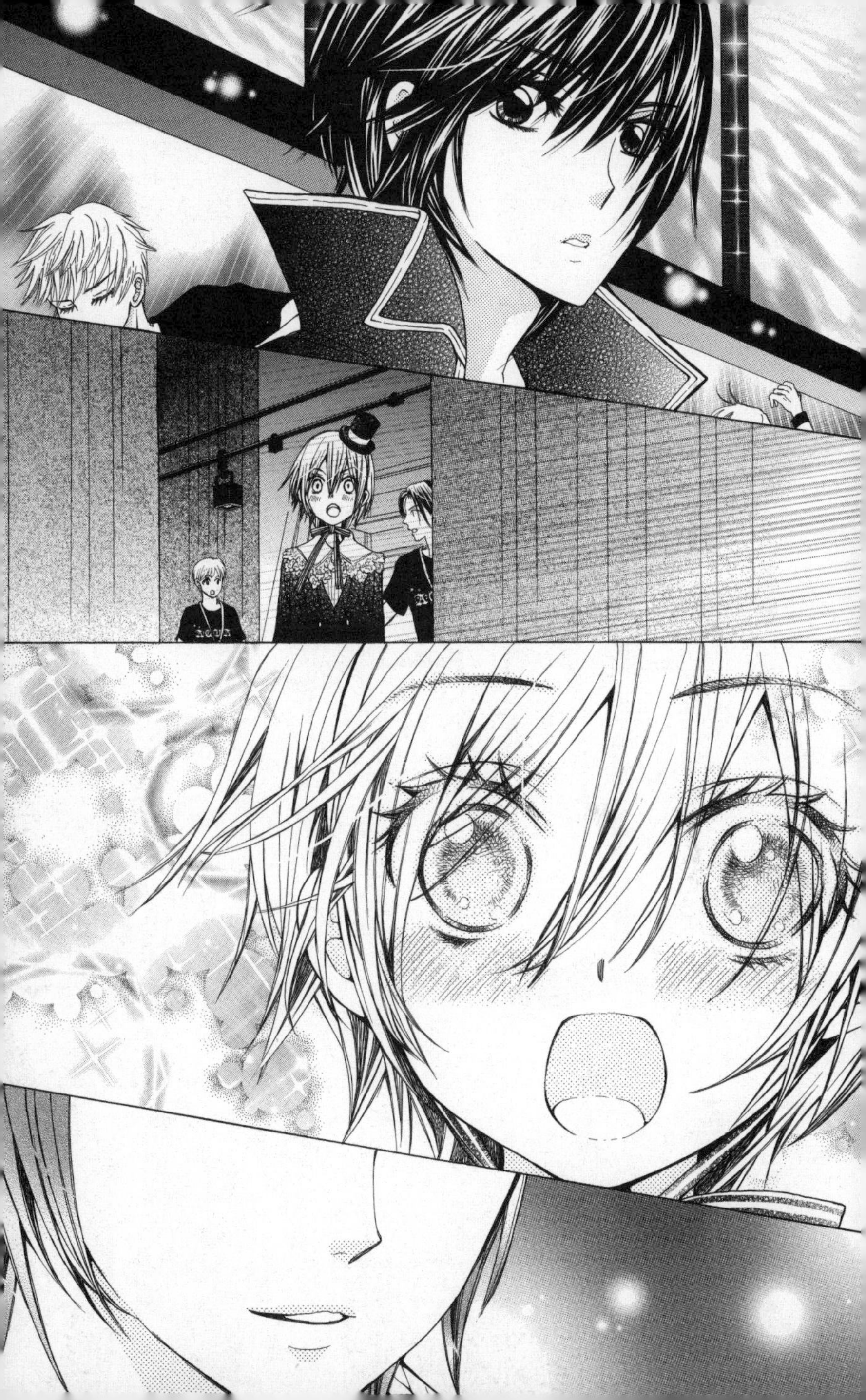

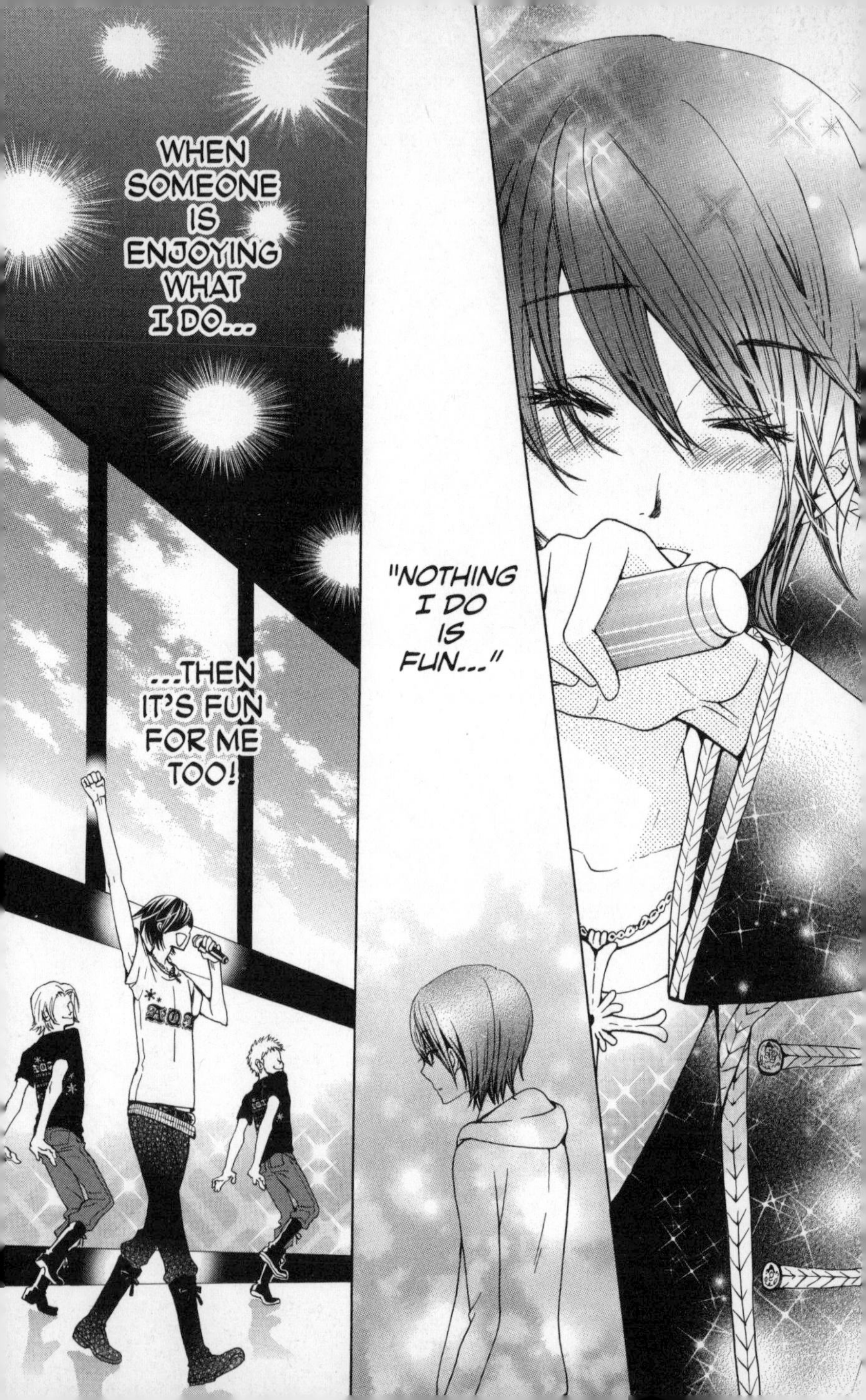
"NOTHING I DO IS FUN..."
WHEN SOMEONE IS ENJOYING WHAT I DO...
...THEN IT'S FUN FOR ME TOO!

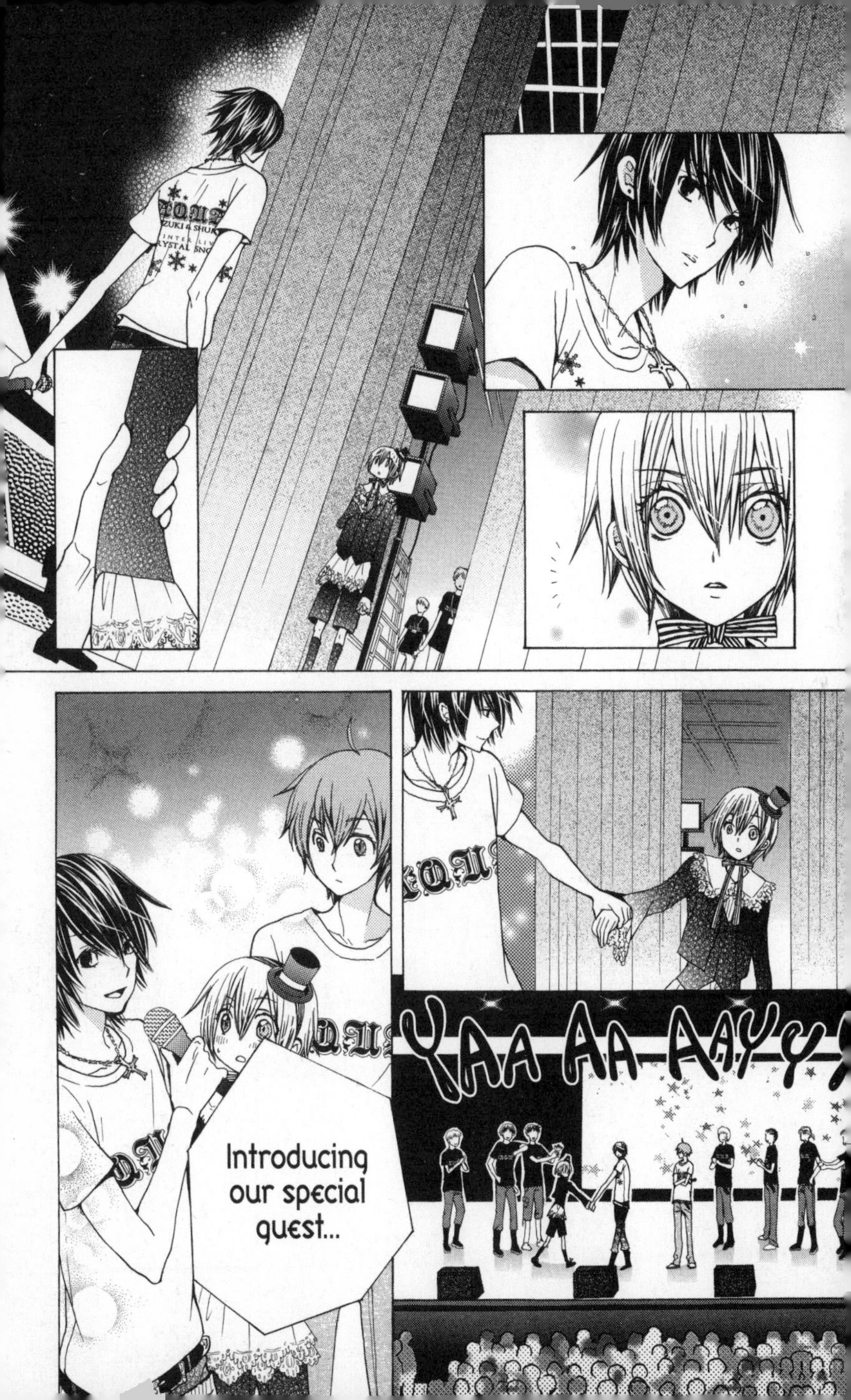
YAA AA AAY!
Introducing our special guest...

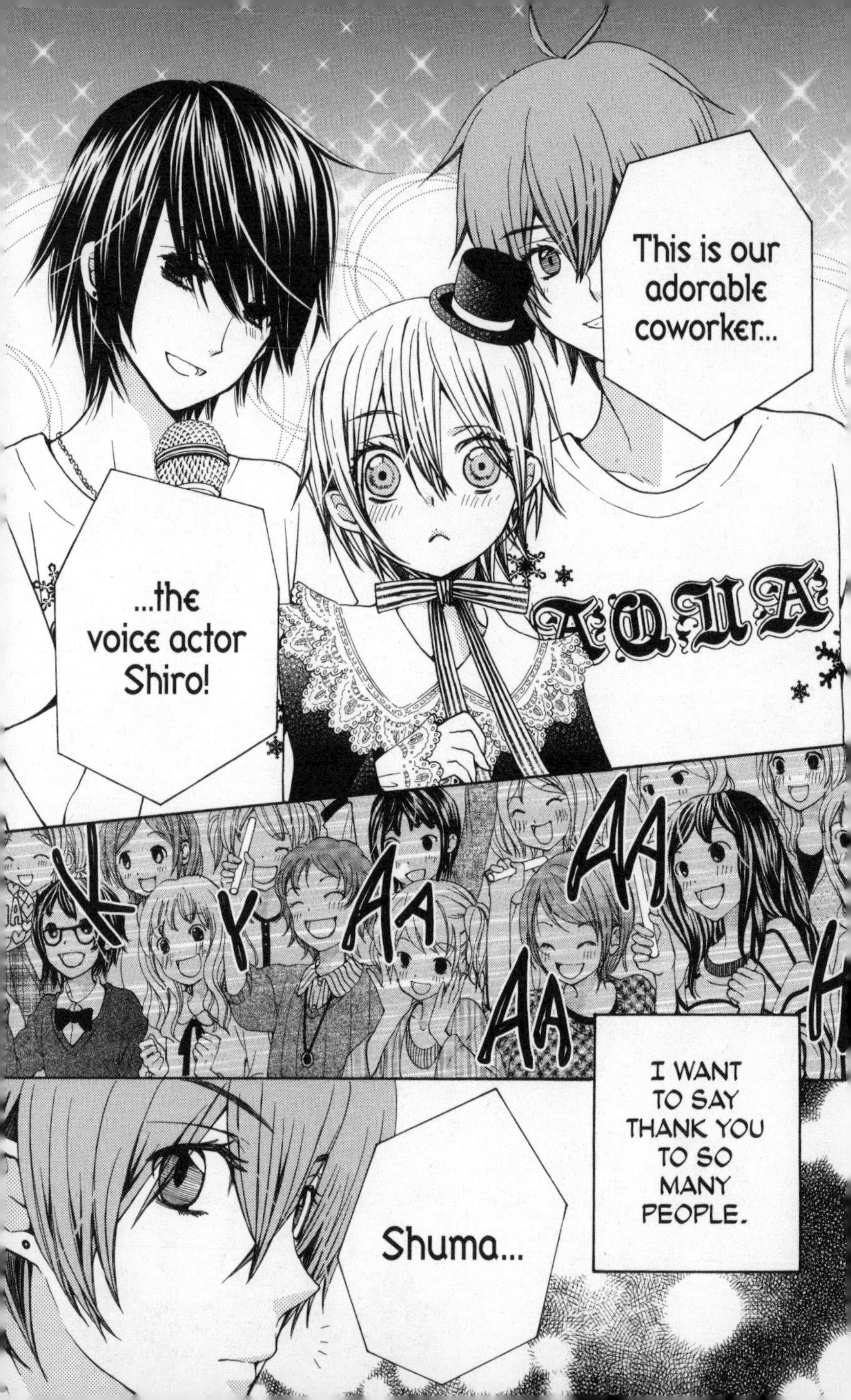

This is our adorable coworker...
...the voice actor Shiro!
AQUA
KYAAAAAAH
I WANT TO SAY THANK YOU TO SO MANY PEOPLE.
Shuma...

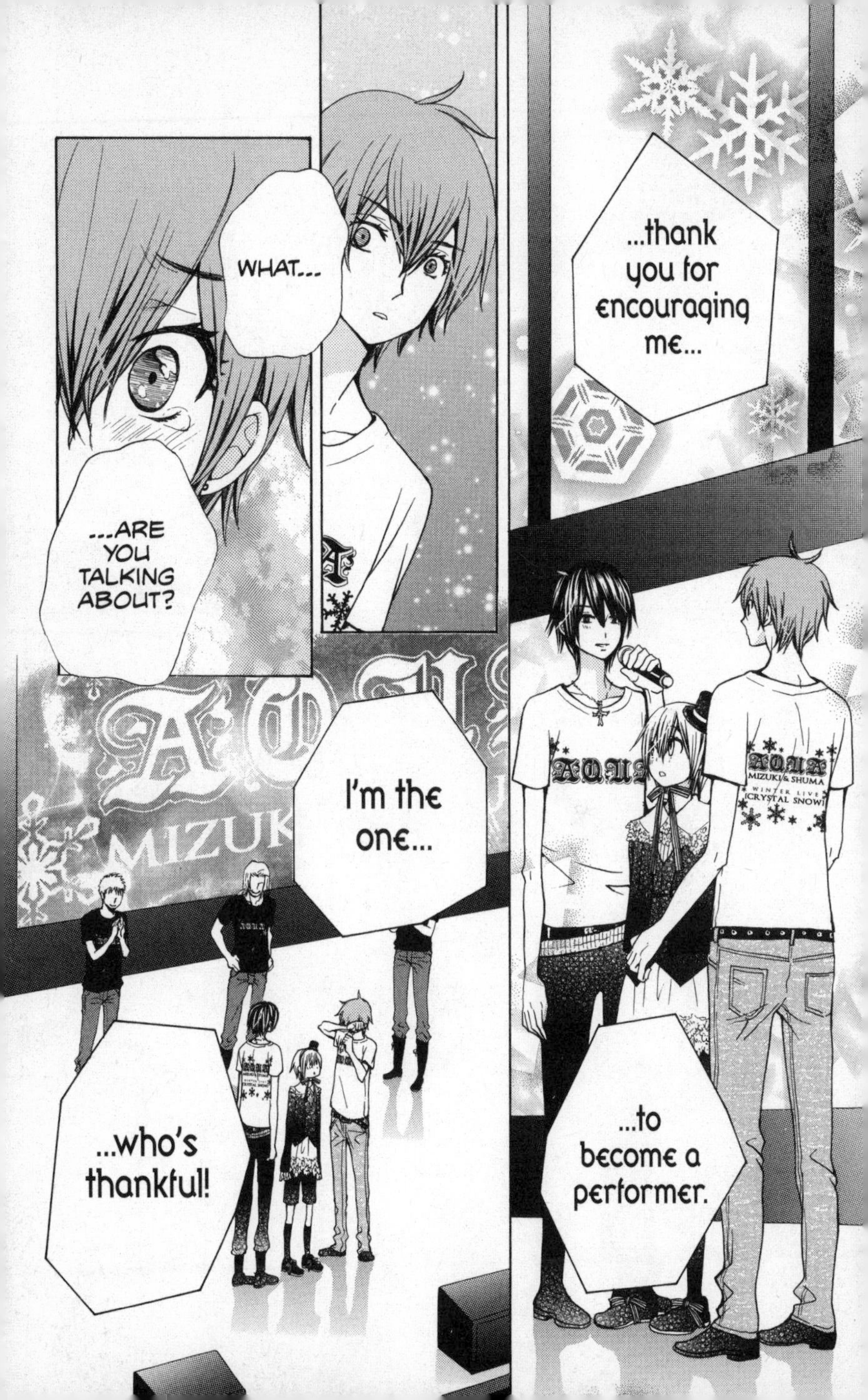
...thank you for encouraging me...
AQUA
MIZUKI & SHUMA
WINTER LIVE
[CRYSTAL SNOW]
...to become a performer.
WHAT...
...ARE YOU TALKING ABOUT?
I'm the one...
...who's thankful!

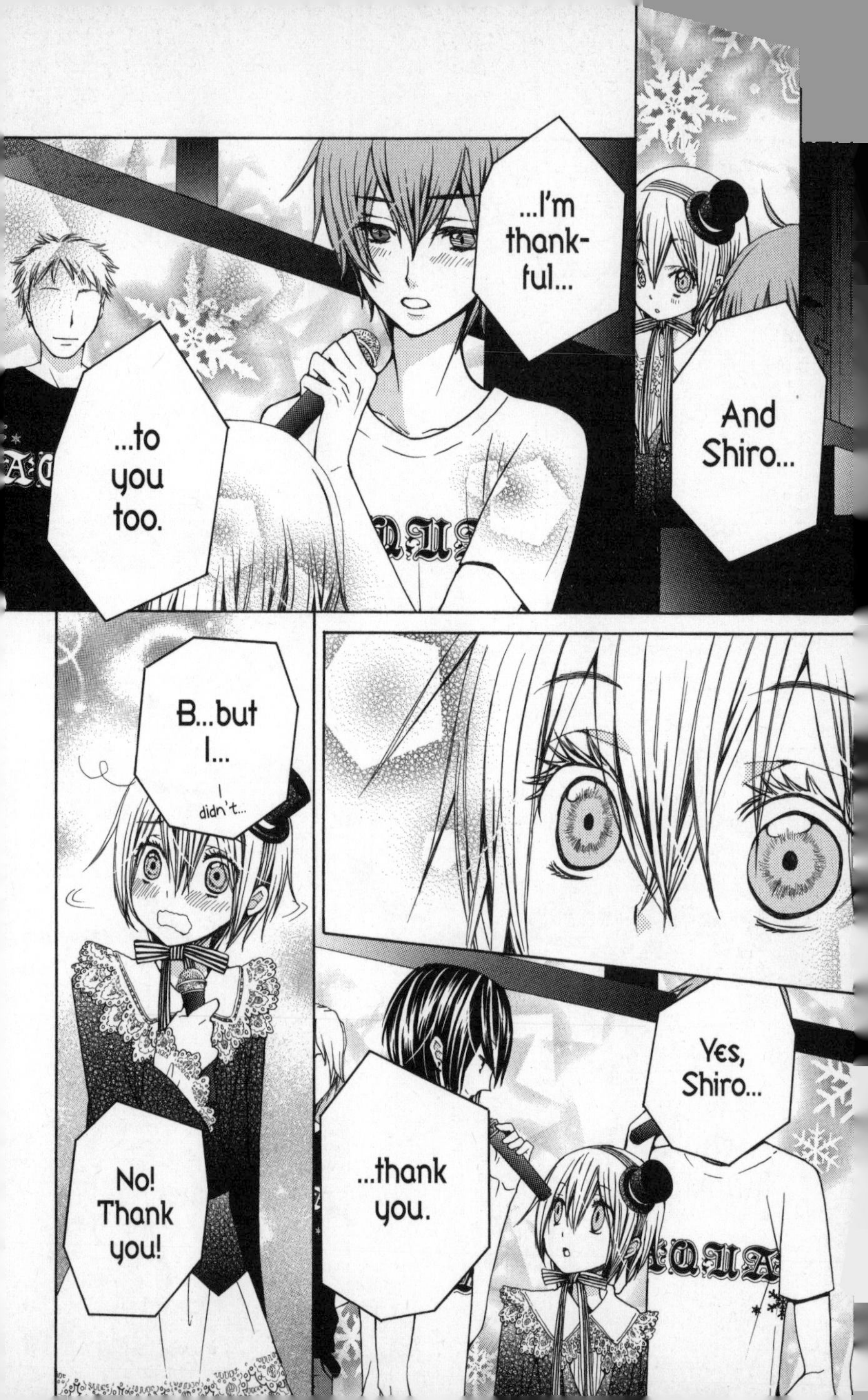
And Shiro...
...I'm thankful...
...to you too.
Yes, Shiro...
...thank you.
B...but I...
I didn't...
No! Thank you!

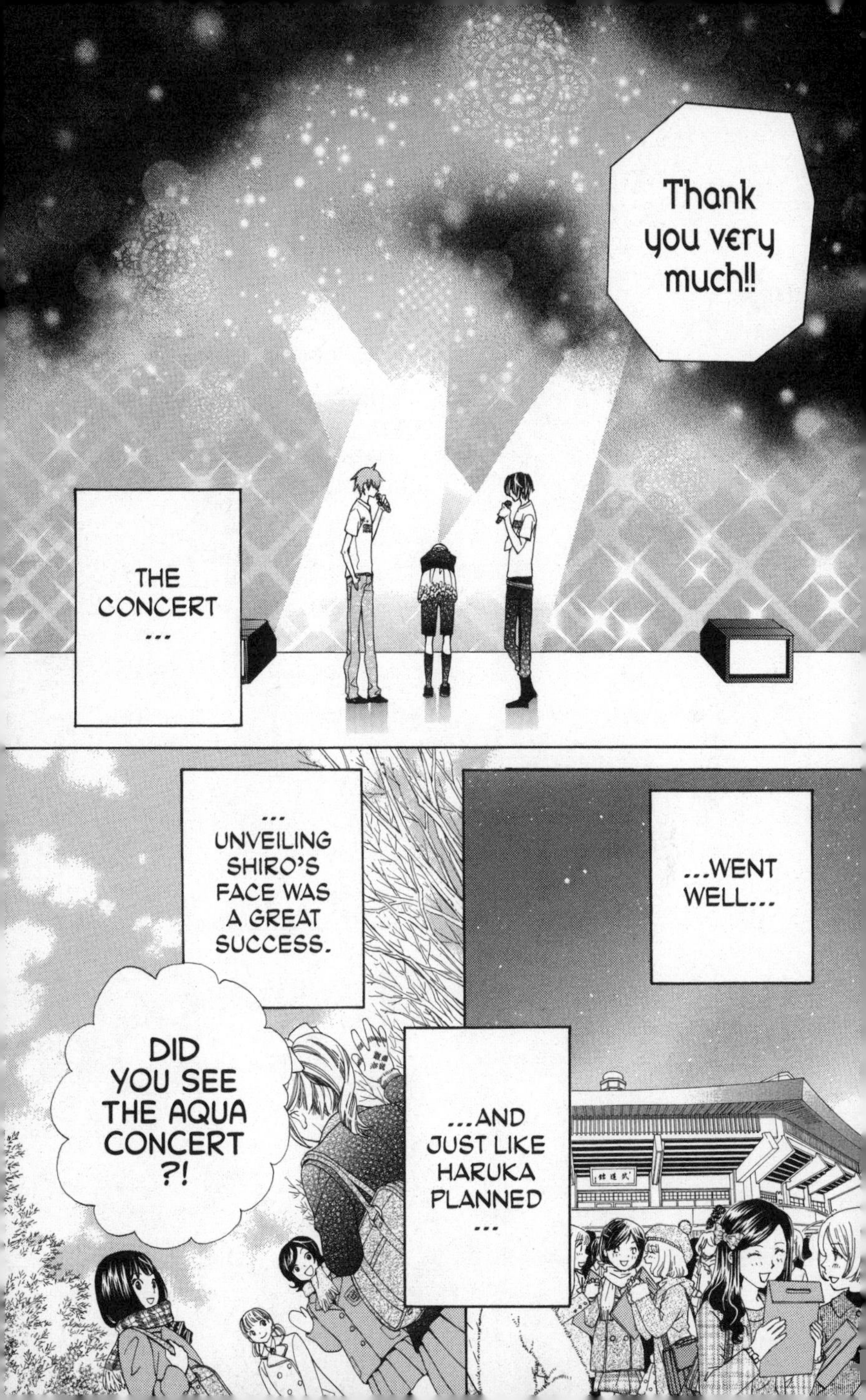
Thank you very much!!
THE CONCERT...
...WENT WELL...
...AND JUST LIKE HARUKA PLANNED...
...UNVEILING SHIRO'S FACE WAS A GREAT SUCCESS.
DID YOU SEE THE AQUA CONCERT?!

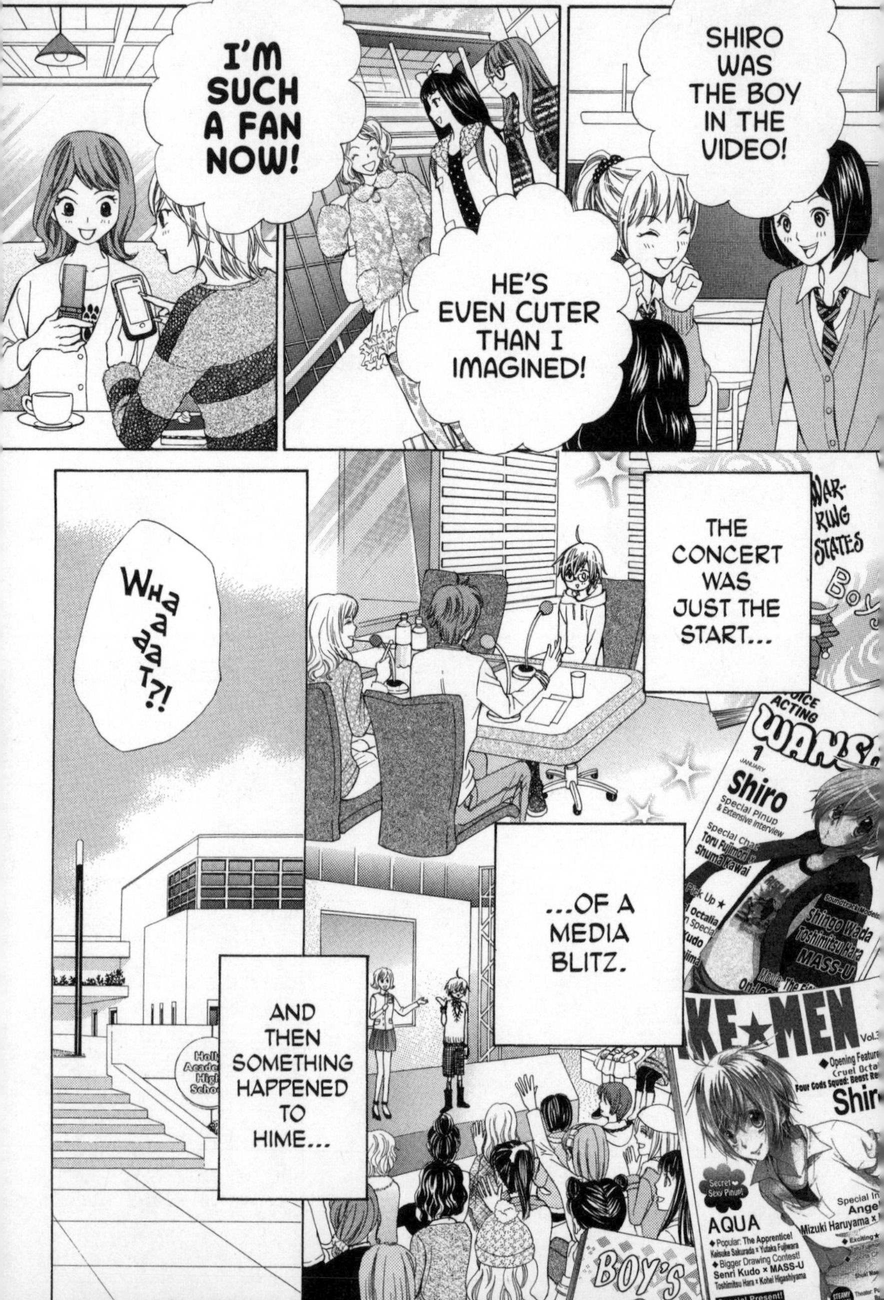
SHIRO WAS THE BOY IN THE VIDEO!
HE'S EVEN CUTER THAN I IMAGINED!
I'M SUCH A FAN NOW!
THE CONCERT WAS JUST THE START...
WAR-RING STATES
Shiro
Special Pinup & Extensive Interview
Shingo Wada
Toshimitsu Hara
MASS-U
...OF A MEDIA BLITZ.
AQUA
Mizuki Haruyama
Popular: The Apprentice!
Bigger Drawing Contest!
Senri Kudo × MASS-U
AND THEN SOMETHING HAPPENED TO HIME...
Whaaaaat?!

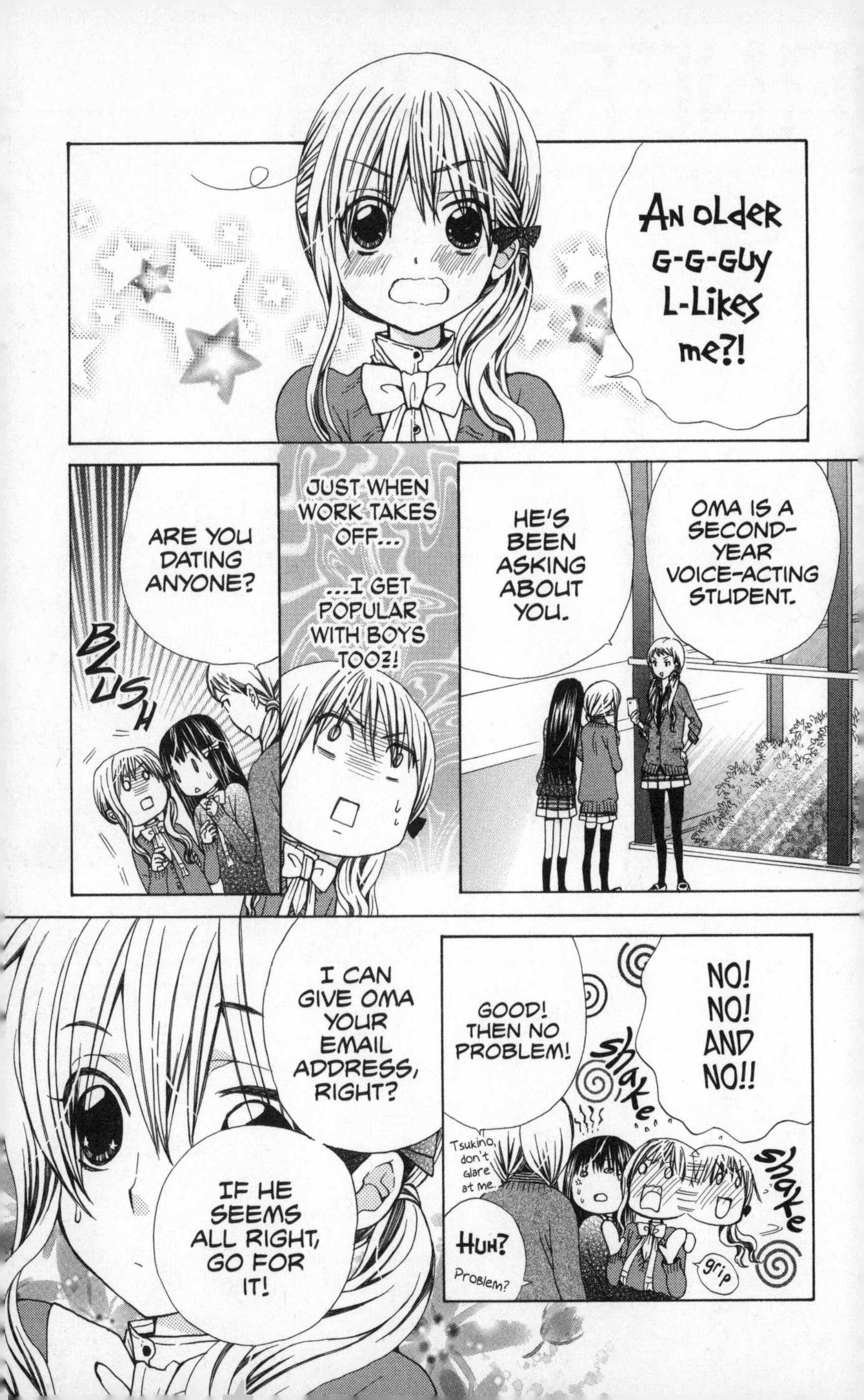
An older G-G-Guy L-Likes me?!
OMA IS A SECOND-YEAR VOICE-ACTING STUDENT.
HE'S BEEN ASKING ABOUT YOU.
JUST WHEN WORK TAKES OFF...
...I GET POPULAR WITH BOYS TOO?!
ARE YOU DATING ANYONE?
BLUSH
NO! NO! AND NO!!
shake
shake
GOOD! THEN NO PROBLEM!
Tsukino, don't glare at me.
grip
HUH?
Problem?
I CAN GIVE OMA YOUR EMAIL ADDRESS, RIGHT?
IF HE SEEMS ALL RIGHT, GO FOR IT!

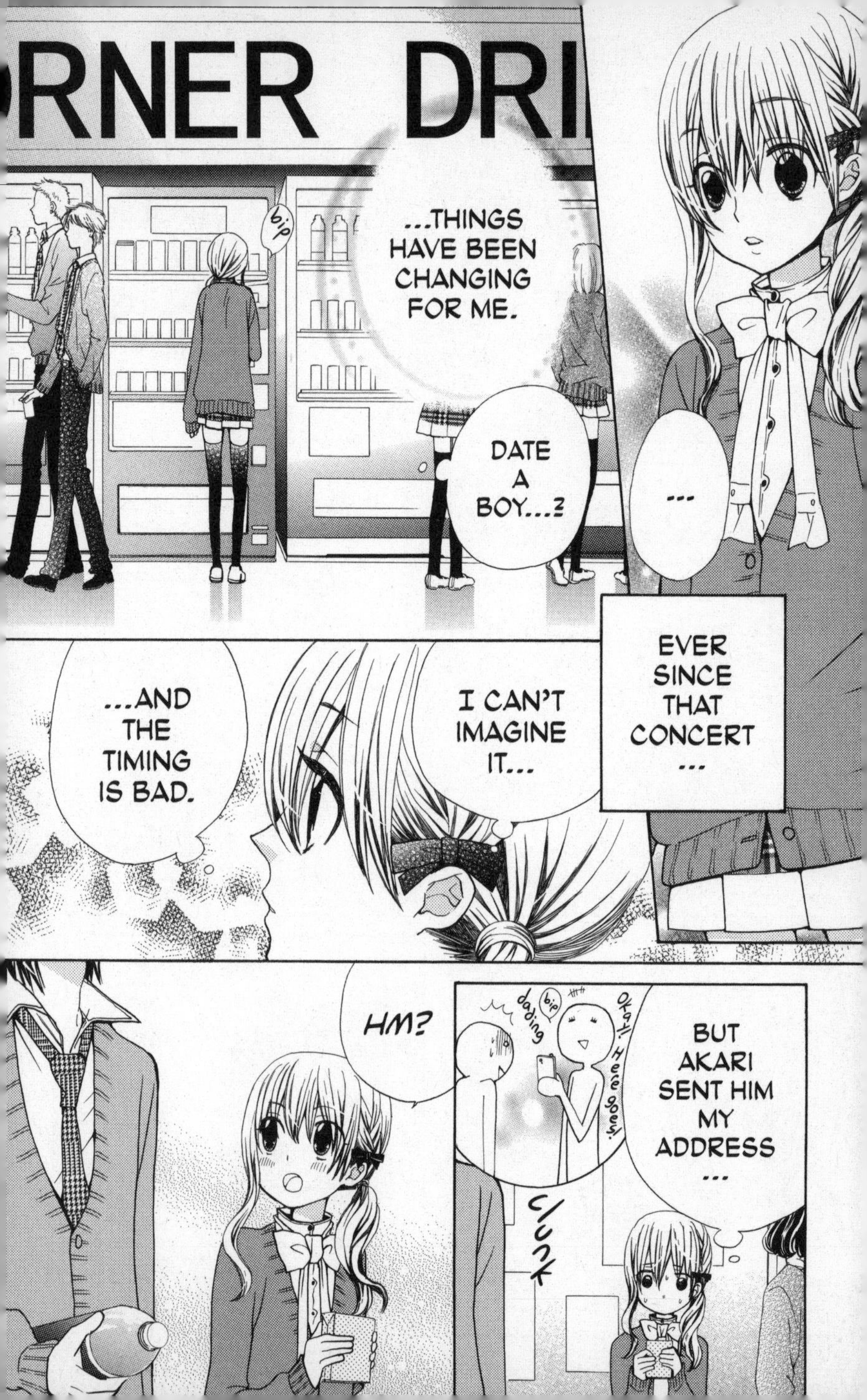
...
EVER SINCE THAT CONCERT ...
RNER DRI
...THINGS HAVE BEEN CHANGING FOR ME.
bip
DATE A BOY...?
I CAN'T IMAGINE IT...
...AND THE TIMING IS BAD.
BUT AKARI SENT HIM MY ADDRESS ...
Okay!! Here goes!
bip
daging
clunk
HM?

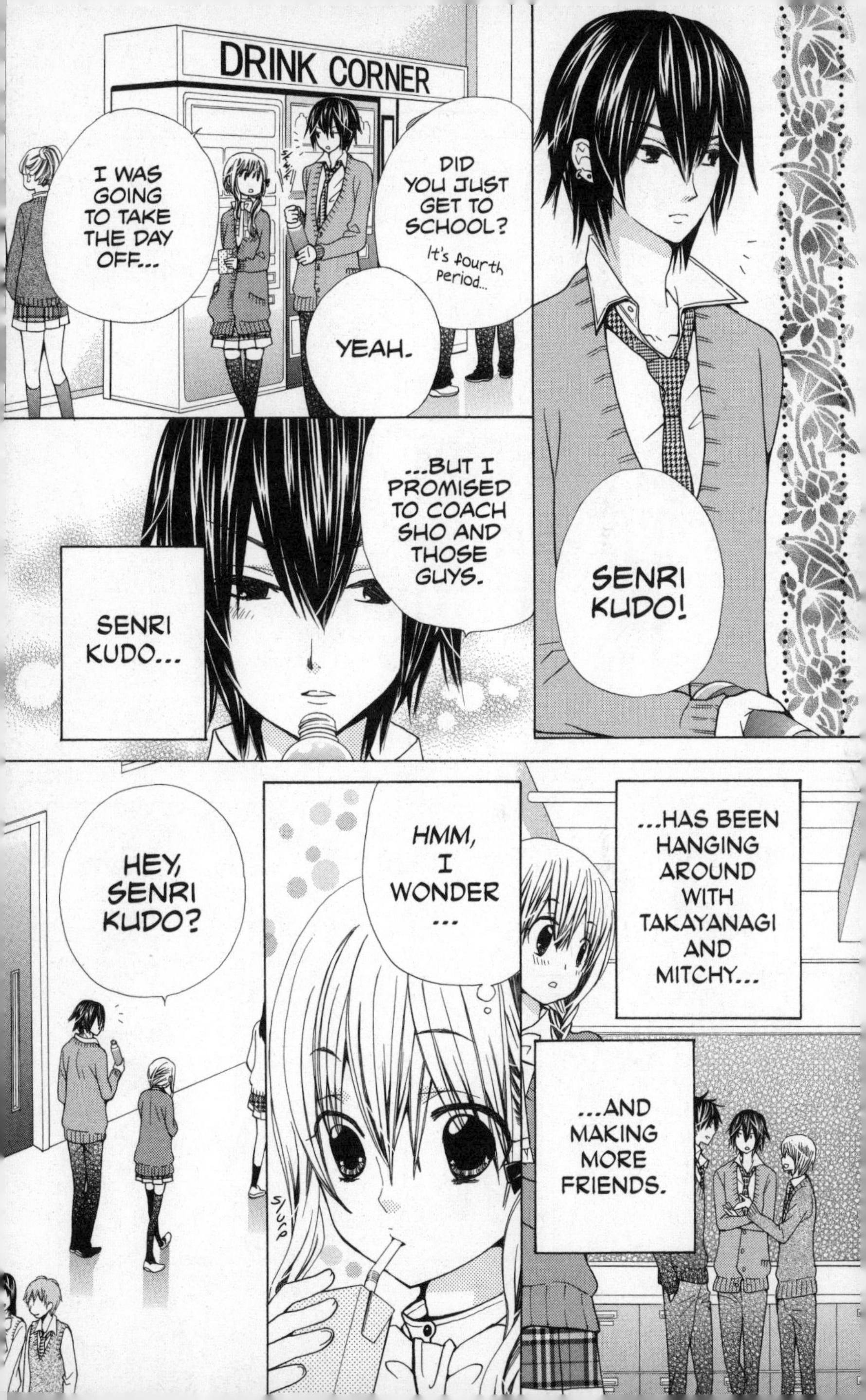
SENRI KUDO!
DRINK CORNER
DID YOU JUST GET TO SCHOOL?
It's fourth period...
YEAH.
I WAS GOING TO TAKE THE DAY OFF...
...BUT I PROMISED TO COACH SHO AND THOSE GUYS.
SENRI KUDO...
...HAS BEEN HANGING AROUND WITH TAKAYANAGI AND MITCHY...
...AND MAKING MORE FRIENDS.
HMM, I WONDER...
SLURP
HEY, SENRI KUDO?

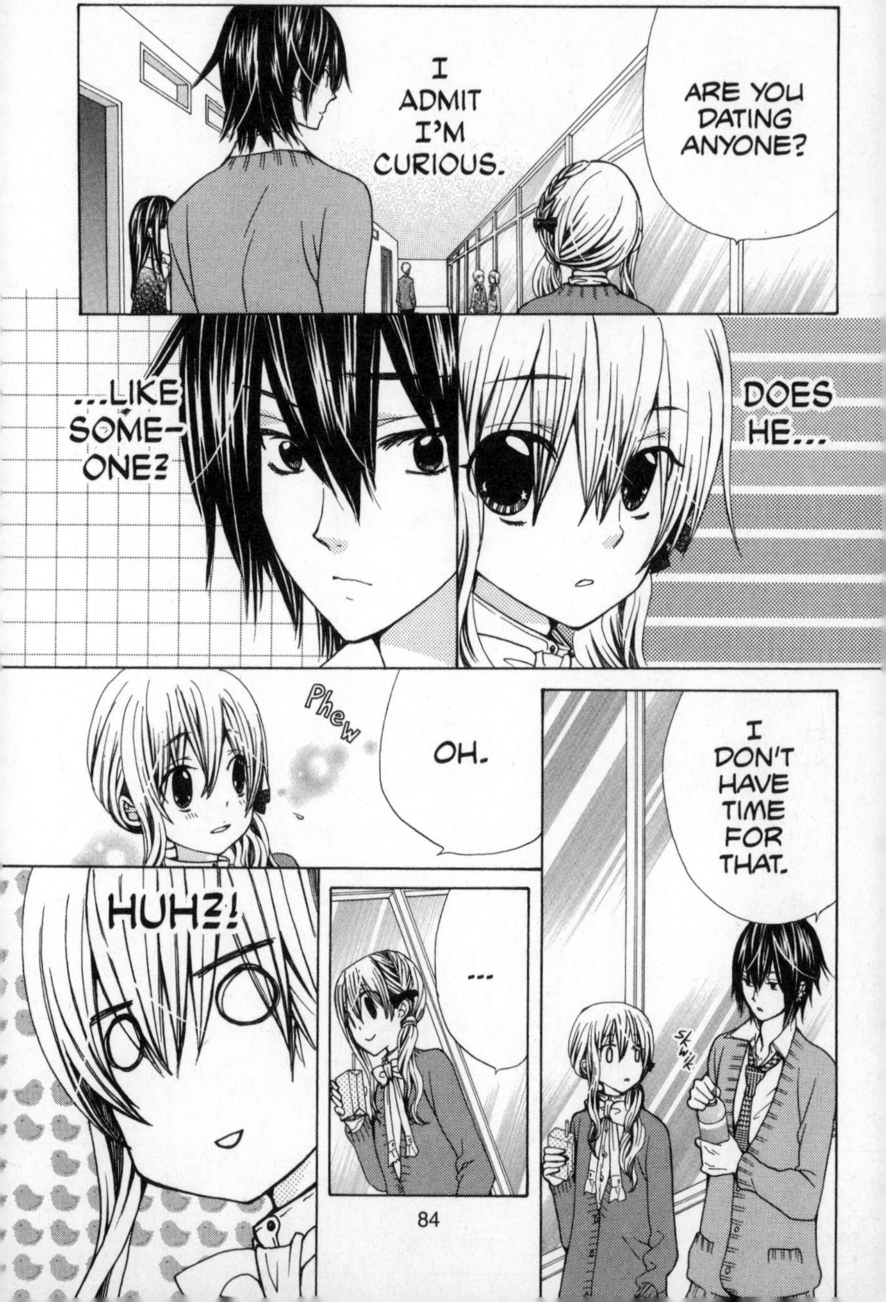
ARE YOU DATING ANYONE?
I ADMIT I'M CURIOUS.
DOES HE...
...LIKE SOMEONE?
I DON'T HAVE TIME FOR THAT.
Phew
OH.
...
HUH?!

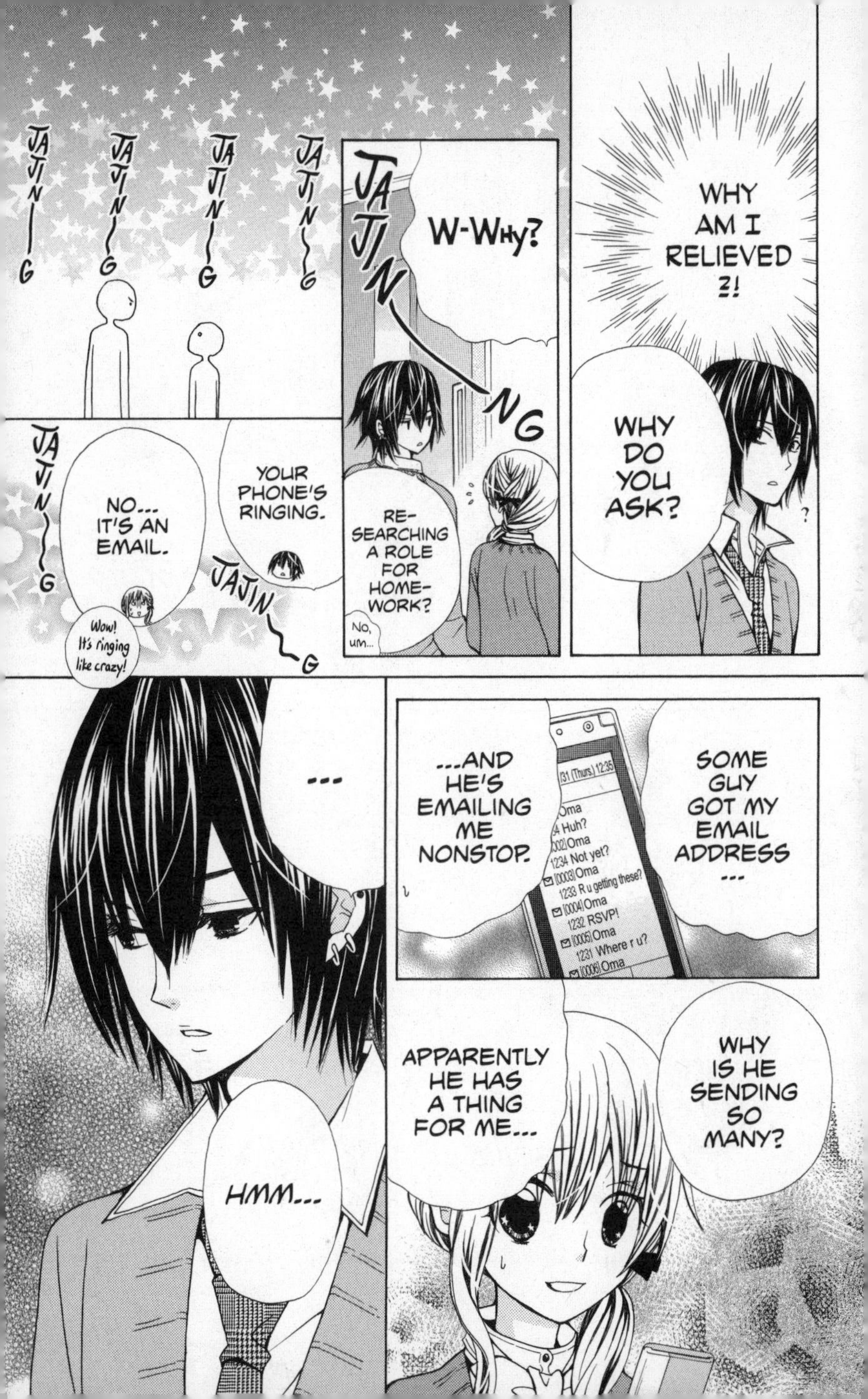
WHY AM I RELIEVED?!
WHY DO YOU ASK?
W-WHY?
JAJIN-NG
RE-SEARCHING A ROLE FOR HOME-WORK?
No, um...
JAJIN-G JAJIN-G JAJIN-G JAJIN-G
YOUR PHONE'S RINGING.
JAJIN-G
NO... IT'S AN EMAIL.
JAJIN-G
Wow! It's ringing like crazy!
SOME GUY GOT MY EMAIL ADDRESS...
...AND HE'S EMAILING ME NONSTOP.
31 (Thurs.) 12:35
Oma
Huh?
[0002] Oma
1234 Not yet?
[0003] Oma
1233 R u getting these?
[0004] Oma
1232 RSVP!
[0005] Oma
1231 Where r u?
[0006] Oma
WHY IS HE SENDING SO MANY?
APPARENTLY HE HAS A THING FOR ME...
...
HMM...

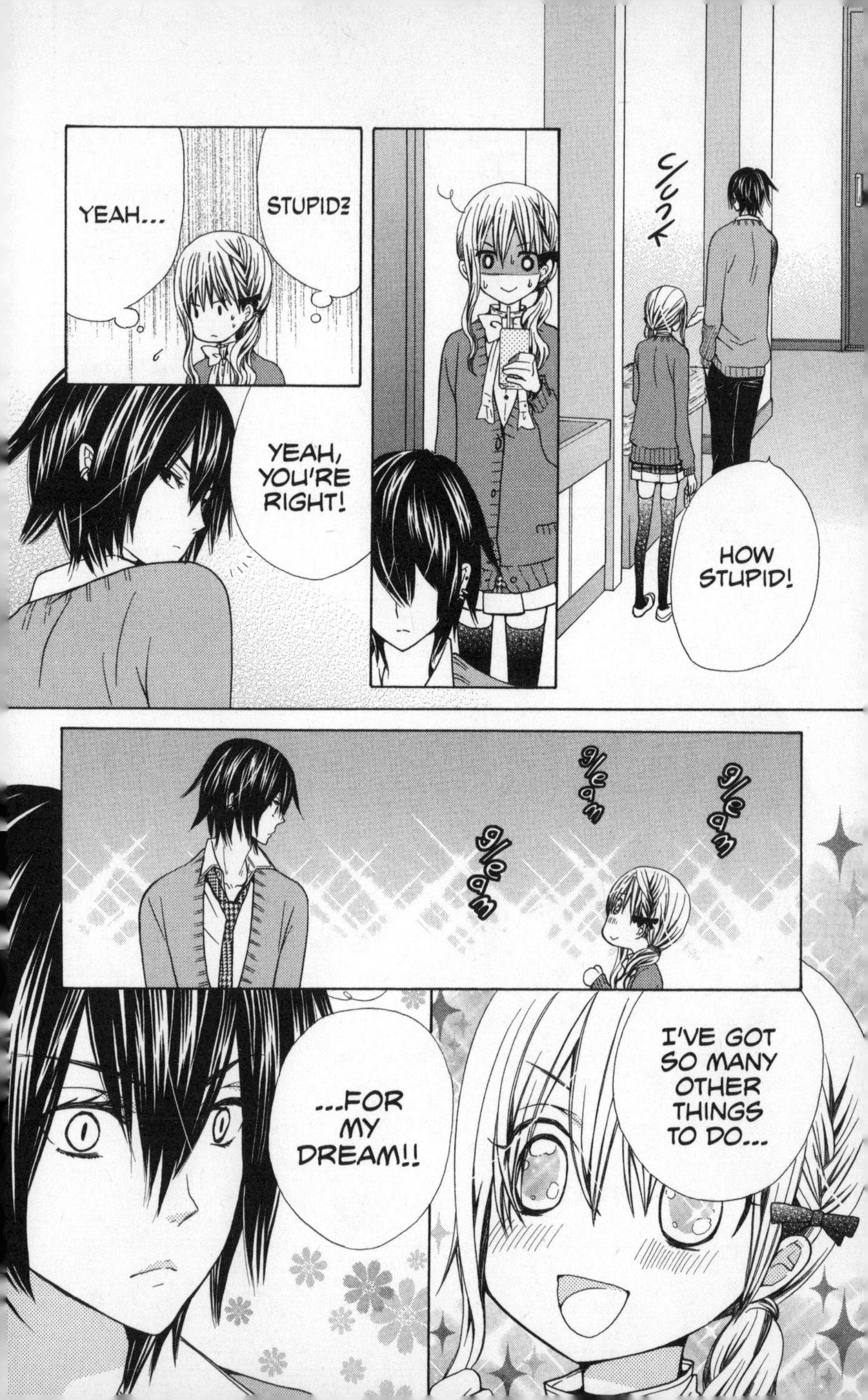
clunk
HOW STUPID!
STUPID?
YEAH...
YEAH, YOU'RE RIGHT!
gleam
gleam
gleam
I'VE GOT SO MANY OTHER THINGS TO DO...
...FOR MY DREAM!!

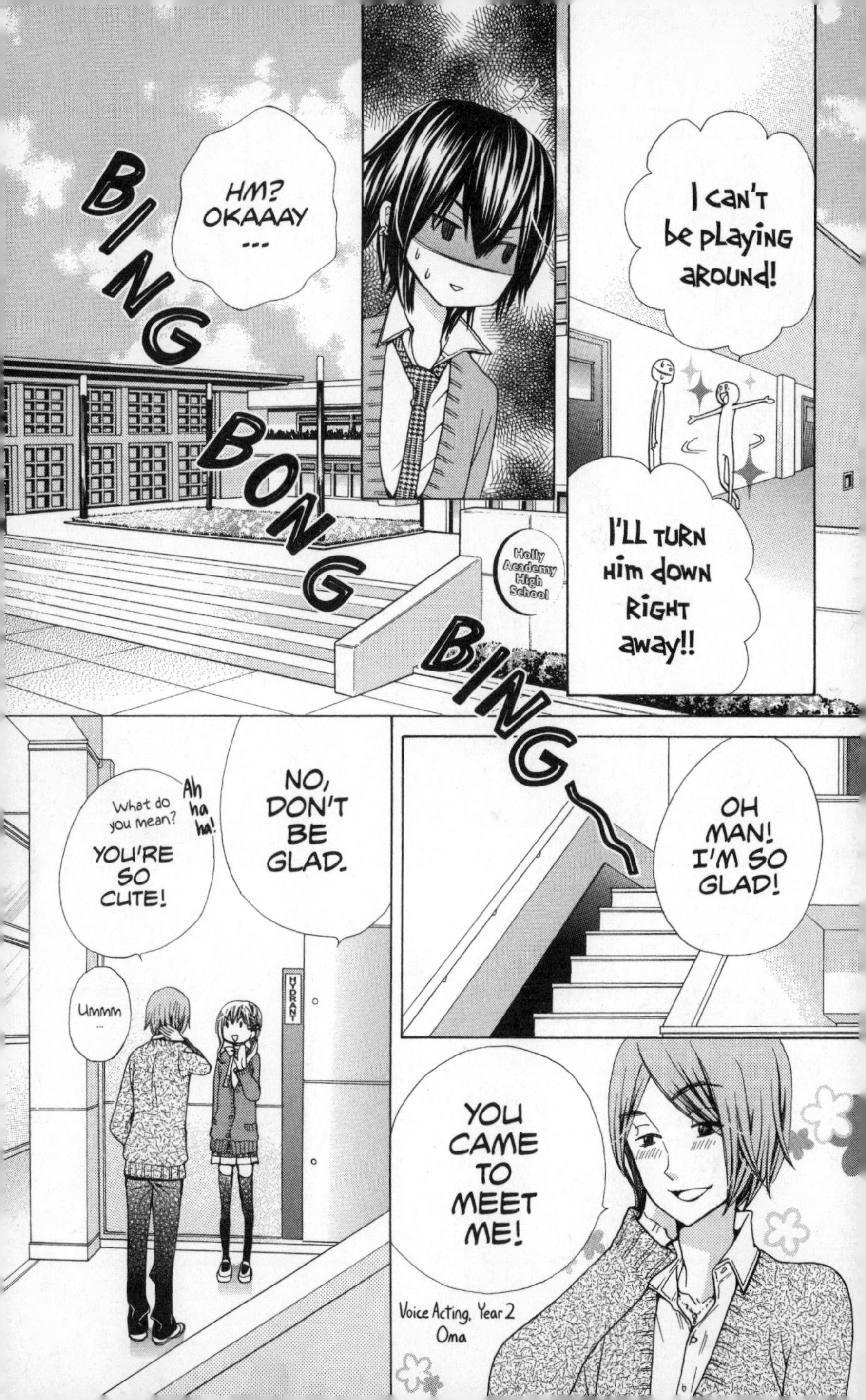
I can't be playing around!
I'LL TURN HIM DOWN RIGHT away!!
HM? OKAAAY ...
BING BONG BING~~
Holly Academy High School
OH MAN! I'M SO GLAD!
YOU CAME TO MEET ME!
Voice Acting, Year 2 Oma
NO, DON'T BE GLAD.
Ah ha ha!
What do you mean? YOU'RE SO CUTE!
Ummm ...
HYDRANT

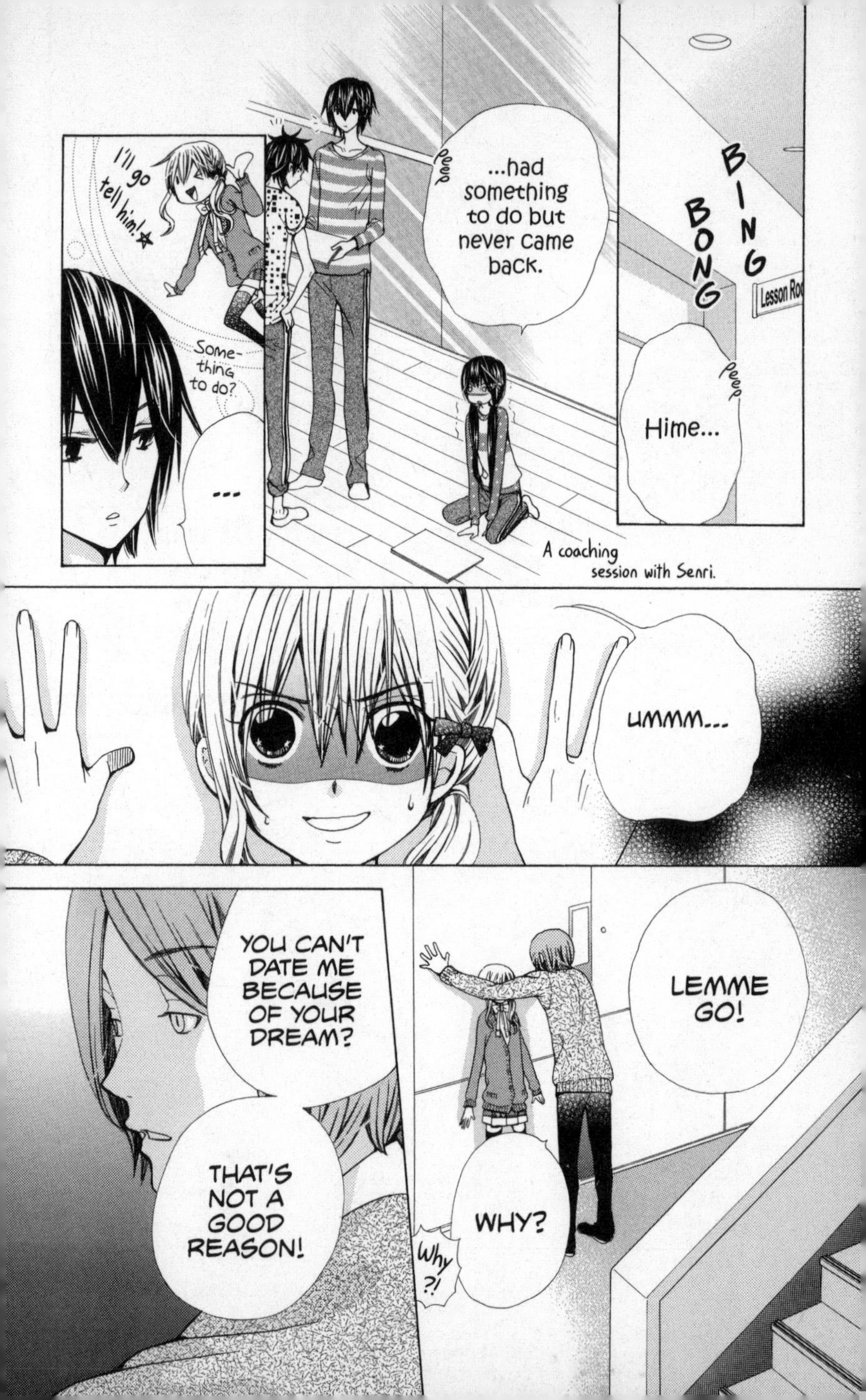
BING
BONG
Peep
Hime...
Peep
...had something to do but never came back.
A coaching session with Senri.
I'll go tell him!☆
Something to do?
...
UMMM...
LEMME GO!
WHY?
Why?!
YOU CAN'T DATE ME BECAUSE OF YOUR DREAM?
THAT'S NOT A GOOD REASON!

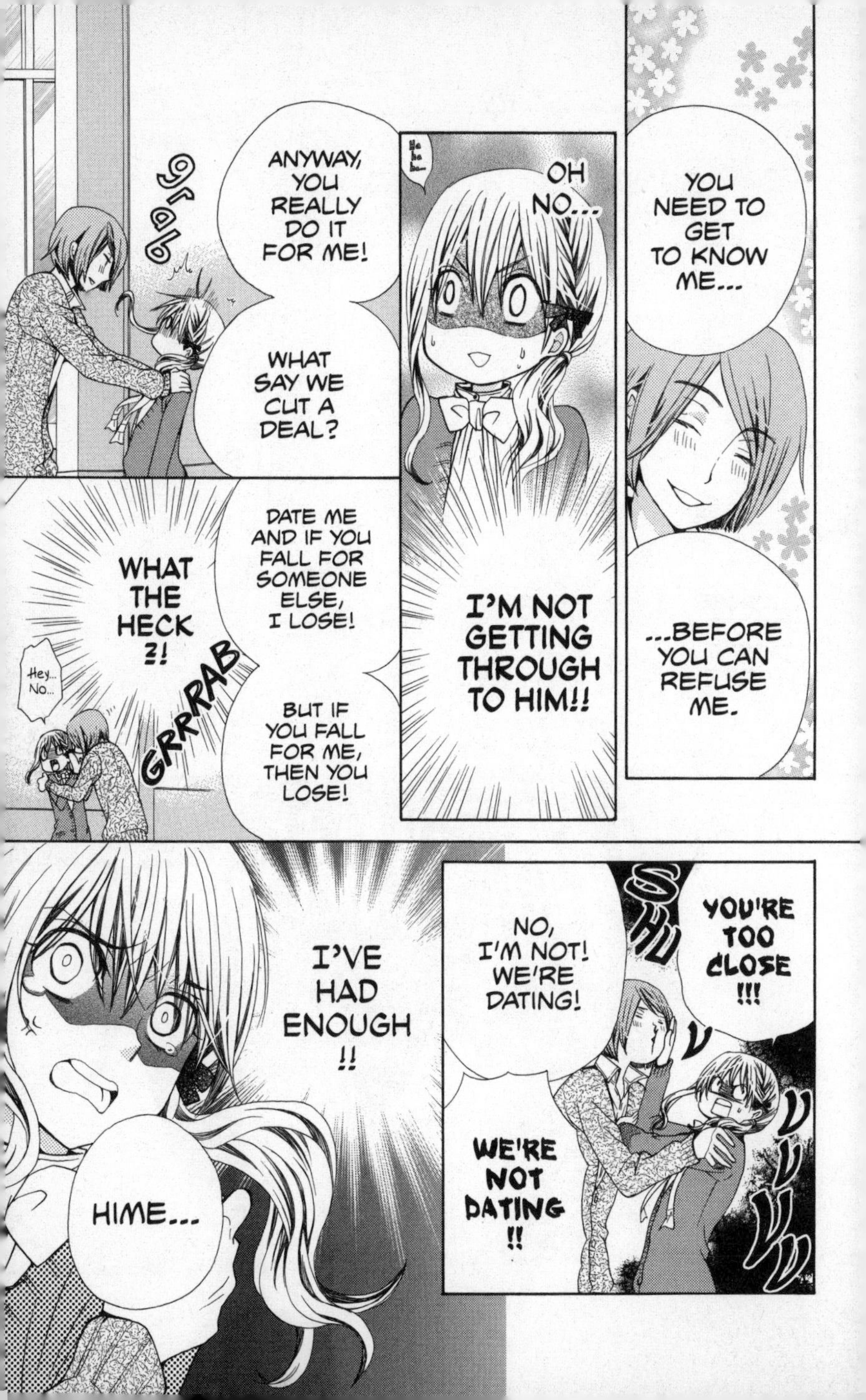
YOU NEED TO GET TO KNOW ME...
...BEFORE YOU CAN REFUSE ME.
OH NO...
I'M NOT GETTING THROUGH TO HIM!!
ANYWAY, YOU REALLY DO IT FOR ME!
grab
WHAT SAY WE CUT A DEAL?
DATE ME AND IF YOU FALL FOR SOMEONE ELSE, I LOSE!
BUT IF YOU FALL FOR ME, THEN YOU LOSE!
WHAT THE HECK?!
GRRRAB
Hey... No...
SHU
YOU'RE TOO CLOSE!!!
NO, I'M NOT! WE'RE DATING!
WE'RE NOT DATING!!
I'VE HAD ENOUGH!!
HIME...

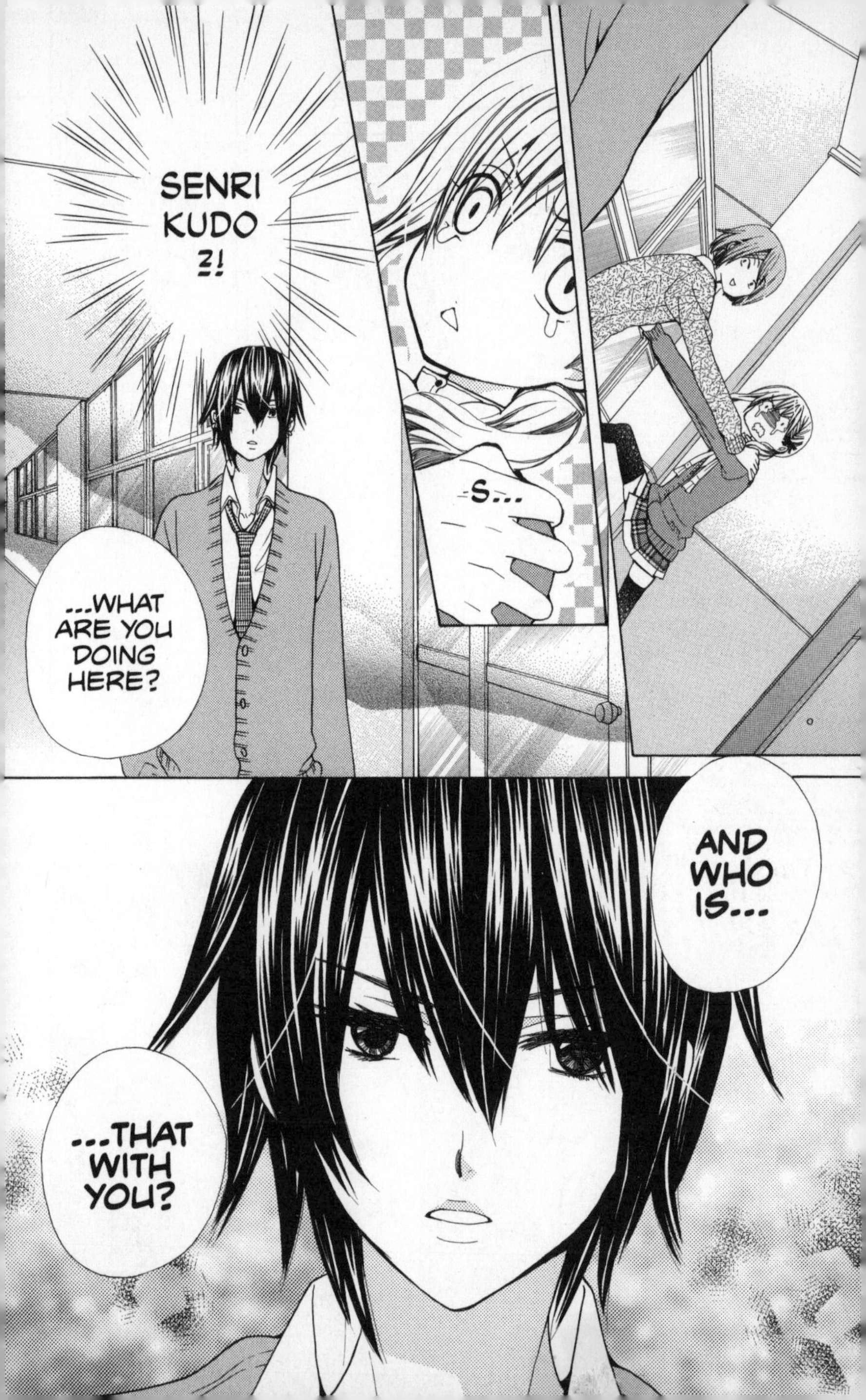
S...
SENRI KUDO?!
...WHAT ARE YOU DOING HERE?
AND WHO IS...
...THAT WITH YOU?

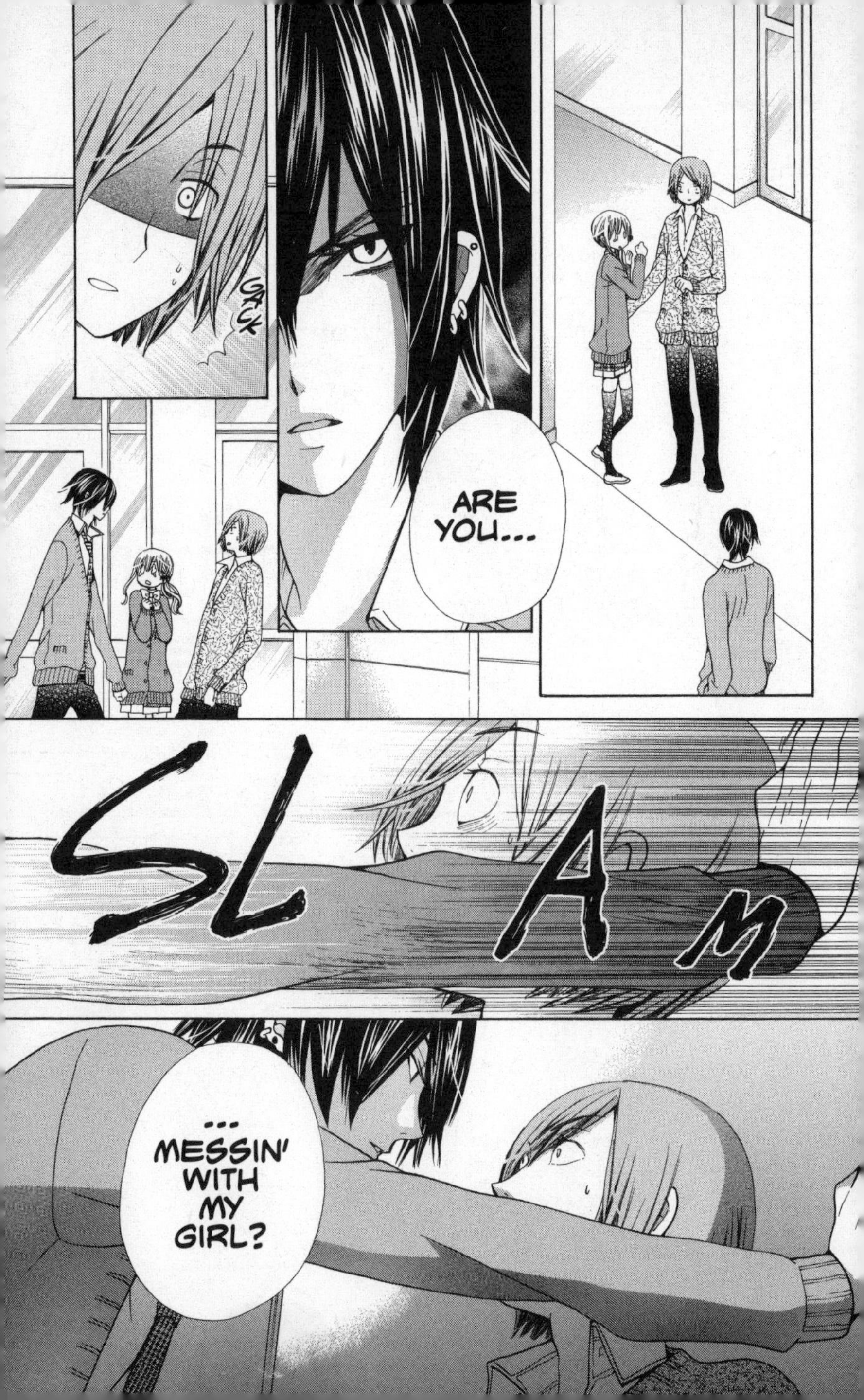
ARE YOU...
GACK
SLAM
...MESSIN' WITH MY GIRL?

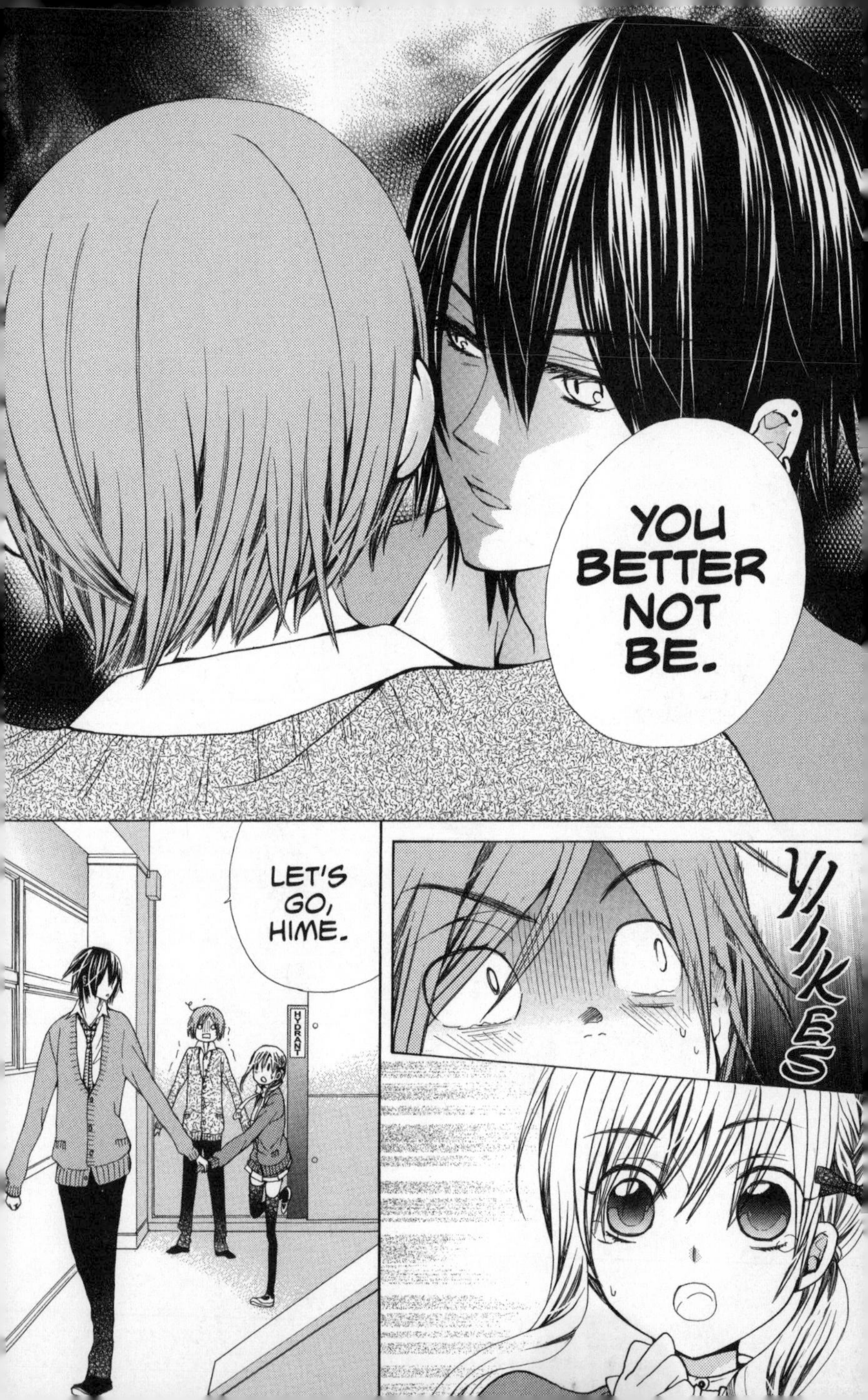
YOU BETTER NOT BE.
YIIIKES
LET'S GO, HIME.
HYDRANT

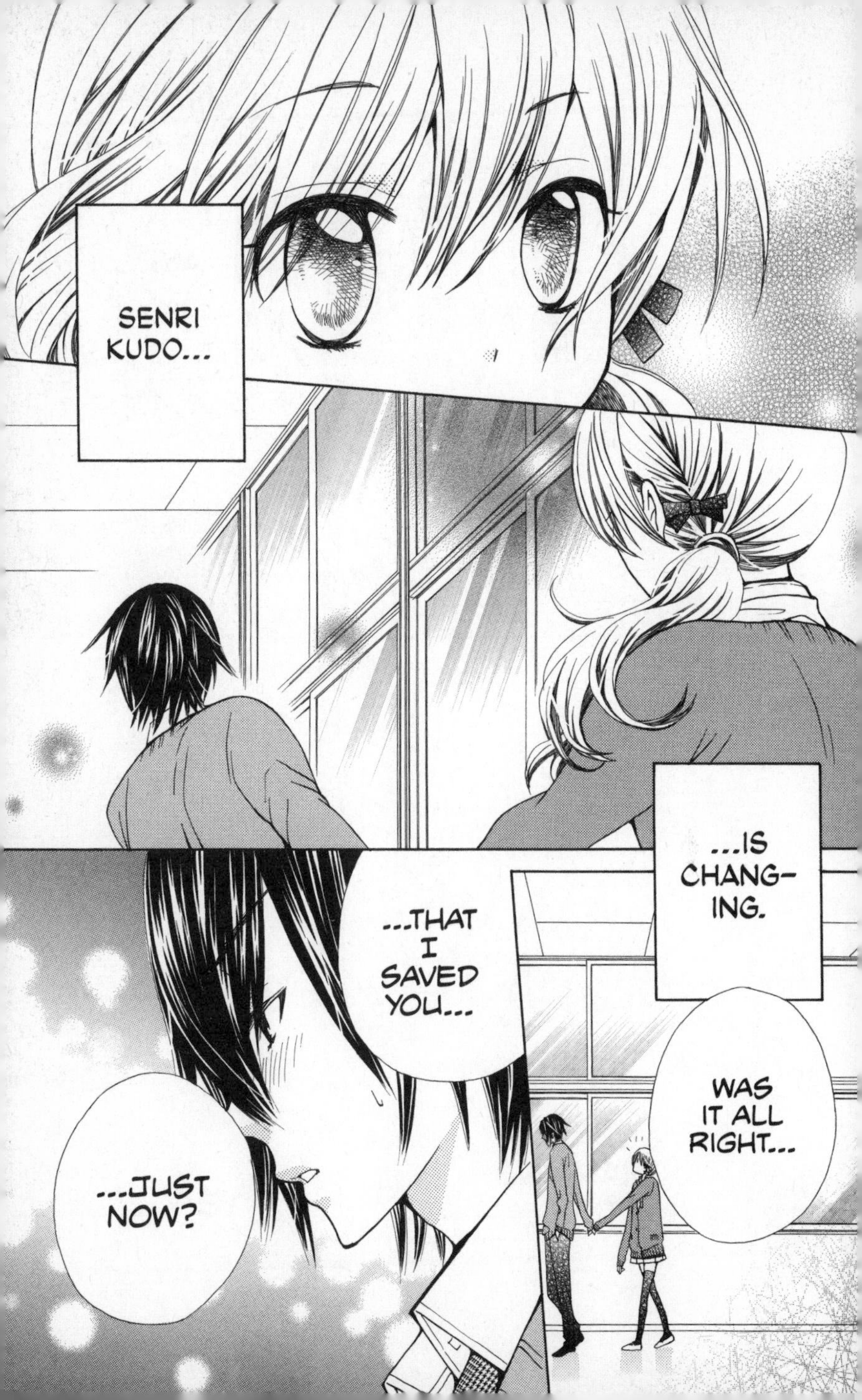
SENRI KUDO...
...IS CHANGING.
WAS IT ALL RIGHT...
...THAT I SAVED YOU...
...JUST NOW?

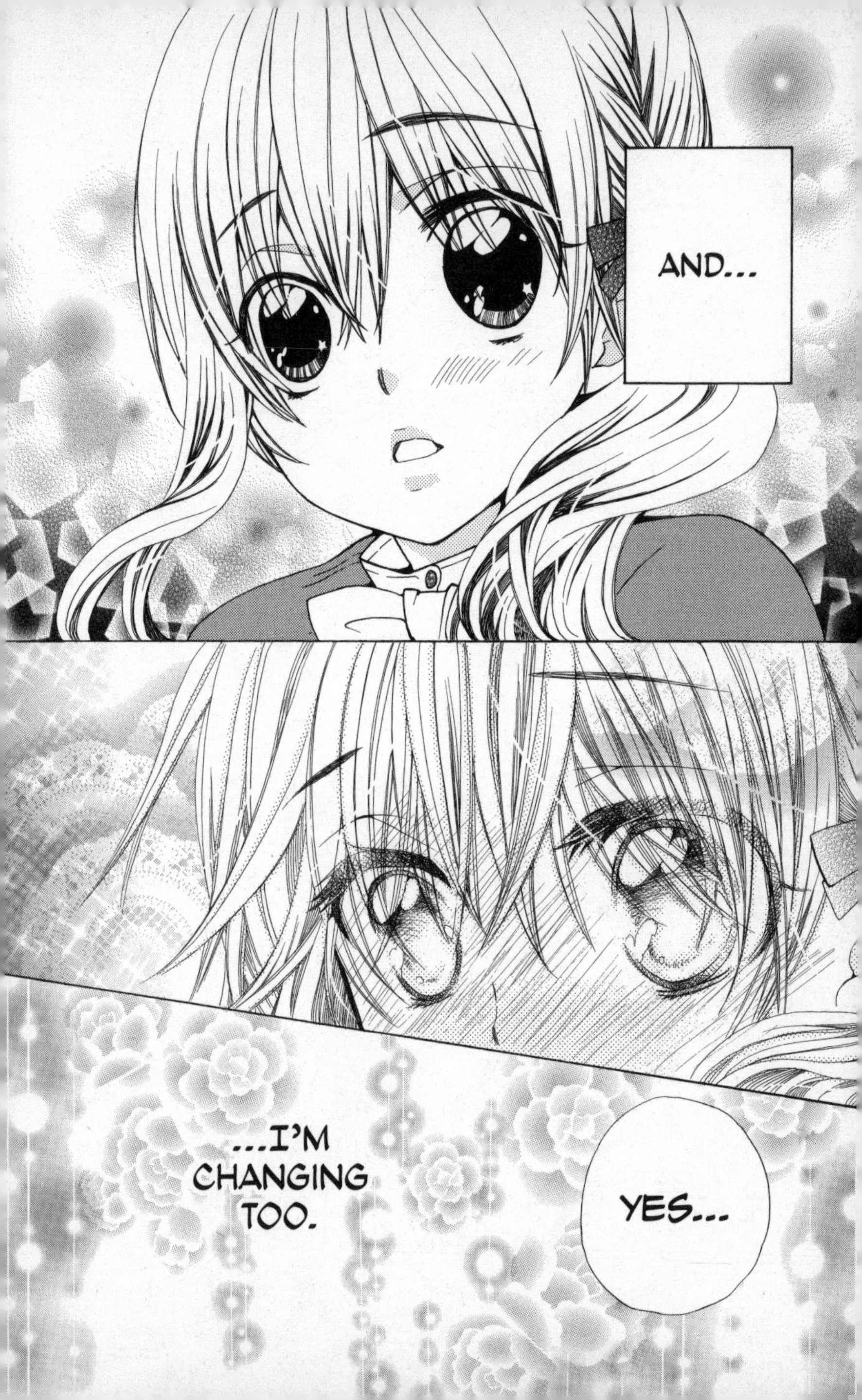
AND...
YES...
...I'M CHANGING TOO.

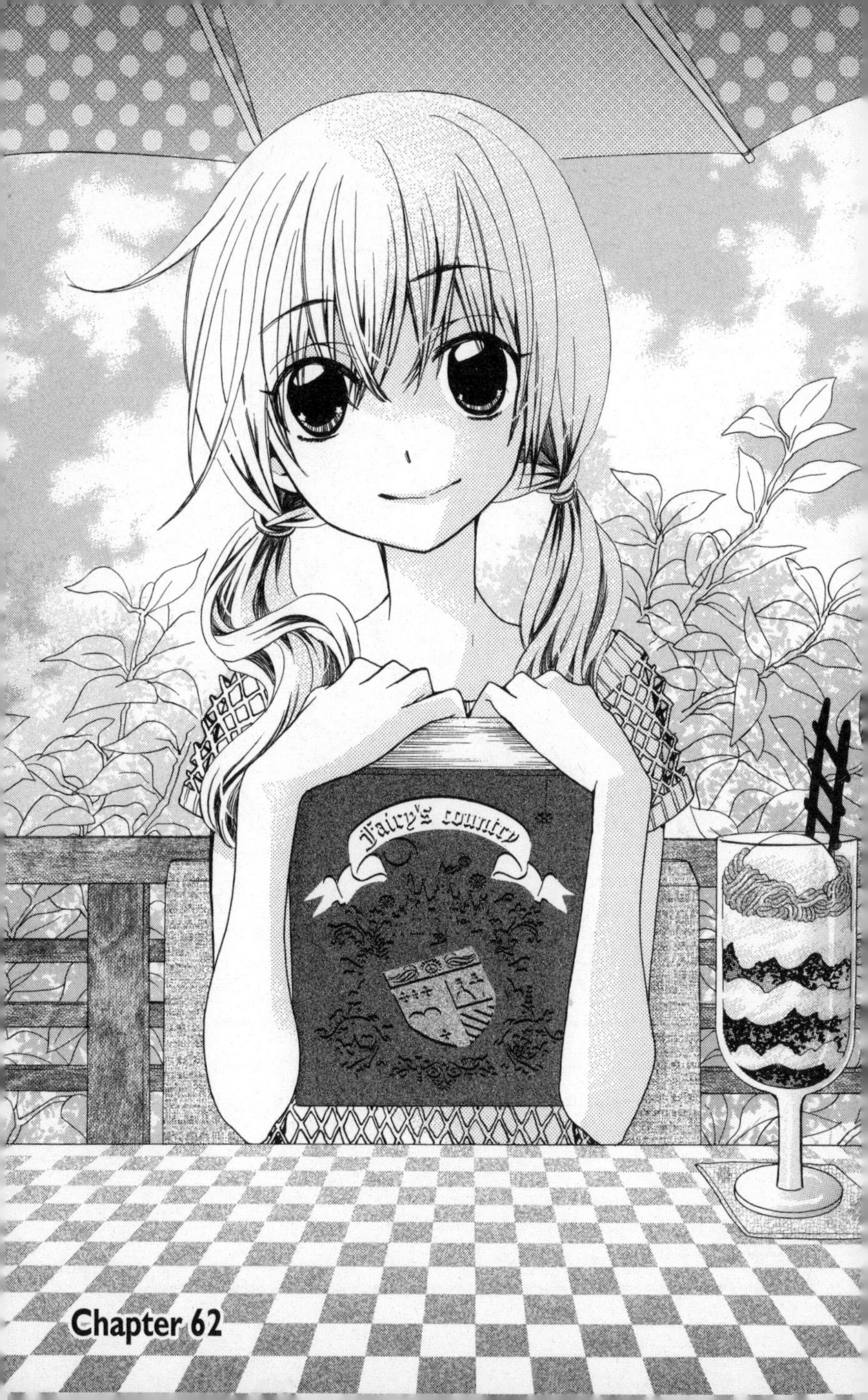
Fairy's country

# Chapter 62

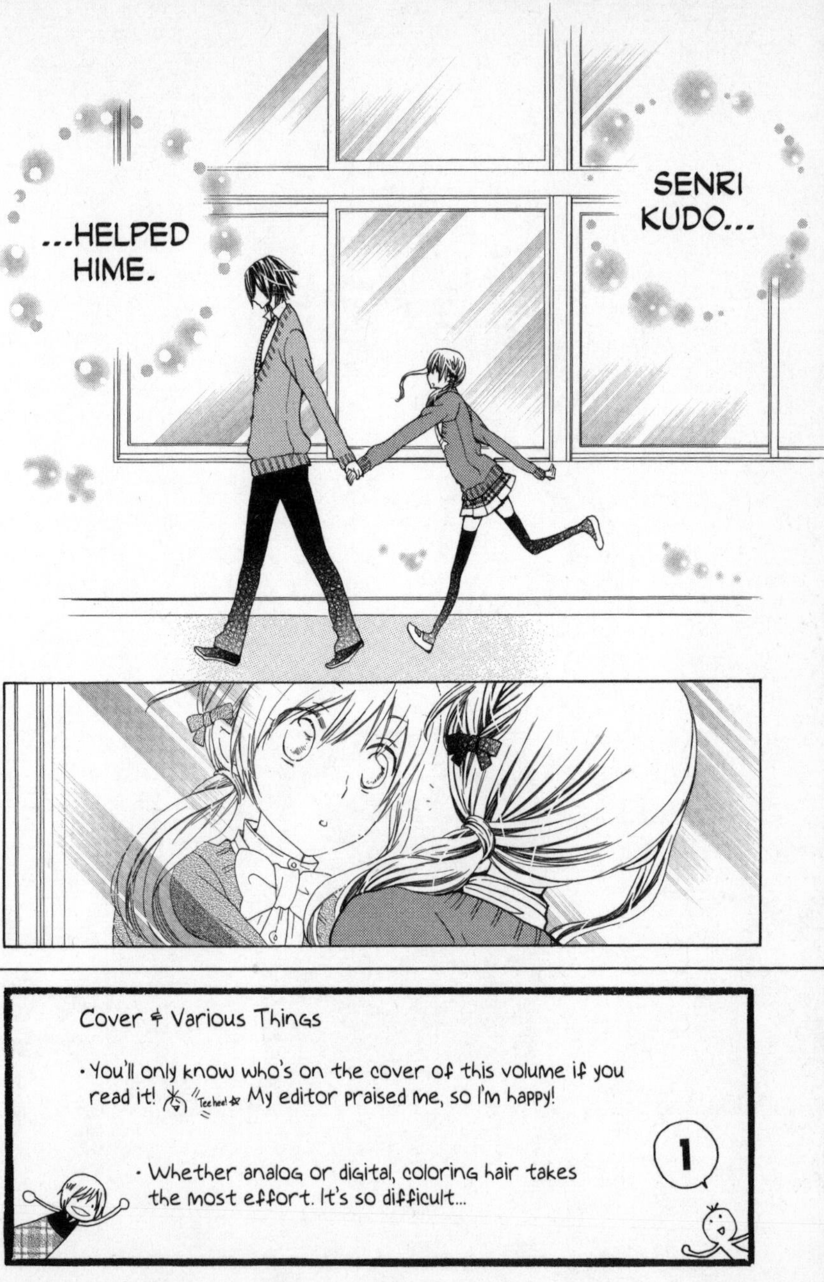
SENRI KUDO...
...HELPED HIME.

Cover & Various Things

• You'll only know who's on the cover of this volume if you read it! Teehee☆ My editor praised me, so I'm happy!

1

• Whether analog or digital, coloring hair takes the most effort. It's so difficult...

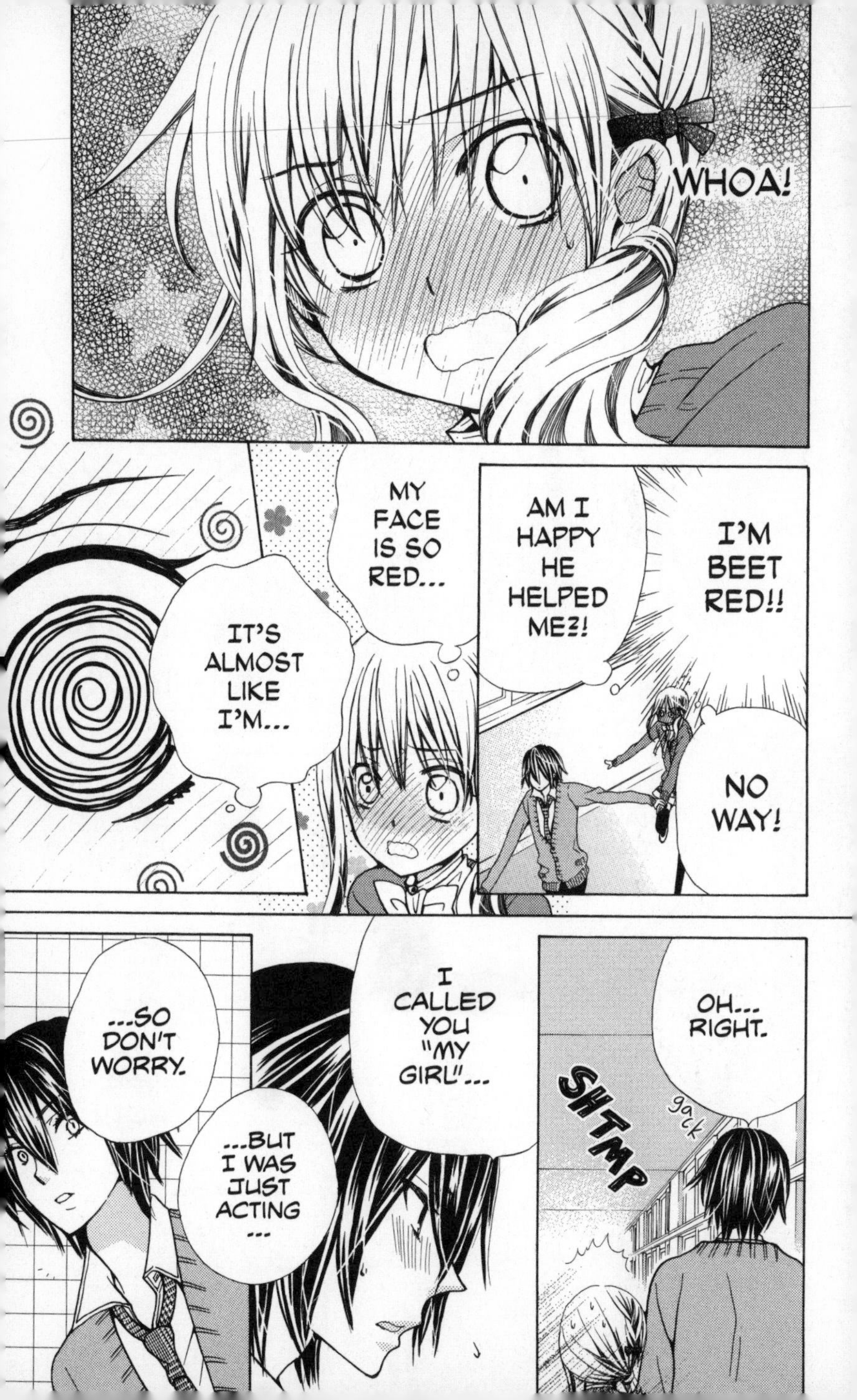
WHOA!
I'M BEET RED!!
AM I HAPPY HE HELPED ME?!
NO WAY!
MY FACE IS SO RED...
IT'S ALMOST LIKE I'M...
OH... RIGHT.
gack
SHTMP
I CALLED YOU "MY GIRL"...
...BUT I WAS JUST ACTING...
...SO DON'T WORRY.

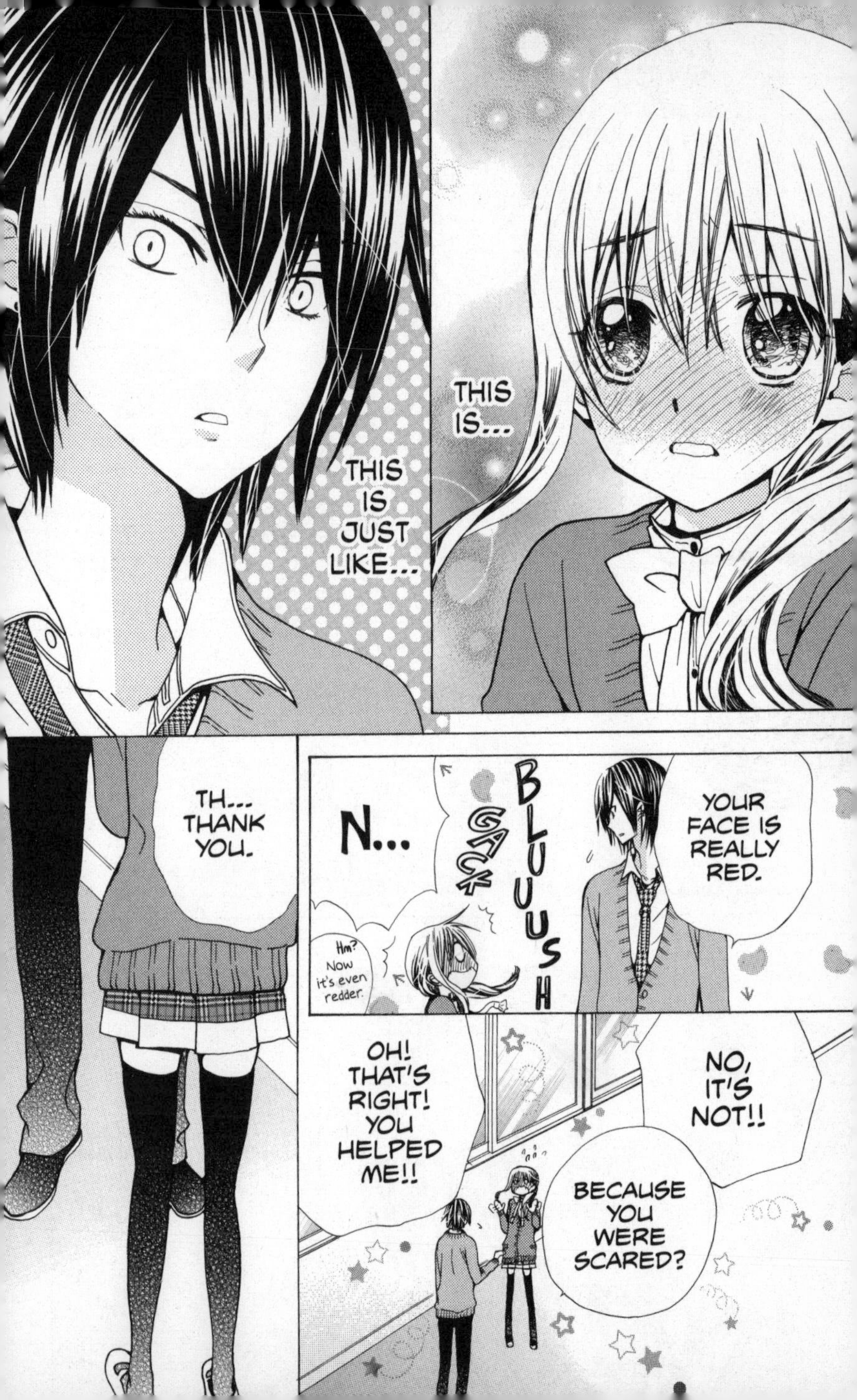
THIS IS...
THIS IS JUST LIKE...
YOUR FACE IS REALLY RED.
BLUUUSH
GACK
N...
Hm? Now it's even redder.
NO, IT'S NOT!!
BECAUSE YOU WERE SCARED?
OH! THAT'S RIGHT! YOU HELPED ME!!
TH... THANK YOU.

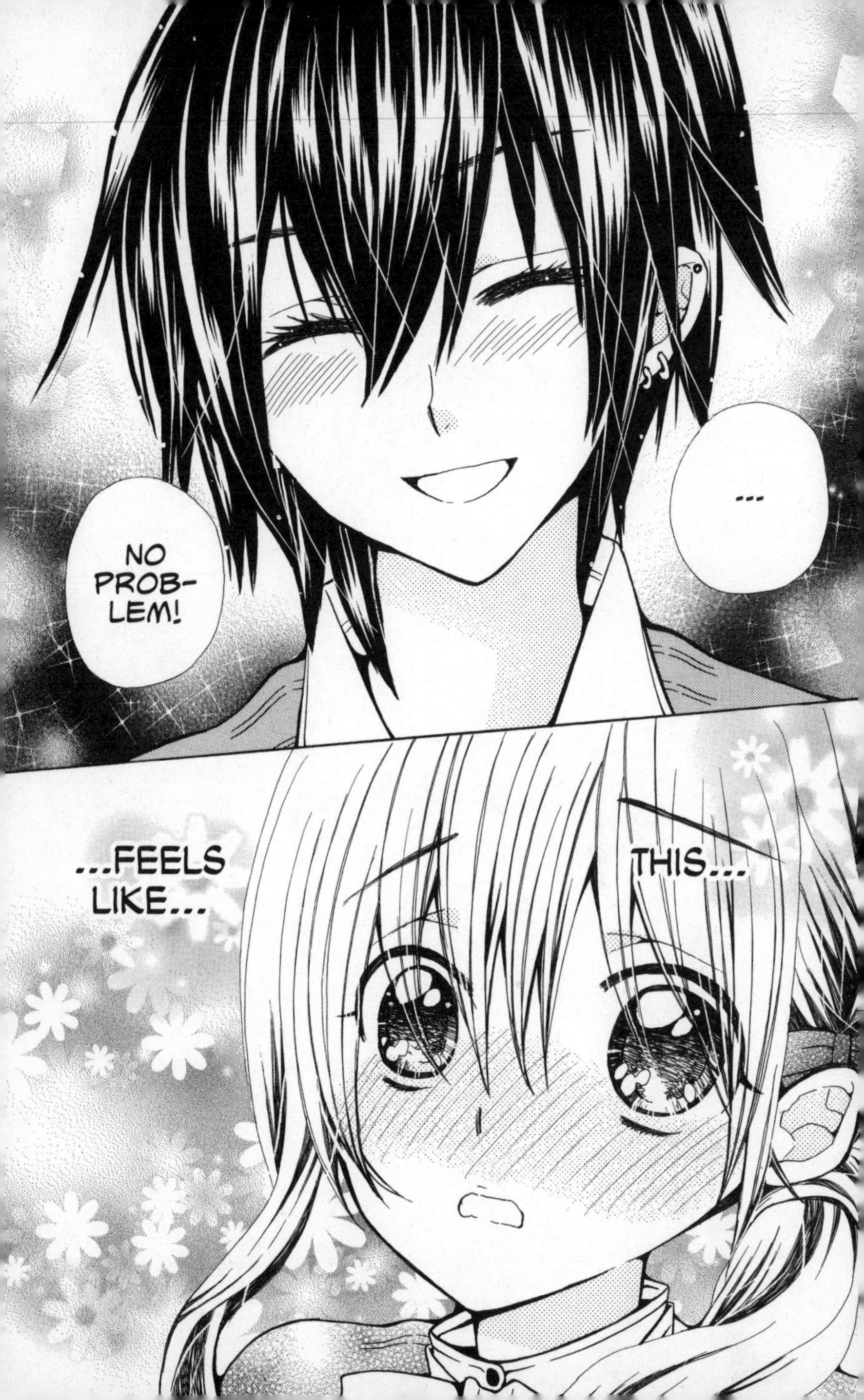
...
NO PROB-LEM!
THIS...
...FEELS LIKE...

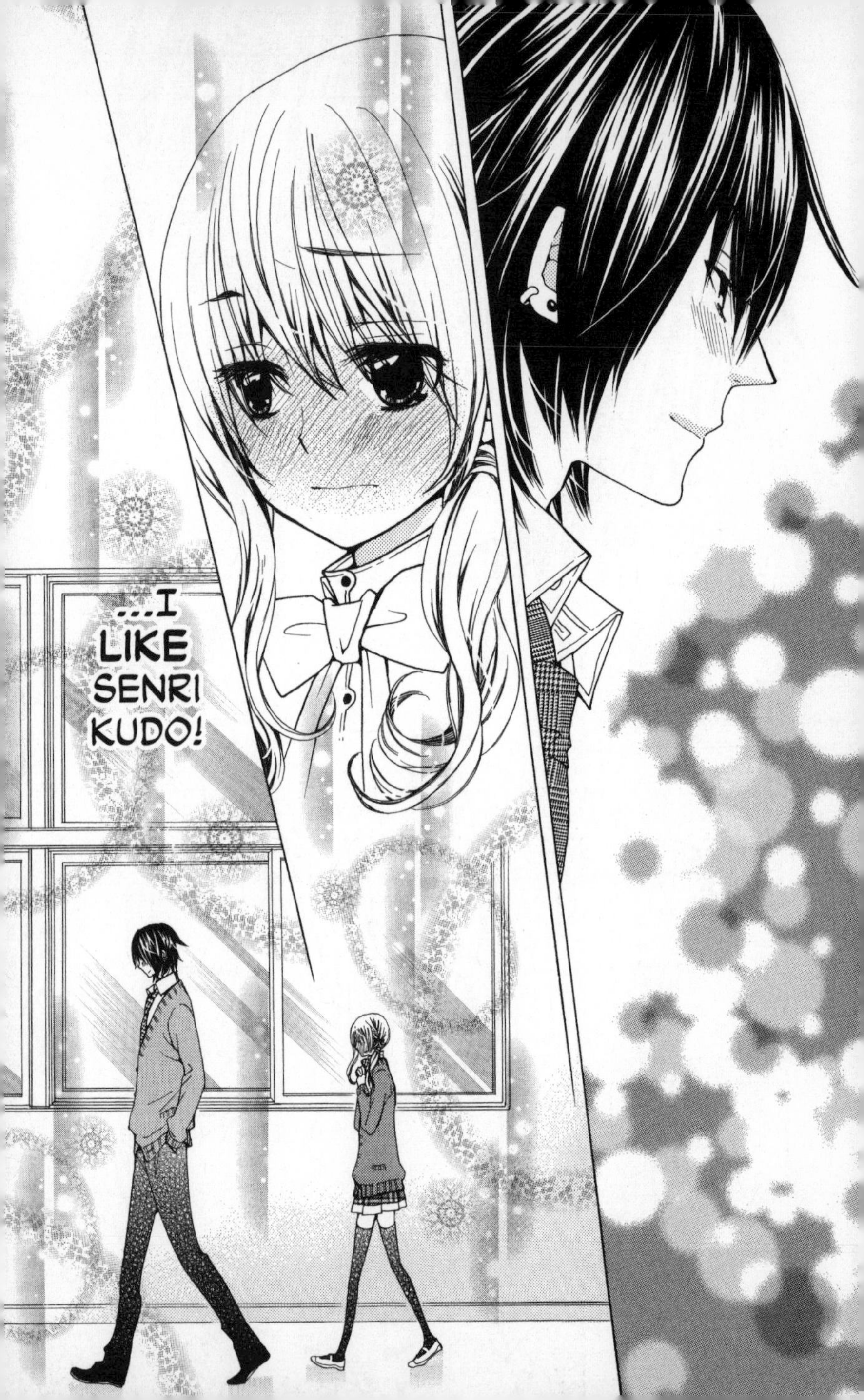
...I LIKE SENRI KUDO!

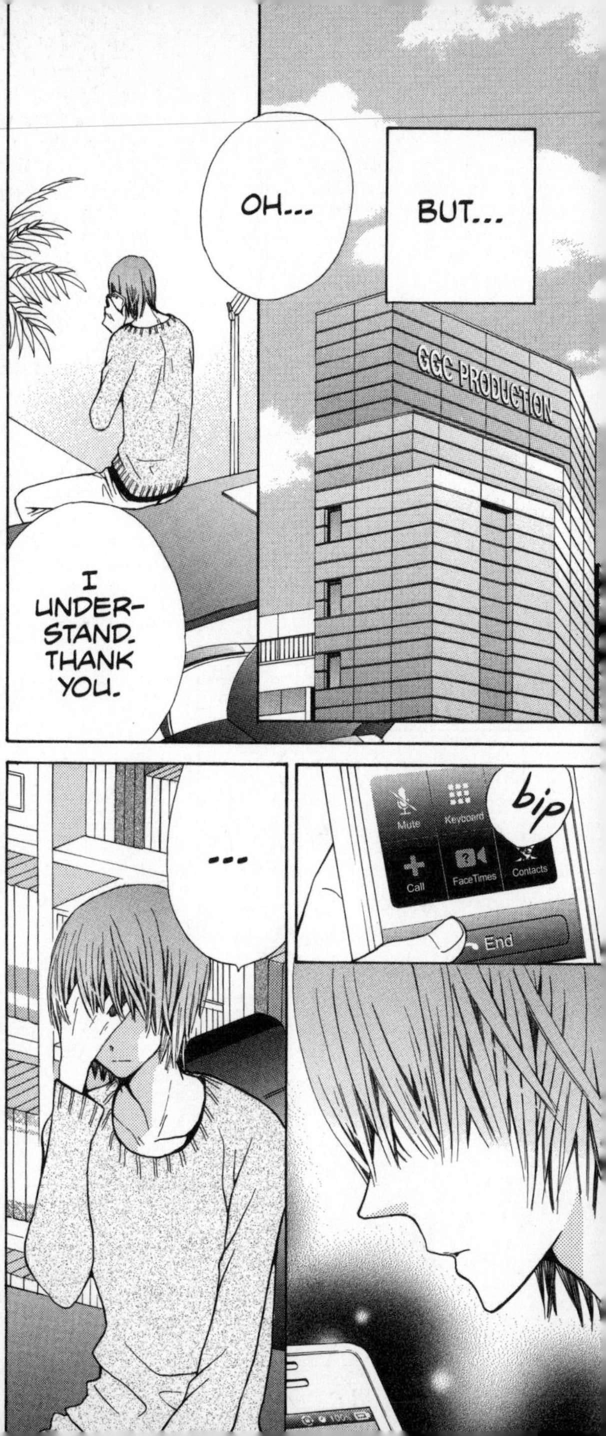
BUT...
GGC PRODUCTION
OH...
I UNDER-STAND. THANK YOU.
bip
Mute
Keyboard
Call
FaceTimes
Contacts
End
...

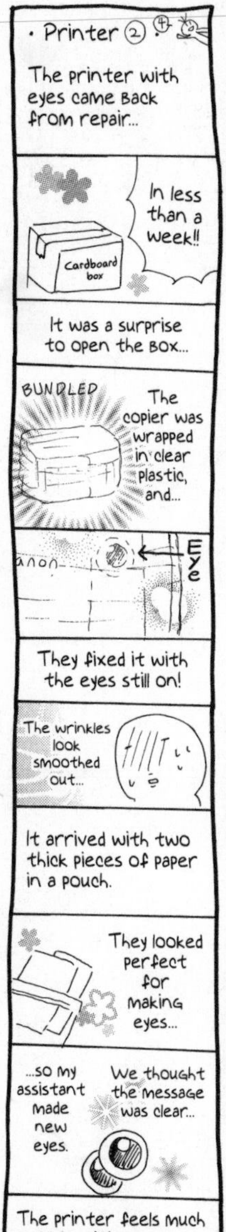
· Printer ②
The printer with eyes came back from repair...
In less than a week!!
Cardboard box
It was a surprise to open the box...
BUNDLED
The copier was wrapped in clear plastic, and...
Eye
They fixed it with the eyes still on!
The wrinkles look smoothed out...
It arrived with two thick pieces of paper in a pouch.
They looked perfect for making eyes...
We thought the message was clear...
...so my assistant made new eyes.
The printer feels much better with new eyes. Thank you, Kanon!

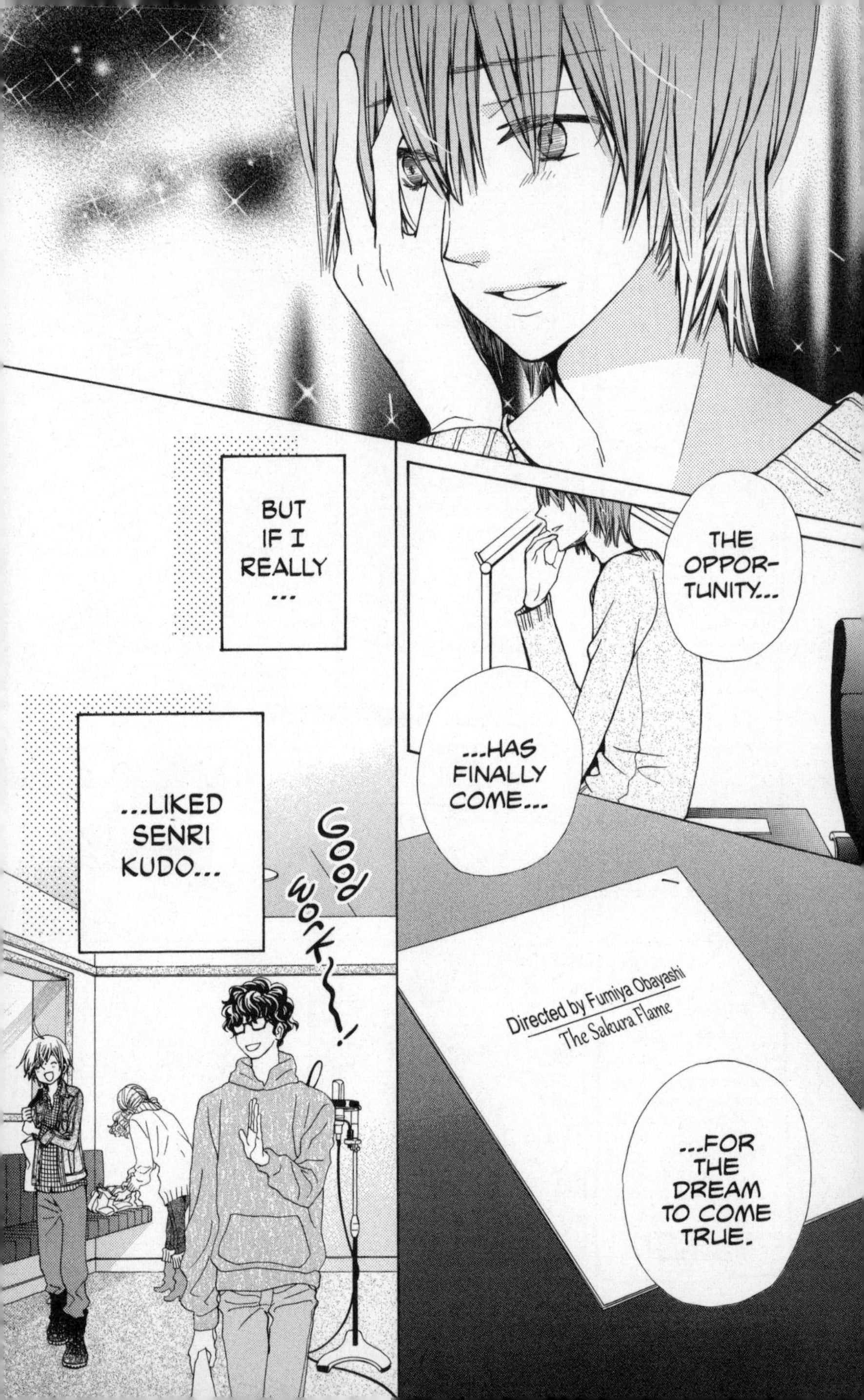
THE OPPORTUNITY...
...HAS FINALLY COME...
The Sakura Flame
Directed by Fumiya Obayashi
...FOR THE DREAM TO COME TRUE.
BUT IF I REALLY...
...LIKED SENRI KUDO...
Good work~~!

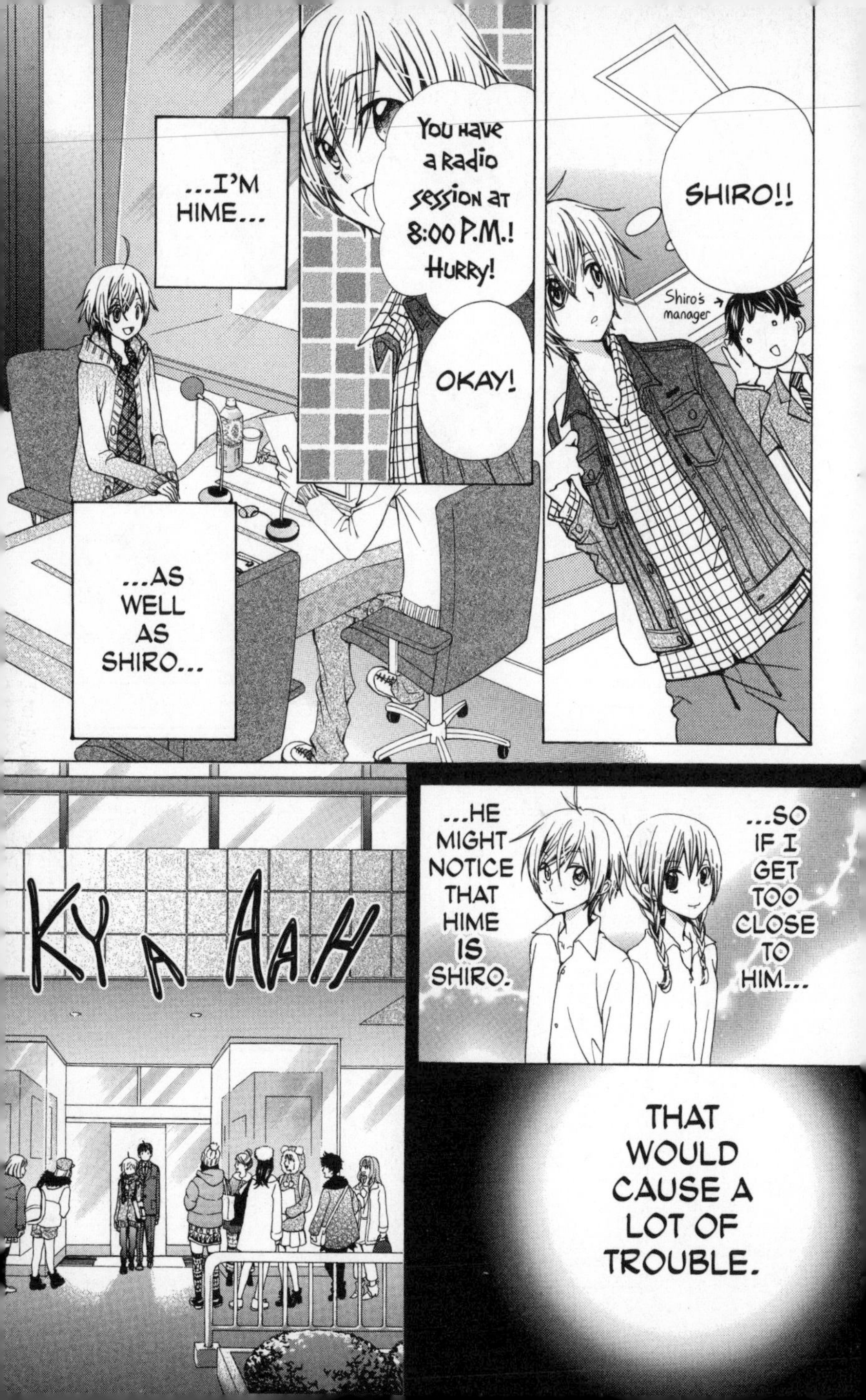
SHIRO!!
Shiro's manager
You have a radio session at 8:00 P.M.! Hurry!
OKAY!
...I'M HIME...
...AS WELL AS SHIRO...
...SO IF I GET TOO CLOSE TO HIM...
...HE MIGHT NOTICE THAT HIME IS SHIRO.
THAT WOULD CAUSE A LOT OF TROUBLE.
KYAAAH

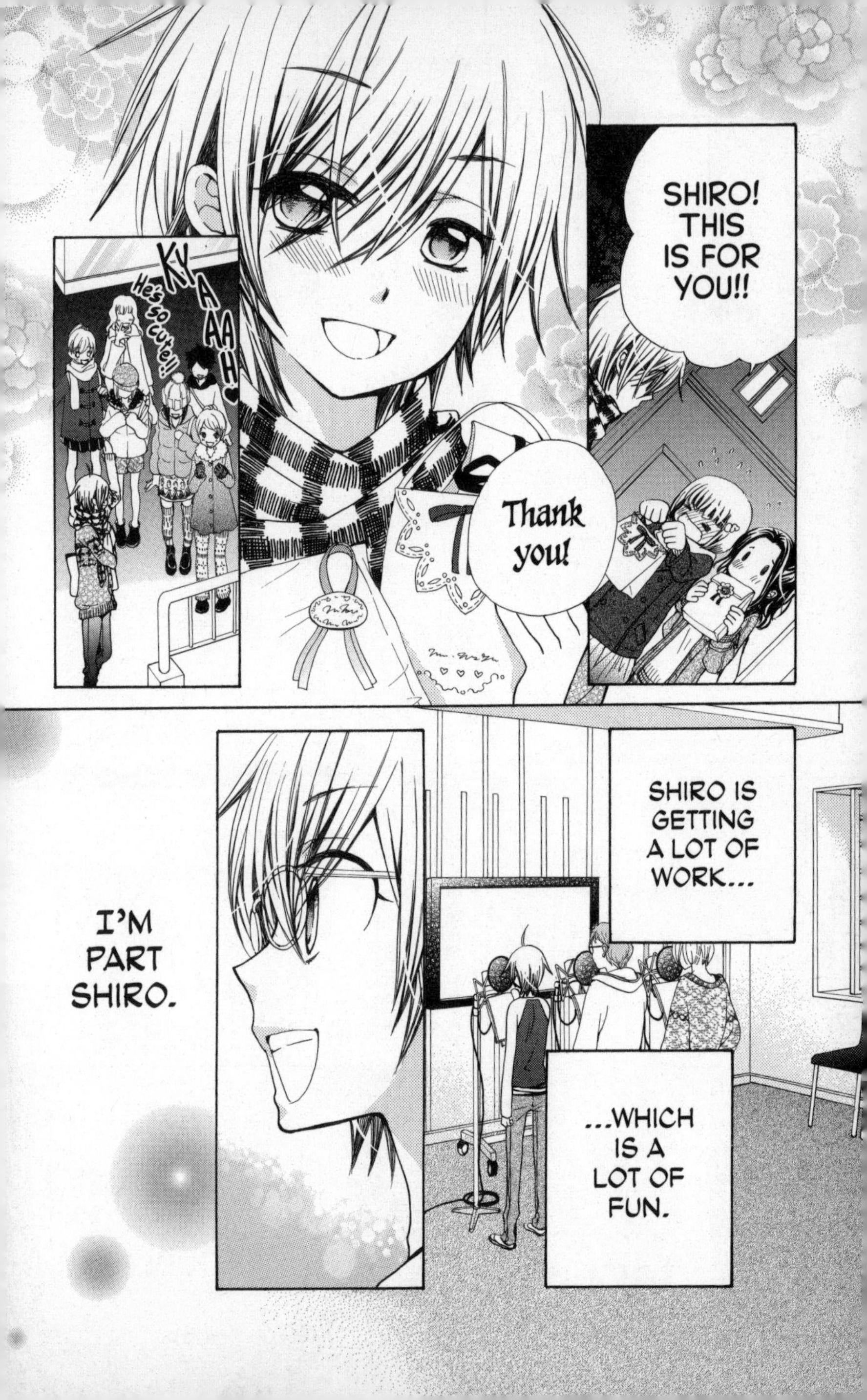
SHIRO! THIS IS FOR YOU!!
Thank you!
KYAAAH♥
He's so cute!!
SHIRO IS GETTING A LOT OF WORK...
...WHICH IS A LOT OF FUN.
I'M PART SHIRO.

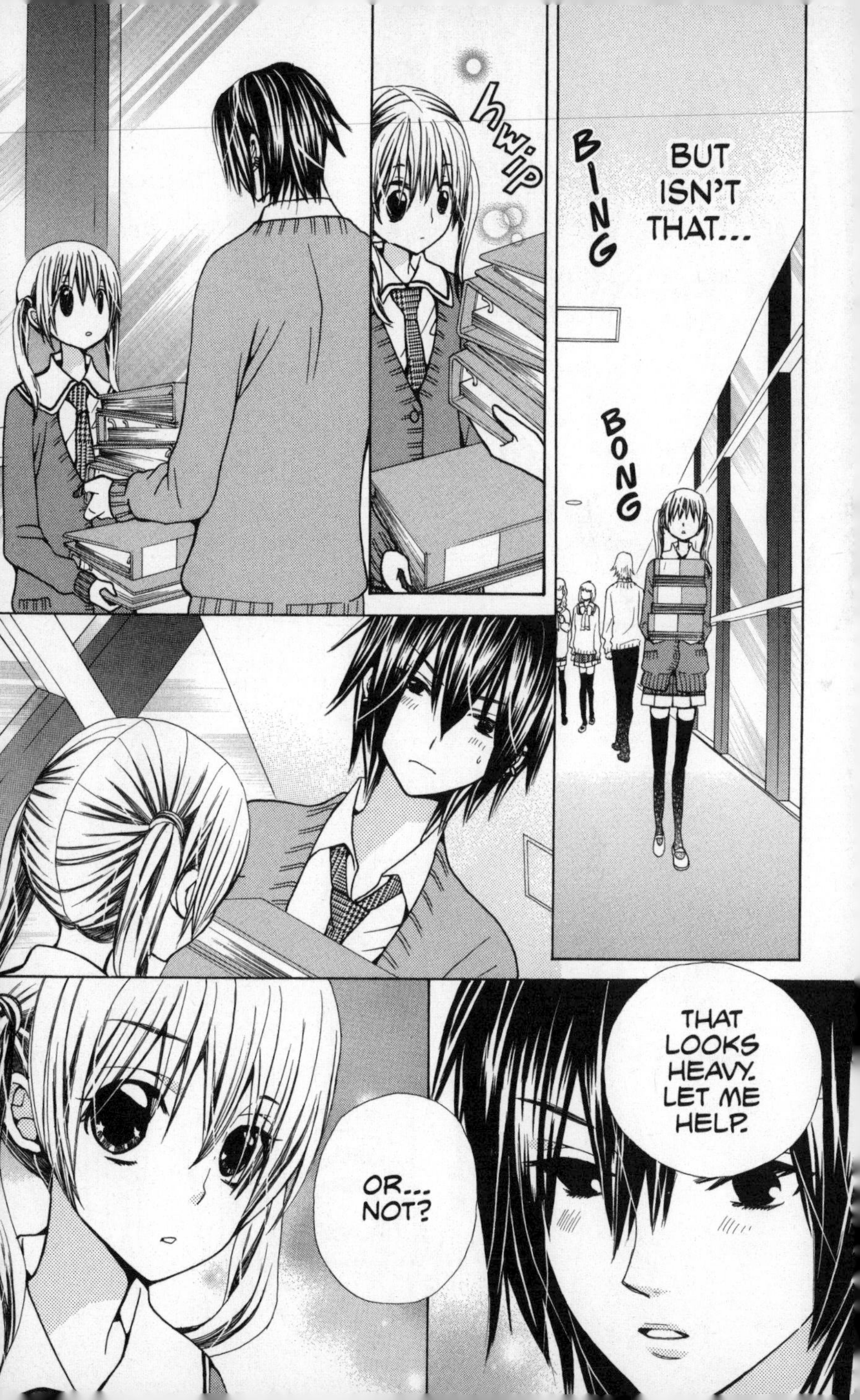
BUT ISN'T THAT...
BING
BONG
hwip
THAT LOOKS HEAVY. LET ME HELP.
OR... NOT?

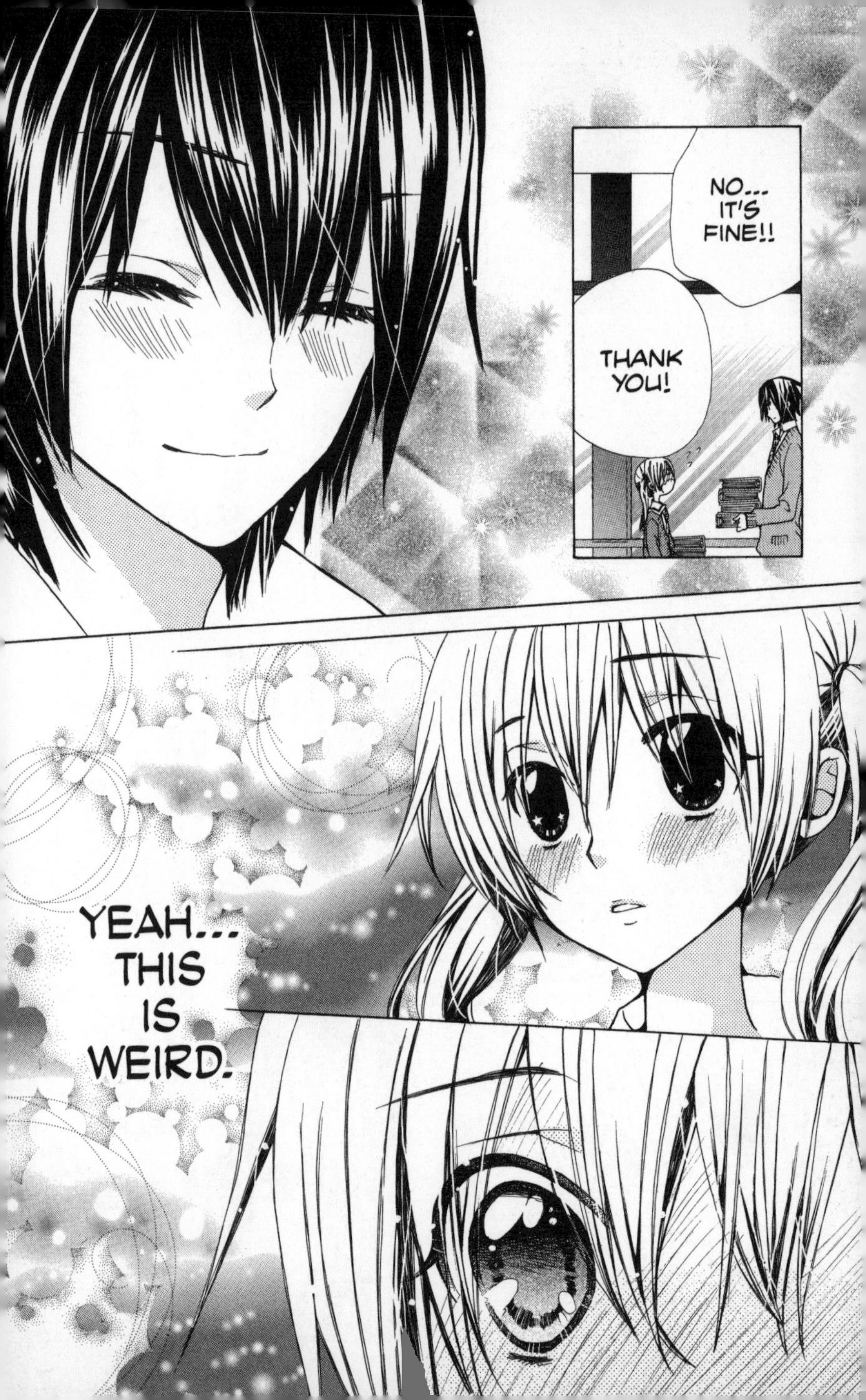
NO... IT'S FINE!!
THANK YOU!
YEAH... THIS IS WEIRD.

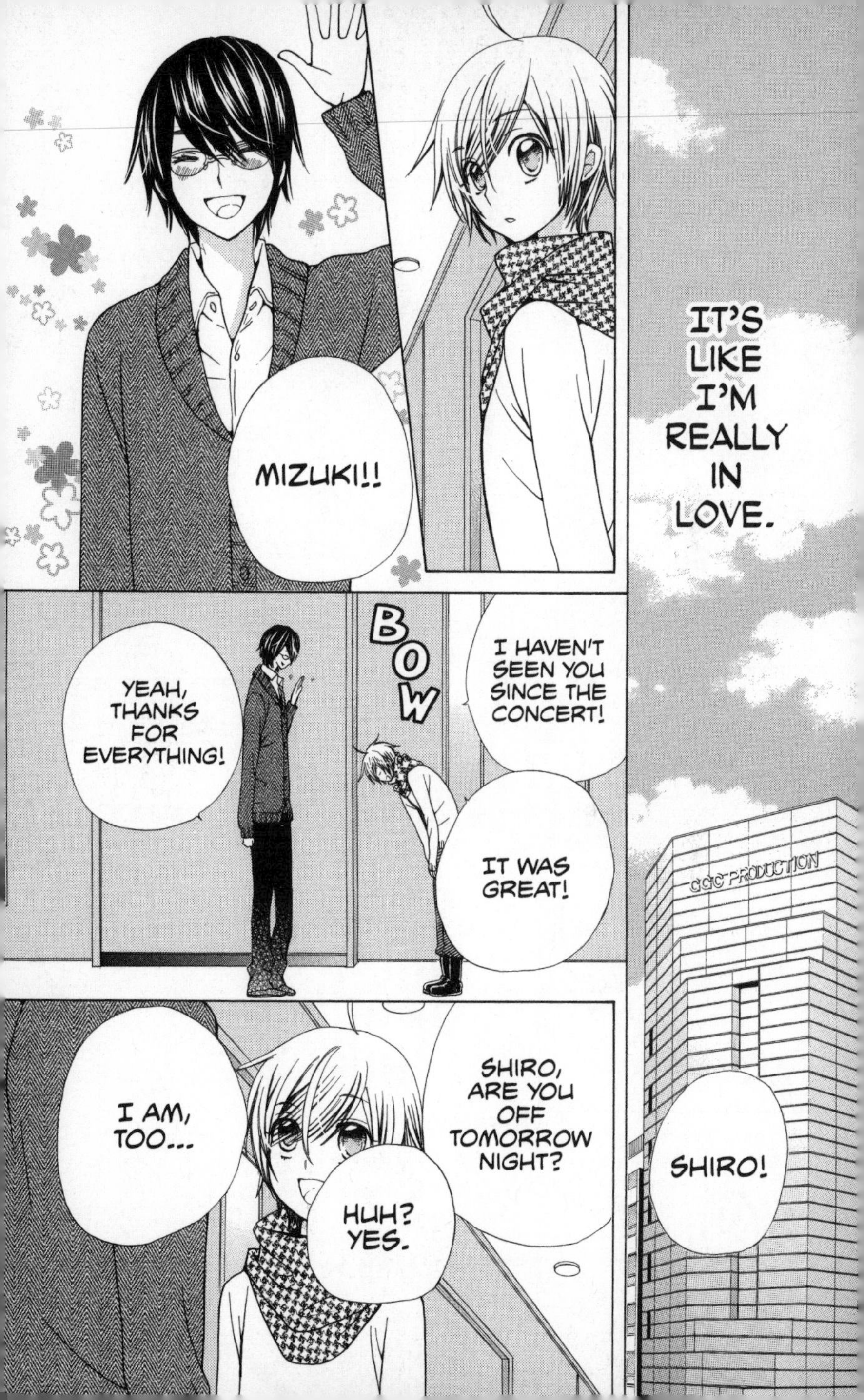
IT'S LIKE I'M REALLY IN LOVE.
GGC PRODUCTION
SHIRO!
MIZUKI!!
I HAVEN'T SEEN YOU SINCE THE CONCERT!
BOW
IT WAS GREAT!
YEAH, THANKS FOR EVERYTHING!
SHIRO, ARE YOU OFF TOMORROW NIGHT?
HUH? YES.
I AM, TOO...

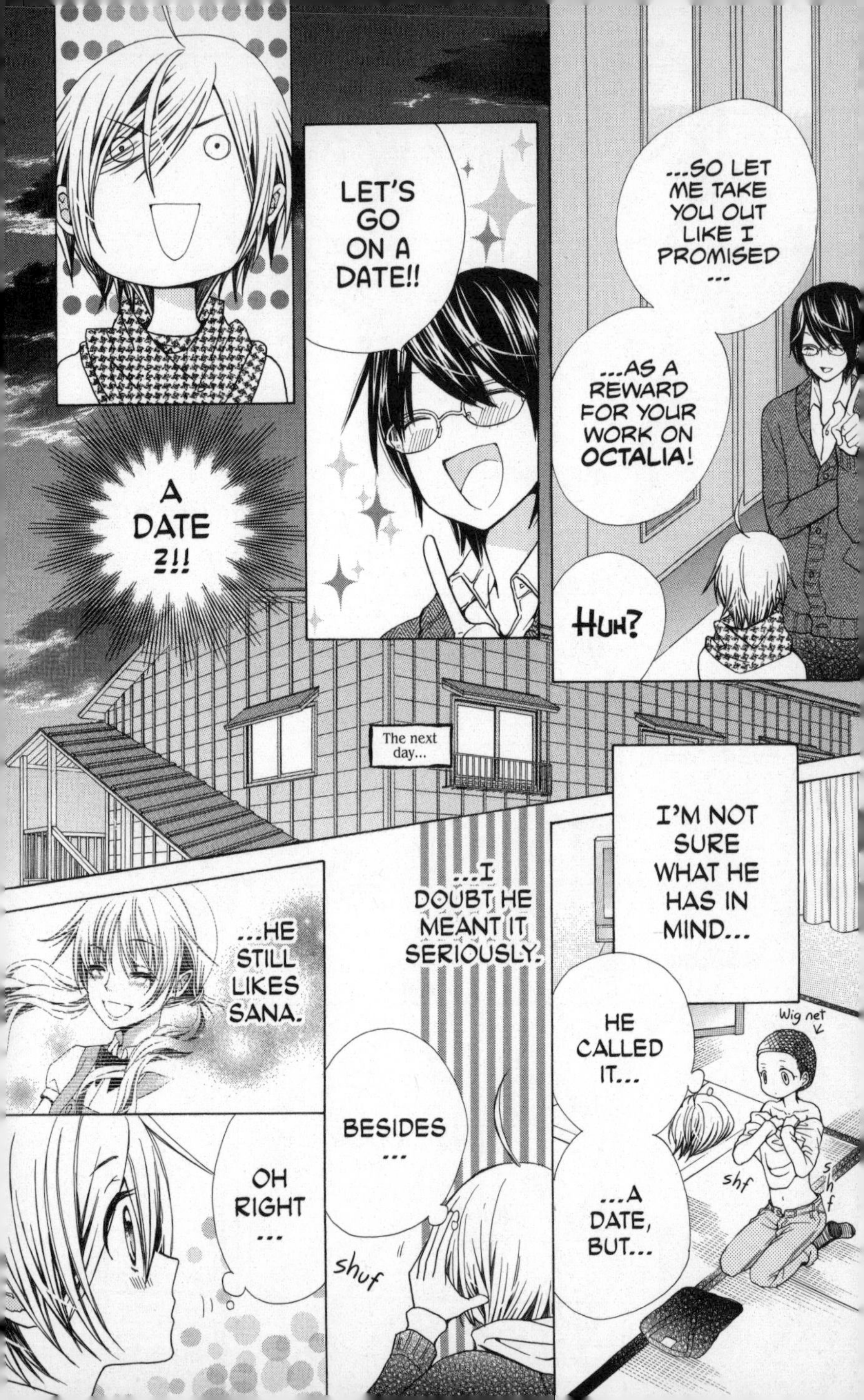
...SO LET ME TAKE YOU OUT LIKE I PROMISED...
...AS A REWARD FOR YOUR WORK ON OCTALIA!
HUH?
LET'S GO ON A DATE!!
A DATE ?!!
The next day...
I'M NOT SURE WHAT HE HAS IN MIND...
HE CALLED IT...
...A DATE, BUT...
Wig net
shf
shf
...I DOUBT HE MEANT IT SERIOUSLY.
BESIDES...
shuf
...HE STILL LIKES SANA.
OH RIGHT...

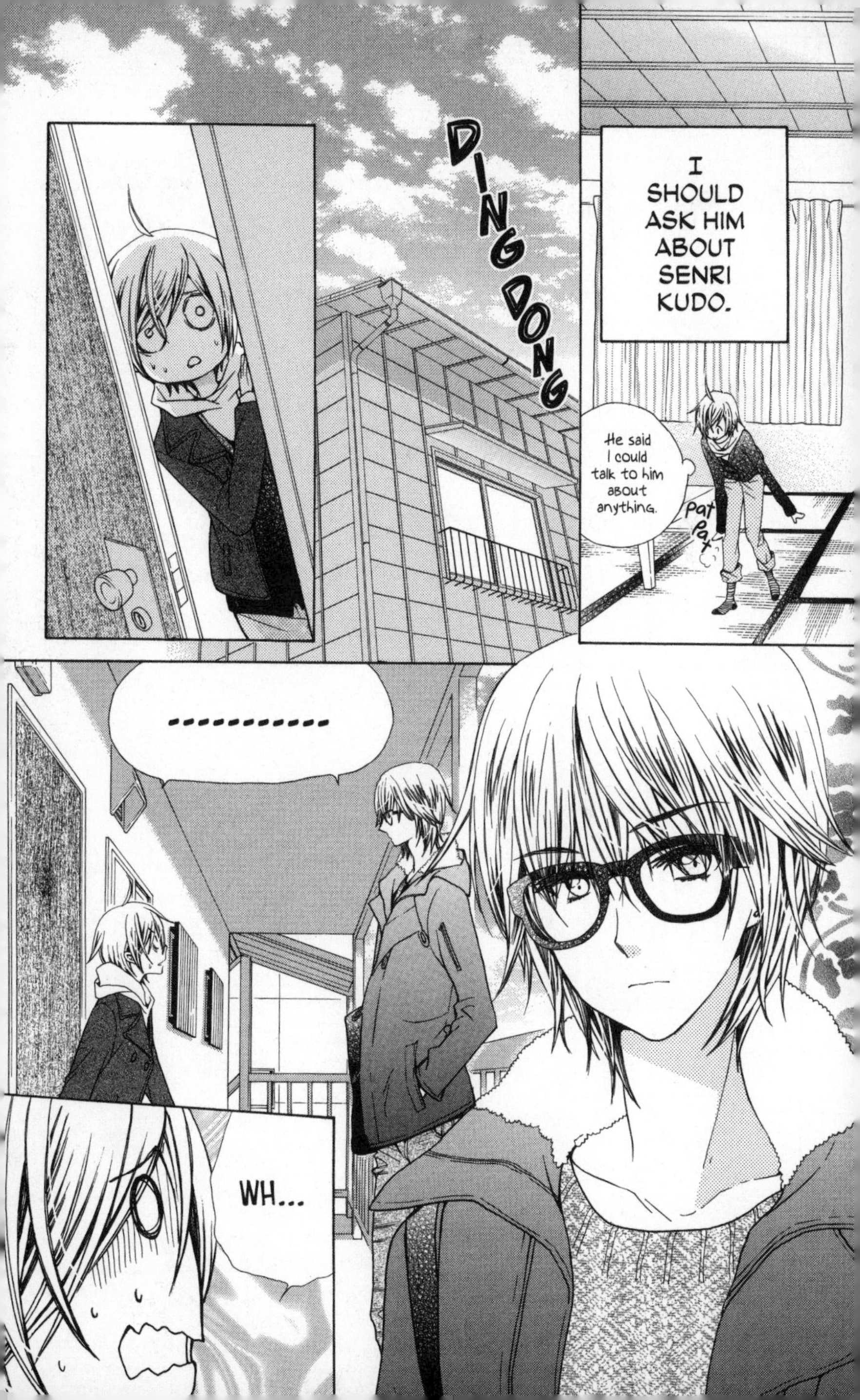
I SHOULD ASK HIM ABOUT SENRI KUDO.
He said I could talk to him about anything.
pat pat
DING DONG
-----------
WH...

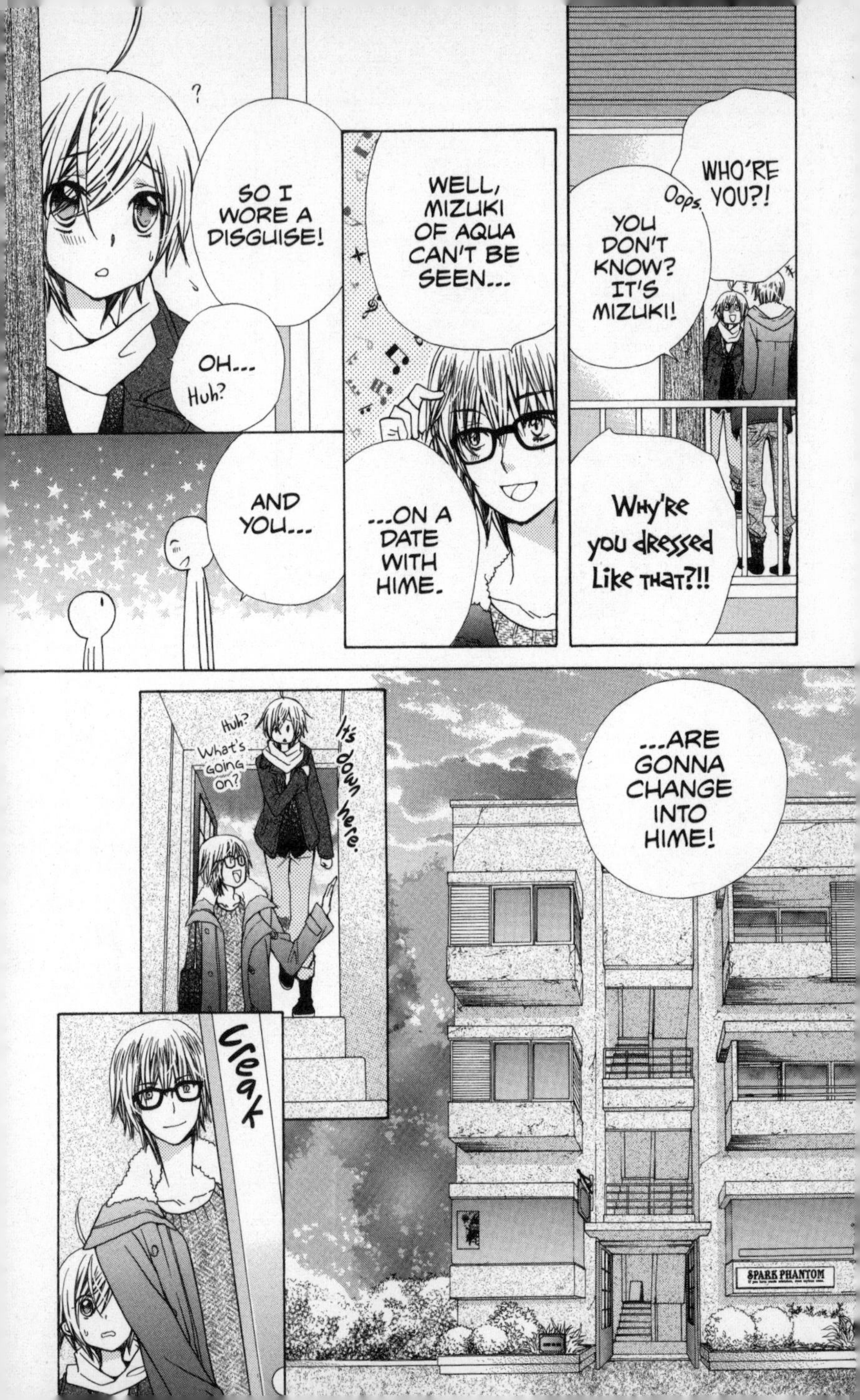
WHO'RE YOU?!
Oops.
YOU DON'T KNOW? IT'S MIZUKI!
Why're you dressed Like that?!!
WELL, MIZUKI OF AQUA CAN'T BE SEEN...
...ON A DATE WITH HIME.
?
SO I WORE A DISGUISE!
OH... Huh?
AND YOU...
...ARE GONNA CHANGE INTO HIME!
SPARK PHANTOM
It's down here.
Huh? What's going on?
Creak

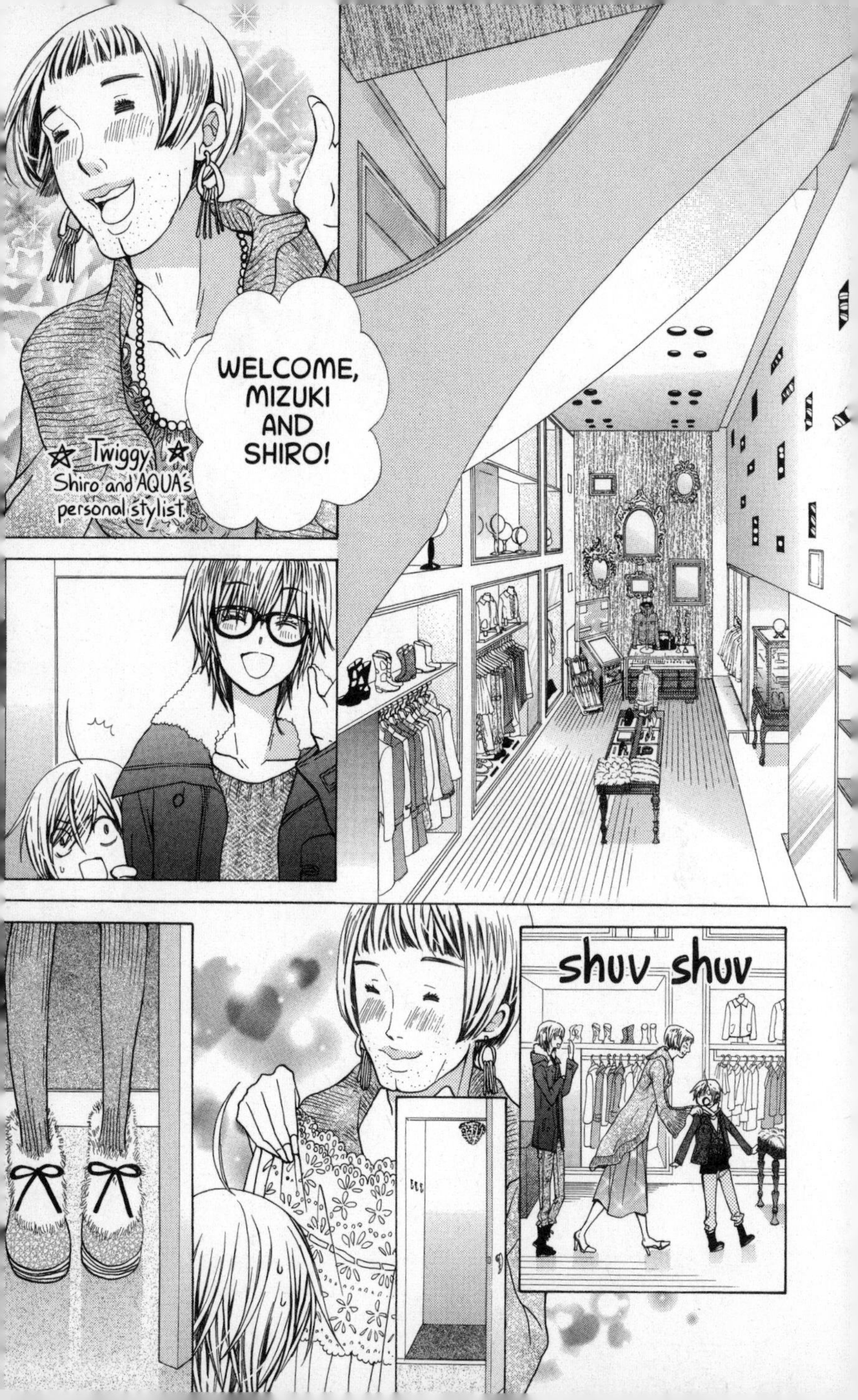

WELCOME, MIZUKI AND SHIRO!
☆ Twiggy ☆ Shiro and AQUA's personal stylist.
shuv shuv

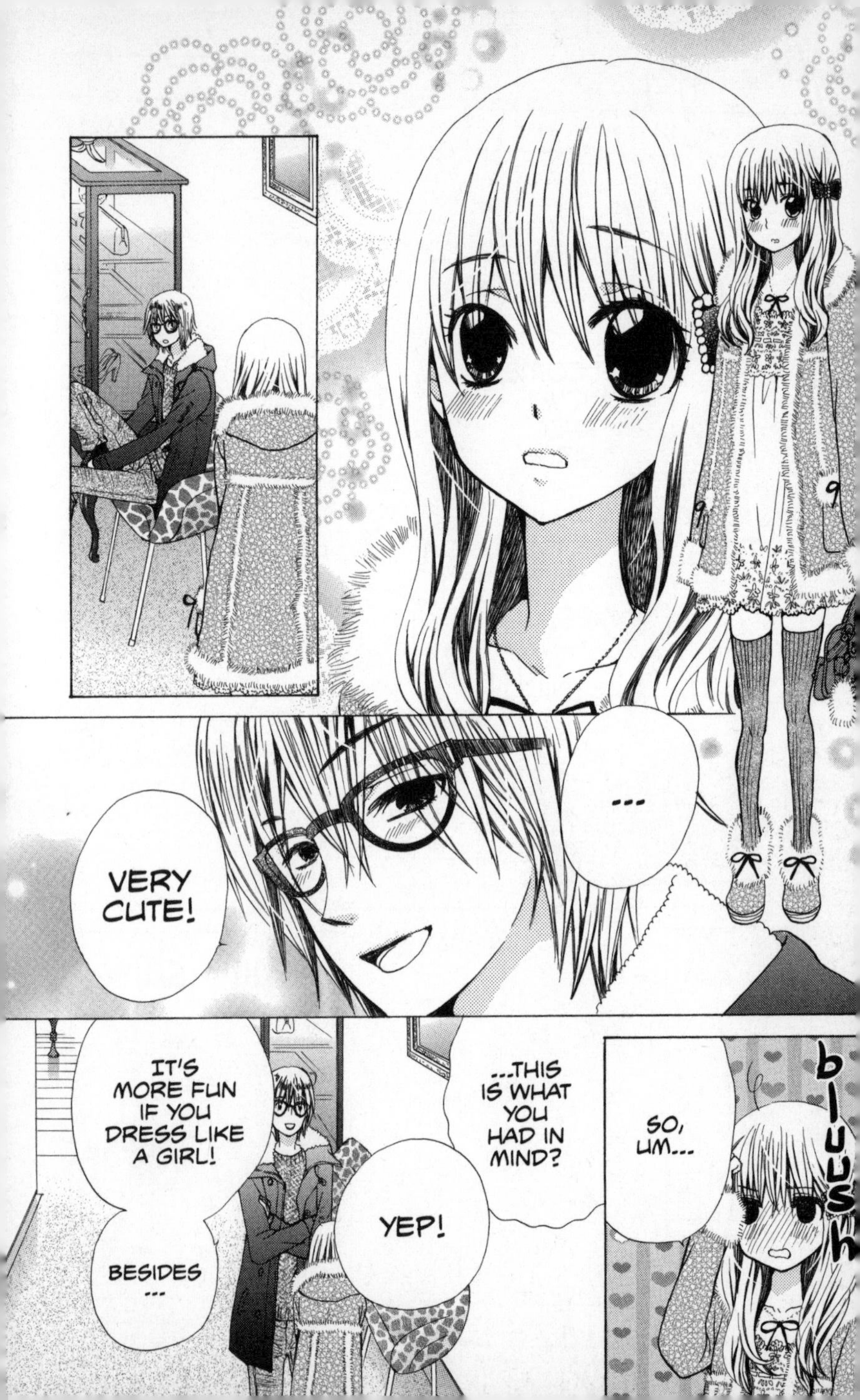
...
VERY CUTE!
bluush
SO, UM...
...THIS IS WHAT YOU HAD IN MIND?
YEP!
IT'S MORE FUN IF YOU DRESS LIKE A GIRL!
BESIDES...

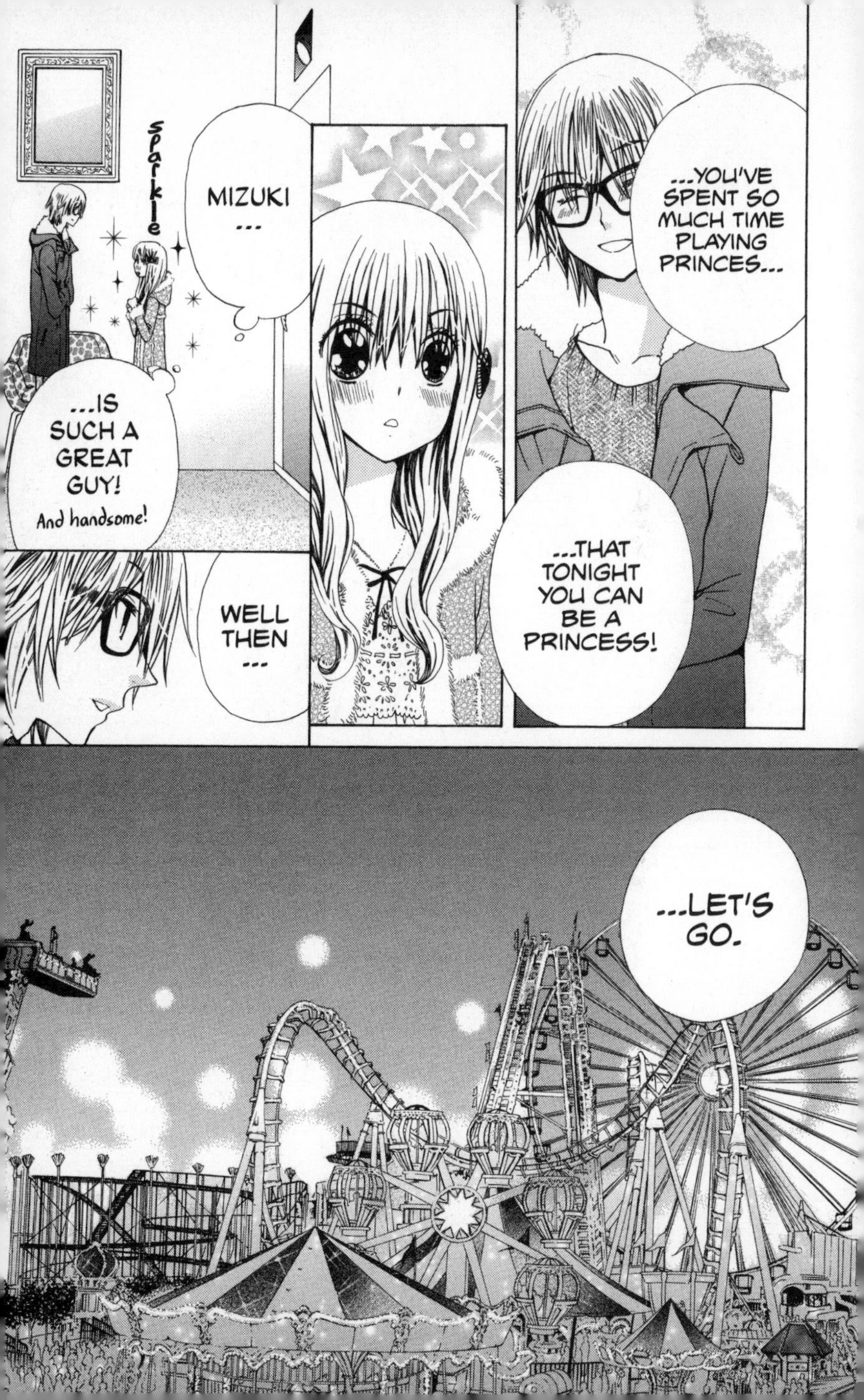
...YOU'VE SPENT SO MUCH TIME PLAYING PRINCES...
...THAT TONIGHT YOU CAN BE A PRINCESS!
MIZUKI ...
Sparkle
...IS SUCH A GREAT GUY!
And handsome!
WELL THEN ...
...LET'S GO.

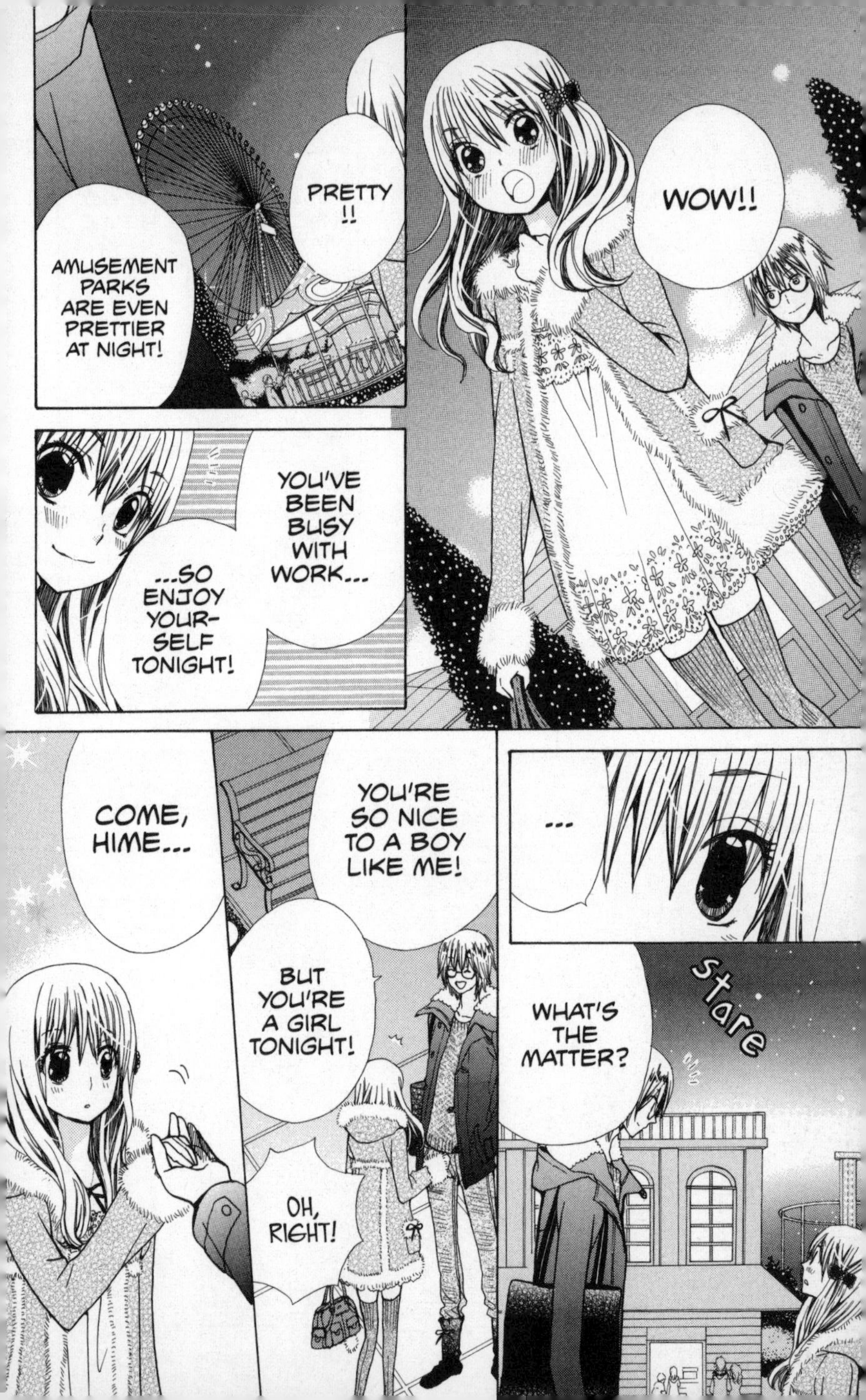
WOW!!
PRETTY!!
AMUSEMENT PARKS ARE EVEN PRETTIER AT NIGHT!
YOU'VE BEEN BUSY WITH WORK...
...SO ENJOY YOURSELF TONIGHT!
...
Stare
WHAT'S THE MATTER?
YOU'RE SO NICE TO A BOY LIKE ME!
BUT YOU'RE A GIRL TONIGHT!
OH, RIGHT!
COME, HIME...

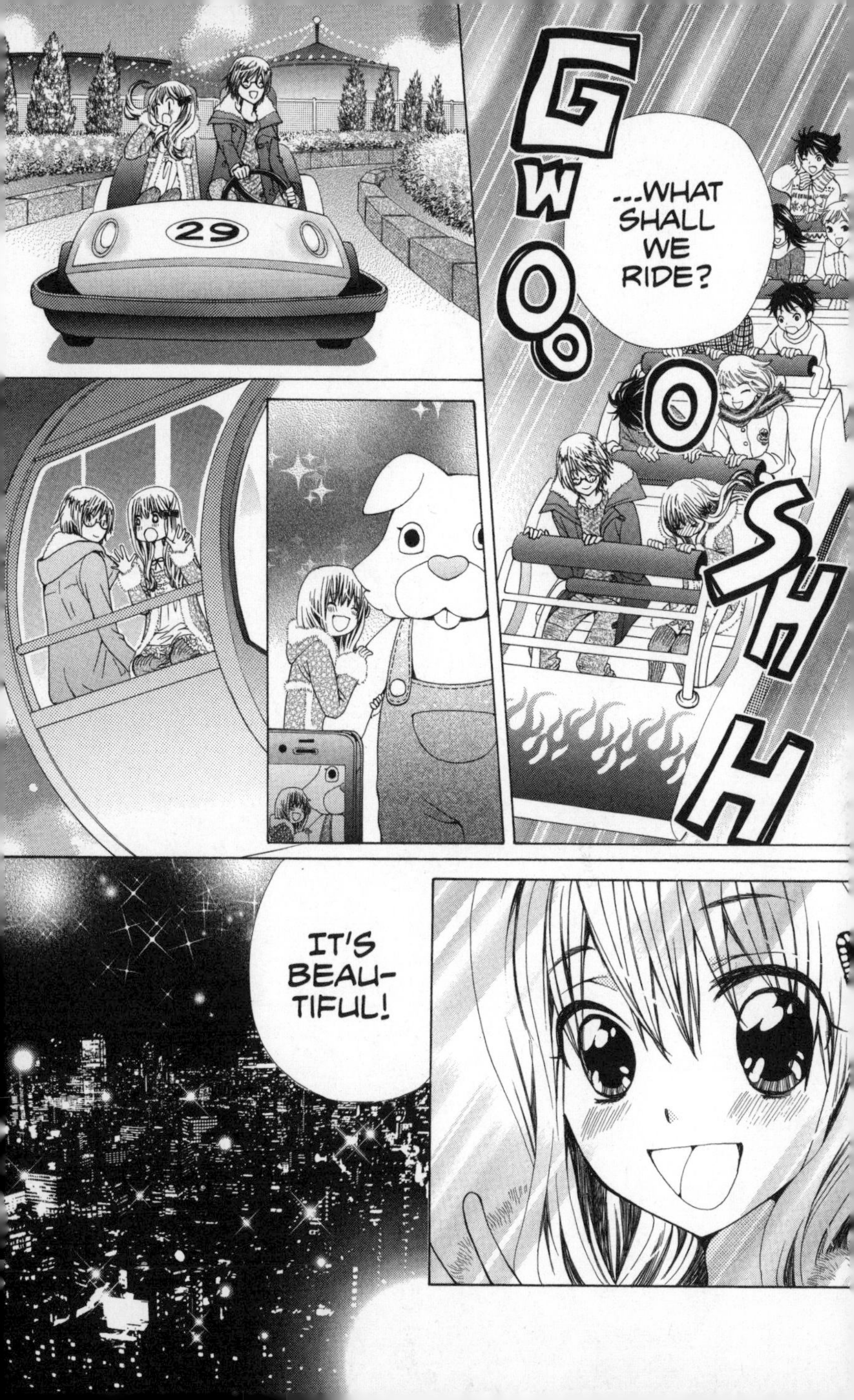

...WHAT SHALL WE RIDE?
GWOOOOSHH
IT'S BEAU-TIFUL!

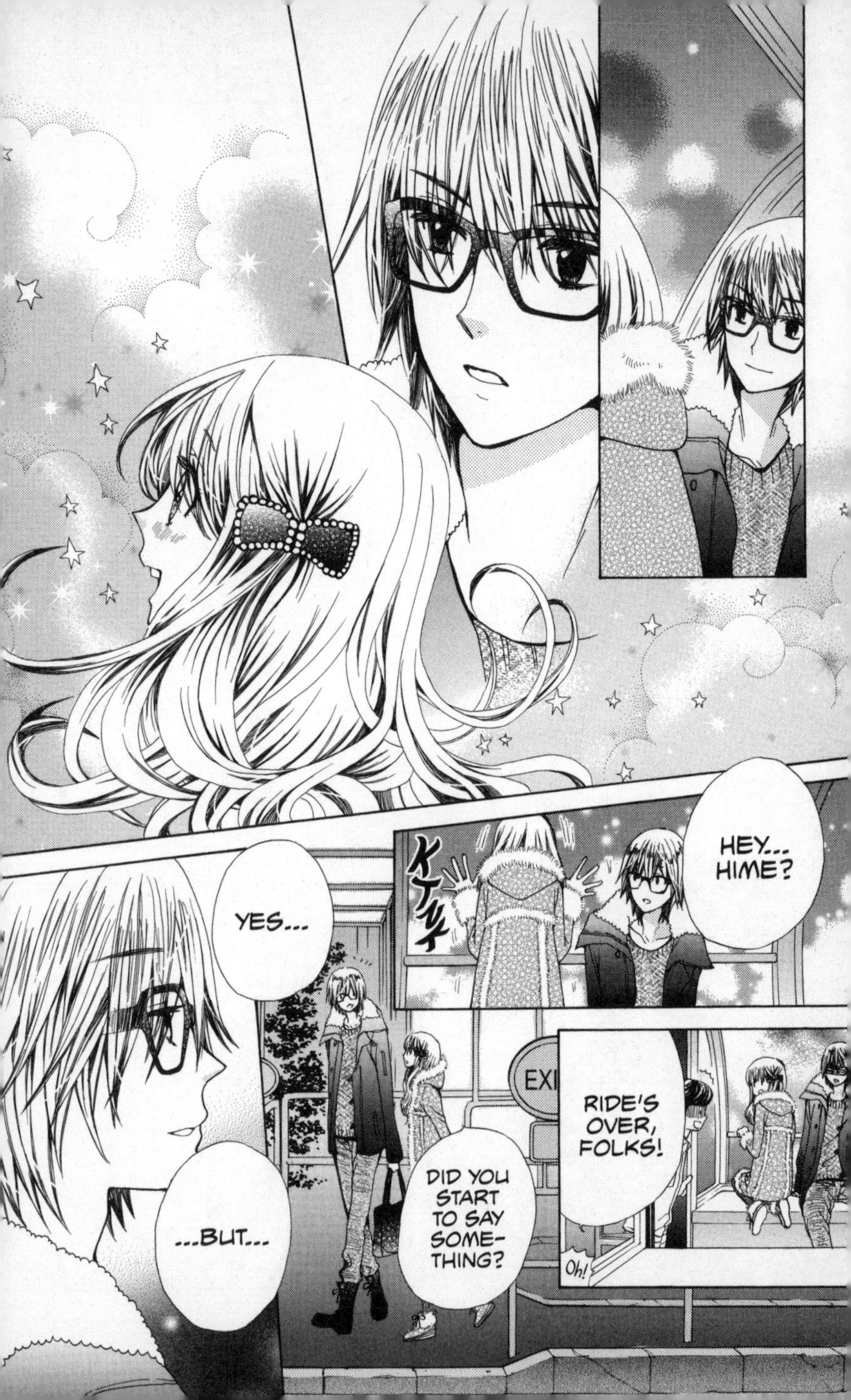

HEY... HIME?
KTNK
RIDE'S OVER, FOLKS!
Oh!
DID YOU START TO SAY SOME-THING?
YES...
...BUT...

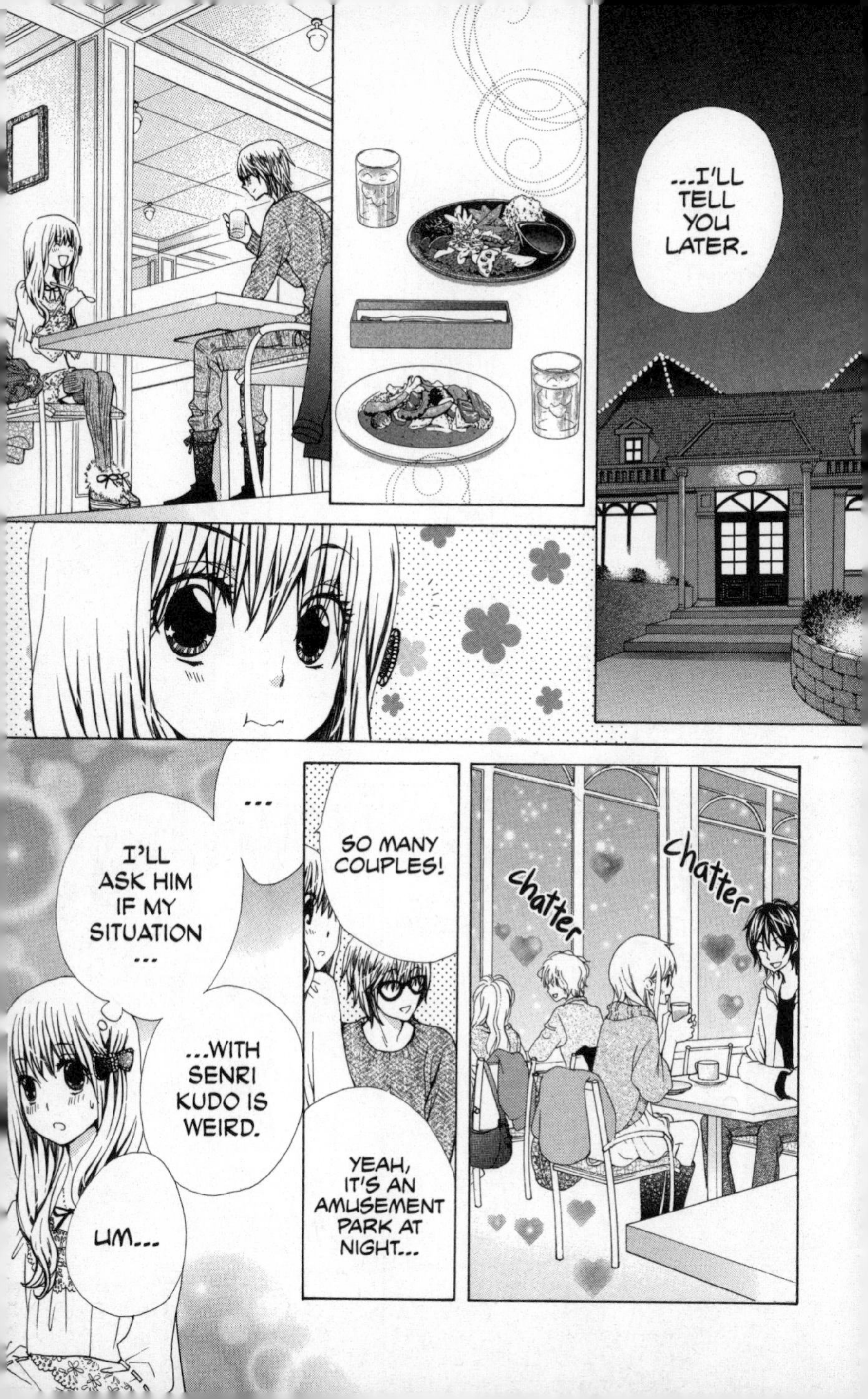
...I'LL TELL YOU LATER.
chatter
chatter
SO MANY COUPLES!
YEAH, IT'S AN AMUSEMENT PARK AT NIGHT...
...
I'LL ASK HIM IF MY SITUATION ...
...WITH SENRI KUDO IS WEIRD.
UM...

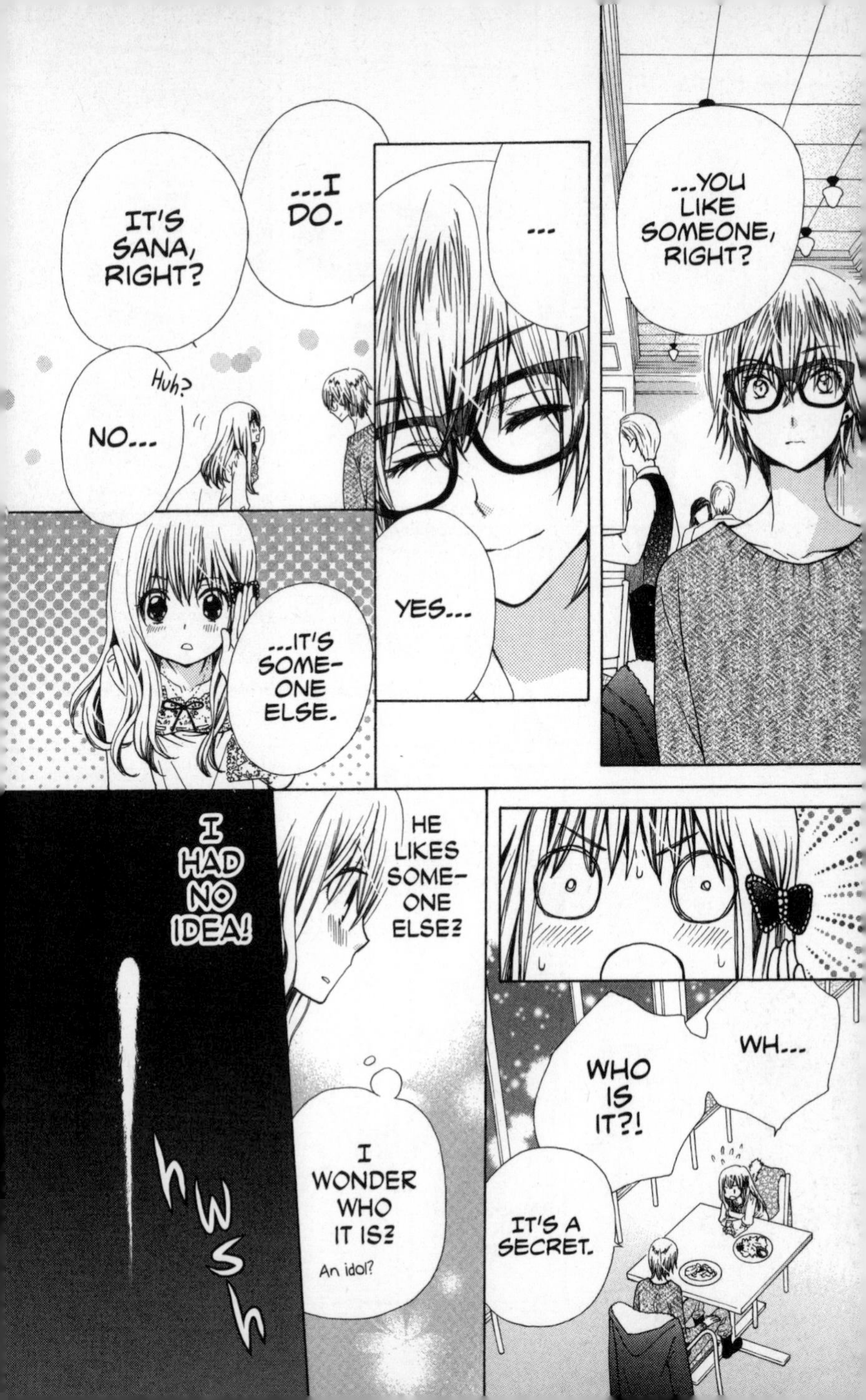
...YOU LIKE SOMEONE, RIGHT?
...
YES...
...I DO.
IT'S SANA, RIGHT?
Huh?
NO...
...IT'S SOME-ONE ELSE.
WH...
WHO IS IT?!
IT'S A SECRET.
HE LIKES SOME-ONE ELSE?
I WONDER WHO IT IS?
An idol?
I HAD NO IDEA!
hwsh

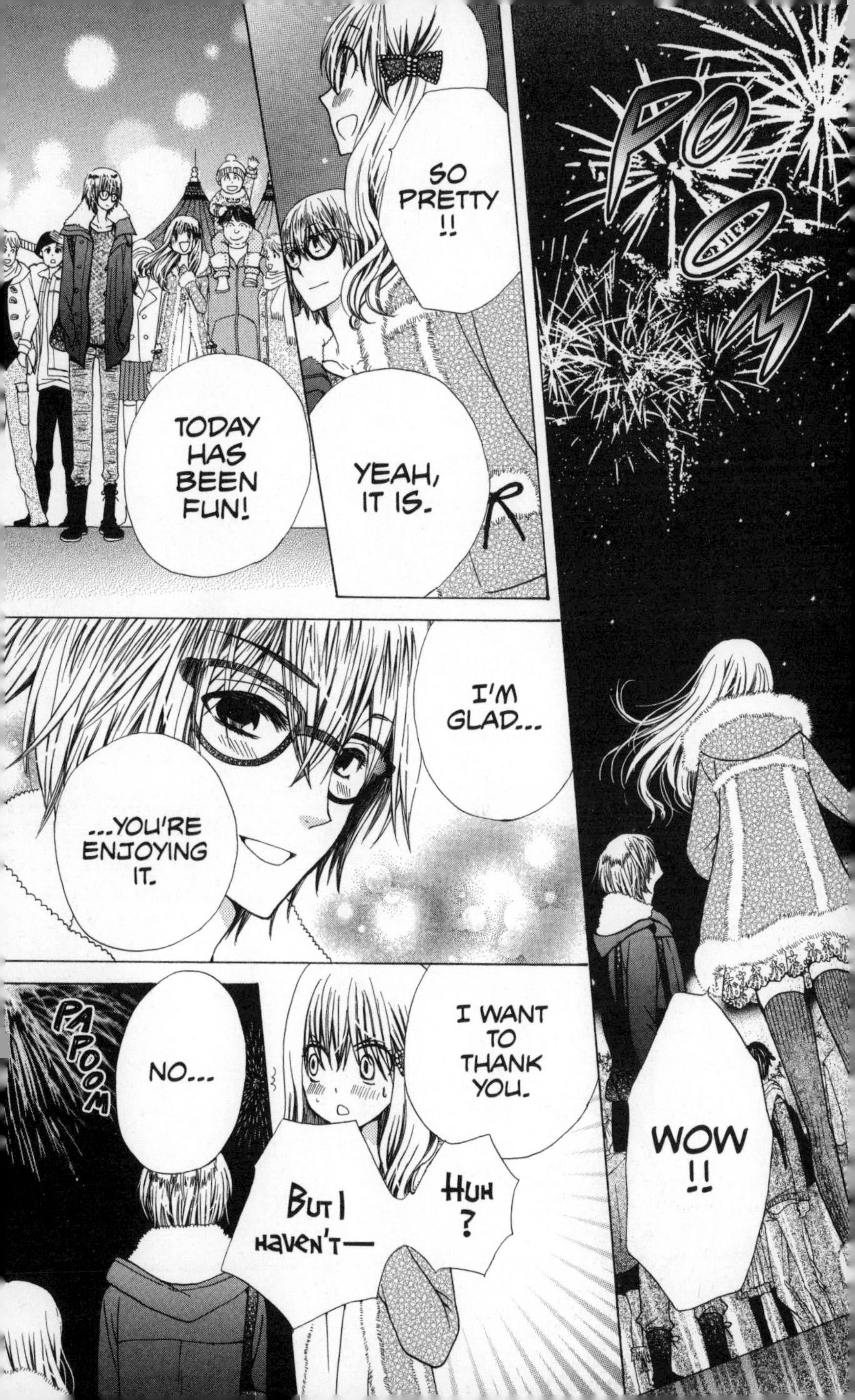
POOM
WOW!!
SO PRETTY!!
YEAH, IT IS.
TODAY HAS BEEN FUN!
I'M GLAD...
...YOU'RE ENJOYING IT.
I WANT TO THANK YOU.
HUH?
But I haven't—
NO...
PAPOOM

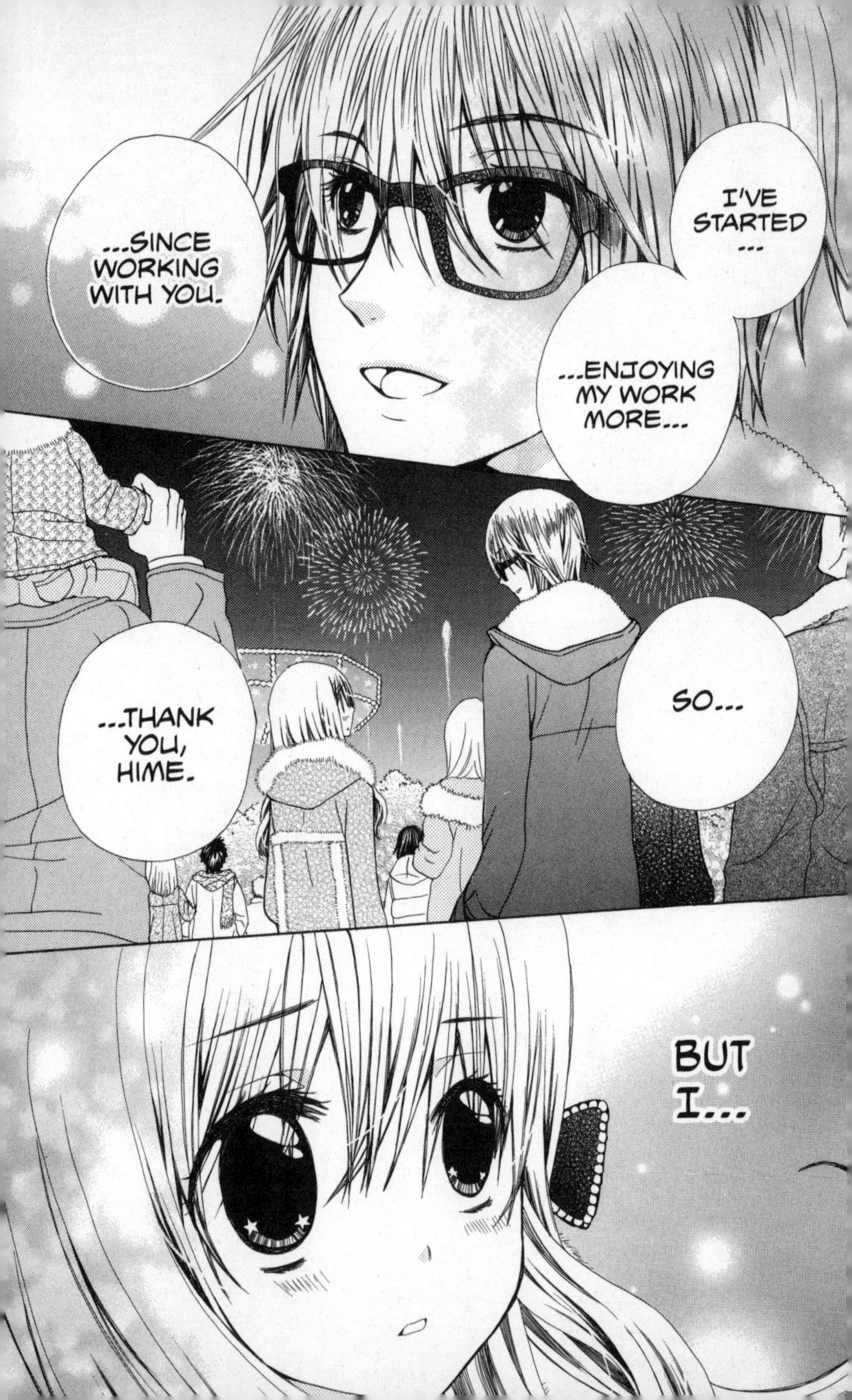
I'VE STARTED ...
...ENJOYING MY WORK MORE...
...SINCE WORKING WITH YOU.
SO...
...THANK YOU, HIME.
BUT I...

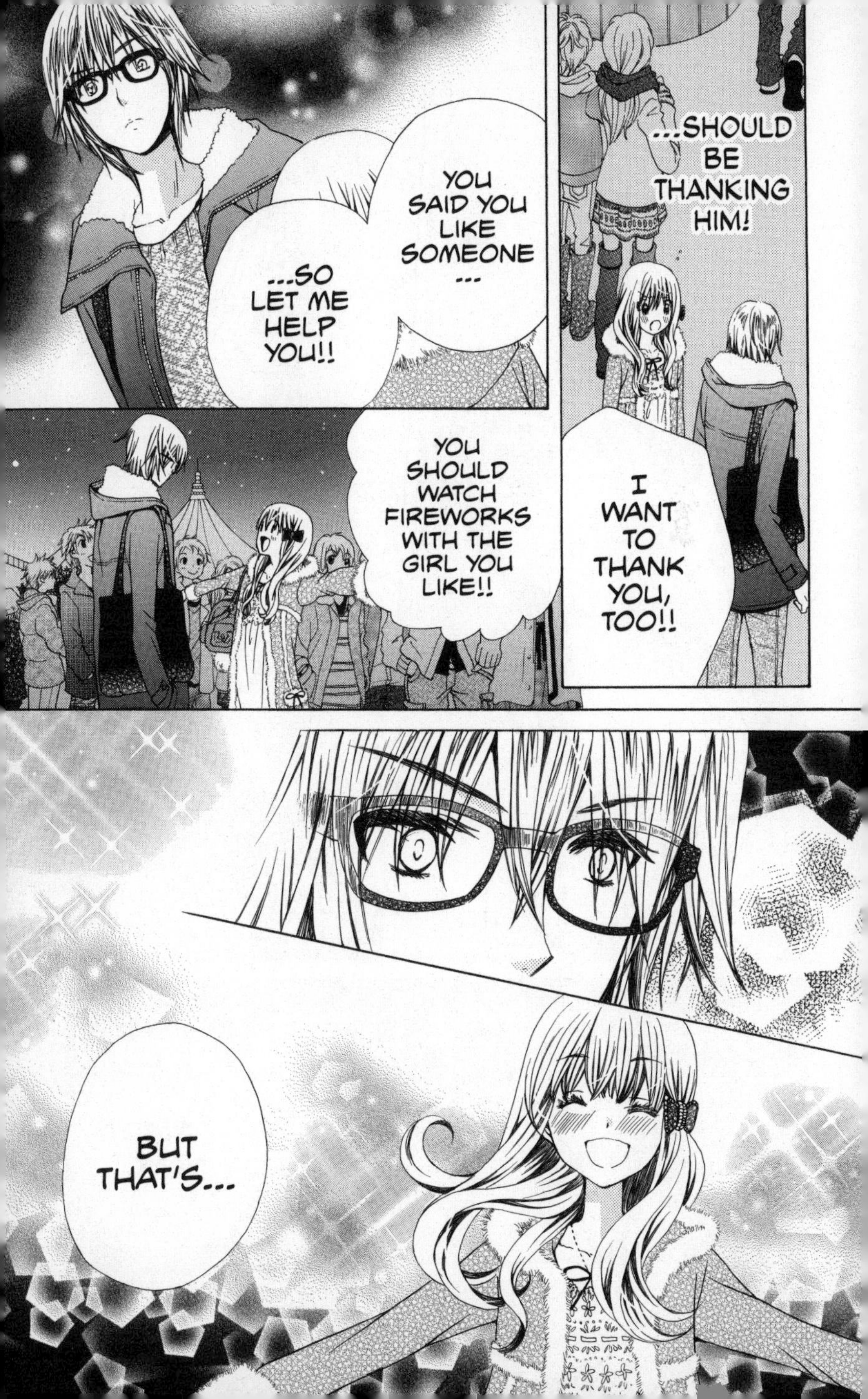
...SHOULD BE THANKING HIM!
I WANT TO THANK YOU, TOO!!
YOU SAID YOU LIKE SOMEONE...
...SO LET ME HELP YOU!!
YOU SHOULD WATCH FIREWORKS WITH THE GIRL YOU LIKE!!
BUT THAT'S...

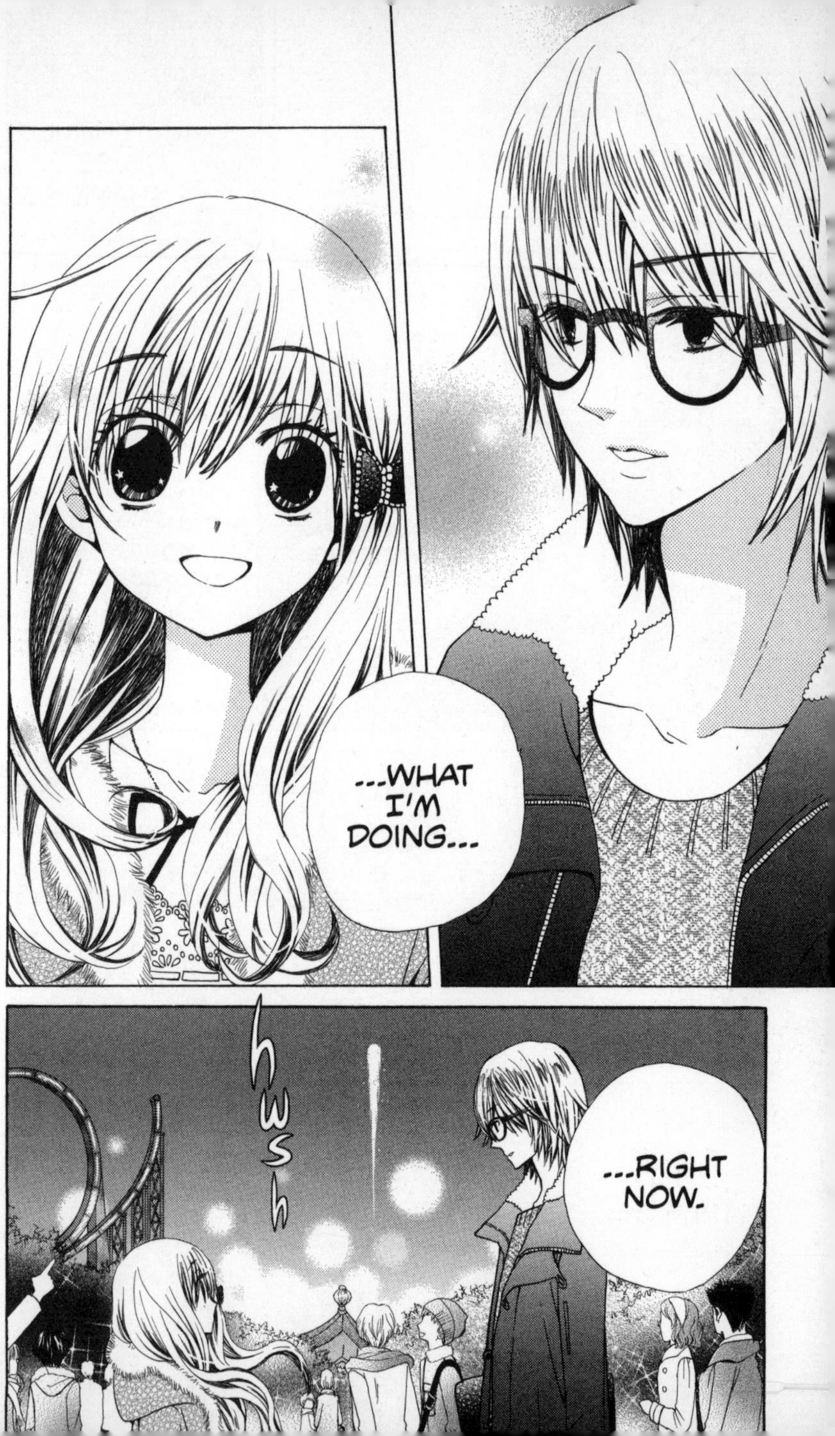
...WHAT I'M DOING...
hwsh
...RIGHT NOW.

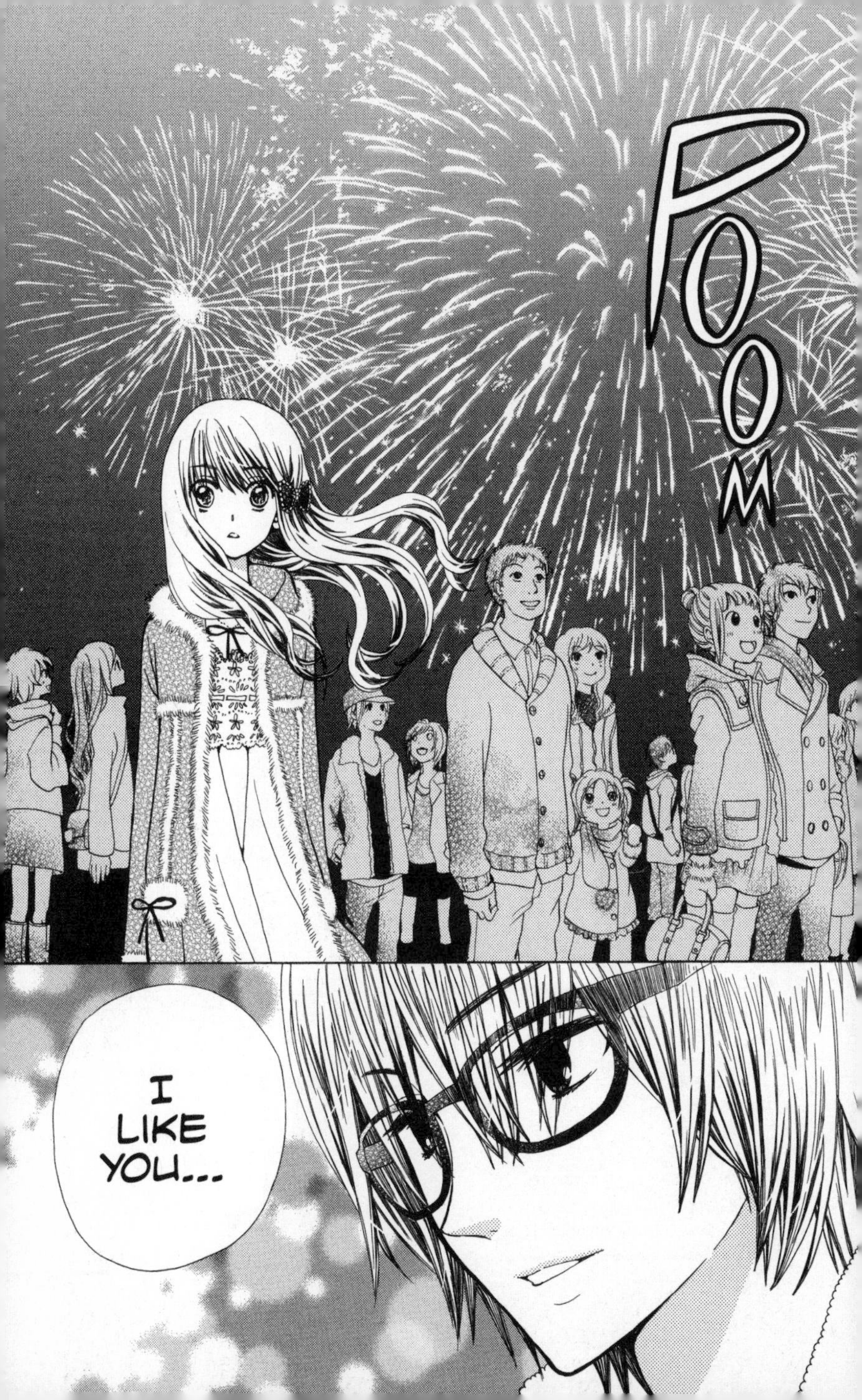
POOOM
I LIKE YOU...

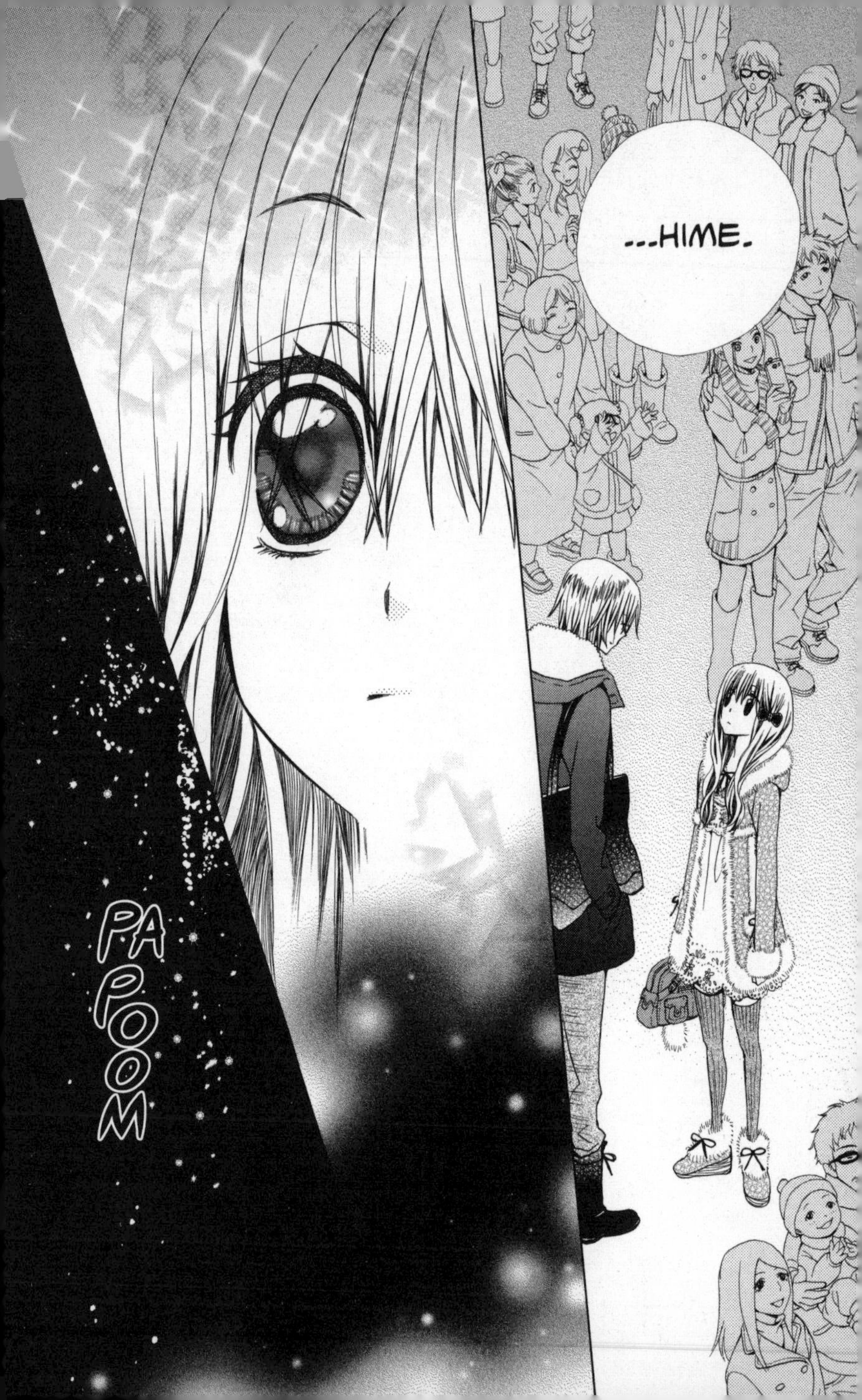
...HIME.
PA POOM

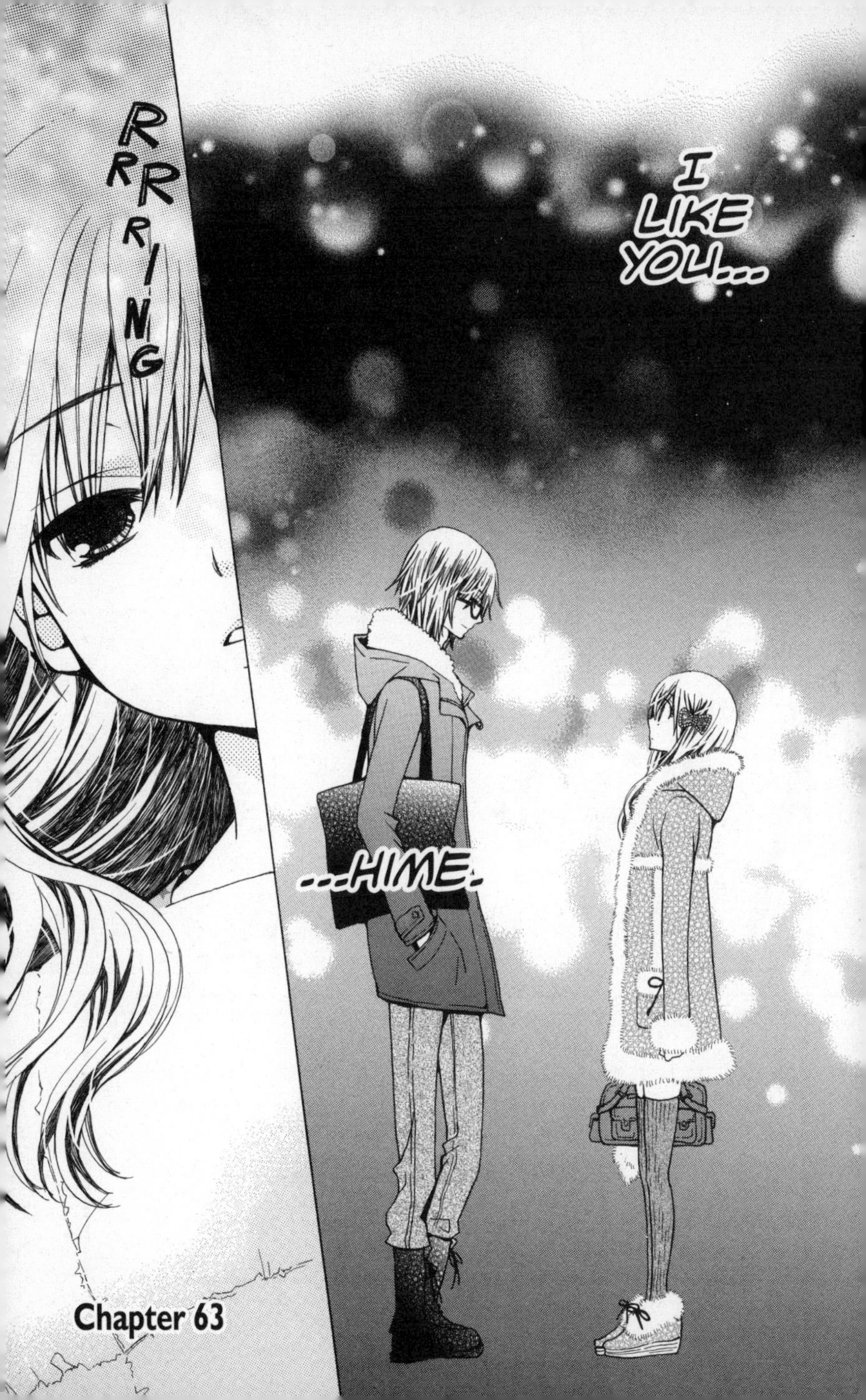
I LIKE YOU...
...HIME.
RRRRING
Chapter 63

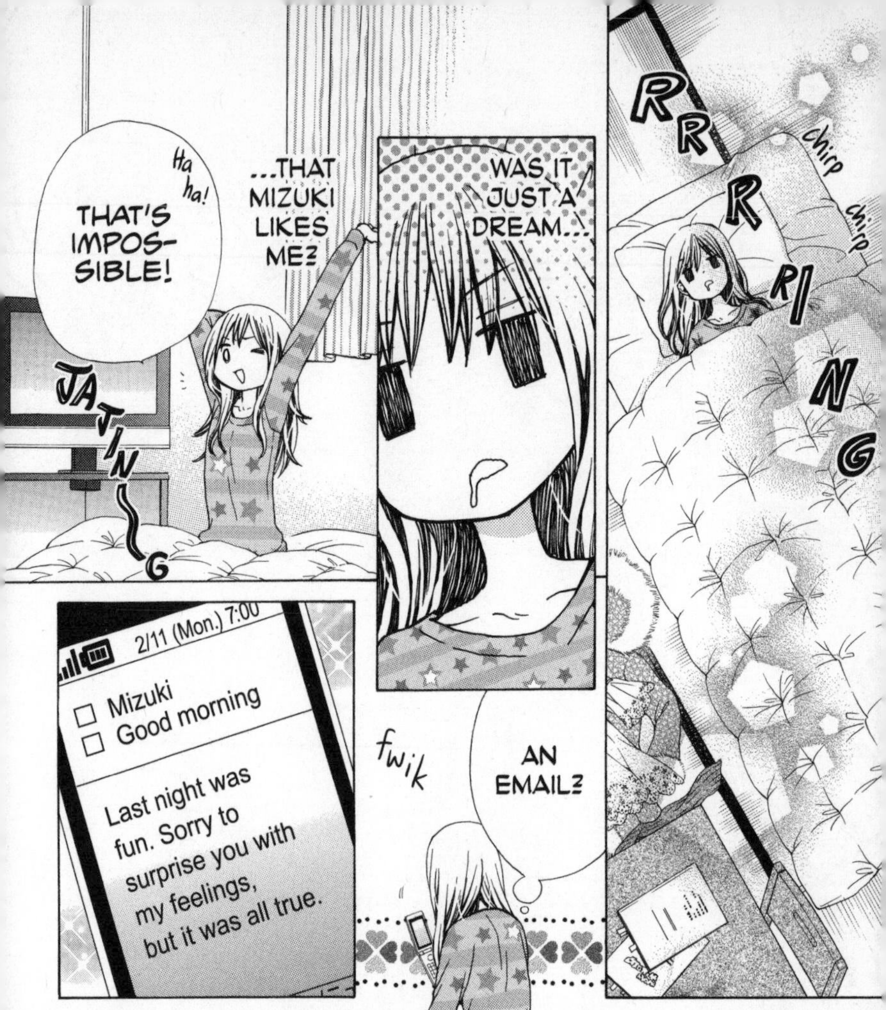
RRRRRIIING
chirp chirp
WAS IT JUST A DREAM...
...THAT MIZUKI LIKES ME?
Ha ha!
THAT'S IMPOSSIBLE!
JAJINGLING
fwik
AN EMAIL?
2/11 (Mon.) 7:00
Mizuki
Good morning
Last night was fun. Sorry to surprise you with my feelings, but it was all true.

◦ Earrings ◦

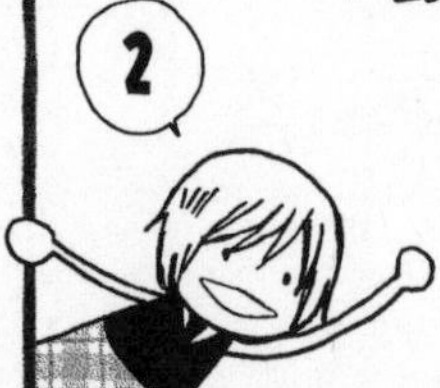
2

I still can't remember where Senri and Takayanagi wear their earrings, so I put a reference sheet up where I'll always see it. It's handy!!

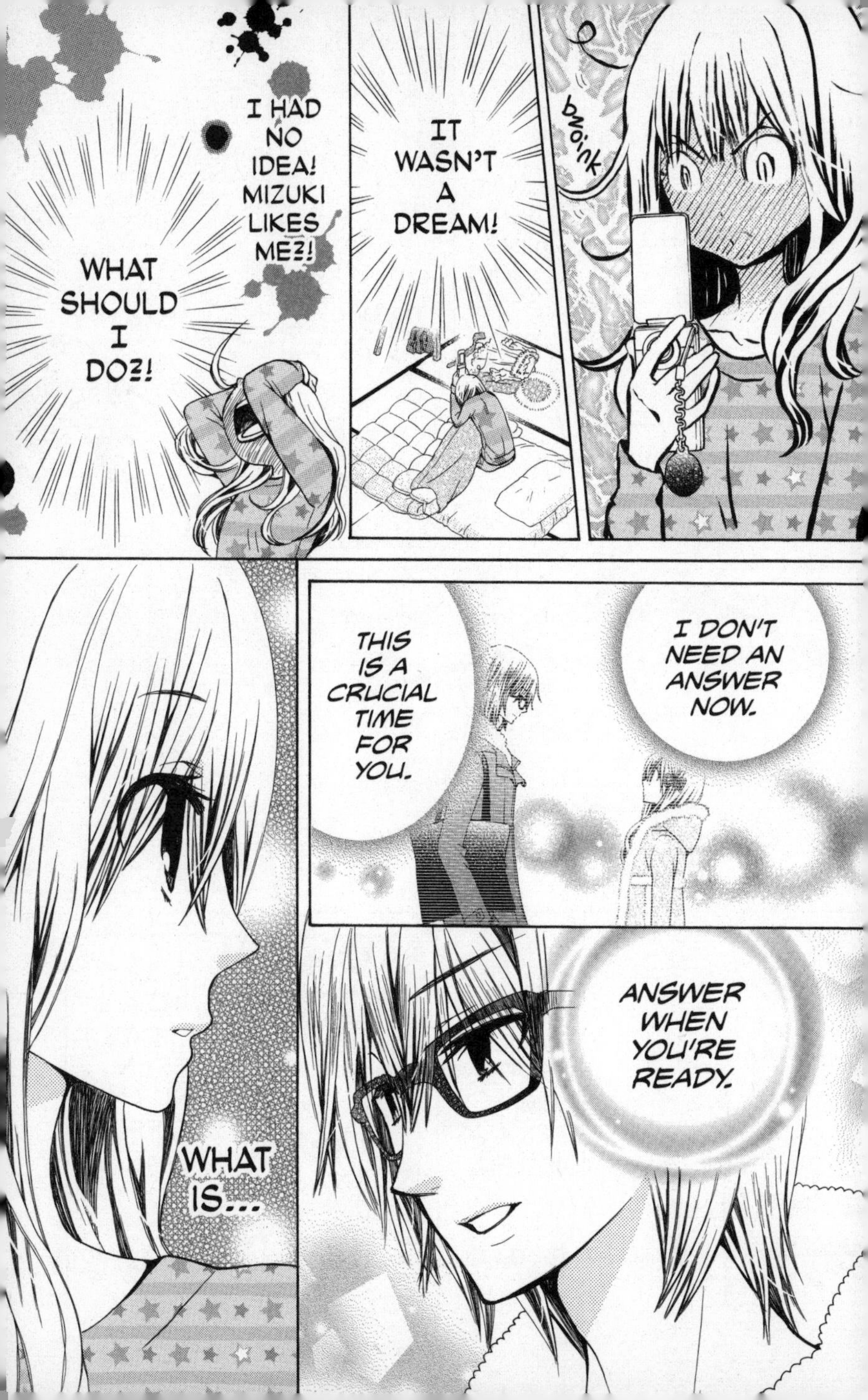
bwoink
IT WASN'T A DREAM!
I HAD NO IDEA! MIZUKI LIKES ME?!
WHAT SHOULD I DO?!
I DON'T NEED AN ANSWER NOW.
THIS IS A CRUCIAL TIME FOR YOU.
ANSWER WHEN YOU'RE READY.
WHAT IS...

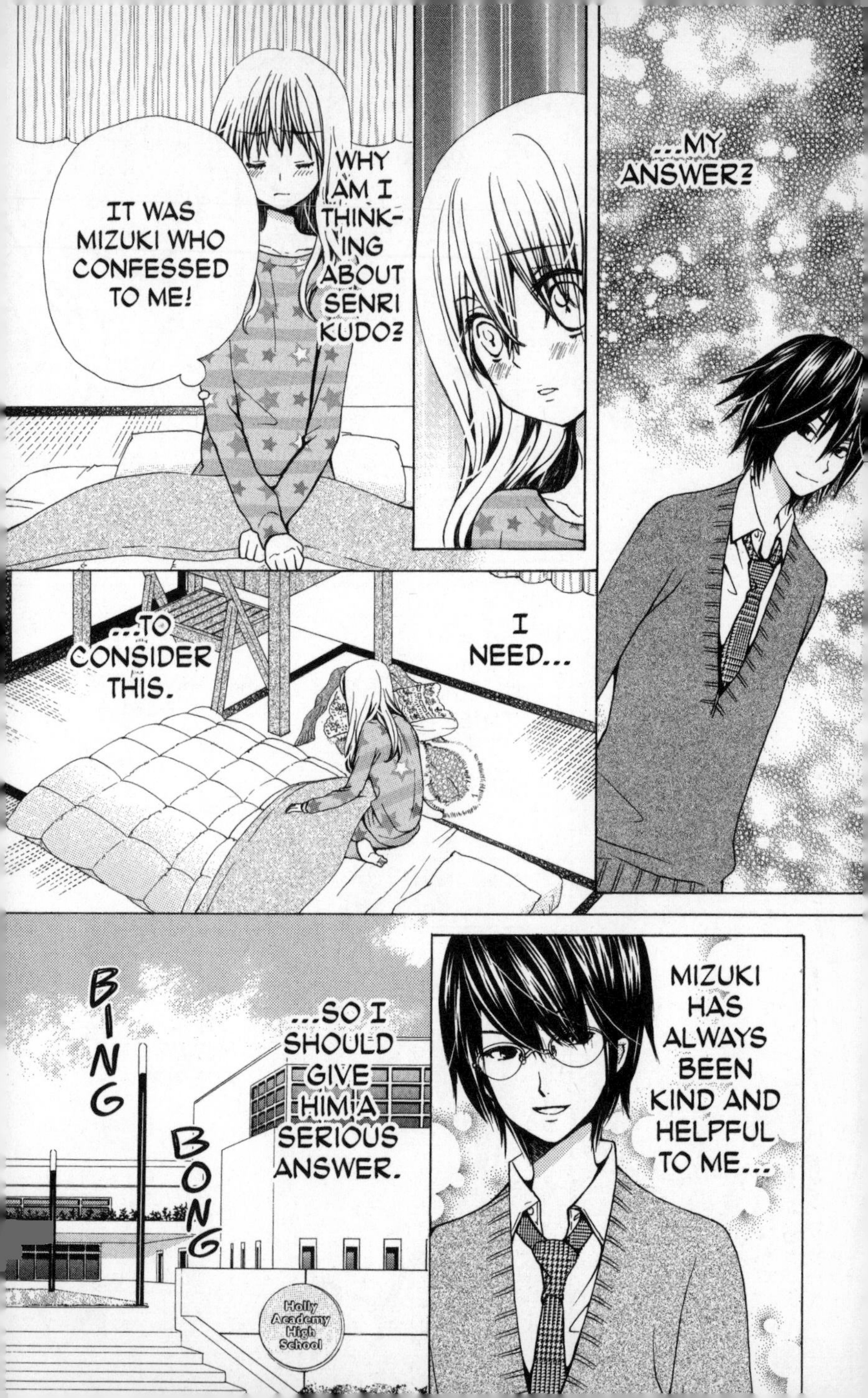
...MY ANSWER?
WHY AM I THINKING ABOUT SENRI KUDO?
IT WAS MIZUKI WHO CONFESSED TO ME!
I NEED...
...TO CONSIDER THIS.
MIZUKI HAS ALWAYS BEEN KIND AND HELPFUL TO ME...
...SO I SHOULD GIVE HIM A SERIOUS ANSWER.
BING
BONG
Holly Academy High School

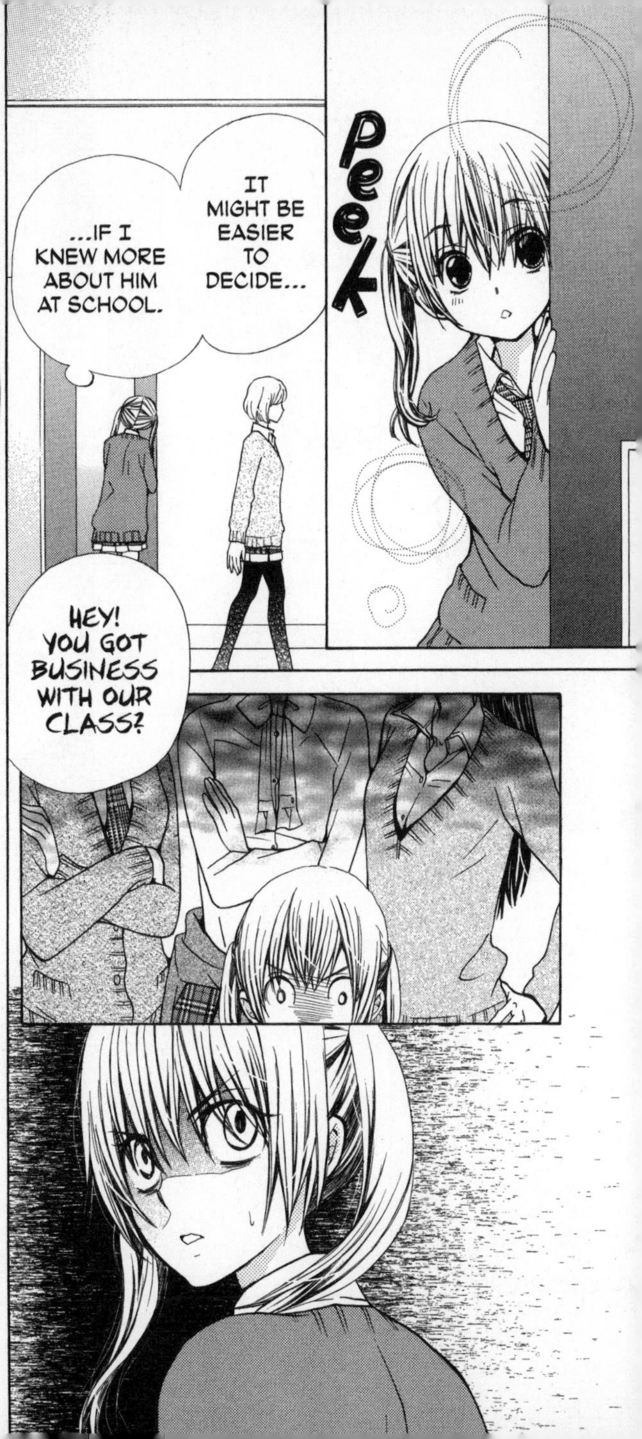
Peek
IT MIGHT BE EASIER TO DECIDE...
...IF I KNEW MORE ABOUT HIM AT SCHOOL.
HEY! YOU GOT BUSINESS WITH OUR CLASS?

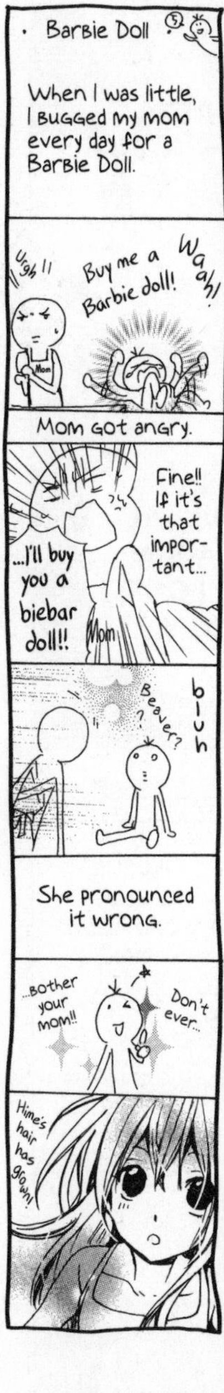
• Barbie Doll 5
When I was little, I bugged my mom every day for a Barbie Doll.
Waah!
Buy me a Barbie doll!
Urgh!!
Mom
Mom got angry.
Fine!! If it's that important...
...I'll buy you a biebar doll!!
Mom
Beaver?
bluh
She pronounced it wrong.
Don't ever...
...bother your mom!!
Hime's hair has grown!

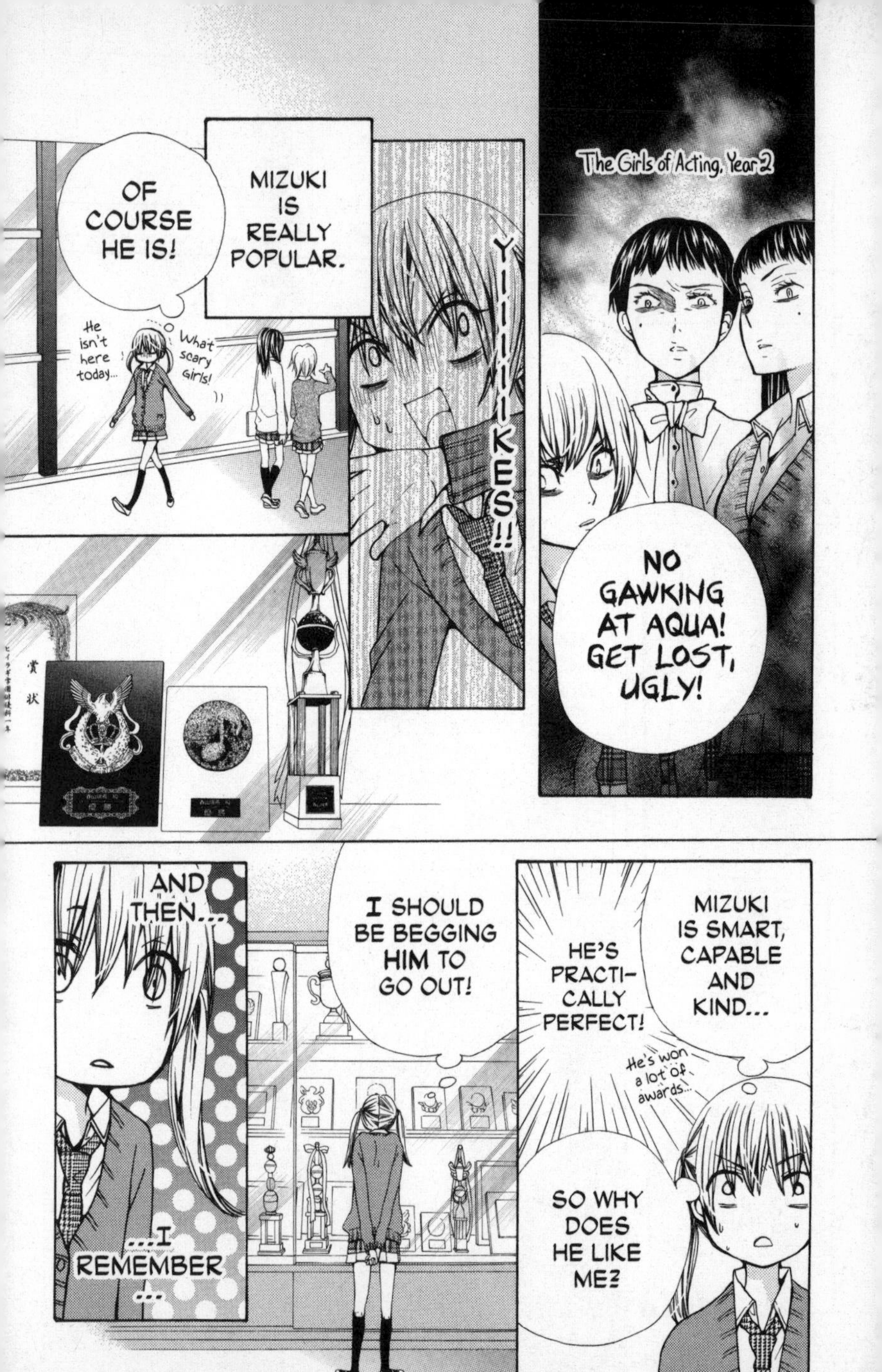
The Girls of Acting, Year 2
NO GAWKING AT AQUA! GET LOST, UGLY!
YIIIIIIIKES!!
MIZUKI IS REALLY POPULAR.
OF COURSE HE IS!
What scary girls!
He isn't here today...
MIZUKI IS SMART, CAPABLE AND KIND...
HE'S PRACTI- CALLY PERFECT!
He's won a lot of awards...
SO WHY DOES HE LIKE ME?
I SHOULD BE BEGGING HIM TO GO OUT!
AND THEN...
...I REMEMBER ...

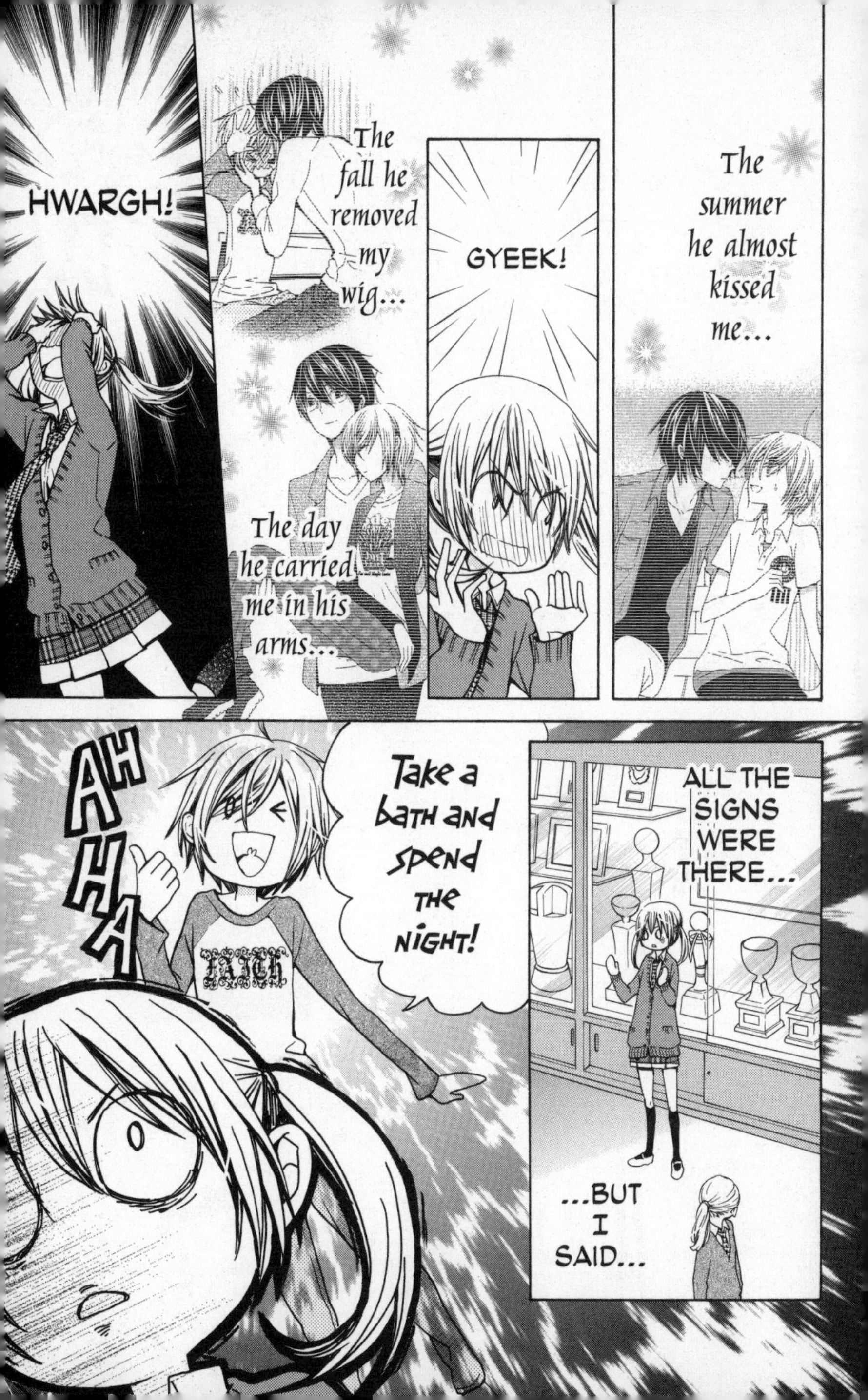
The summer he almost kissed me...
GYEEK!
The fall he removed my wig...
The day he carried me in his arms...
HWARGH!
ALL THE SIGNS WERE THERE...
...BUT I SAID...
Take a bath and spend the night!
AH HA HA

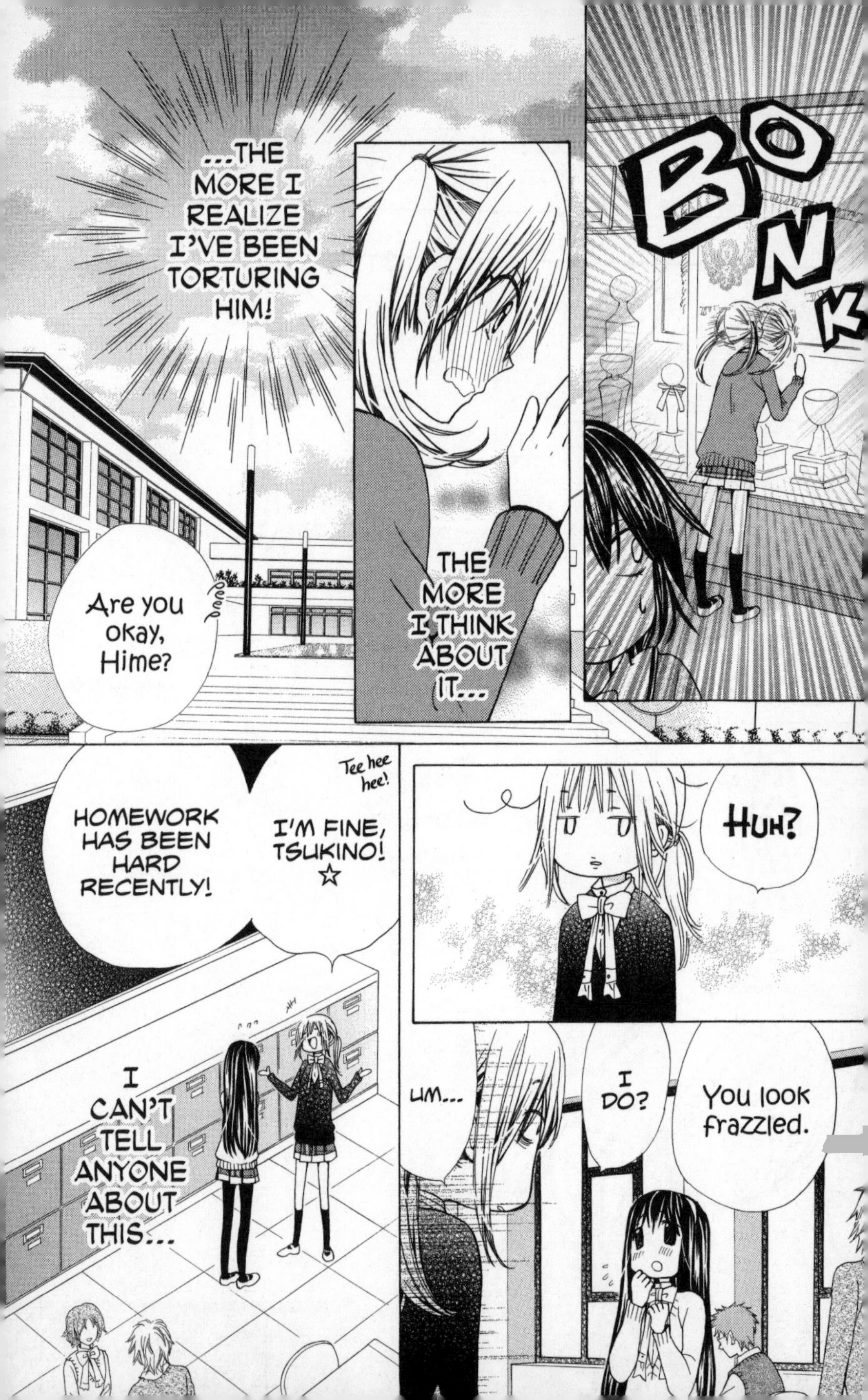
BONK
THE MORE I THINK ABOUT IT...
...THE MORE I REALIZE I'VE BEEN TORTURING HIM!
Are you okay, Hime?
HUH?
You look frazzled.
I DO?
UM...
Tee hee hee!
I'M FINE, TSUKINO! ☆
HOMEWORK HAS BEEN HARD RECENTLY!
I CAN'T TELL ANYONE ABOUT THIS...

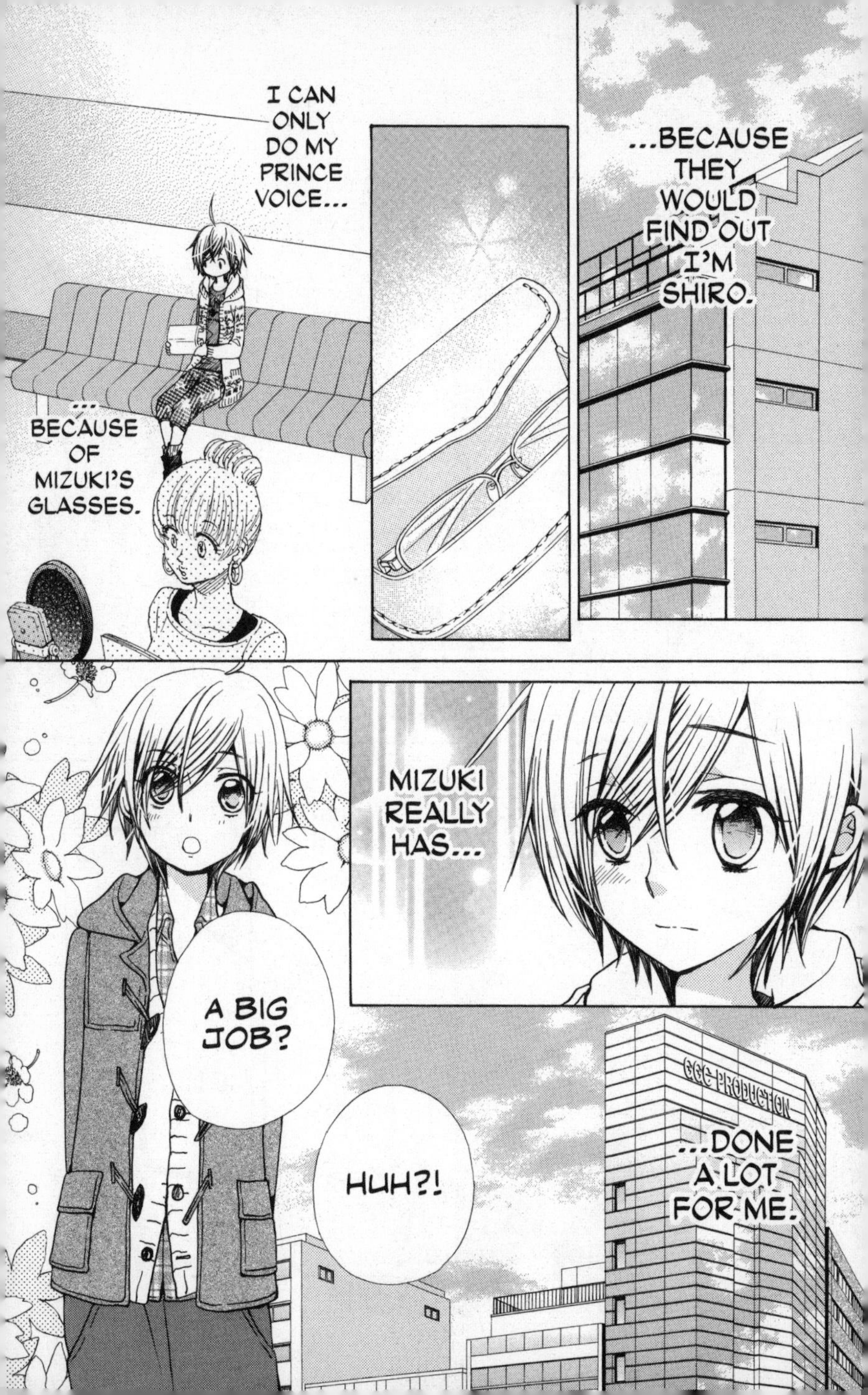
...BECAUSE THEY WOULD FIND OUT I'M SHIRO.
I CAN ONLY DO MY PRINCE VOICE...
...BECAUSE OF MIZUKI'S GLASSES.
MIZUKI REALLY HAS...
GGG PRODUCTION
...DONE A LOT FOR ME.
A BIG JOB?
HUH?!

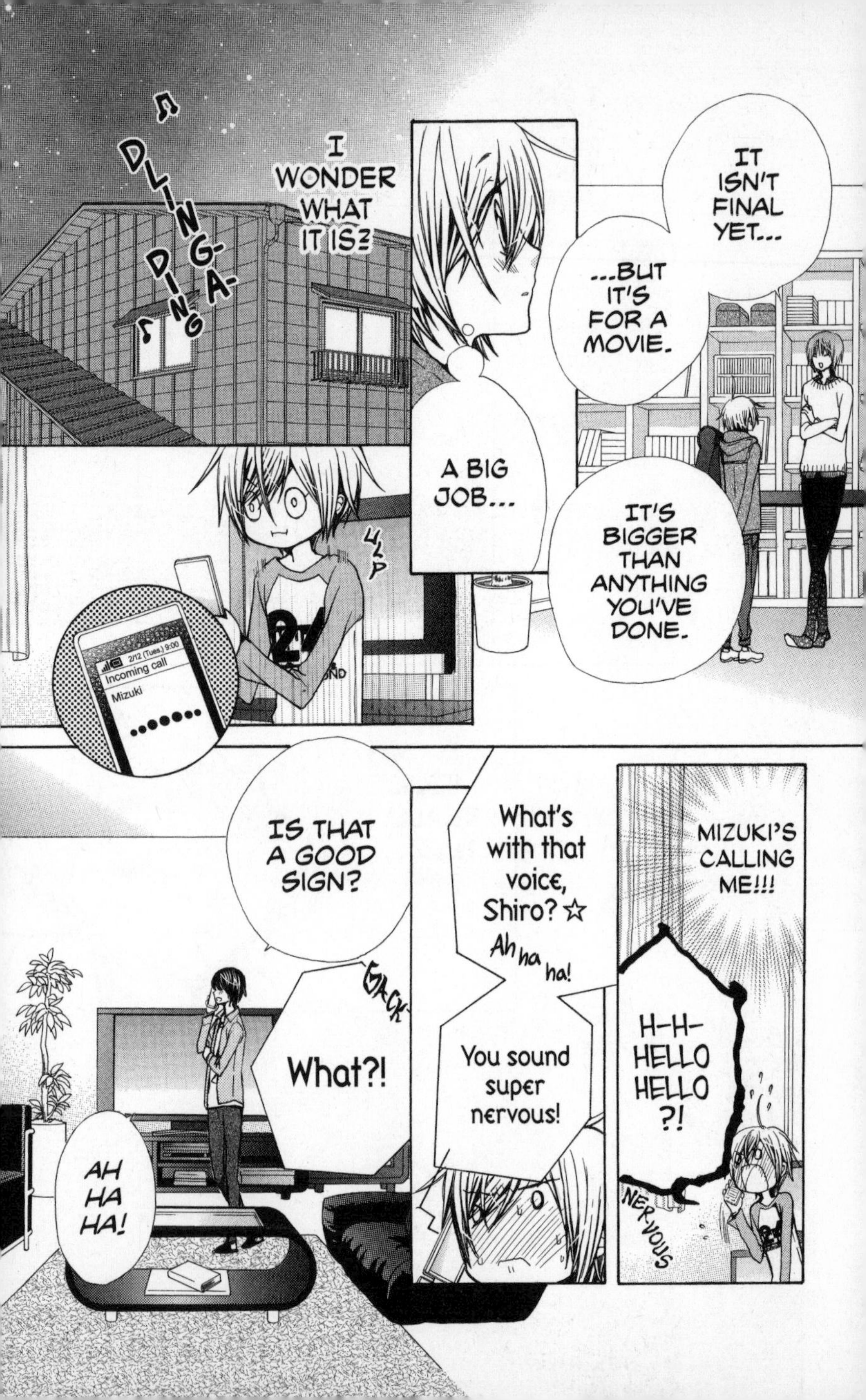
IT ISN'T FINAL YET...
...BUT IT'S FOR A MOVIE.
IT'S BIGGER THAN ANYTHING YOU'VE DONE.
A BIG JOB...
DLING-A-DING
I WONDER WHAT IT IS?
ULP
2/12 (Tues.) 9:00
Incoming call
Mizuki
MIZUKI'S CALLING ME!!!
H-H-HELLO HELLO?!
NERVOUS
What's with that voice, Shiro? ☆
Ah ha ha!
You sound super nervous!
GACK
What?!
IS THAT A GOOD SIGN?
AH HA HA!

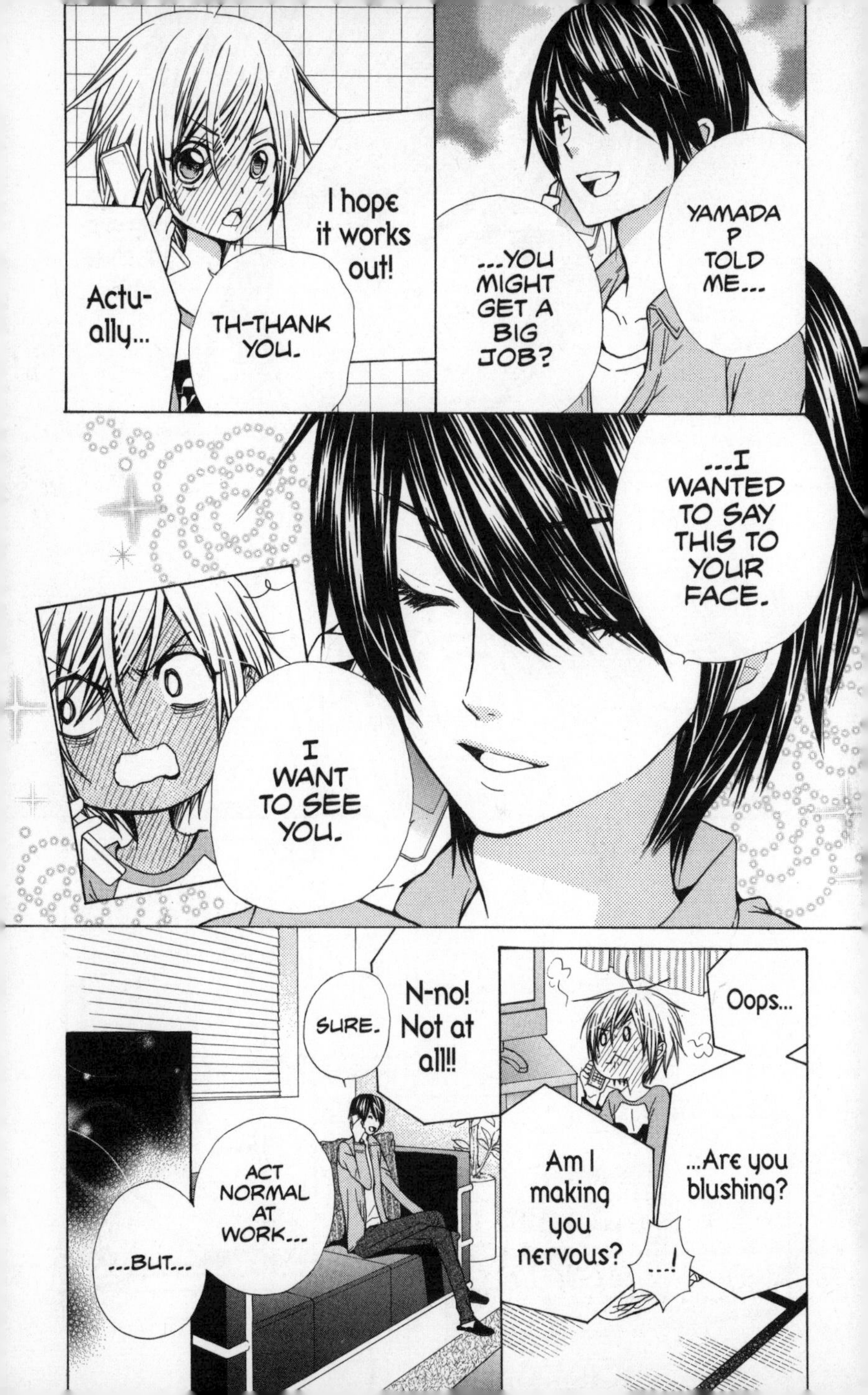
YAMADA P TOLD ME...
...YOU MIGHT GET A BIG JOB?
I hope it works out!
TH-THANK YOU.
Actu-ally...
...I WANTED TO SAY THIS TO YOUR FACE.
I WANT TO SEE YOU.
Oops...
...Are you blushing?
Am I making you nervous?
...!
N-no! Not at all!!
SURE.
ACT NORMAL AT WORK...
...BUT...

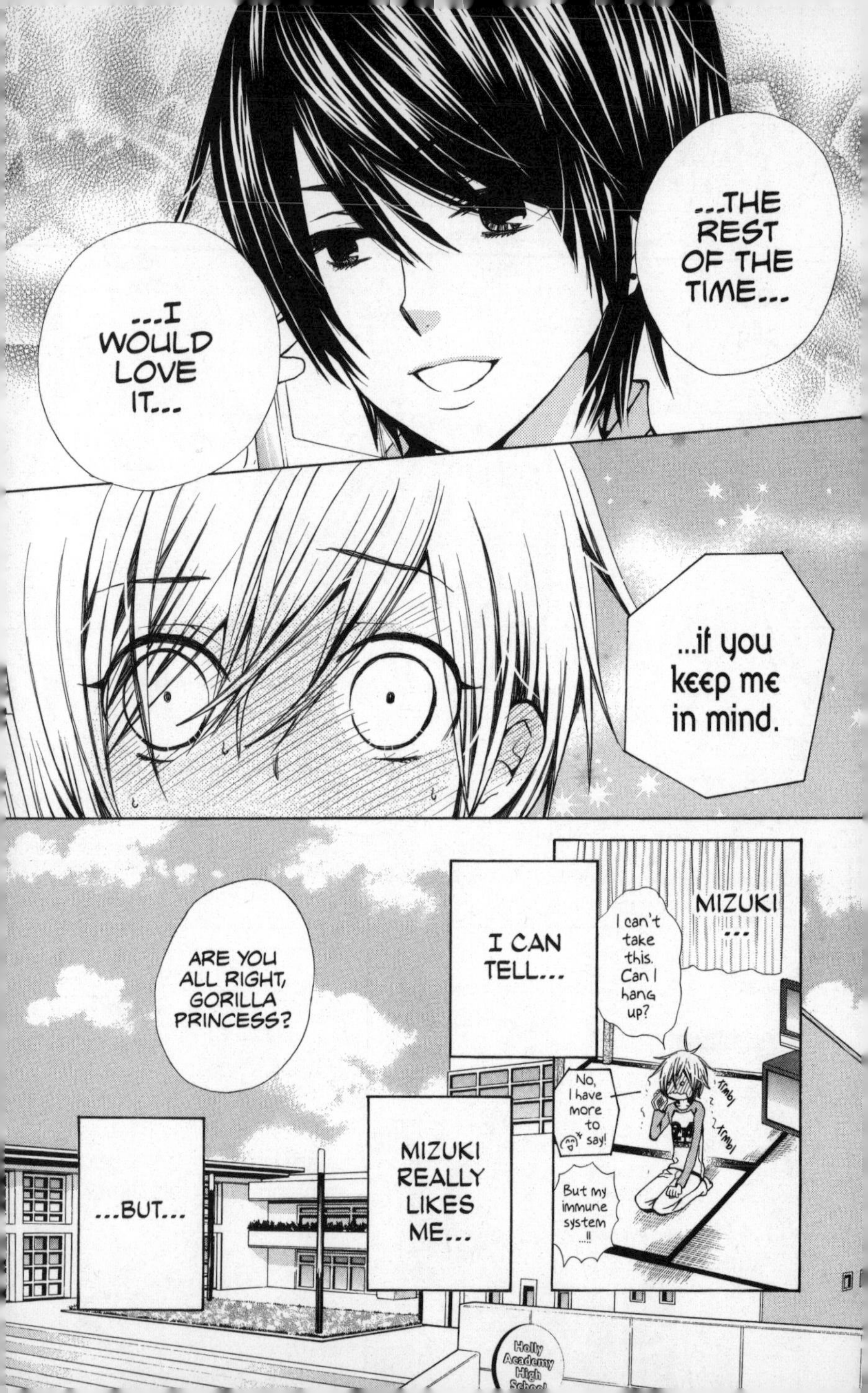
...THE REST OF THE TIME...
...I WOULD LOVE IT...
...if you keep me in mind.
MIZUKI...
I can't take this. Can I hang up?
No, I have more to say!
But my immune system...!!
I CAN TELL...
ARE YOU ALL RIGHT, GORILLA PRINCESS?
MIZUKI REALLY LIKES ME...
...BUT...
Holly Academy High School

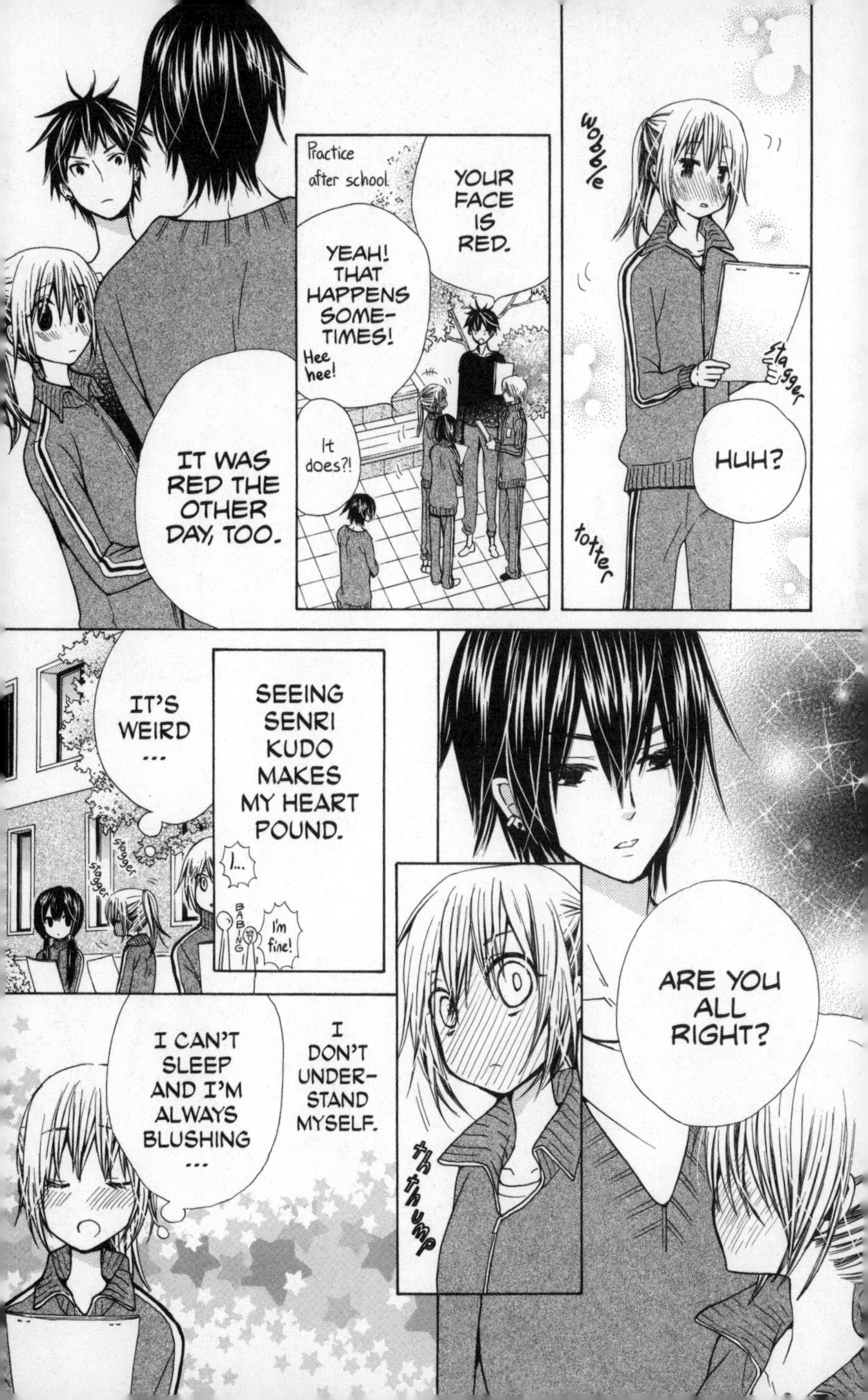
wobble
HUH?
stagger
totter
Practice after school.
YOUR FACE IS RED.
YEAH! THAT HAPPENS SOME-TIMES!
Hee hee!
It does?!
IT WAS RED THE OTHER DAY, TOO.
ARE YOU ALL RIGHT?
thump thump
SEEING SENRI KUDO MAKES MY HEART POUND.
I...
BABING
I'm fine!
IT'S WEIRD...
stagger
stagger
I DON'T UNDER-STAND MYSELF.
I CAN'T SLEEP AND I'M ALWAYS BLUSHING...

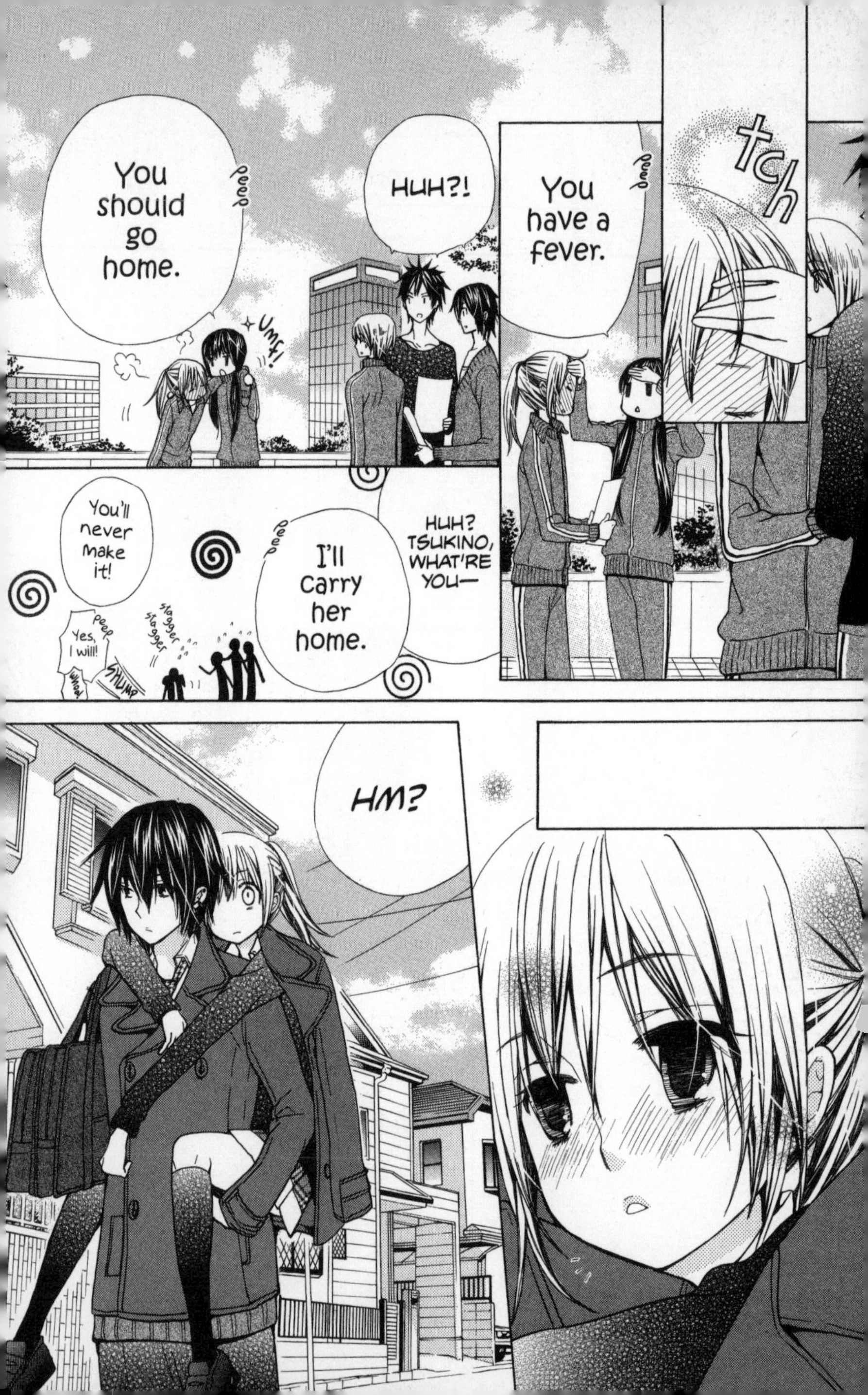
tch
You have a fever.
peep
HUH?!
You should go home.
peep
Umf!
HUH? TSUKINO, WHAT'RE YOU—
I'll carry her home.
peep
You'll never make it!
stagger stagger
peep
Yes, I will!
SHUMP
whoa
HM?

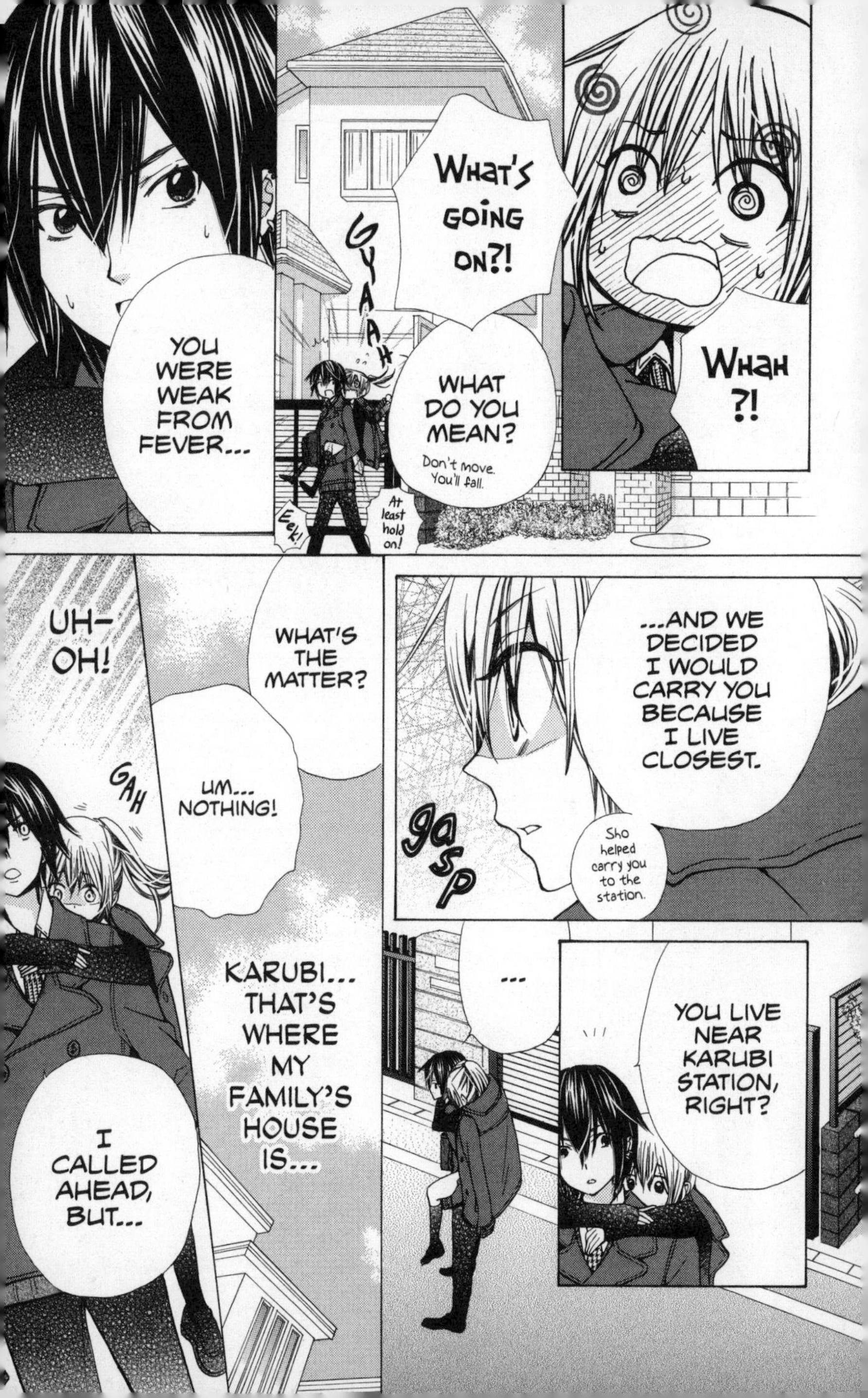
WHAH ?!
WHAT'S GOING ON?!
GYAAAH
WHAT DO YOU MEAN?
Don't move. You'll fall.
At least hold on!
Eek!
YOU WERE WEAK FROM FEVER...
...AND WE DECIDED I WOULD CARRY YOU BECAUSE I LIVE CLOSEST.
Sho helped carry you to the station.
gasp
YOU LIVE NEAR KARUBI STATION, RIGHT?
...
KARUBI... THAT'S WHERE MY FAMILY'S HOUSE IS...
WHAT'S THE MATTER?
UH-OH!
UM... NOTHING!
GAH
I CALLED AHEAD, BUT...

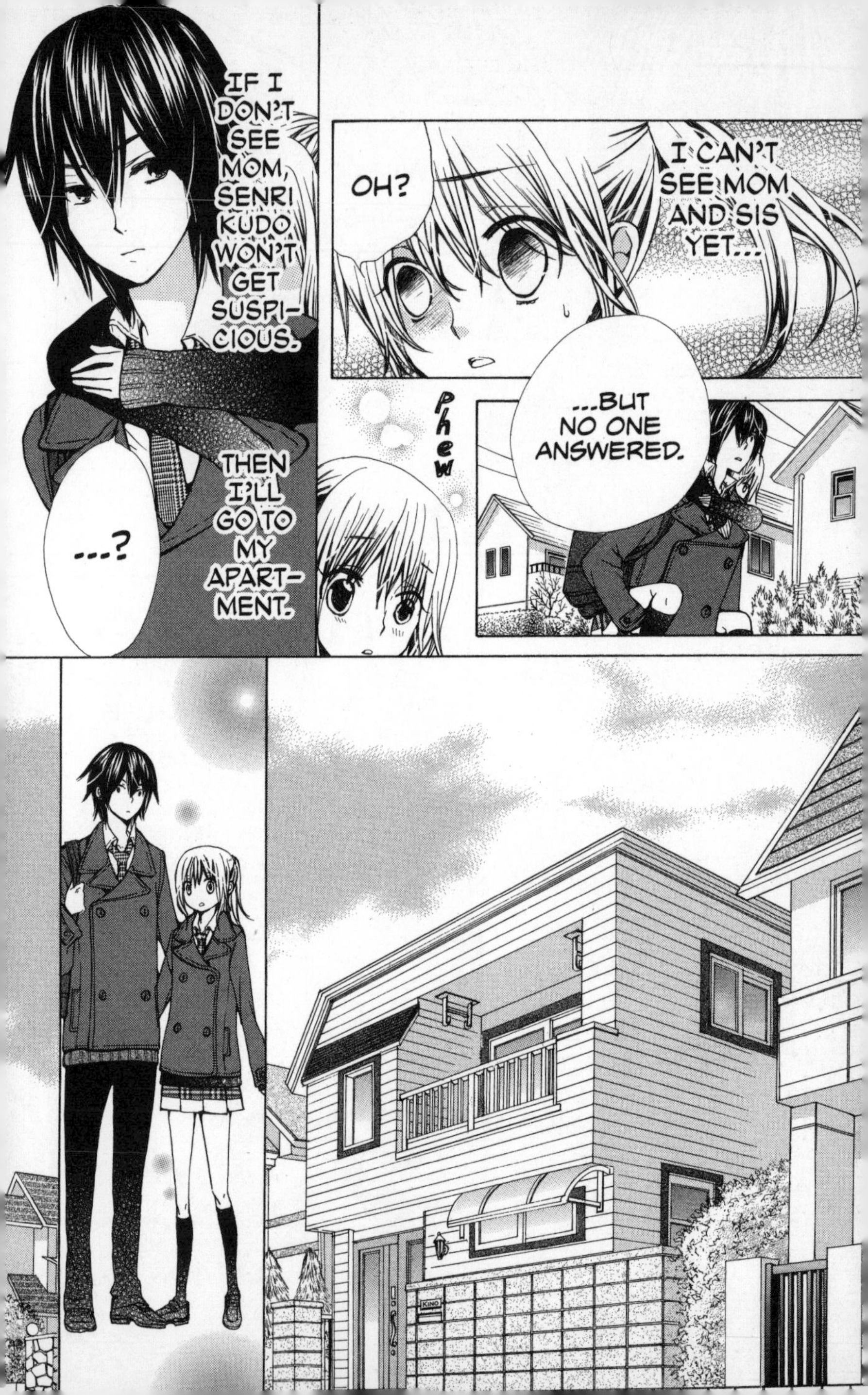
I CAN'T SEE MOM AND SIS YET...
OH?
...BUT NO ONE ANSWERED.
Phew
IF I DON'T SEE MOM, SENRI KUDO WON'T GET SUSPICIOUS.
THEN I'LL GO TO MY APARTMENT.
...?
KINO

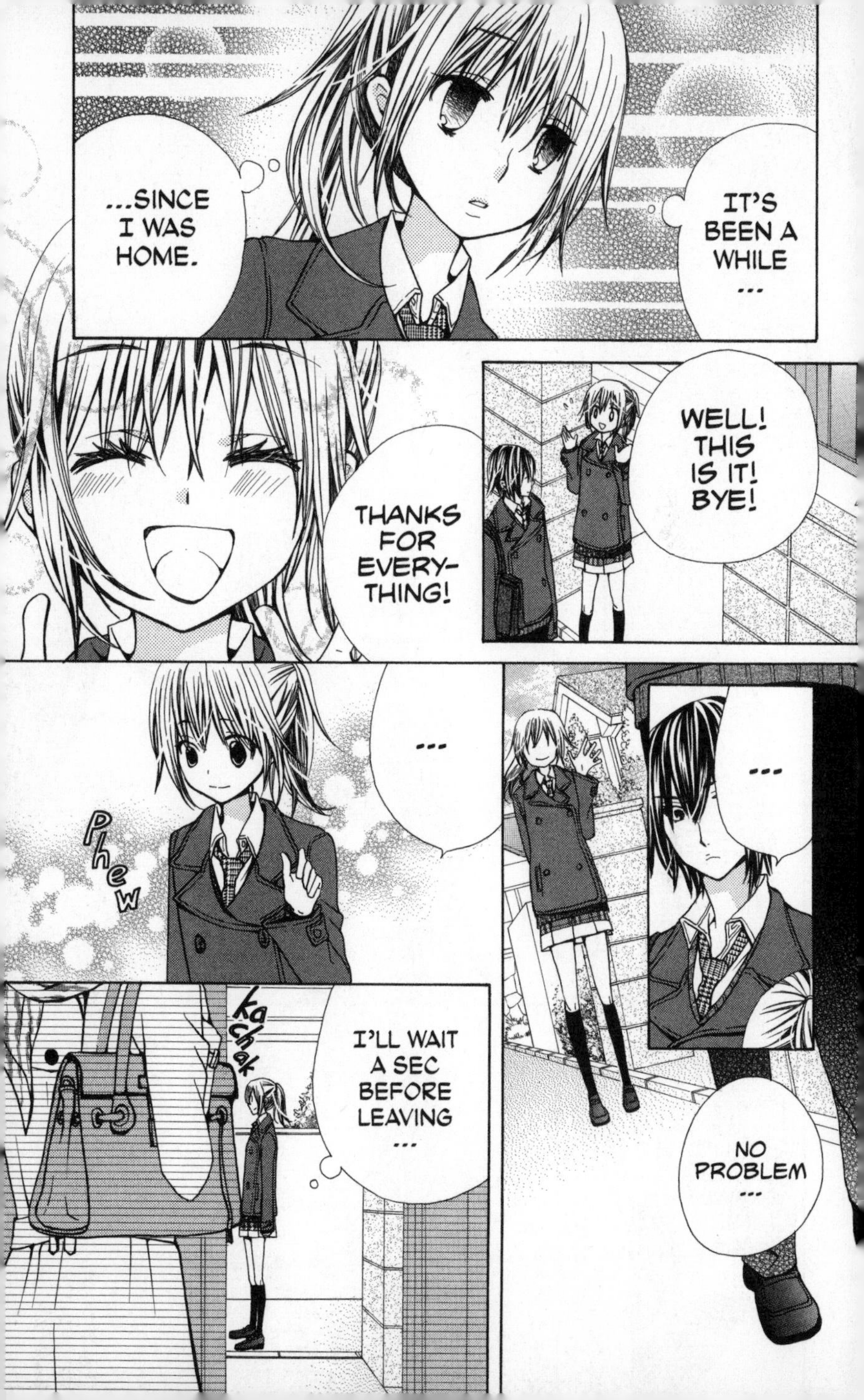
IT'S BEEN A WHILE ...
...SINCE I WAS HOME.
WELL! THIS IS IT! BYE!
THANKS FOR EVERY-THING!
...
NO PROBLEM ...
...
Phew
kachak
I'LL WAIT A SEC BEFORE LEAVING ...

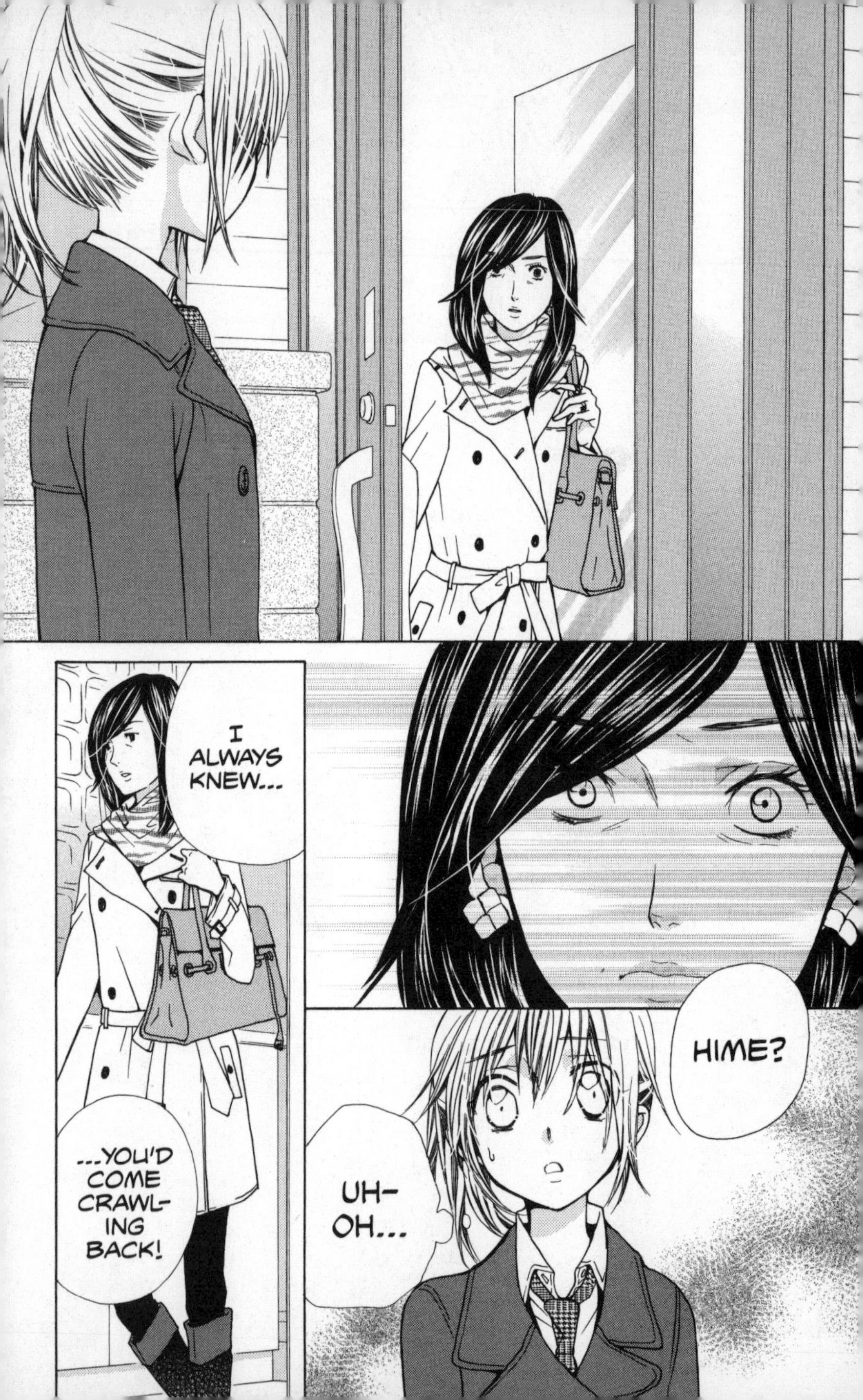
HIME?
UH-OH...
I ALWAYS KNEW...
...YOU'D COME CRAWLING BACK!

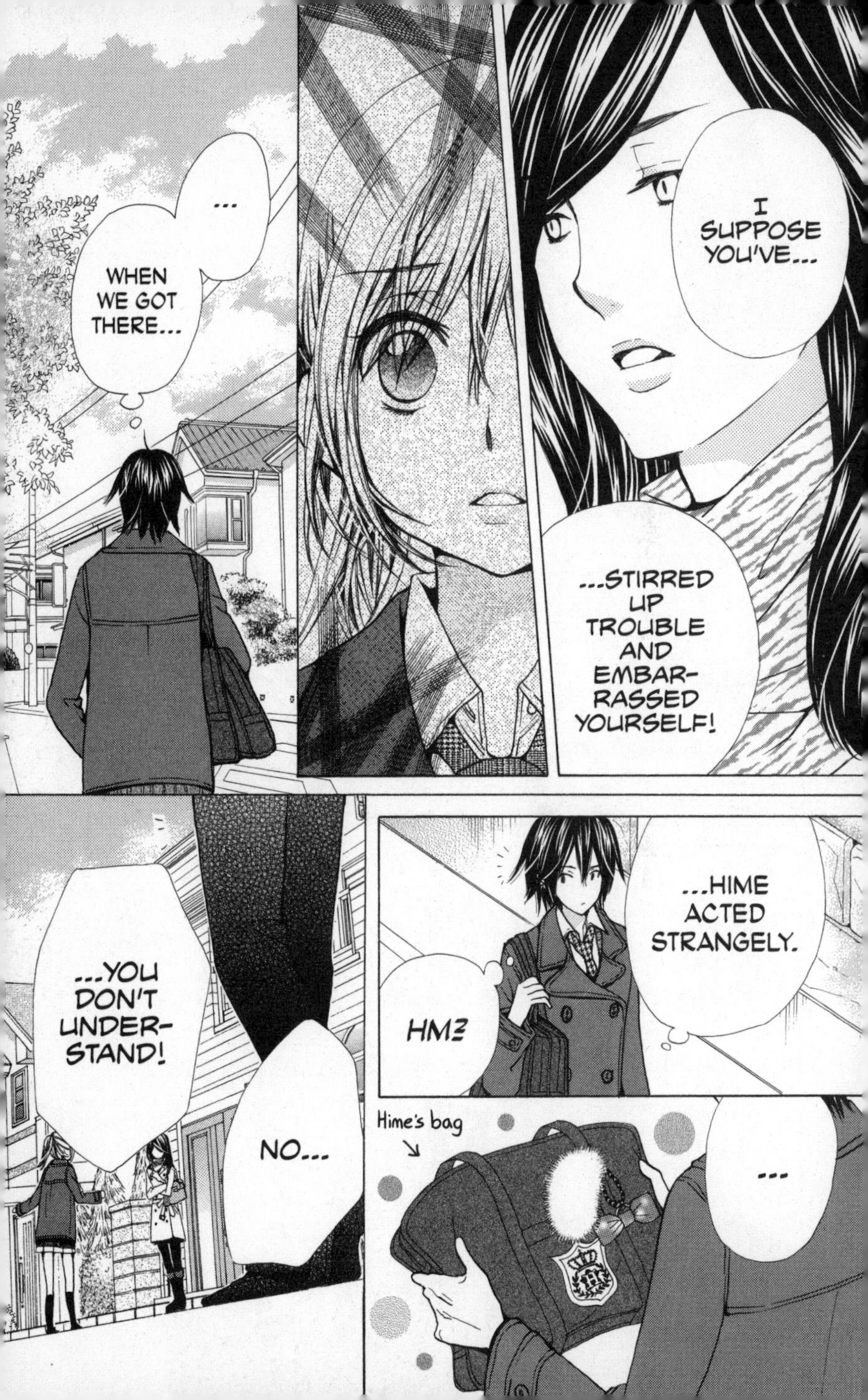
I SUPPOSE YOU'VE...
...STIRRED UP TROUBLE AND EMBARRASSED YOURSELF!
...
WHEN WE GOT THERE...
...HIME ACTED STRANGELY.
HM?
Hime's bag
...
...YOU DON'T UNDERSTAND!
NO...

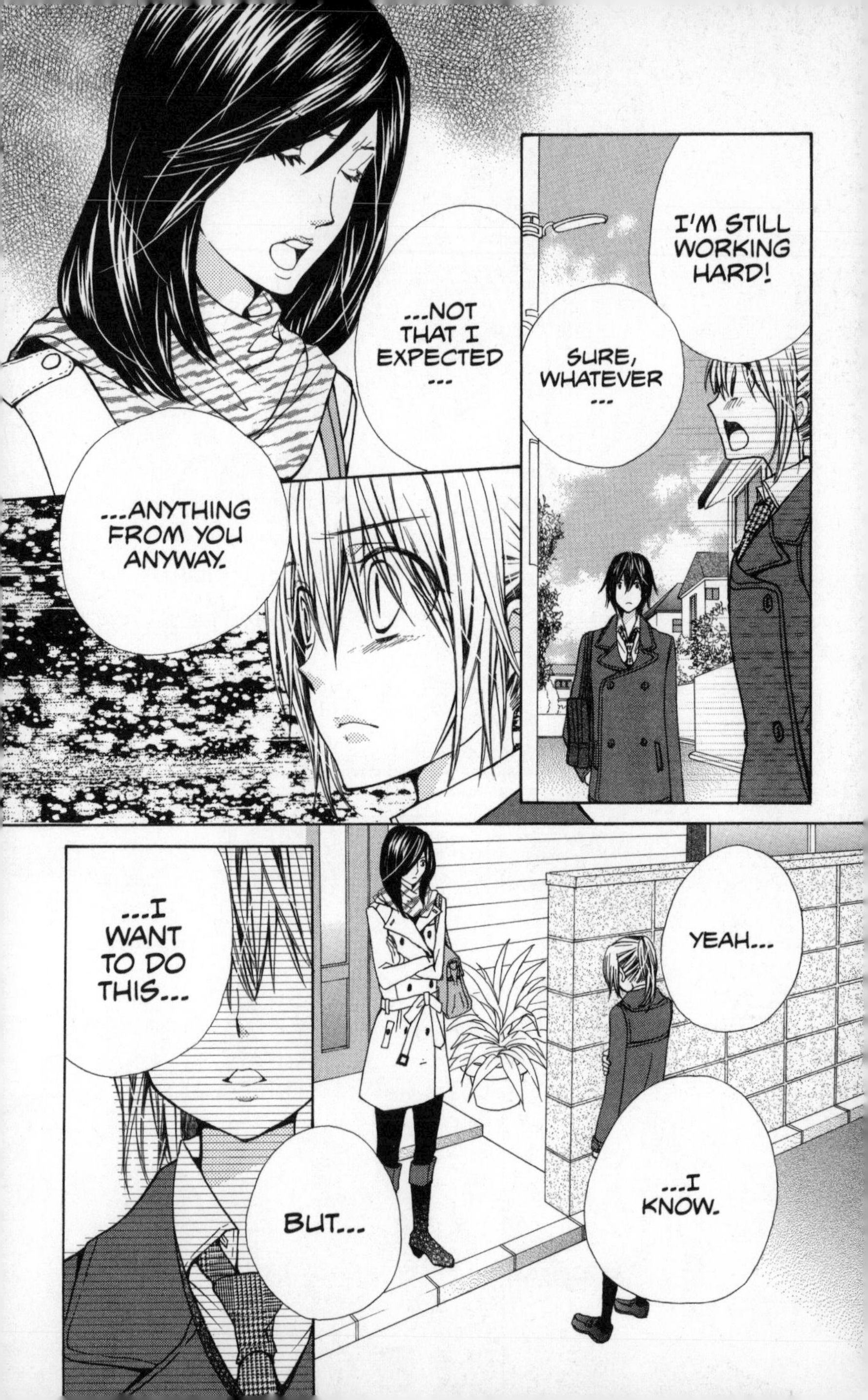
I'M STILL WORKING HARD!
SURE, WHATEVER ...
...NOT THAT I EXPECTED ...
...ANYTHING FROM YOU ANYWAY.
YEAH...
...I KNOW.
...I WANT TO DO THIS...
BUT...

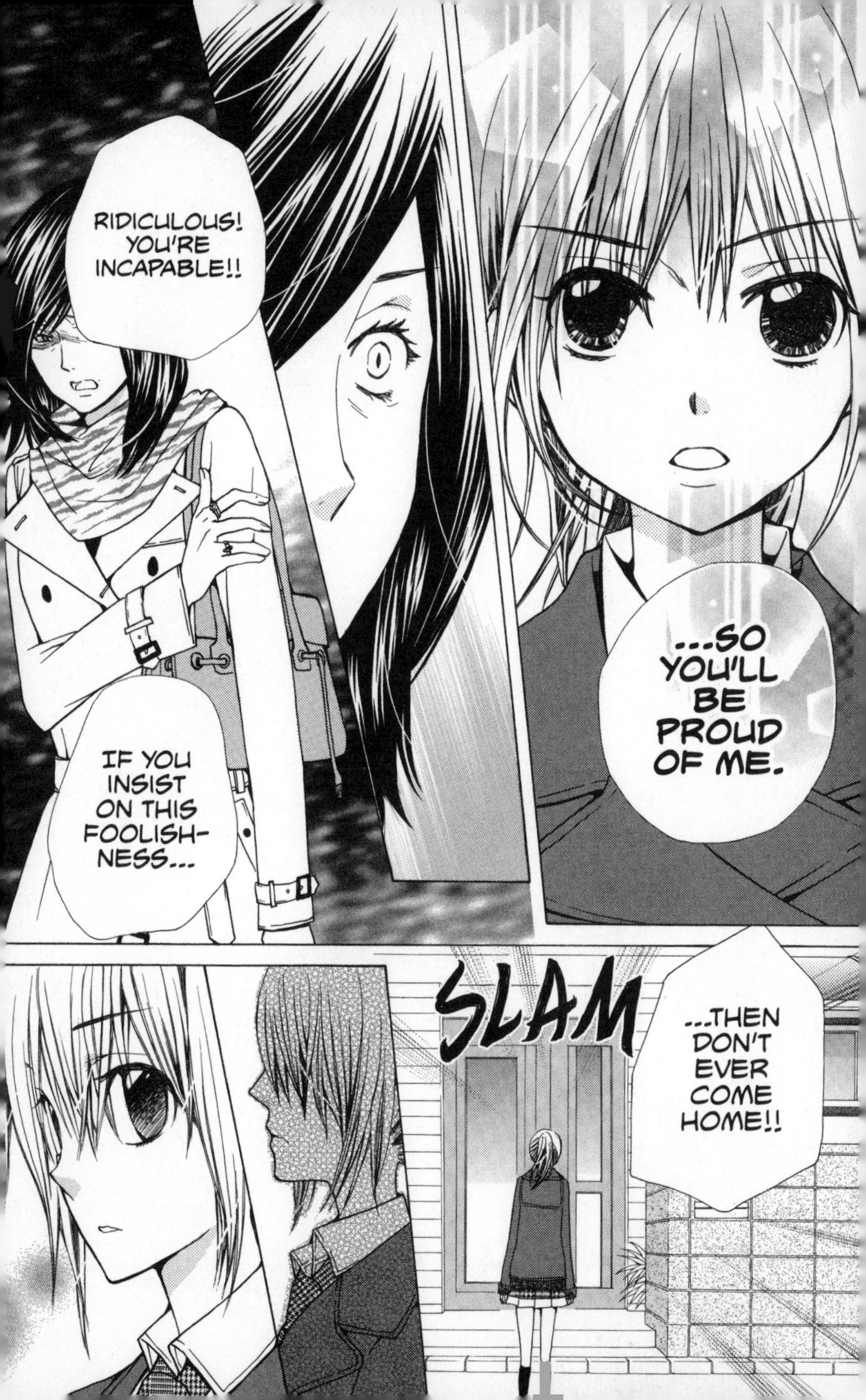
...SO YOU'LL BE PROUD OF ME.
RIDICULOUS! YOU'RE INCAPABLE!!
IF YOU INSIST ON THIS FOOLISH-NESS...
...THEN DON'T EVER COME HOME!!
SLAM

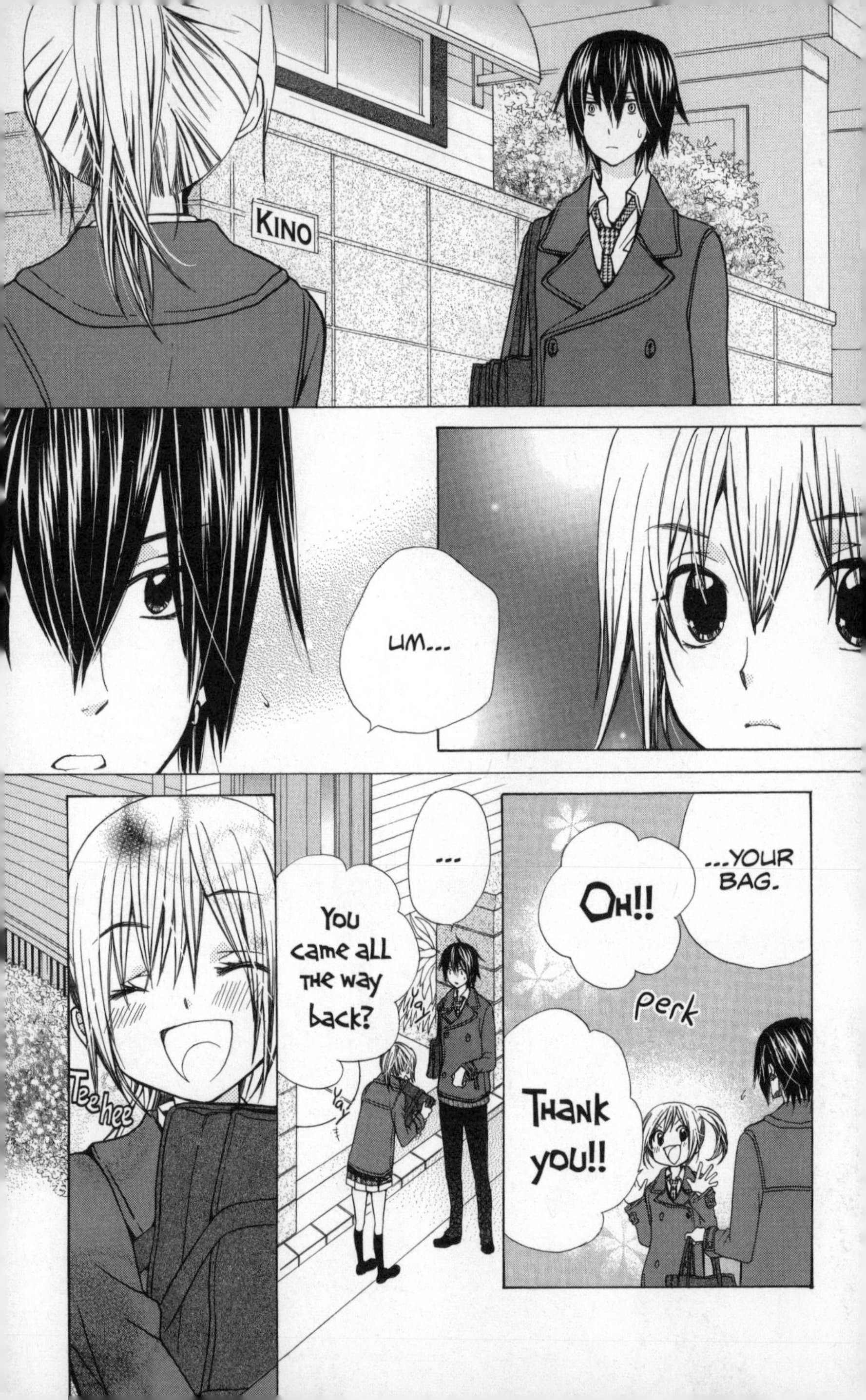
KINO
UM...
...YOUR BAG.
OH!!
perk
THANK YOU!!
...
You came all the way back?
Yay
Yay
Teehee

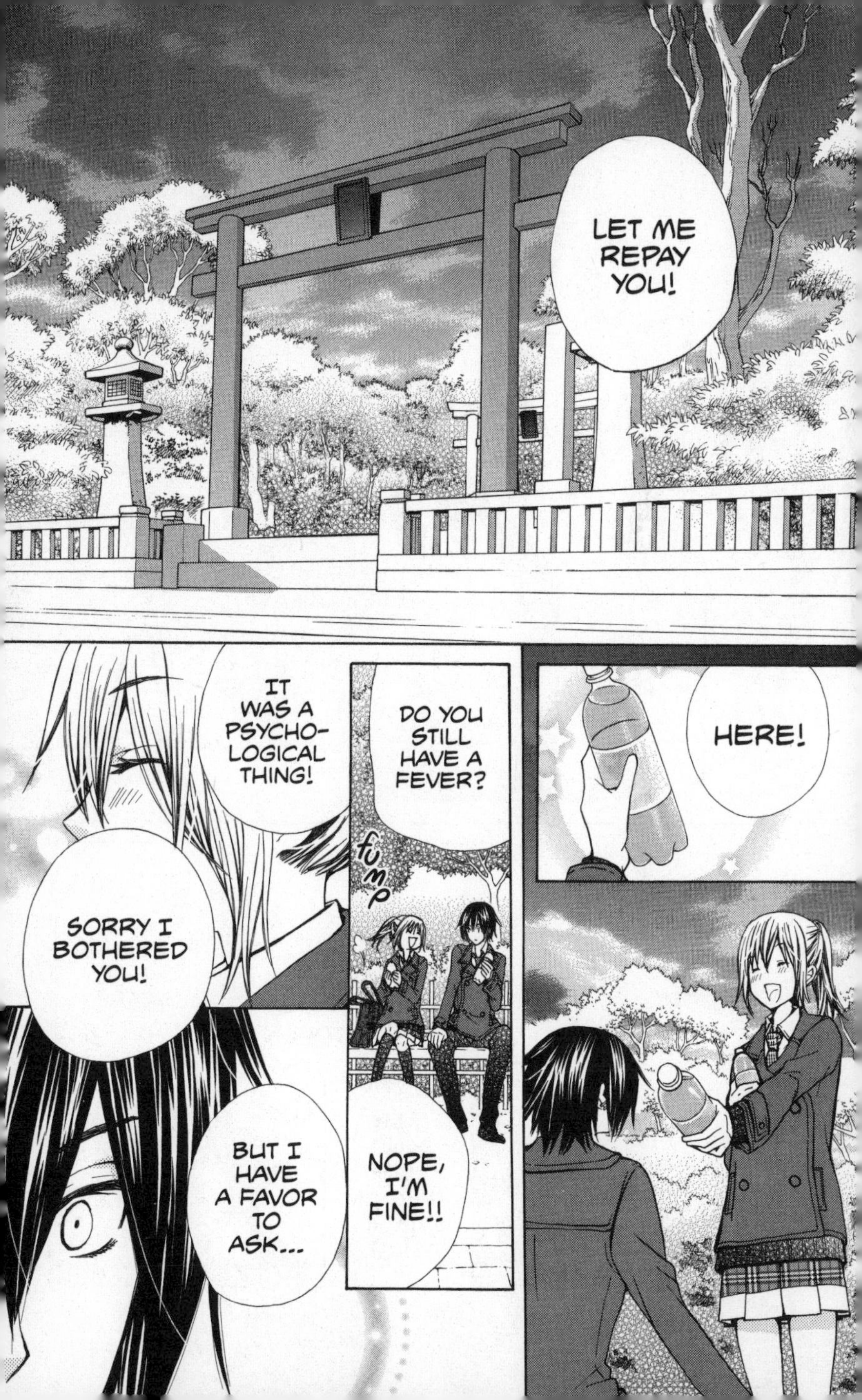
LET ME REPAY YOU!
HERE!
DO YOU STILL HAVE A FEVER?
fump
NOPE, I'M FINE!!
IT WAS A PSYCHOLOGICAL THING!
SORRY I BOTHERED YOU!
BUT I HAVE A FAVOR TO ASK...

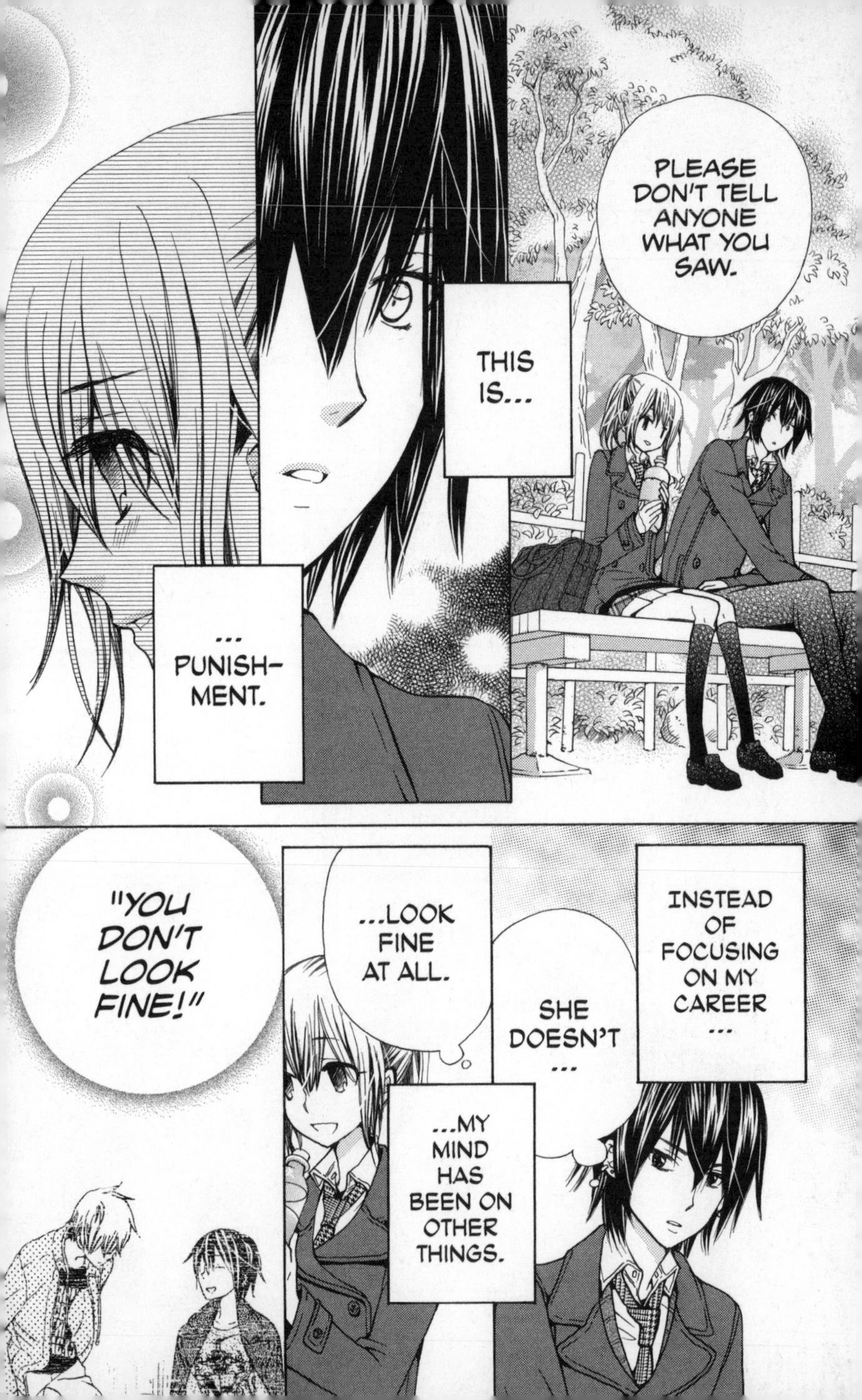
PLEASE DON'T TELL ANYONE WHAT YOU SAW.
THIS IS...
...PUNISHMENT.
INSTEAD OF FOCUSING ON MY CAREER...
SHE DOESN'T...
...LOOK FINE AT ALL.
...MY MIND HAS BEEN ON OTHER THINGS.
"YOU DON'T LOOK FINE!"

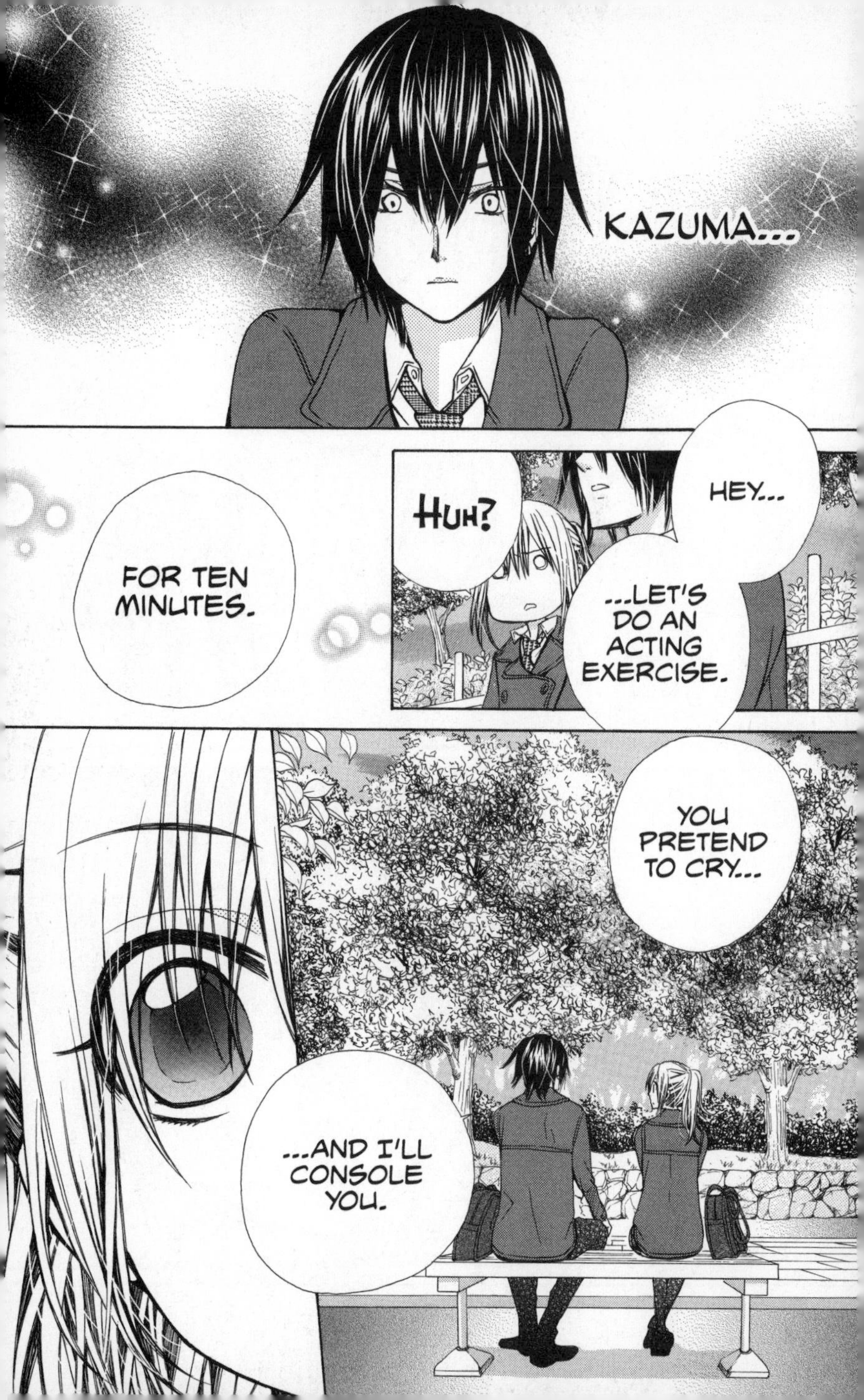
KAZUMA...
HEY...
HUH?
...LET'S DO AN ACTING EXERCISE.
FOR TEN MINUTES.
YOU PRETEND TO CRY...
...AND I'LL CONSOLE YOU.

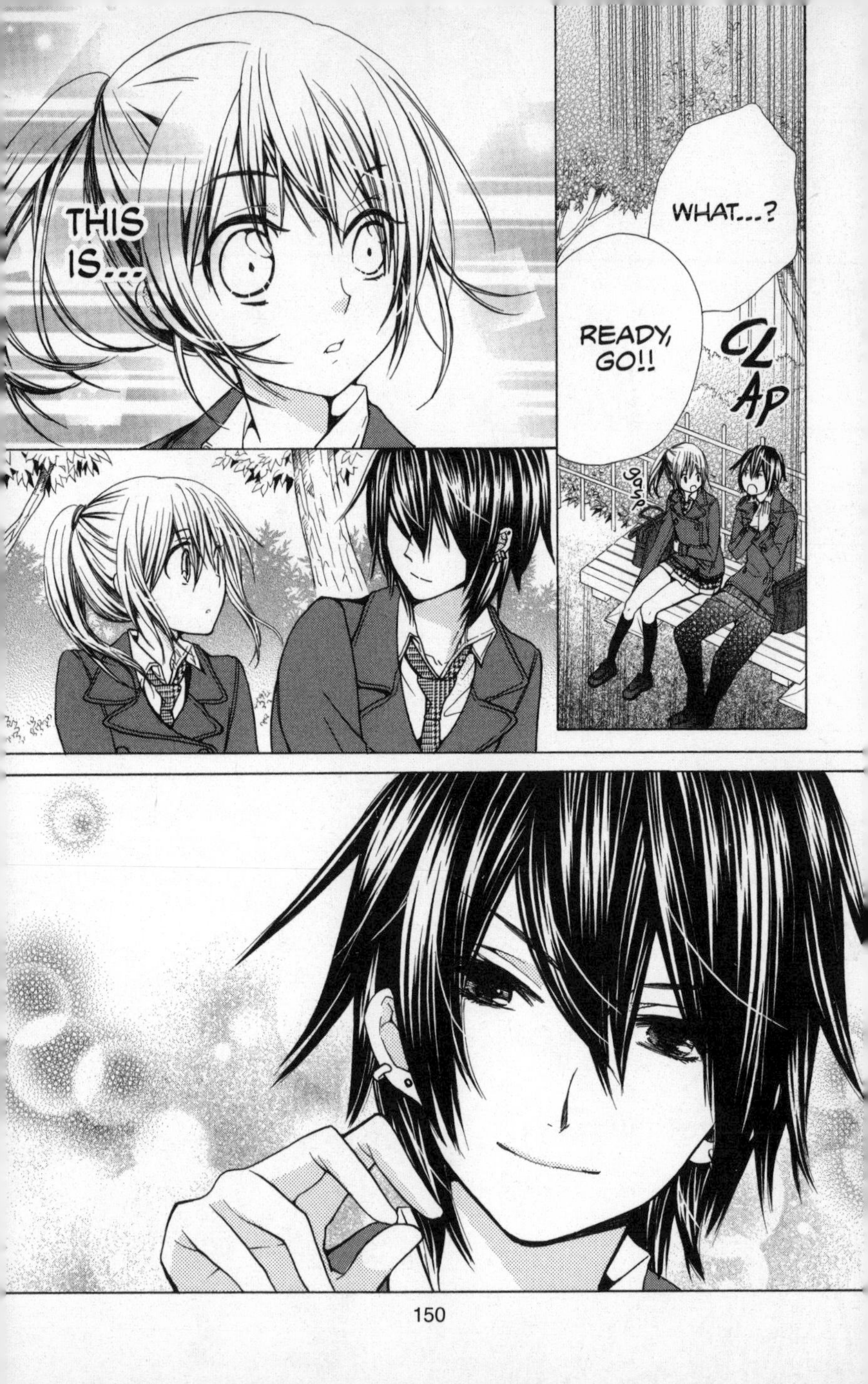

WHAT...?
READY, GO!!
CLAP
gasp
THIS IS...

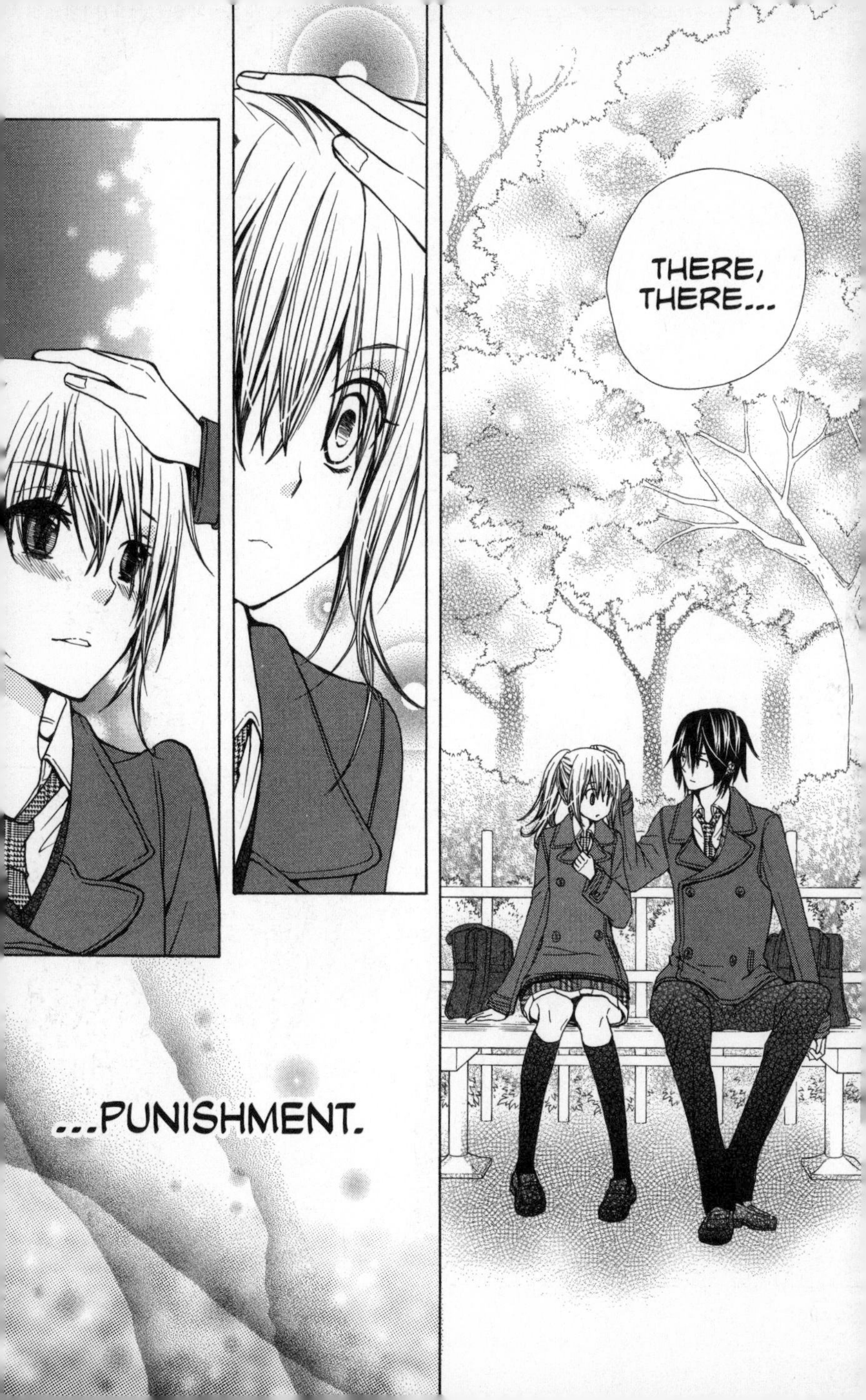
THERE, THERE...
...PUNISHMENT.

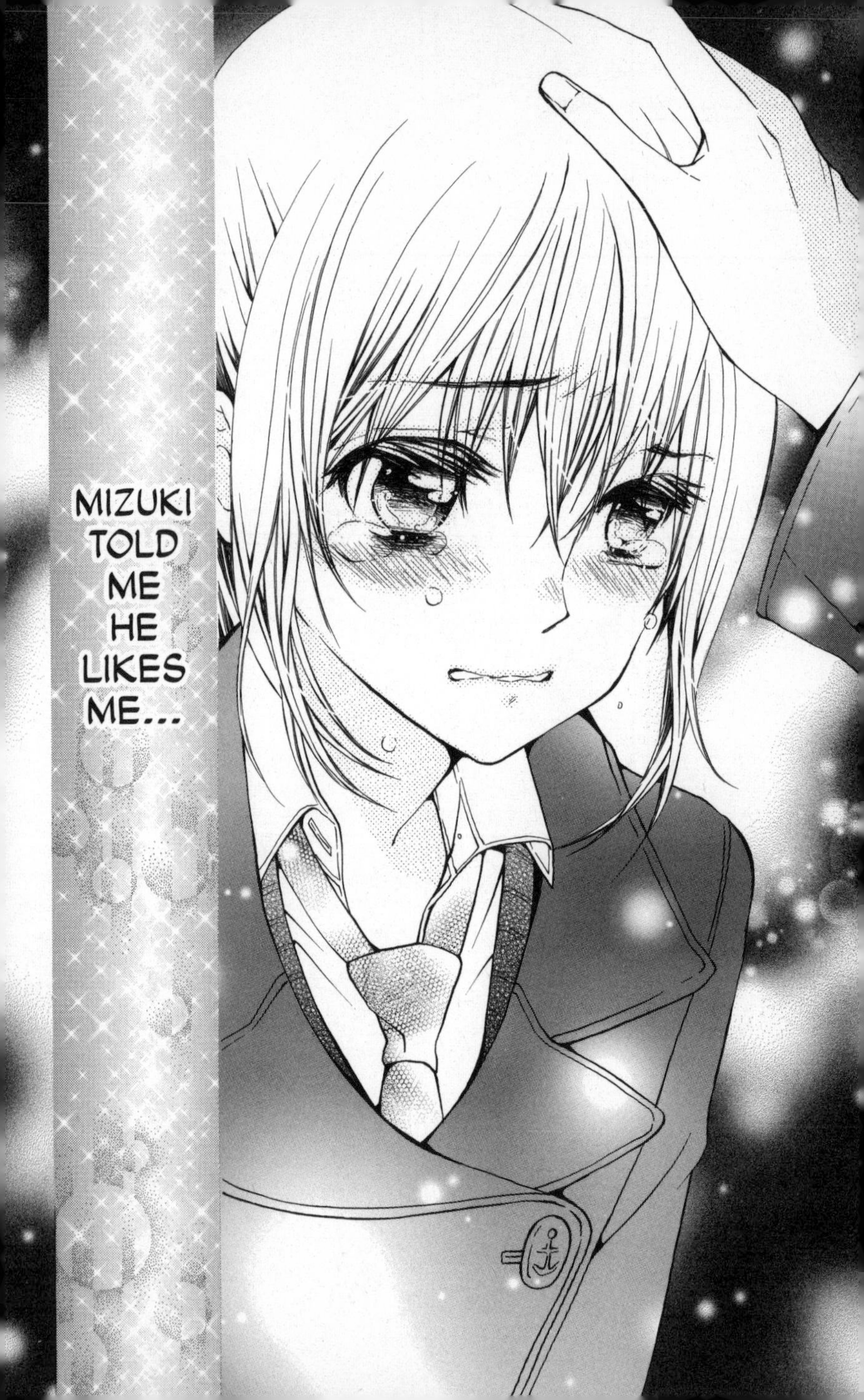
MIZUKI TOLD ME HE LIKES ME...

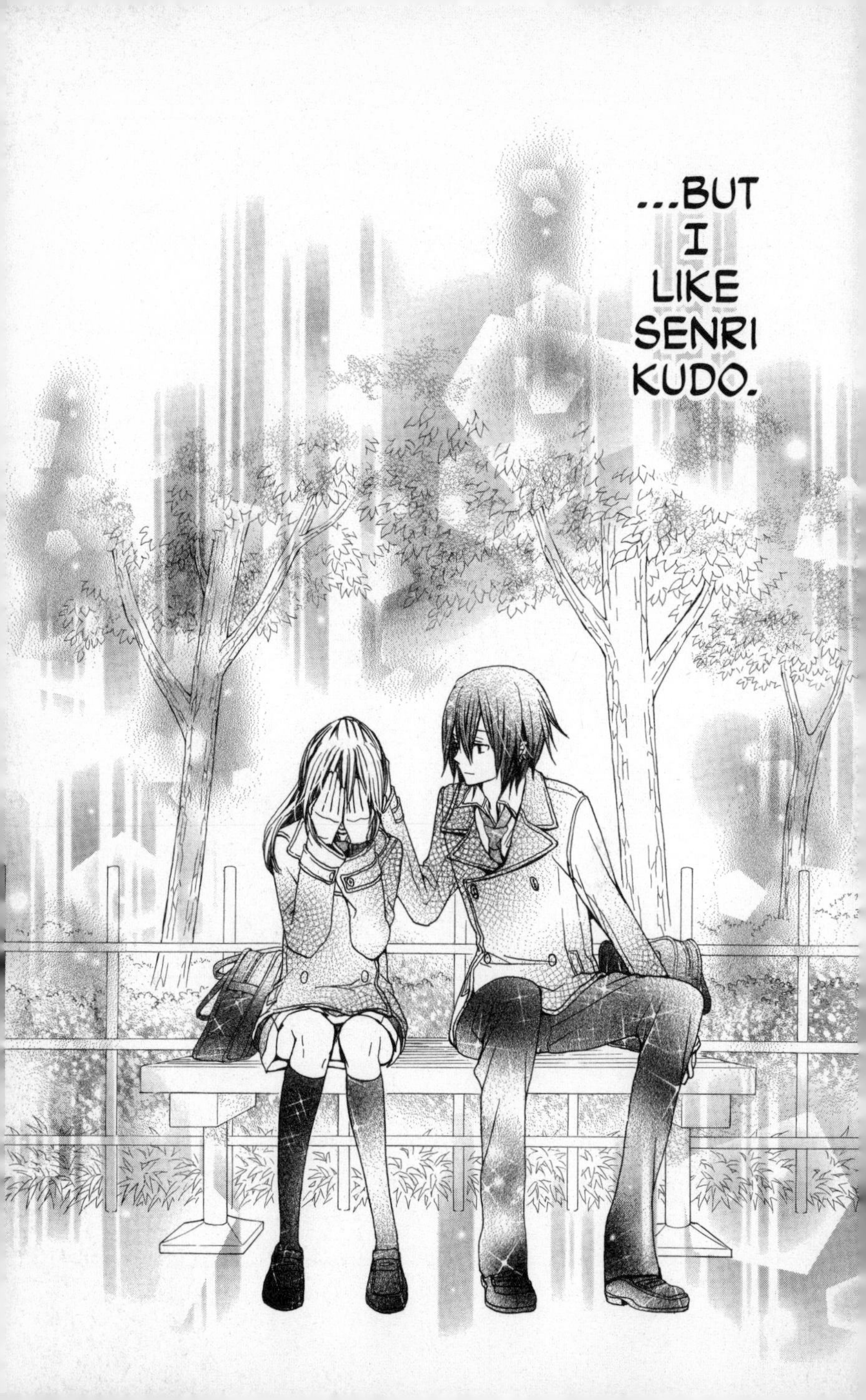
...BUT I LIKE SENRI KUDO.

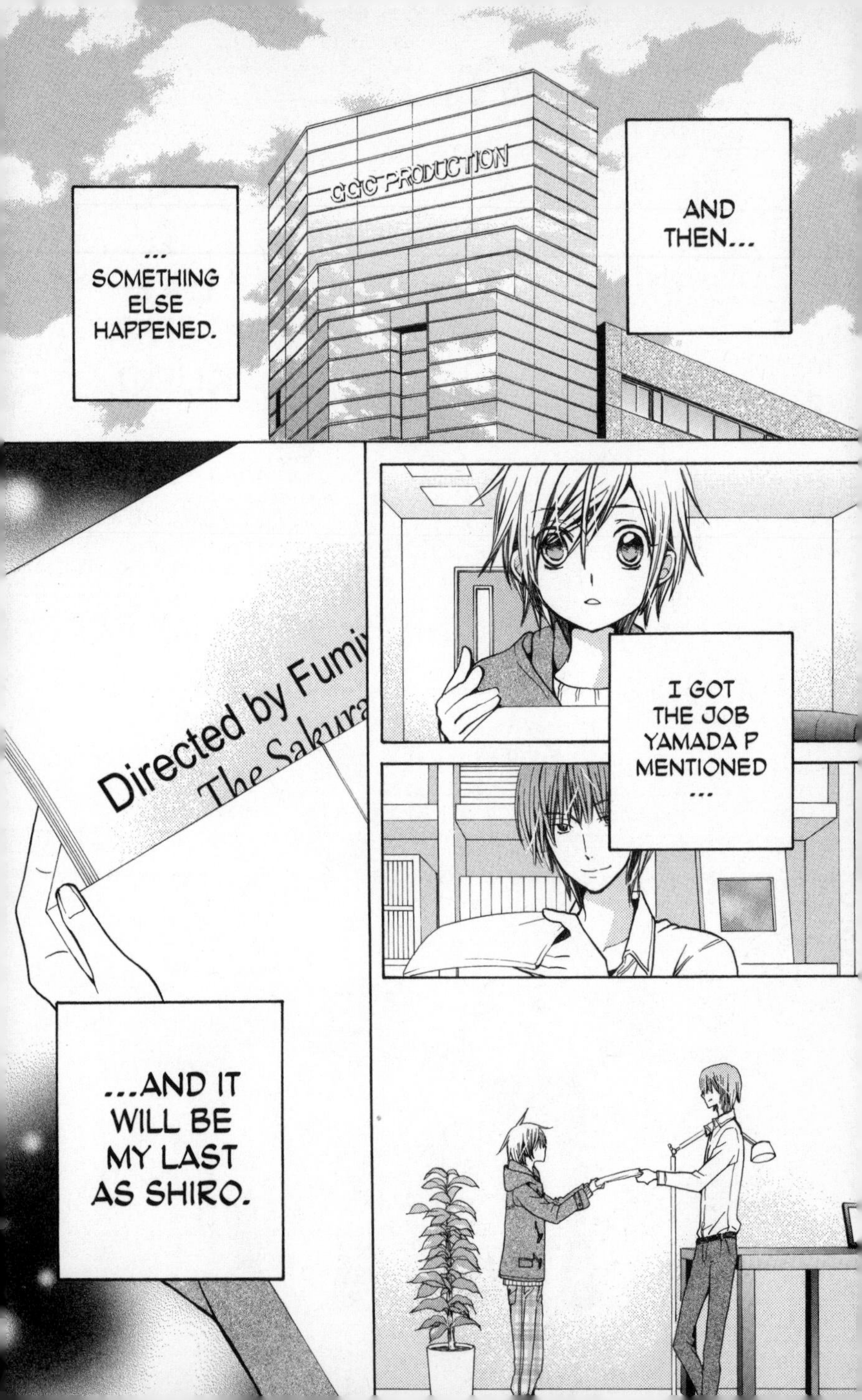
AND THEN...
GGC PRODUCTION
... SOMETHING ELSE HAPPENED.
I GOT THE JOB YAMADA P MENTIONED ...
Directed by
...AND IT WILL BE MY LAST AS SHIRO.

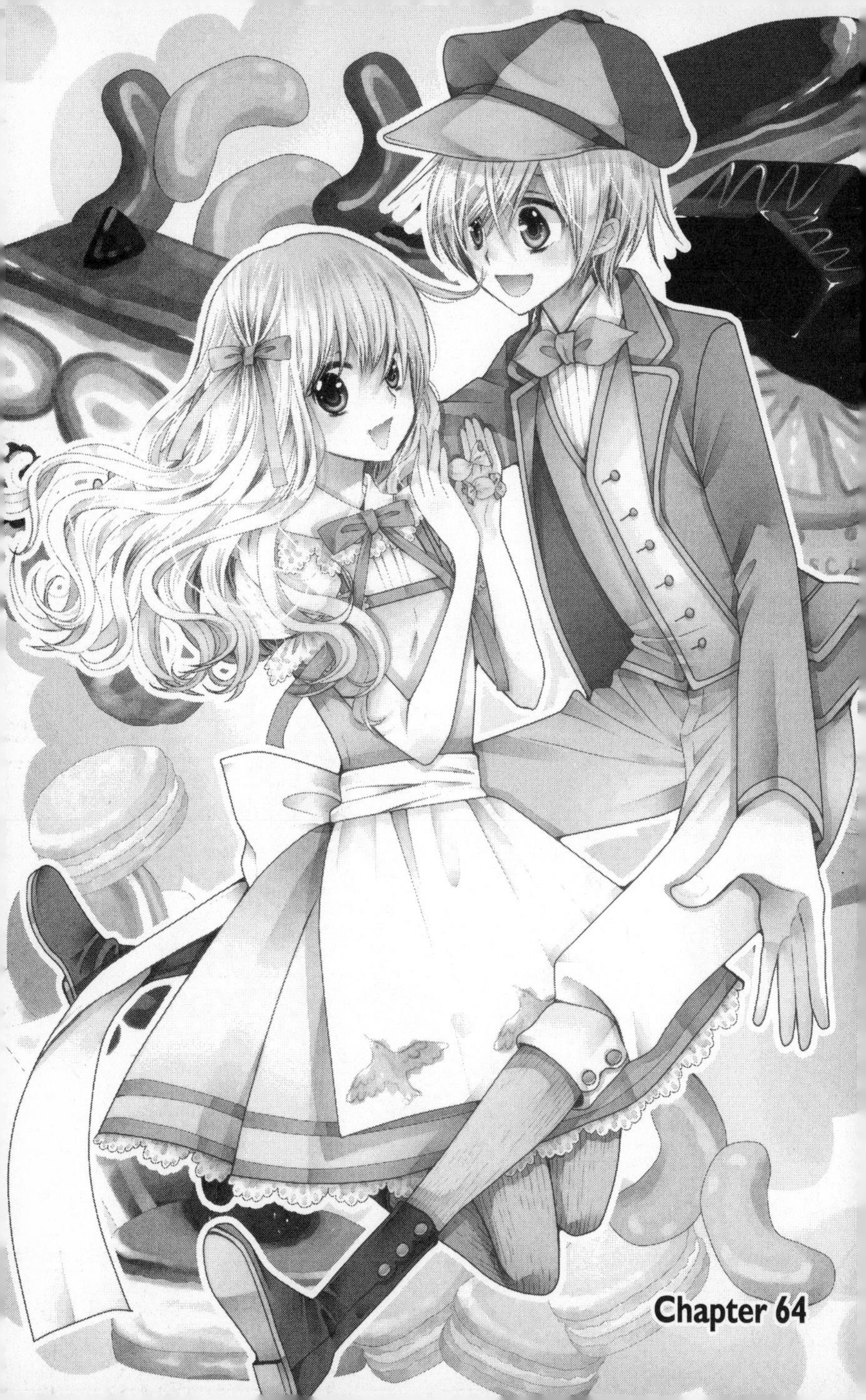

# Chapter 64

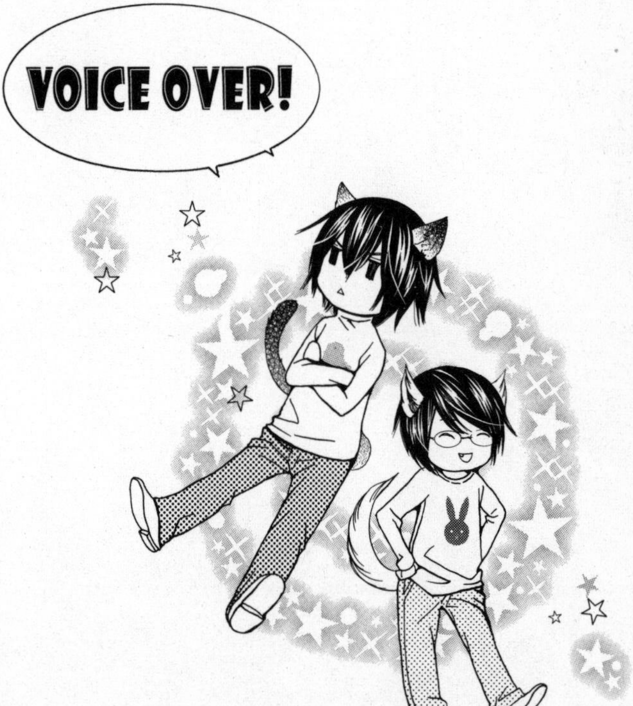
VOICE OVER!

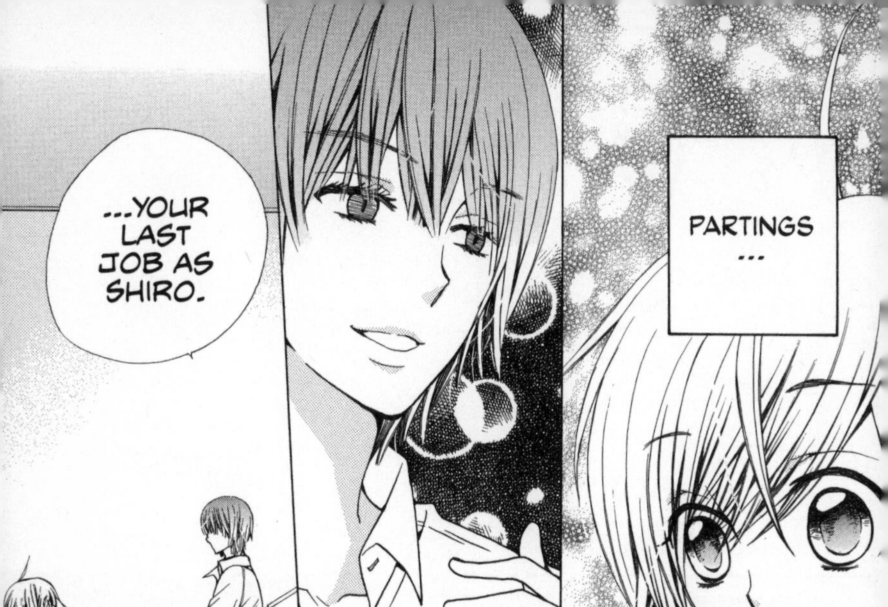
PARTINGS...
...COME SUDDENLY.
THIS IS...
...YOUR LAST JOB AS SHIRO.

• Blue Lead •

When I do rough sketches, I always use a blue mechanical pencil, but I haven't been able to find any recently. I hope it's just a temporary shortage. It's sad to see analog supplies disappearing.

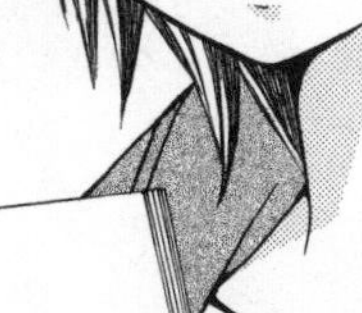
3

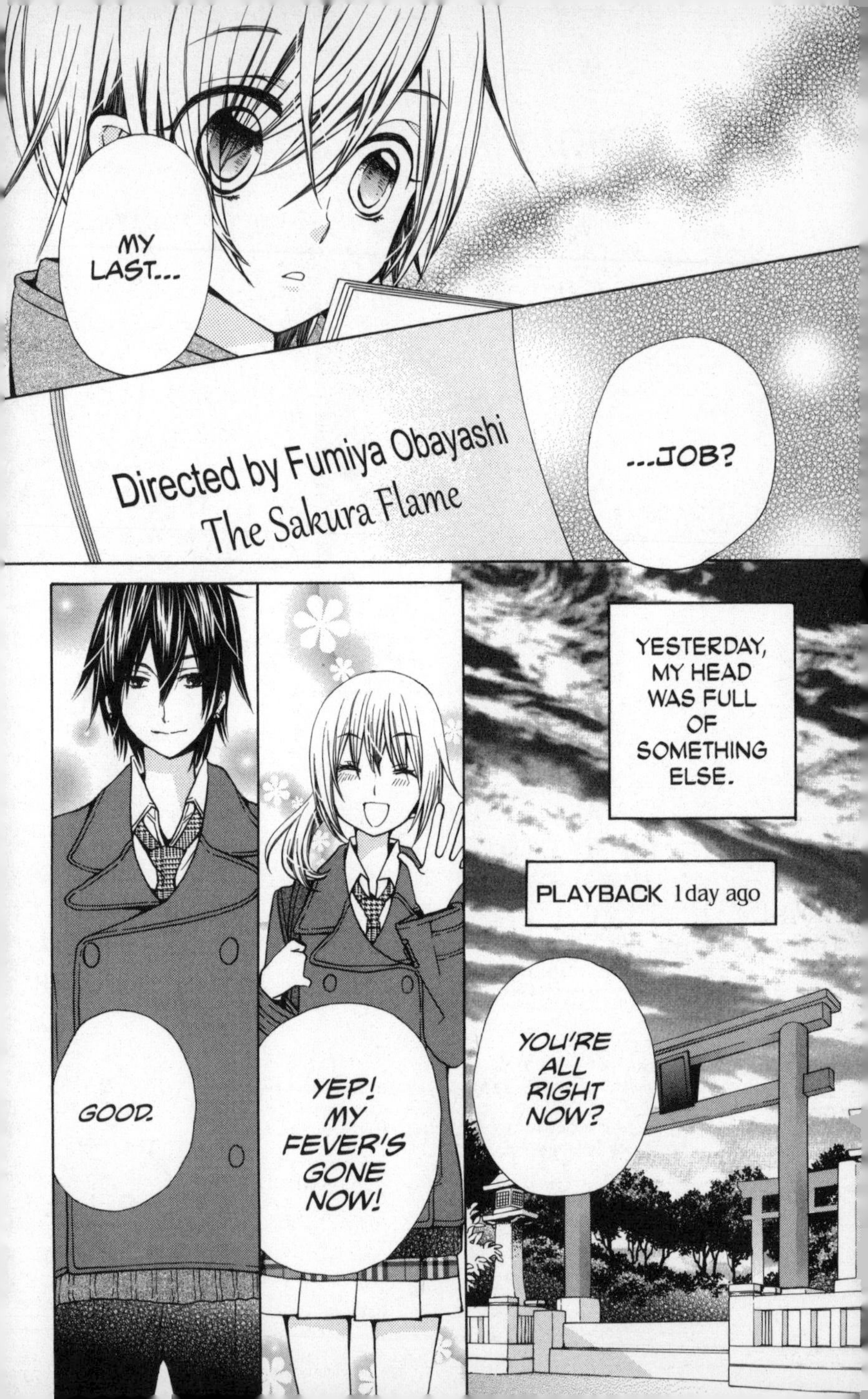
MY LAST...
...JOB?
Directed by Fumiya Obayashi
The Sakura Flame
YESTERDAY, MY HEAD WAS FULL OF SOMETHING ELSE.
PLAYBACK 1day ago
YOU'RE ALL RIGHT NOW?
YEP! MY FEVER'S GONE NOW!
GOOD.

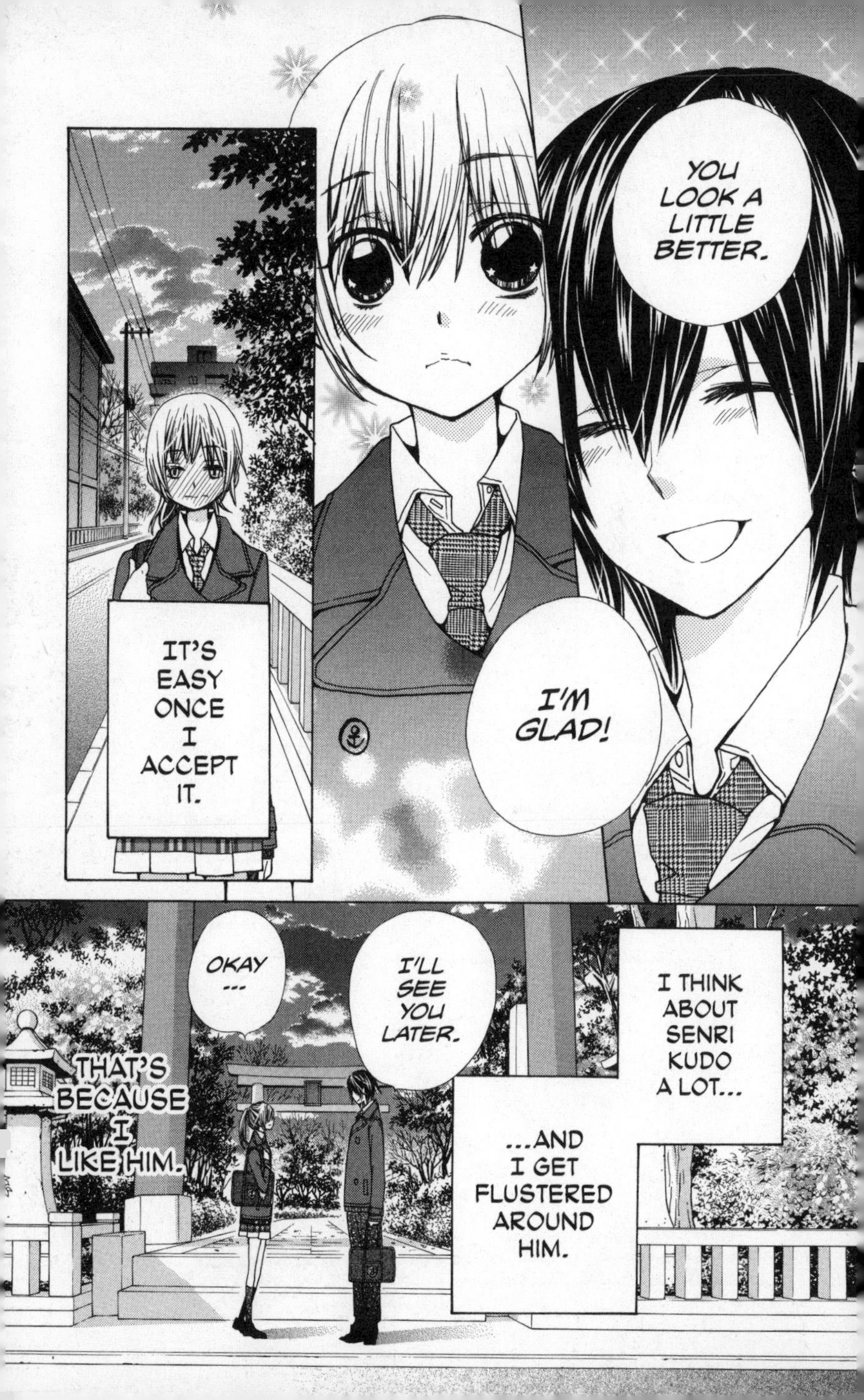
YOU LOOK A LITTLE BETTER.
I'M GLAD!
IT'S EASY ONCE I ACCEPT IT.
I THINK ABOUT SENRI KUDO A LOT...
...AND I GET FLUSTERED AROUND HIM.
I'LL SEE YOU LATER.
OKAY...
THAT'S BECAUSE I LIKE HIM.

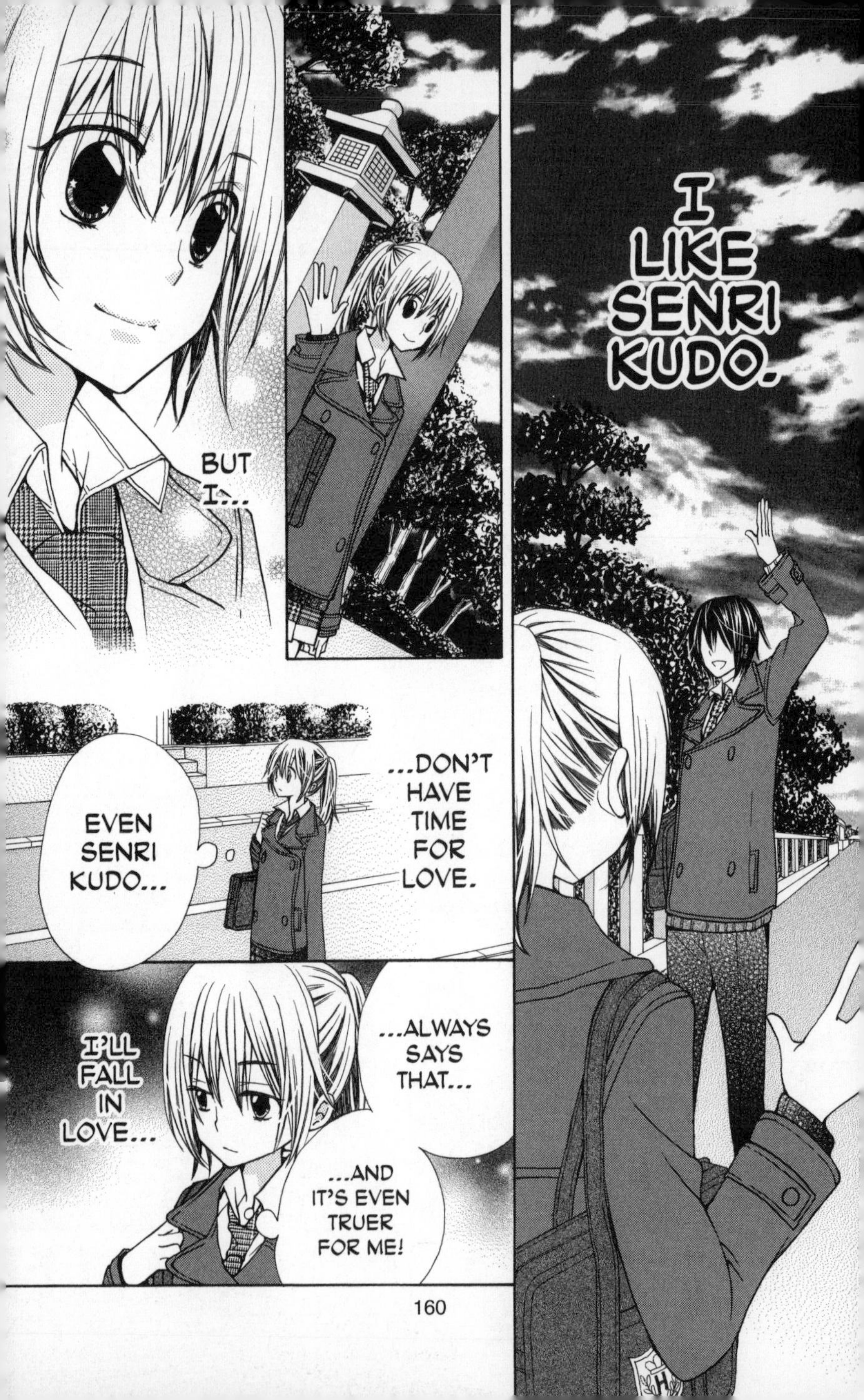
I LIKE SENRI KUDO.
BUT I...
...DON'T HAVE TIME FOR LOVE.
EVEN SENRI KUDO...
...ALWAYS SAYS THAT...
...AND IT'S EVEN TRUER FOR ME!
I'LL FALL IN LOVE...

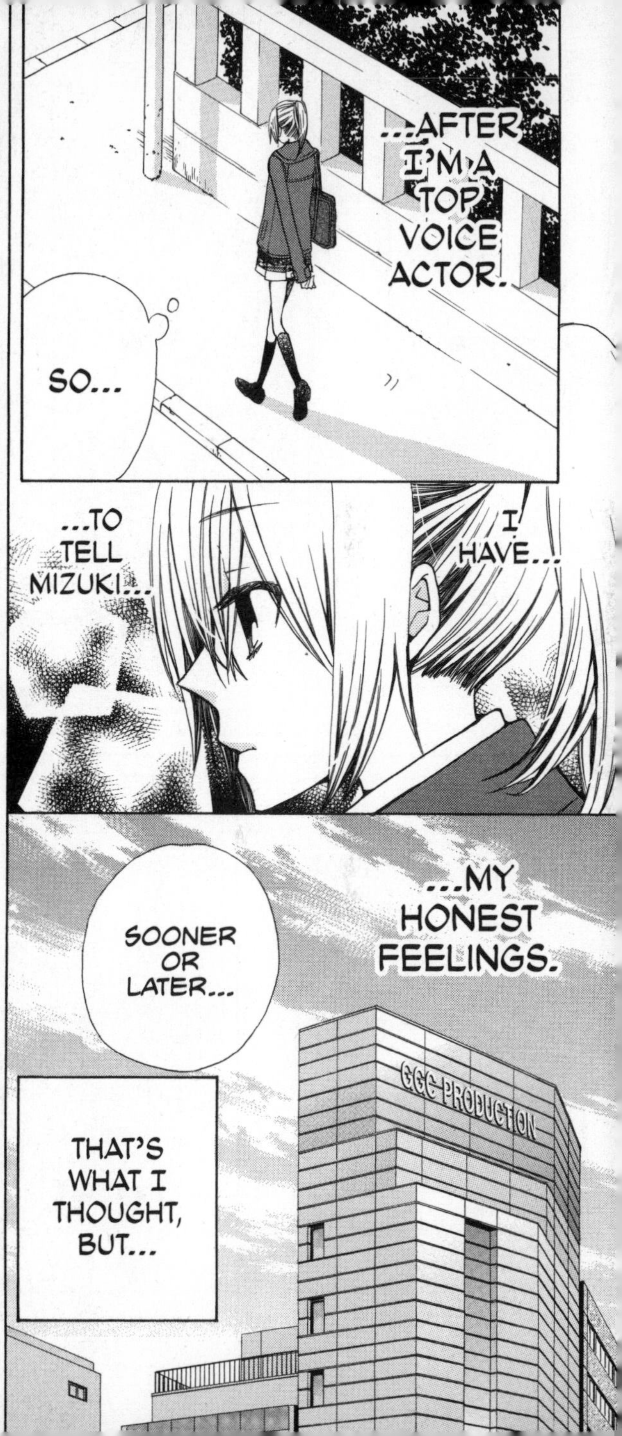
...AFTER I'M A TOP VOICE ACTOR.
SO...
I HAVE...
...TO TELL MIZUKI...
...MY HONEST FEELINGS.
SOONER OR LATER...
GGC PRODUCTION
THAT'S WHAT I THOUGHT, BUT...

• A Few Words •

This is the last sidebar. Thank you for reading this far!

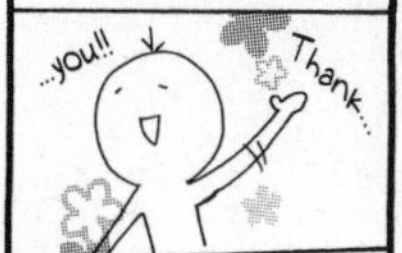
Thank...
...you!!

The neighborhood got a new convenience store. How handy!

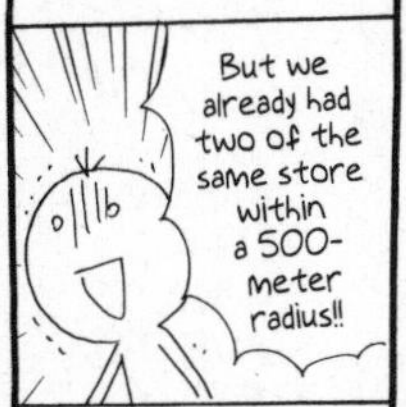
But we already had two of the same store within a 500-meter radius!!

Is it okay to have three of the same one?!

And now...much thanks to everyone who read this far, everyone who helped with research, everyone who worked on the graphic novel, my editor, everyone who helped with composition, all my assistants, my friends and my family!!

♡ If you feel like it, lemme hear your thoughts! ♡

Maki Minami
c/o Shojo Beat
P.O. Box 77010
San Francisco, CA
94107

Maki Minami

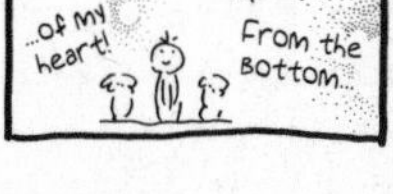
From the bottom...
...of my heart!

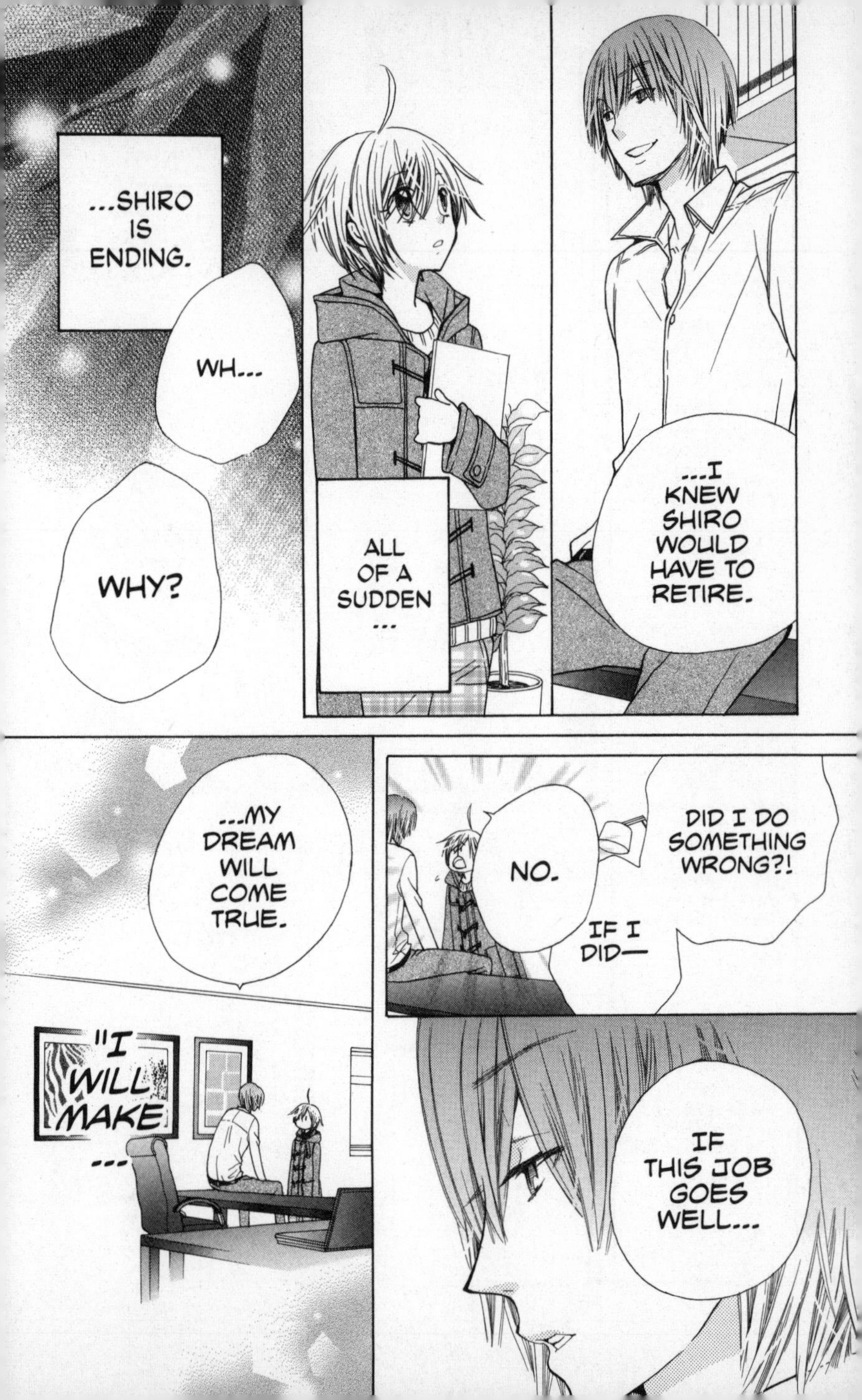
...I KNEW SHIRO WOULD HAVE TO RETIRE.
ALL OF A SUDDEN...
...SHIRO IS ENDING.
WH...
WHY?
DID I DO SOMETHING WRONG?!
NO.
IF I DID—
IF THIS JOB GOES WELL...
...MY DREAM WILL COME TRUE.
"I WILL MAKE ...

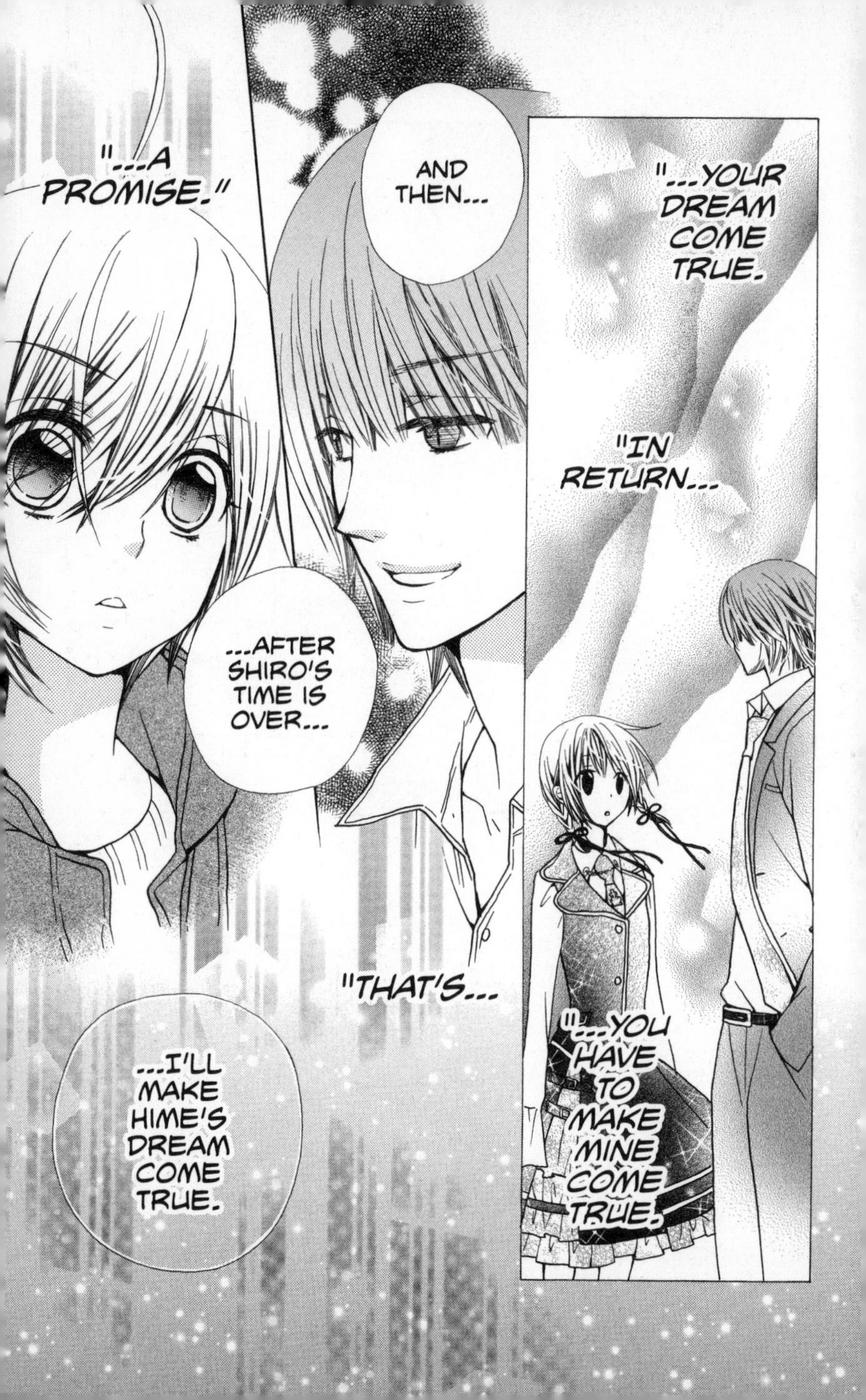
"...YOUR DREAM COME TRUE.
"IN RETURN...
"...YOU HAVE TO MAKE MINE COME TRUE.
"...A PROMISE."
AND THEN...
...AFTER SHIRO'S TIME IS OVER...
"THAT'S...
...I'LL MAKE HIME'S DREAM COME TRUE.

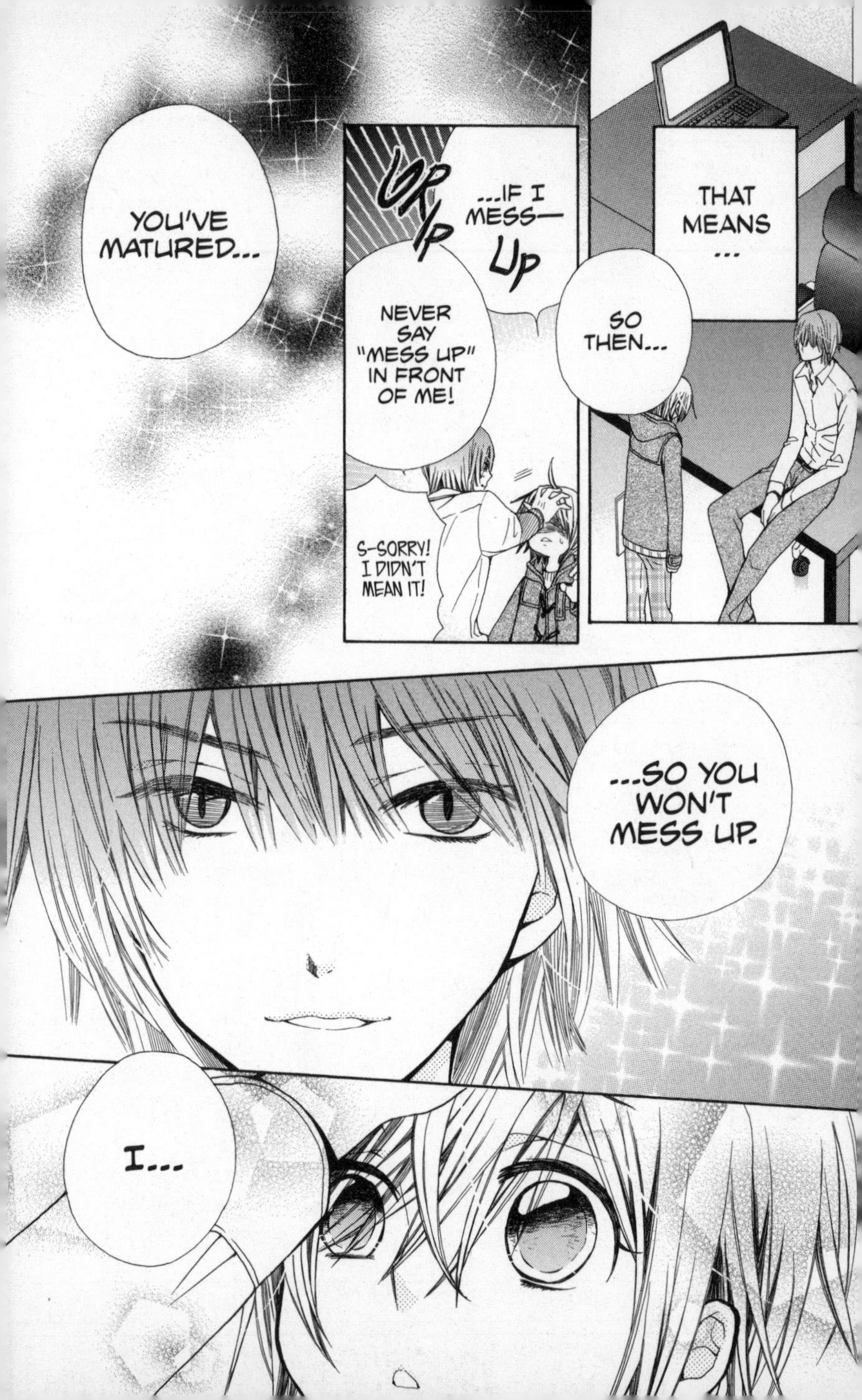
THAT MEANS ...
SO THEN...
...IF I MESS—
RIP
UP
NEVER SAY "MESS UP" IN FRONT OF ME!
S-SORRY! I DIDN'T MEAN IT!
YOU'VE MATURED...
...SO YOU WON'T MESS UP.
I...

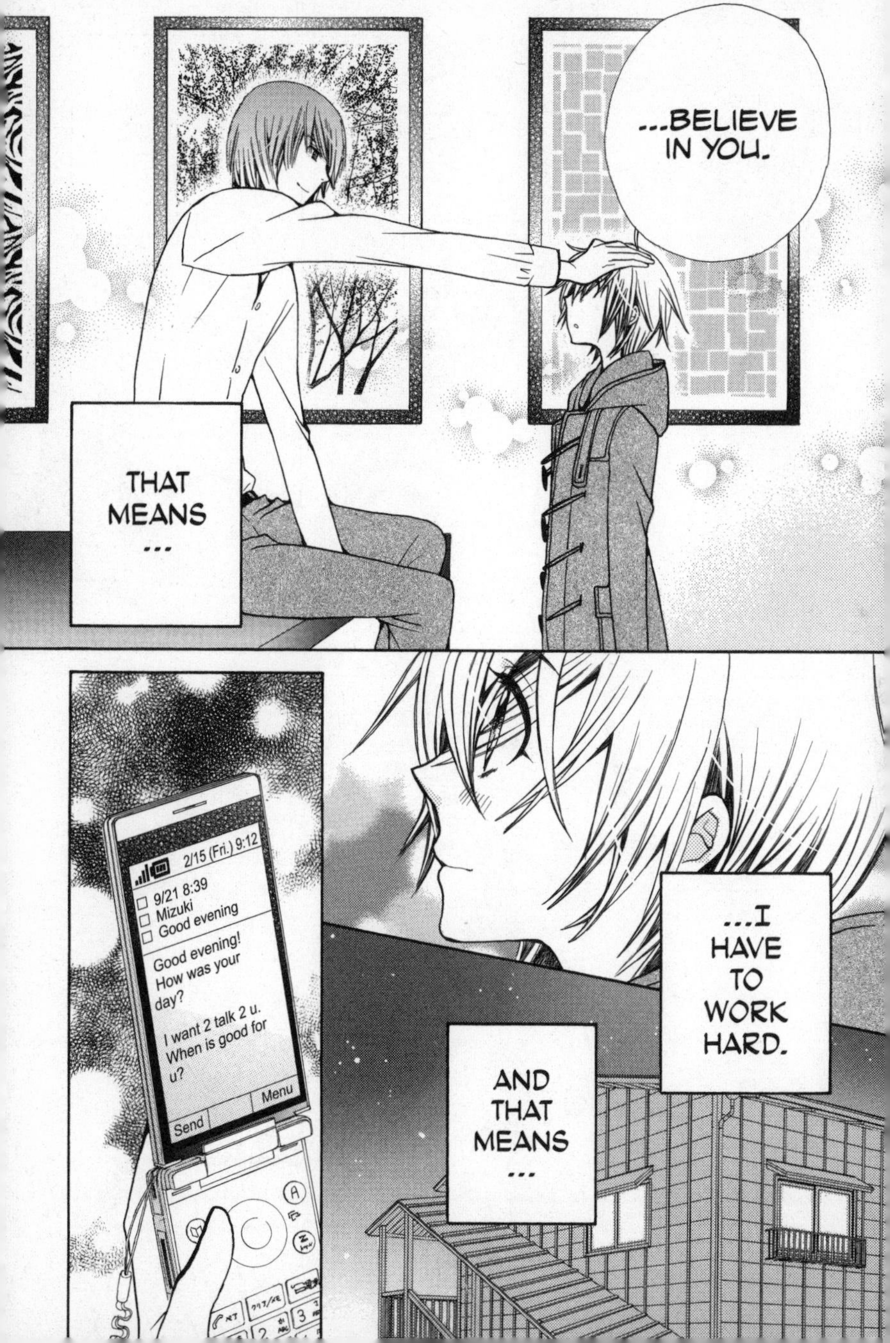
...BELIEVE IN YOU.
THAT MEANS ...
...I HAVE TO WORK HARD.
AND THAT MEANS ...
2/15 (Fri.) 9:12
9/21 8:39
Mizuki
Good evening
Good evening! How was your day?
I want 2 talk 2 u. When is good for u?
Menu
Send

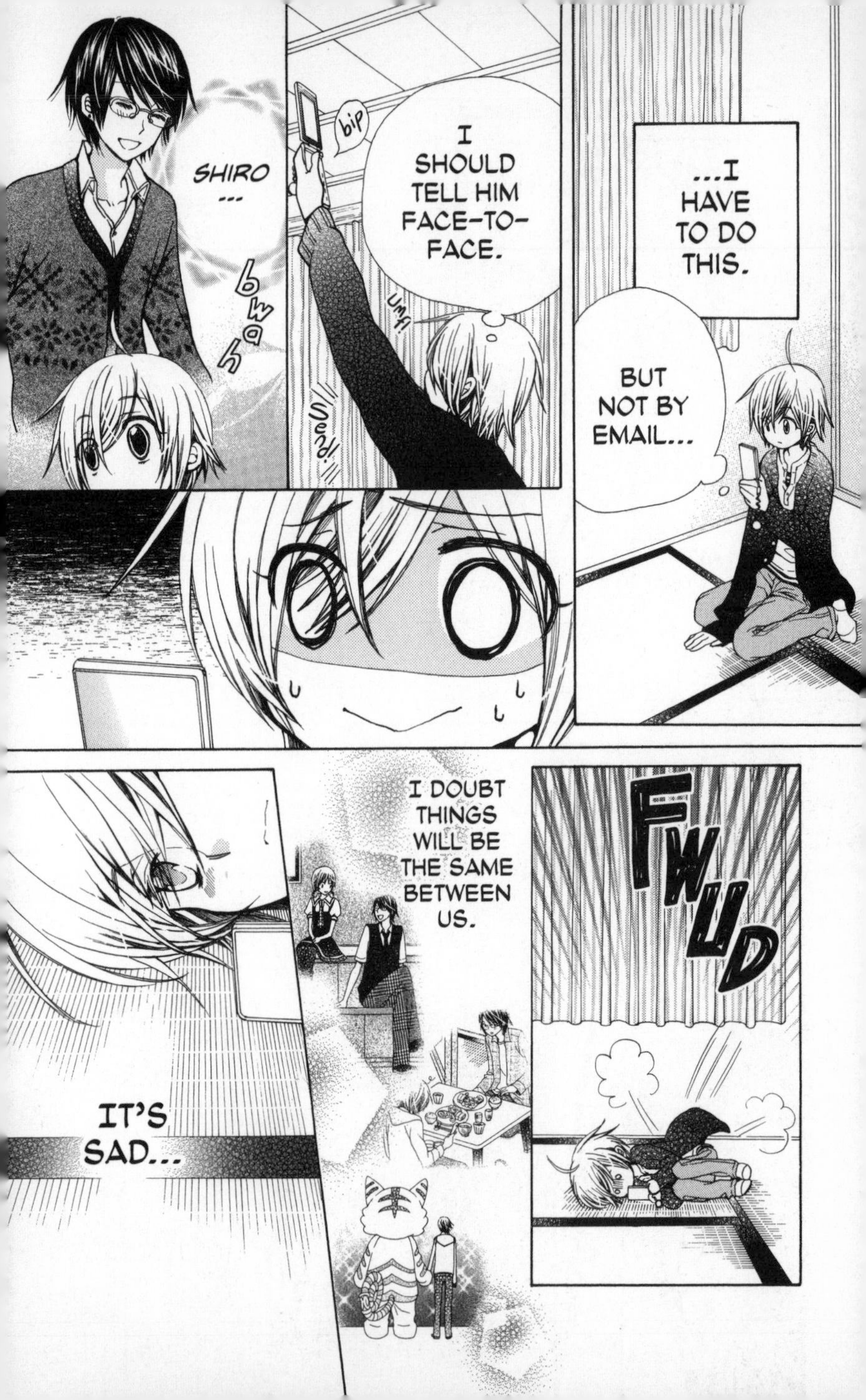
...I HAVE TO DO THIS.
BUT NOT BY EMAIL...
I SHOULD TELL HIM FACE-TO-FACE.
bip
umf!
Send!
SHIRO ...
bwah
FWUD
I DOUBT THINGS WILL BE THE SAME BETWEEN US.
IT'S SAD...

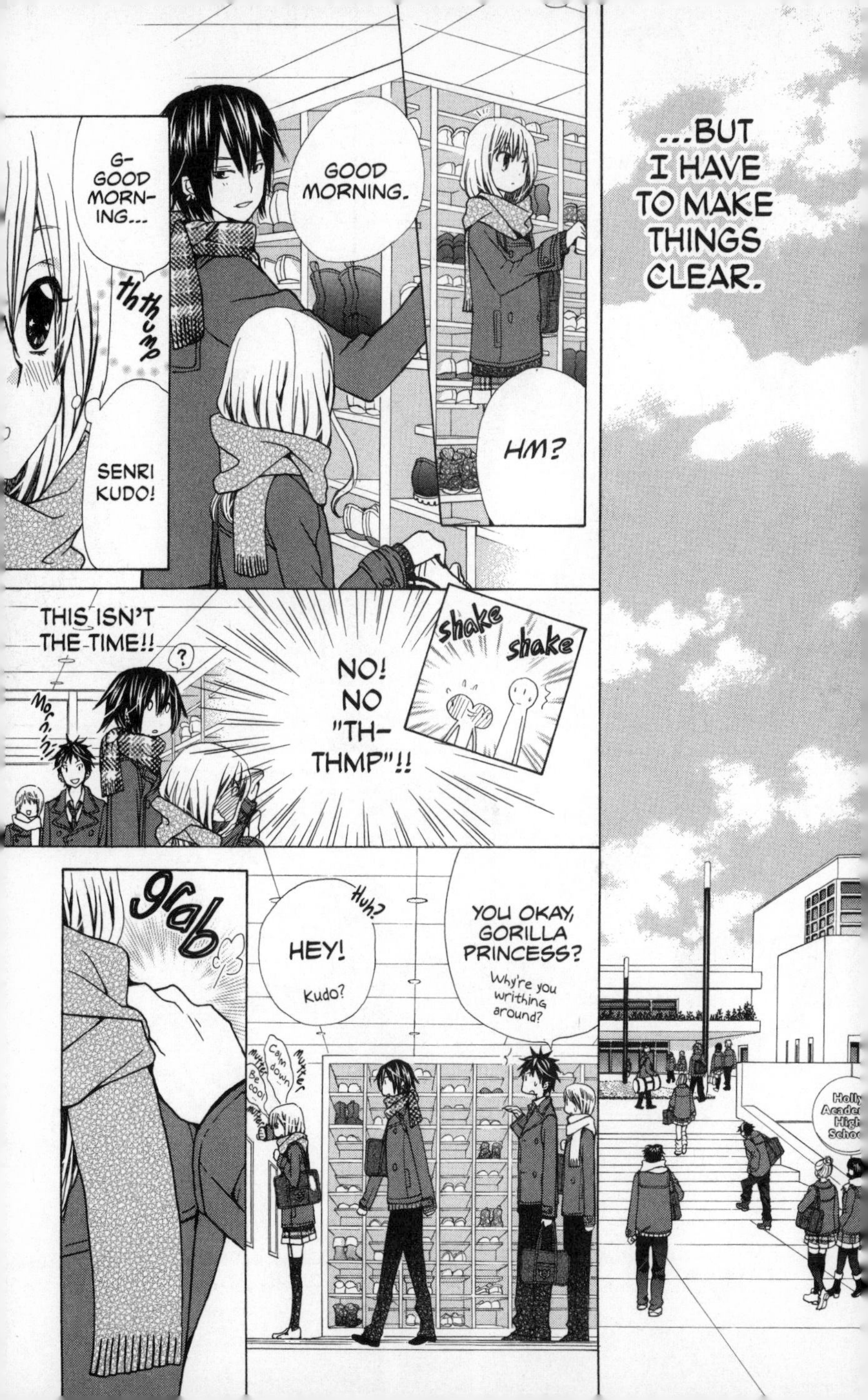
...BUT I HAVE TO MAKE THINGS CLEAR.
HM?
GOOD MORNING.
G-GOOD MORN-ING...
thth-ump
SENRI KUDO!
shake shake
NO! NO "TH-THMP"!!
THIS ISN'T THE TIME!!
?
Mornin'!
YOU OKAY, GORILLA PRINCESS?
Why're you writhing around?
Huh?
HEY!
Kudo?
mutter
Calm down...
mutter
Be cool...
mutter
grab

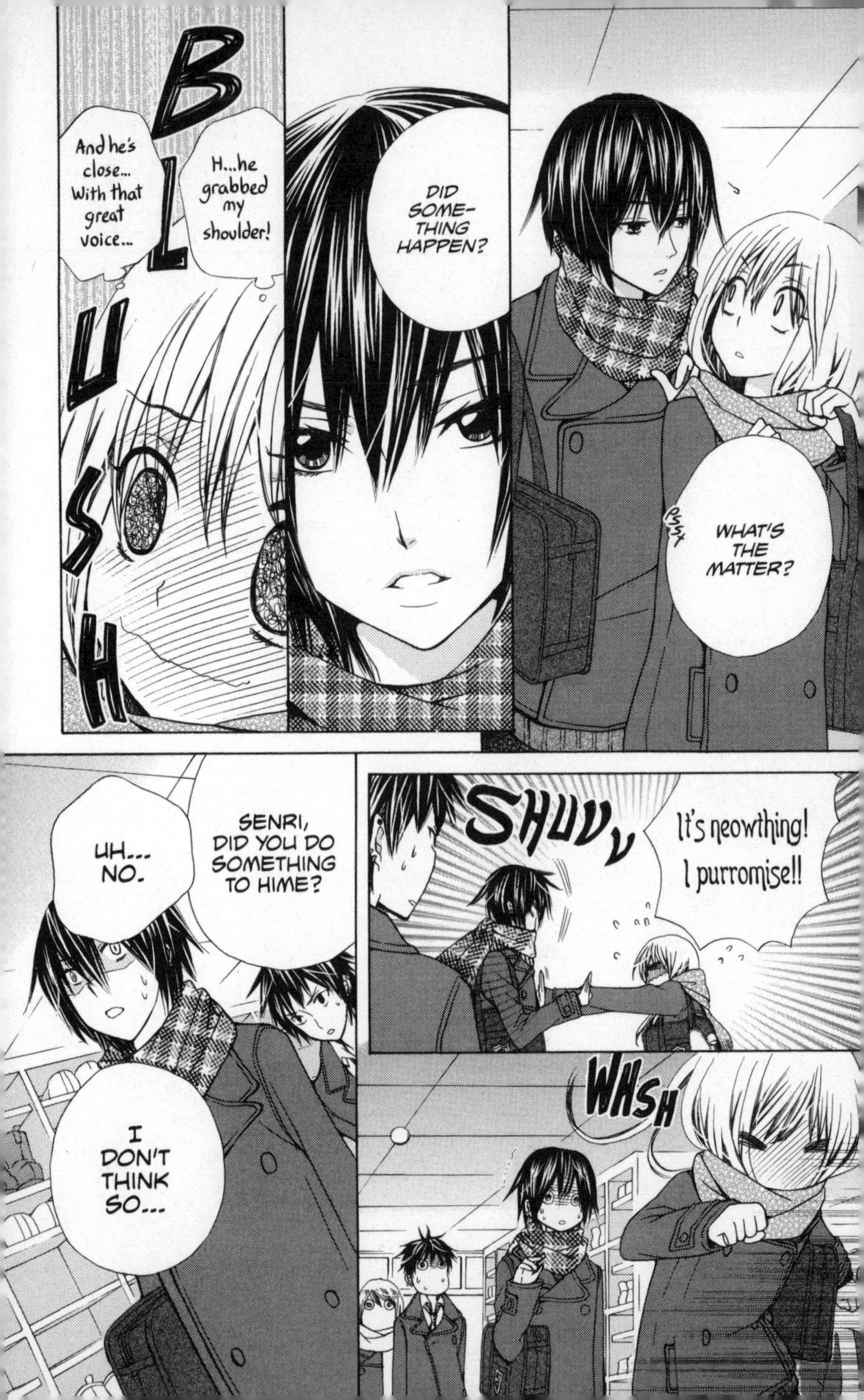
PSST
WHAT'S THE MATTER?
DID SOMETHING HAPPEN?
H...he grabbed my shoulder!
And he's close... With that great voice...
BLUSH
SHUVV
It's neowthing! I purromise!!
WHSH
SENRI, DID YOU DO SOMETHING TO HIME?
UH... NO.
I DON'T THINK SO...

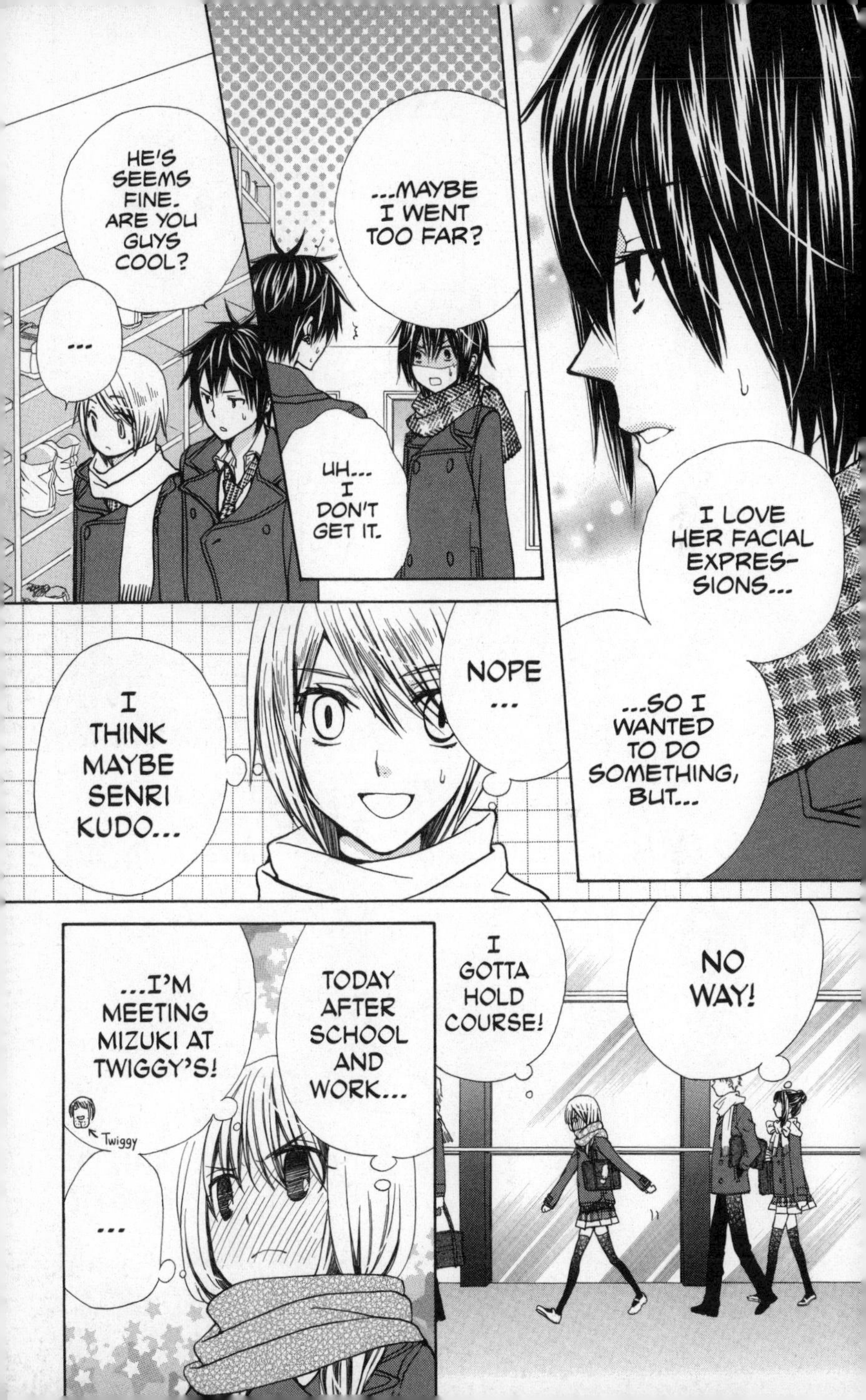
I LOVE HER FACIAL EXPRES-SIONS...
...SO I WANTED TO DO SOMETHING, BUT...
...MAYBE I WENT TOO FAR?
HE'S SEEMS FINE. ARE YOU GUYS COOL?
...
UH... I DON'T GET IT.
NOPE ...
I THINK MAYBE SENRI KUDO...
NO WAY!
I GOTTA HOLD COURSE!
TODAY AFTER SCHOOL AND WORK...
...I'M MEETING MIZUKI AT TWIGGY'S!
Twiggy
...

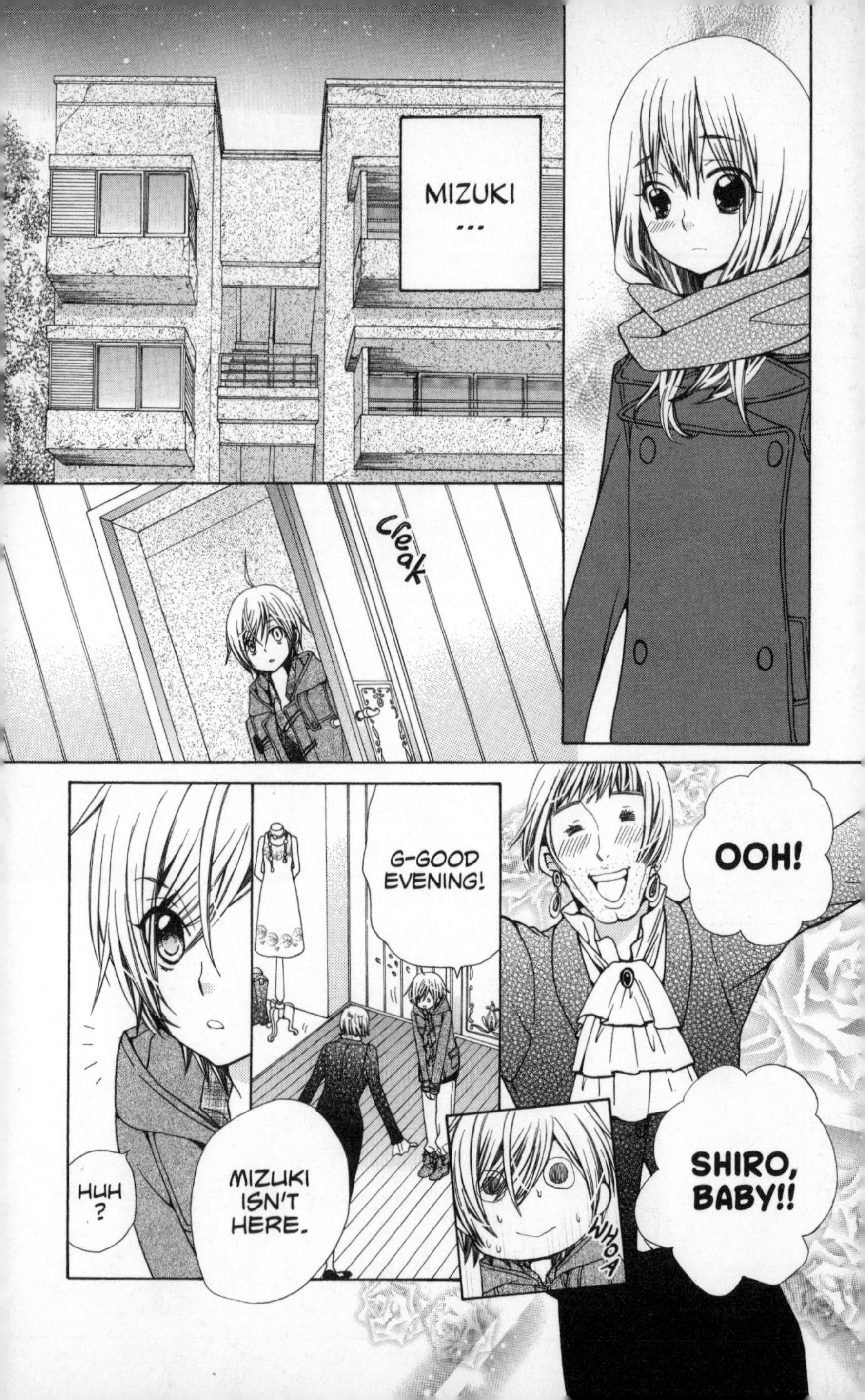
MIZUKI ...
Creak
OOH!
SHIRO, BABY!!
WHOA
G-GOOD EVENING!
MIZUKI ISN'T HERE.
HUH?

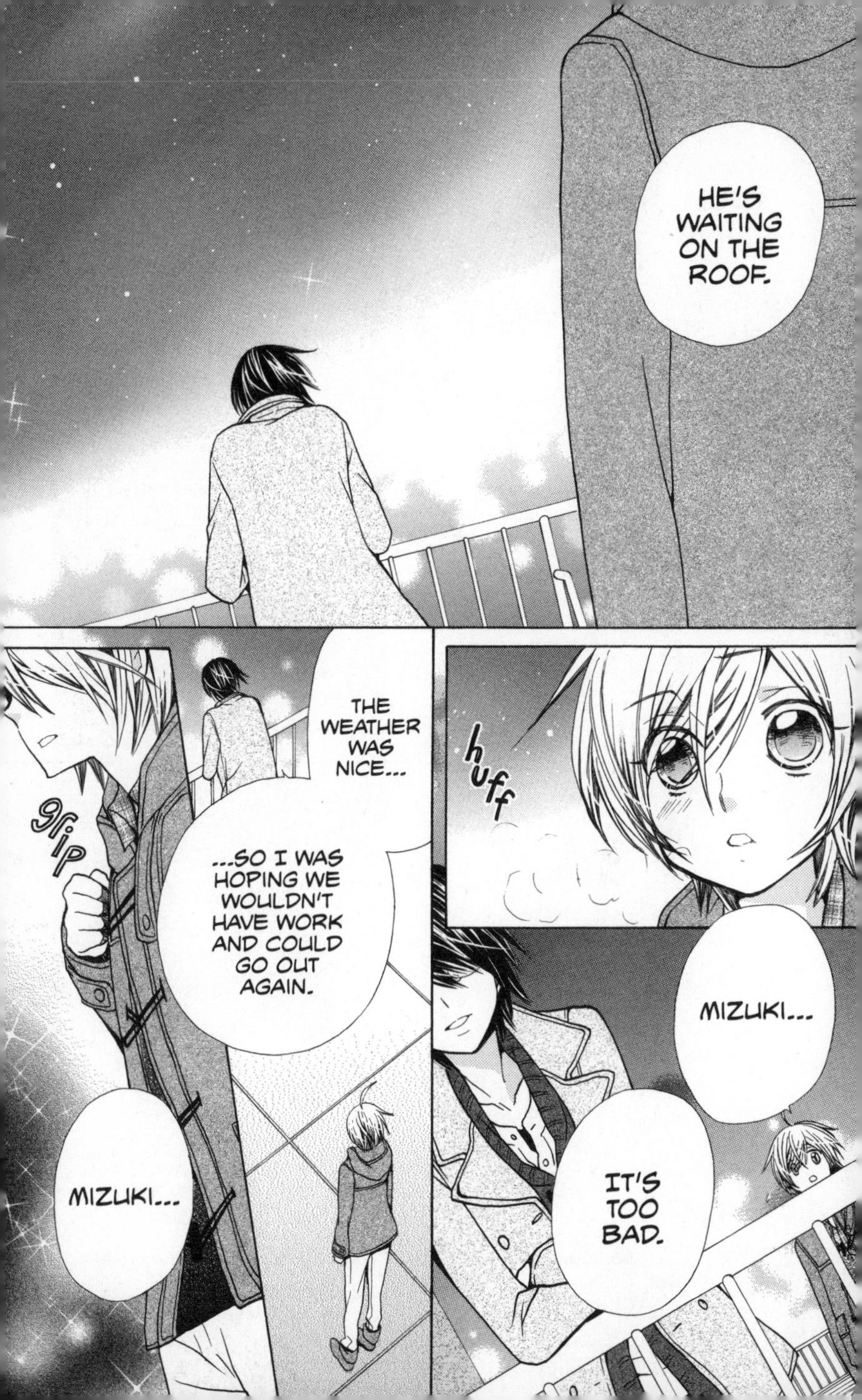
HE'S WAITING ON THE ROOF.
huff
MIZUKI...
IT'S TOO BAD.
THE WEATHER WAS NICE...
...SO I WAS HOPING WE WOULDN'T HAVE WORK AND COULD GO OUT AGAIN.
grip
MIZUKI...

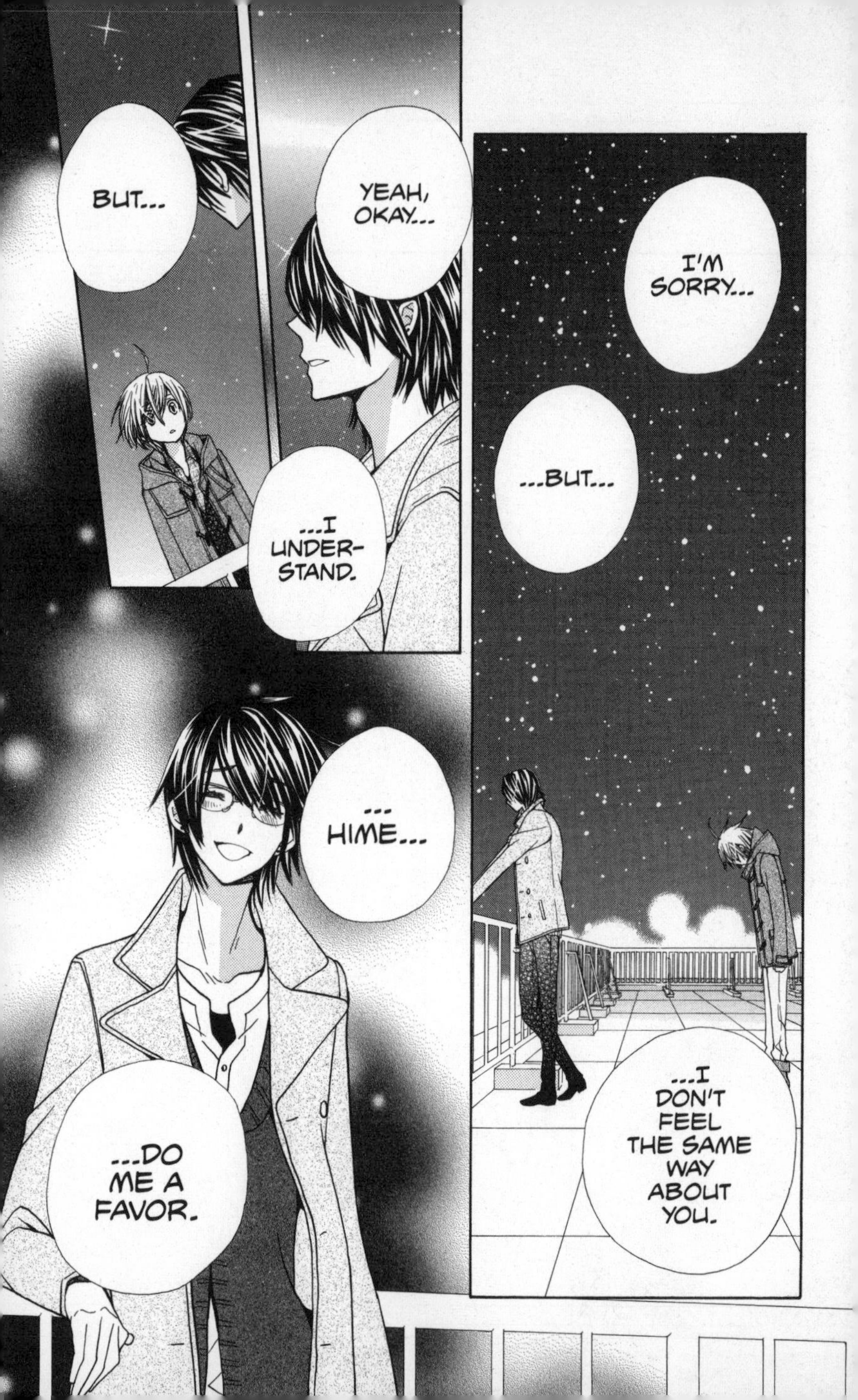
I'M SORRY...
...BUT...
...I DON'T FEEL THE SAME WAY ABOUT YOU.
YEAH, OKAY...
...I UNDERSTAND.
BUT...
...HIME...
...DO ME A FAVOR.

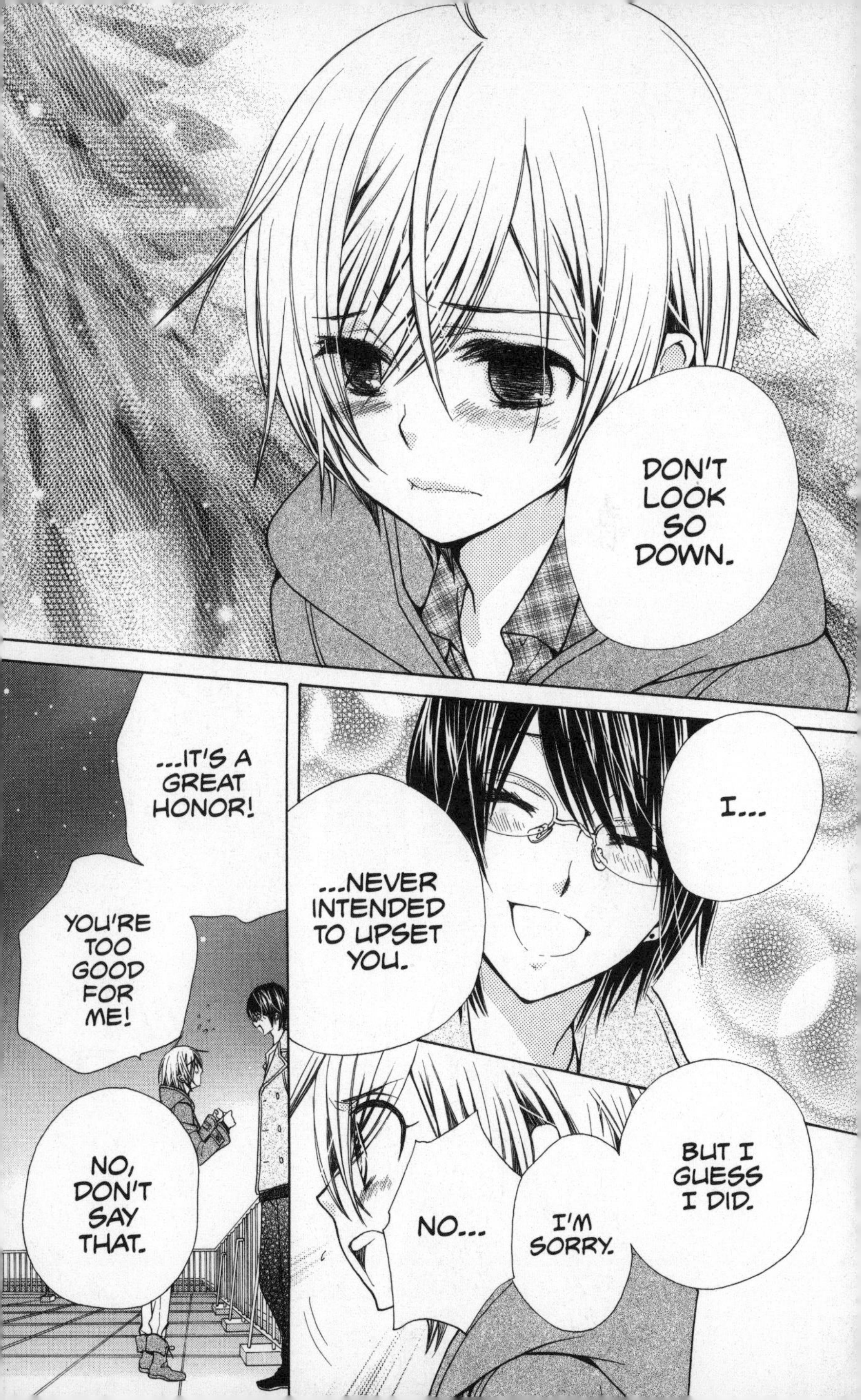
DON'T LOOK SO DOWN.
I...
...NEVER INTENDED TO UPSET YOU.
BUT I GUESS I DID.
I'M SORRY.
NO...
...IT'S A GREAT HONOR!
YOU'RE TOO GOOD FOR ME!
NO, DON'T SAY THAT.

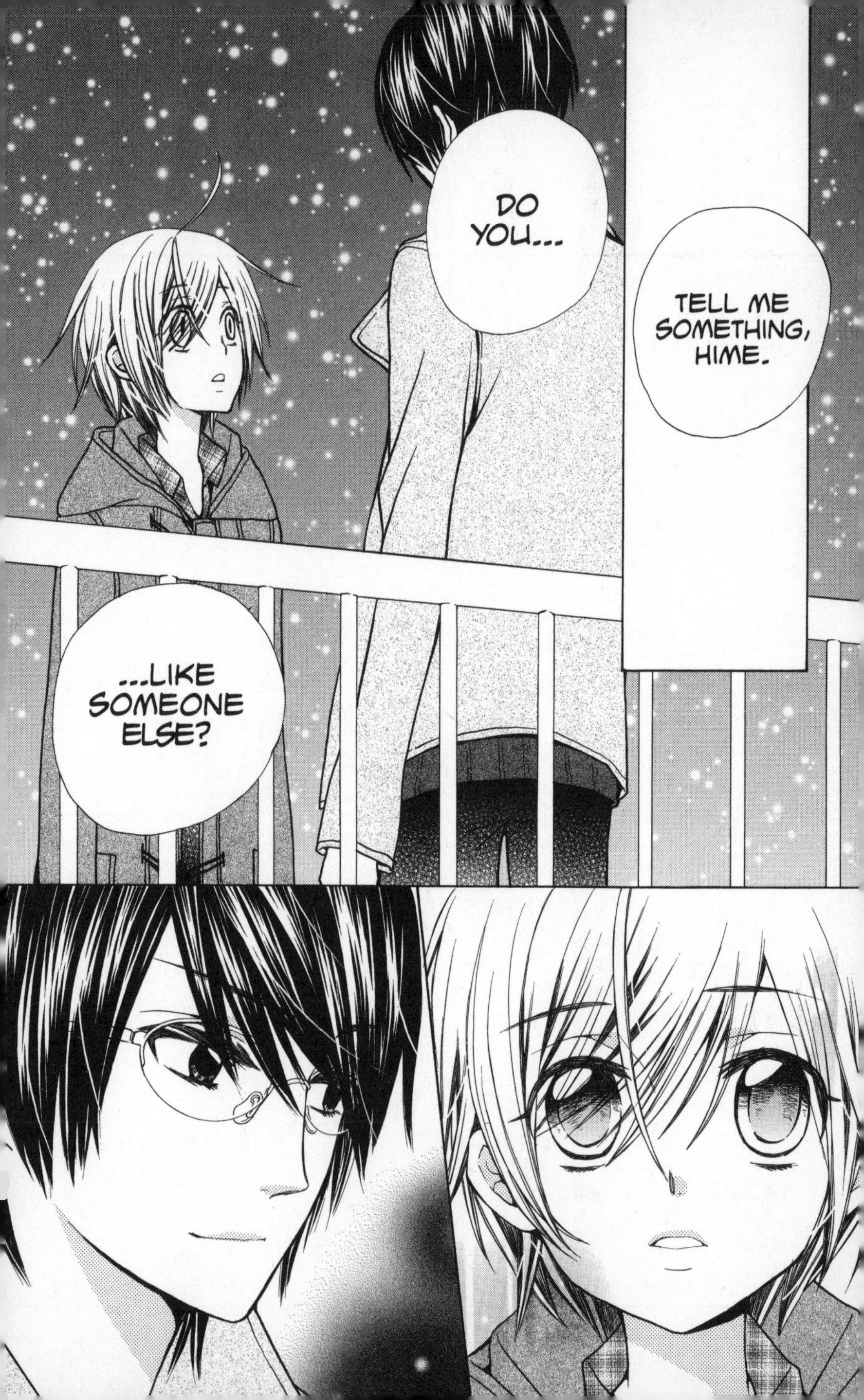
TELL ME SOMETHING, HIME.
DO YOU...
...LIKE SOMEONE ELSE?

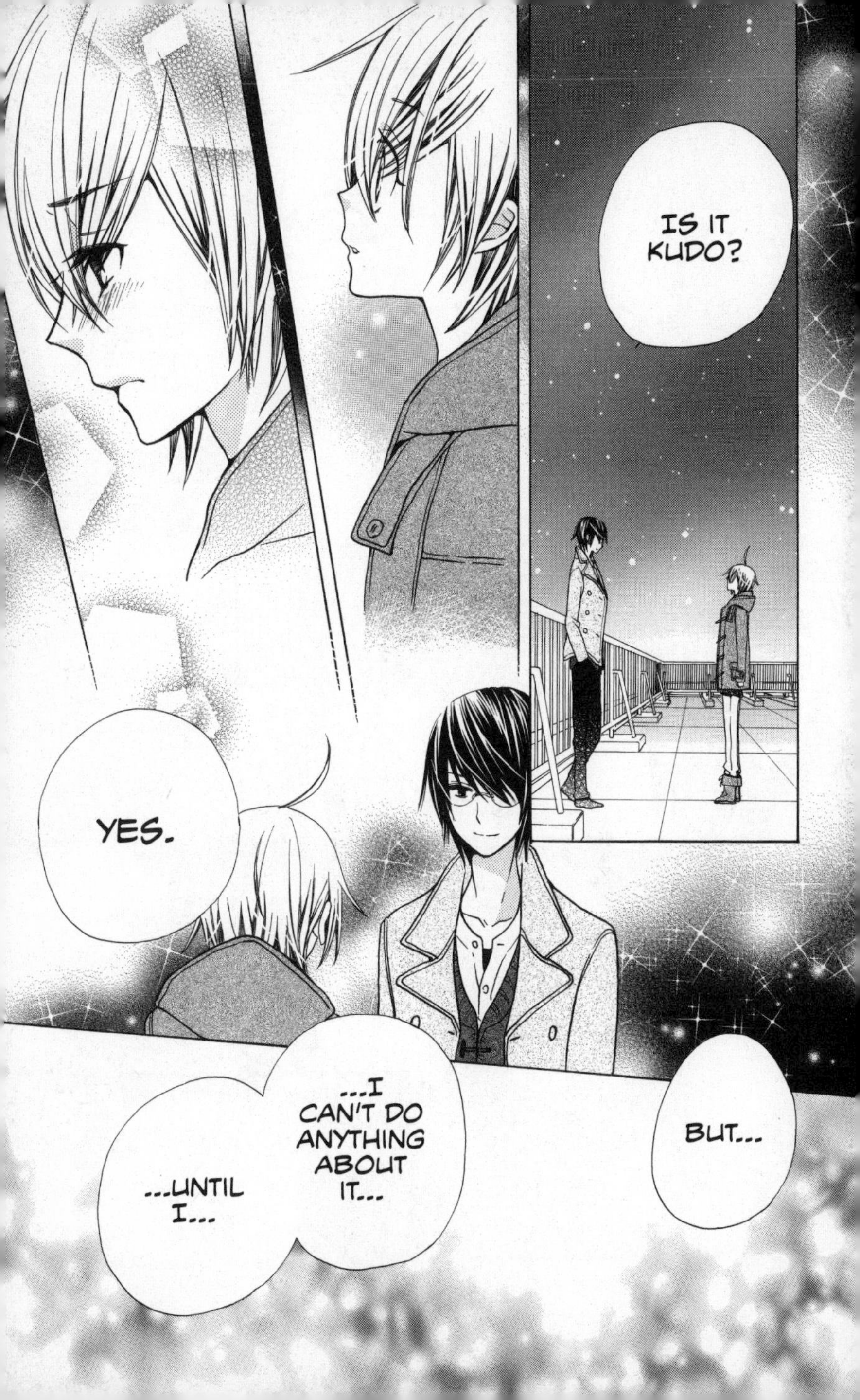
IS IT KUDO?
YES.
BUT...
...I CAN'T DO ANYTHING ABOUT IT...
...UNTIL I...

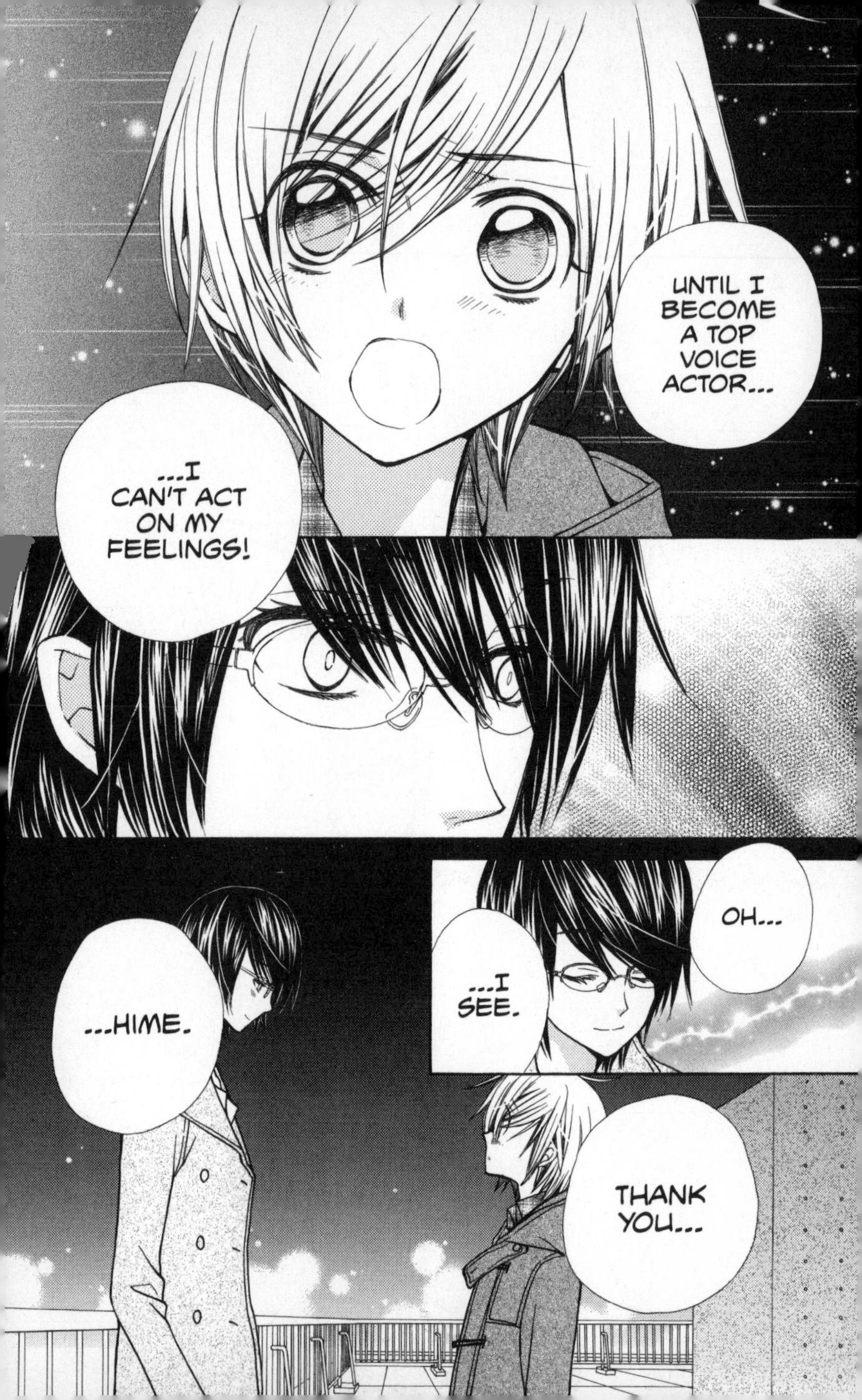
UNTIL I BECOME A TOP VOICE ACTOR...
...I CAN'T ACT ON MY FEELINGS!
OH...
...I SEE.
...HIME.
THANK YOU...

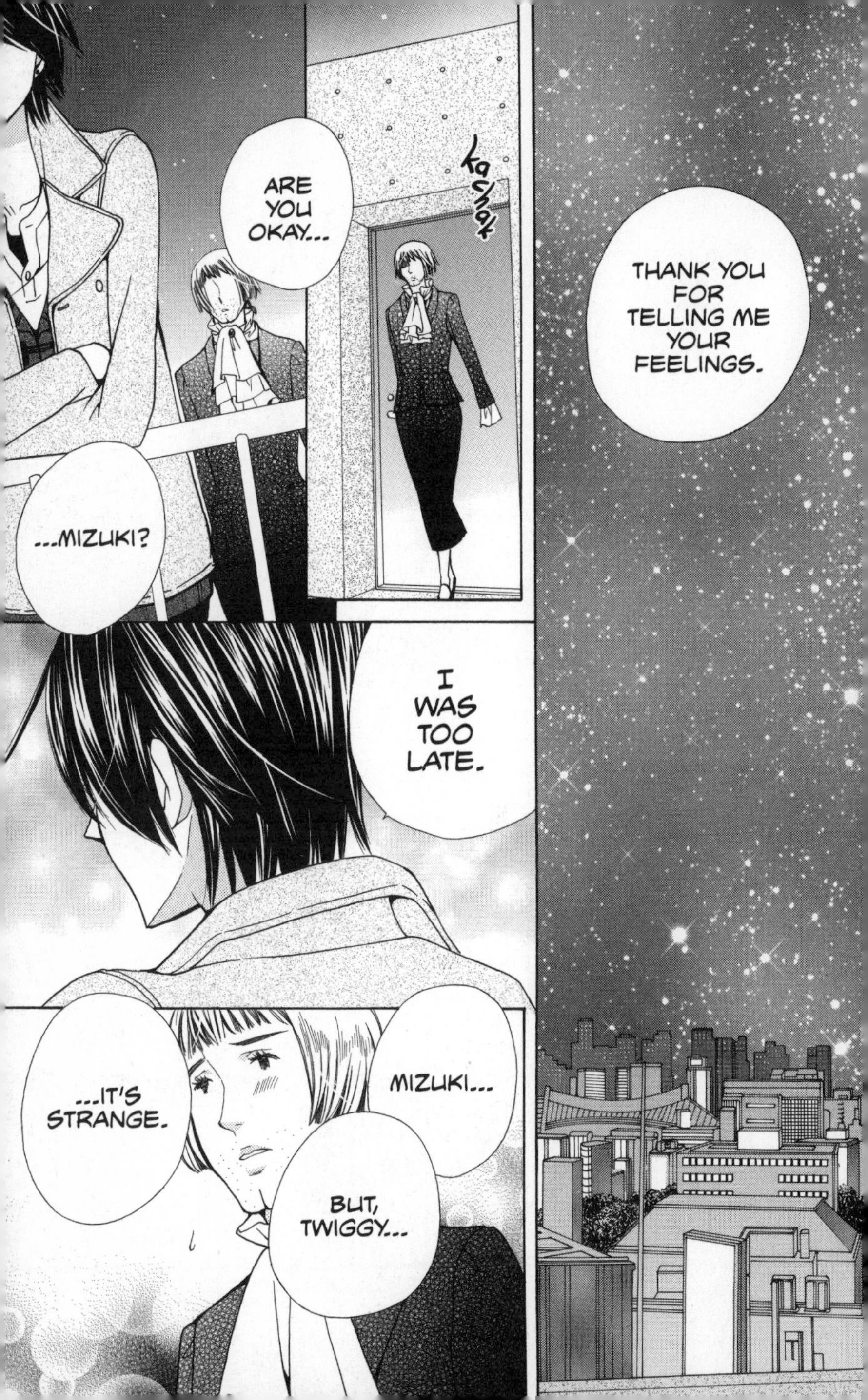
THANK YOU FOR TELLING ME YOUR FEELINGS.
kachak
ARE YOU OKAY...
...MIZUKI?
I WAS TOO LATE.
MIZUKI...
...IT'S STRANGE.
BUT, TWIGGY...

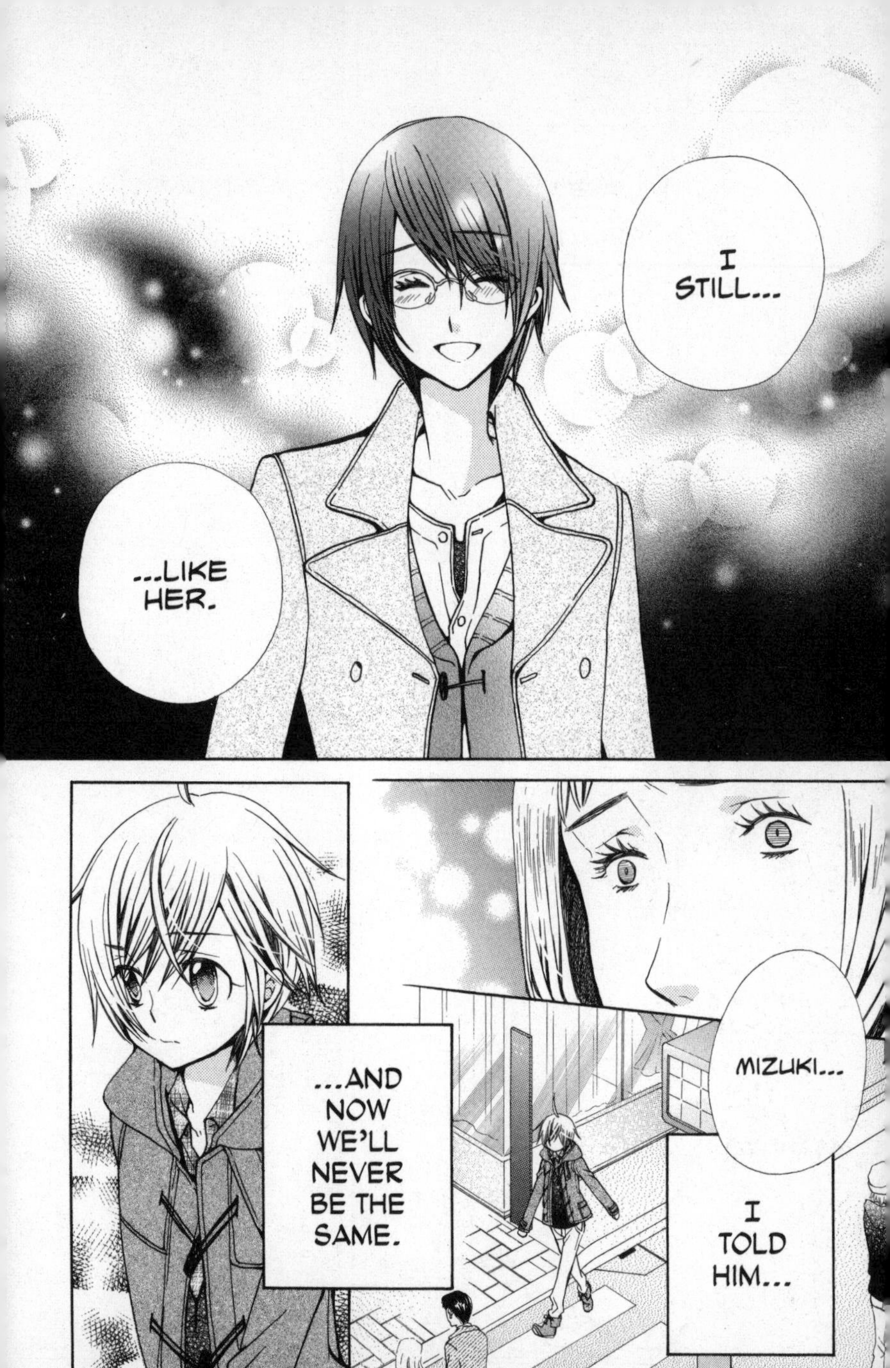
I STILL...
...LIKE HER.
MIZUKI...
I TOLD HIM...
...AND NOW WE'LL NEVER BE THE SAME.

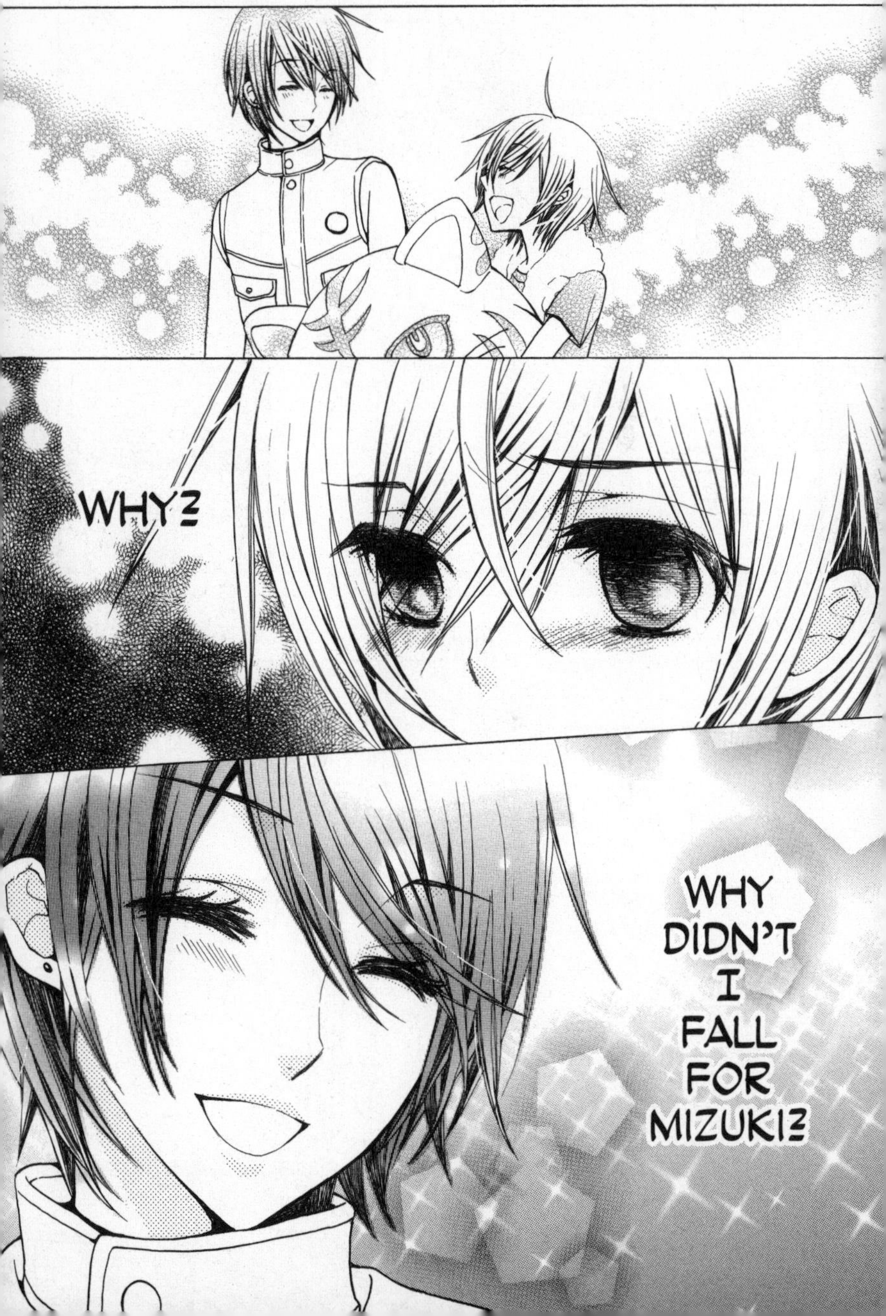
WHY?
WHY DIDN'T I FALL FOR MIZUKI?

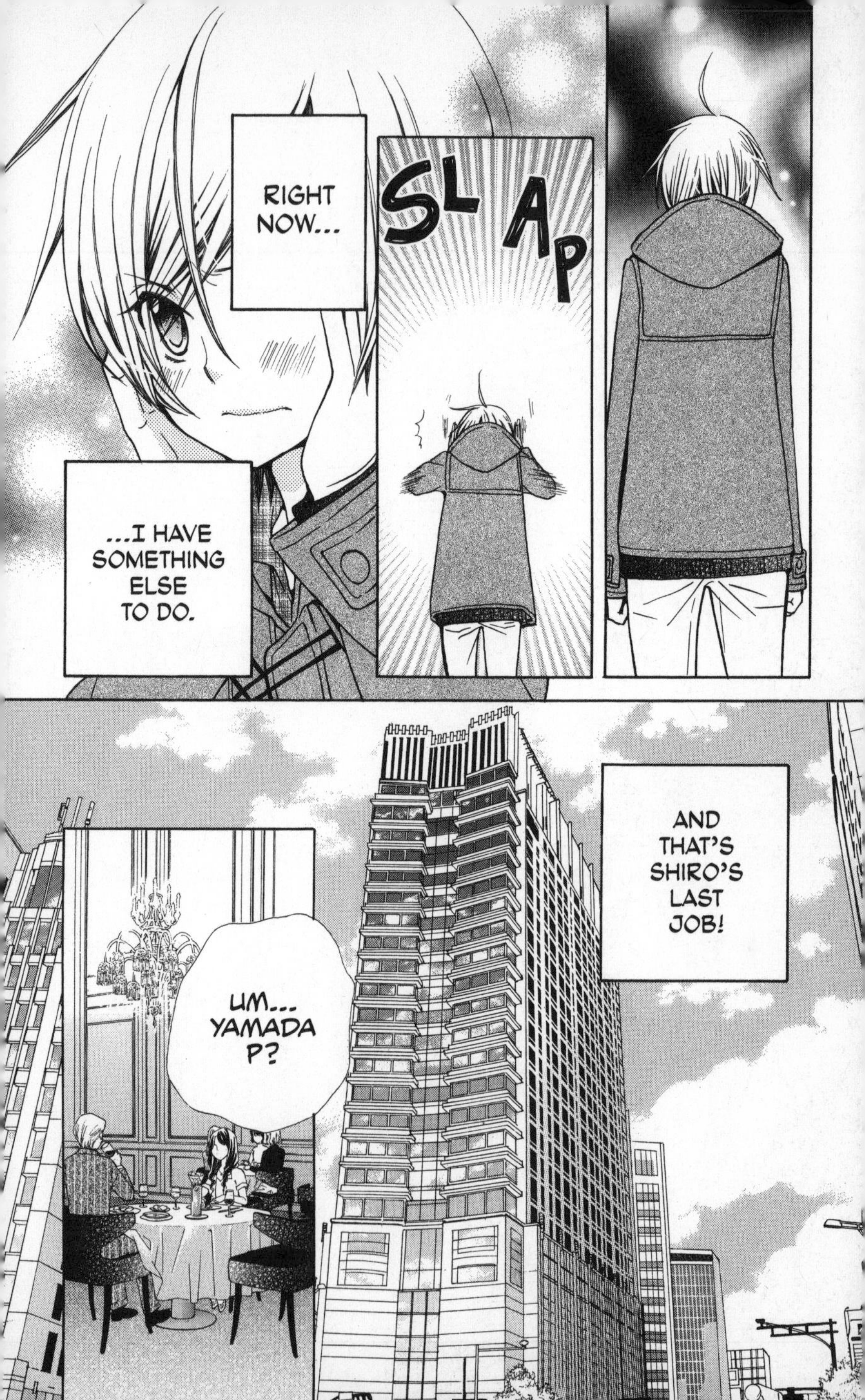
SLAP
RIGHT NOW...
...I HAVE SOMETHING ELSE TO DO.
AND THAT'S SHIRO'S LAST JOB!
UM... YAMADA P?

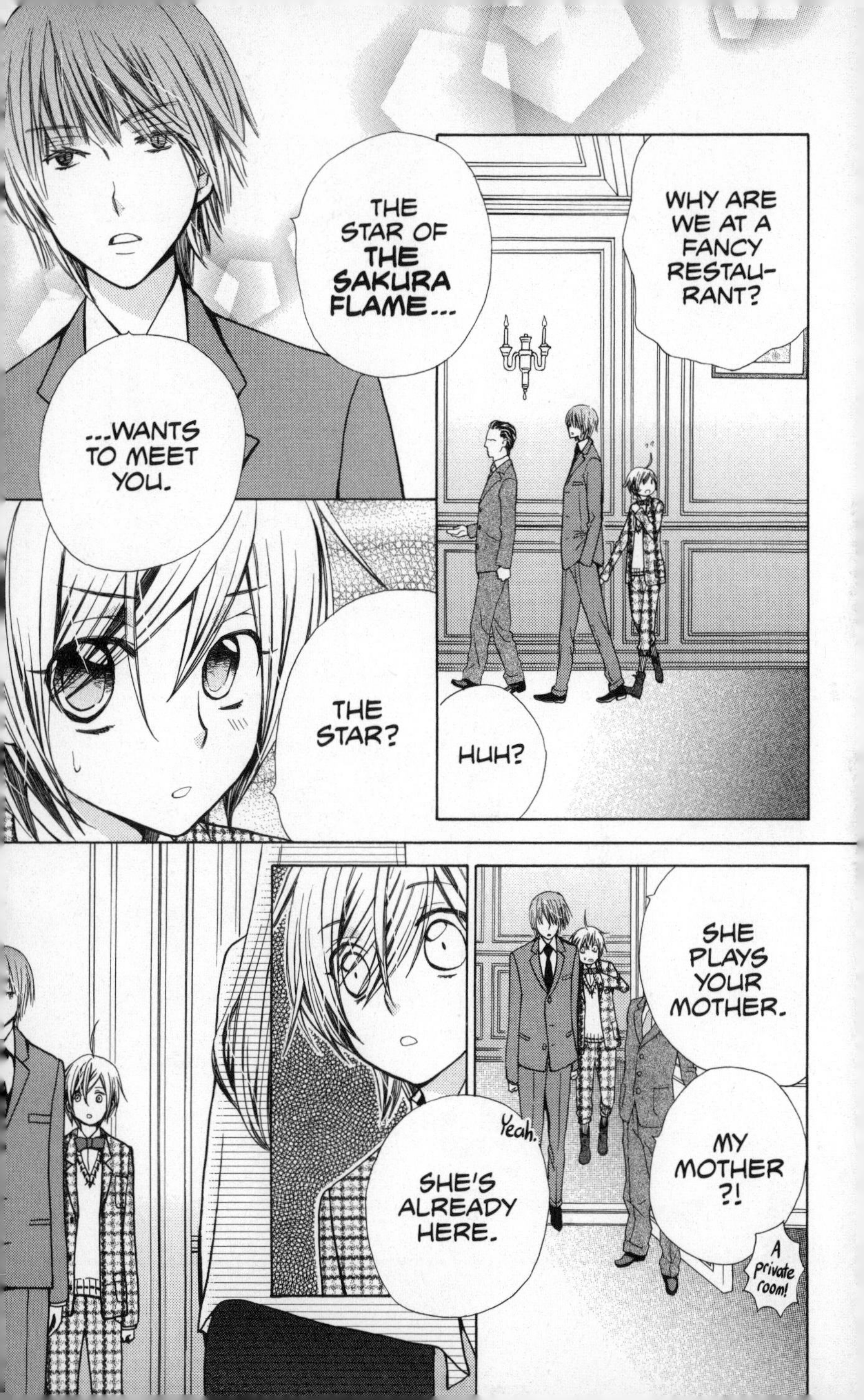
WHY ARE WE AT A FANCY RESTAURANT?
HUH?
THE STAR OF THE SAKURA FLAME...
...WANTS TO MEET YOU.
THE STAR?
SHE PLAYS YOUR MOTHER.
MY MOTHER?!
A private room!
Yeah.
SHE'S ALREADY HERE.

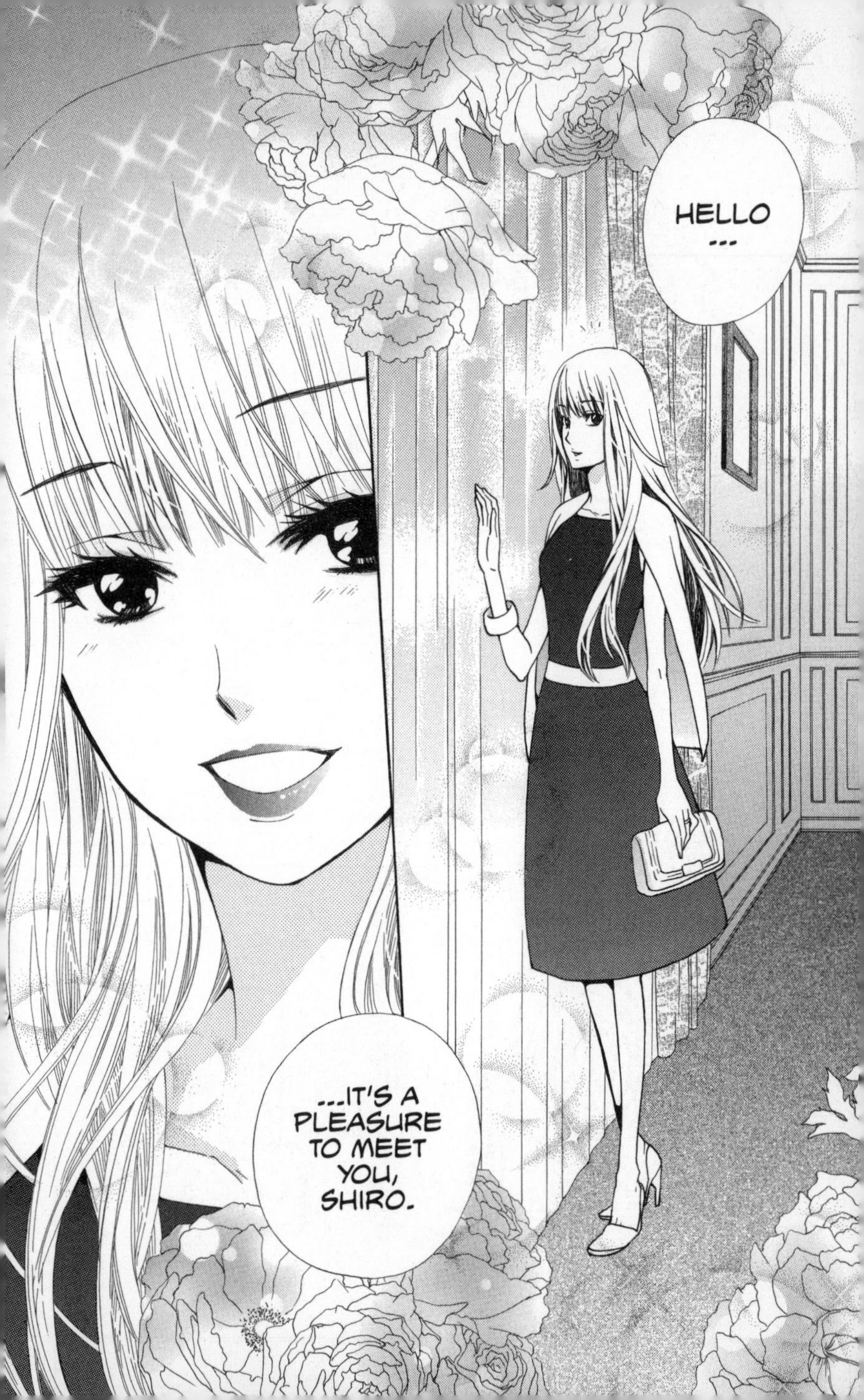
HELLO...
...IT'S A PLEASURE TO MEET YOU, SHIRO.

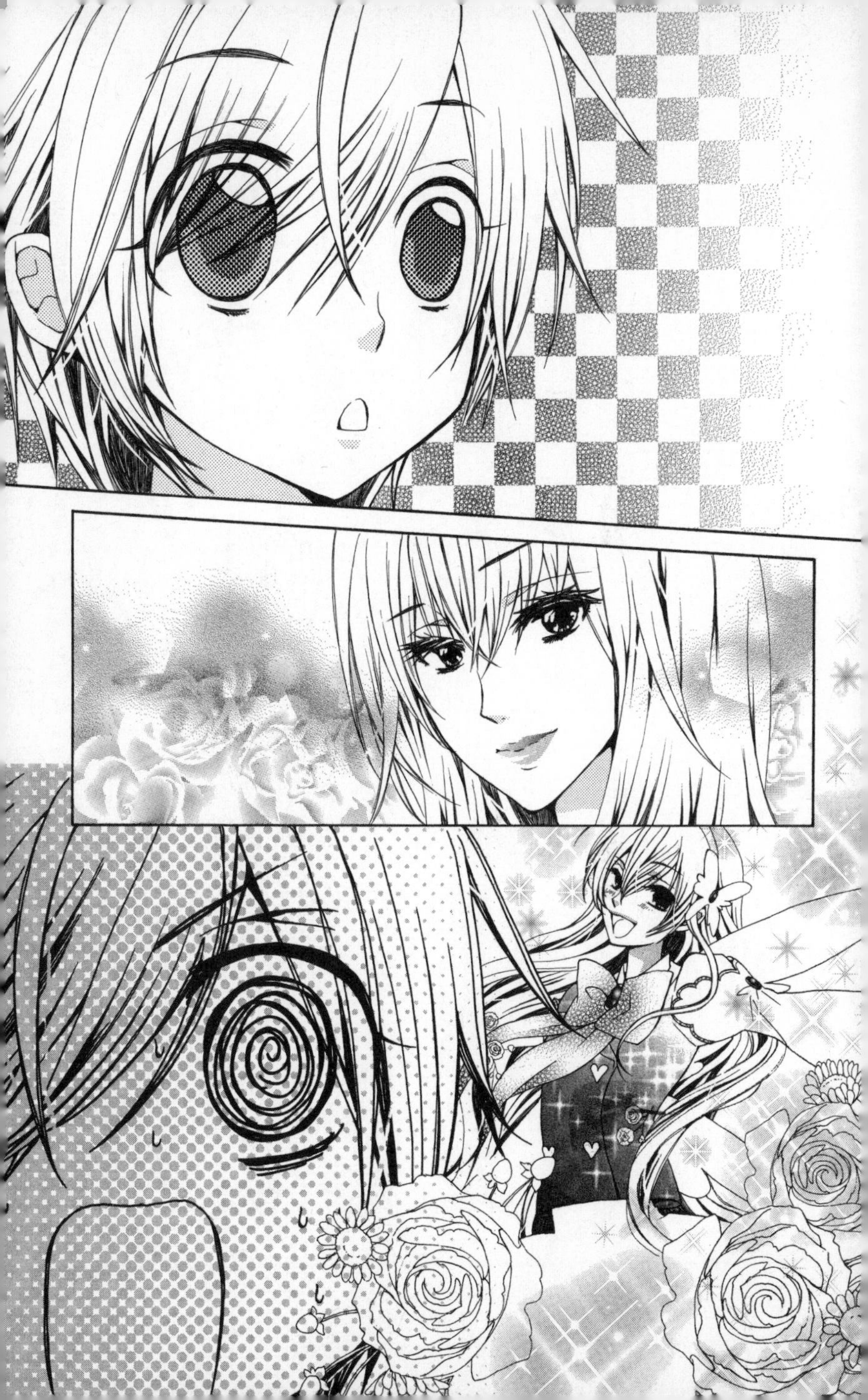

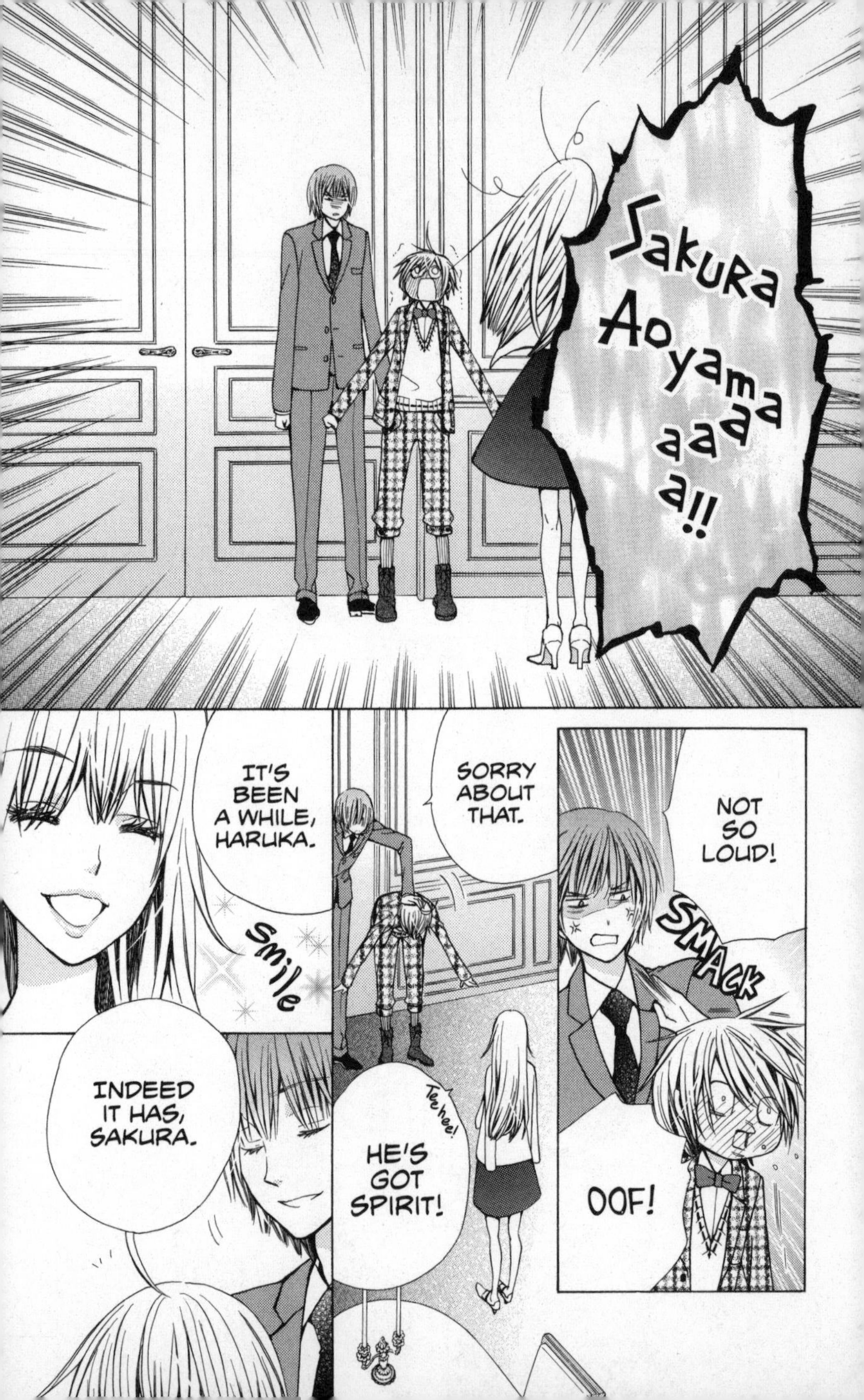
Sakura Aoyamaaaaa!!
NOT SO LOUD!
SMACK
OOF!
SORRY ABOUT THAT.
Teehee!
HE'S GOT SPIRIT!
IT'S BEEN A WHILE, HARUKA.
Smile
INDEED IT HAS, SAKURA.

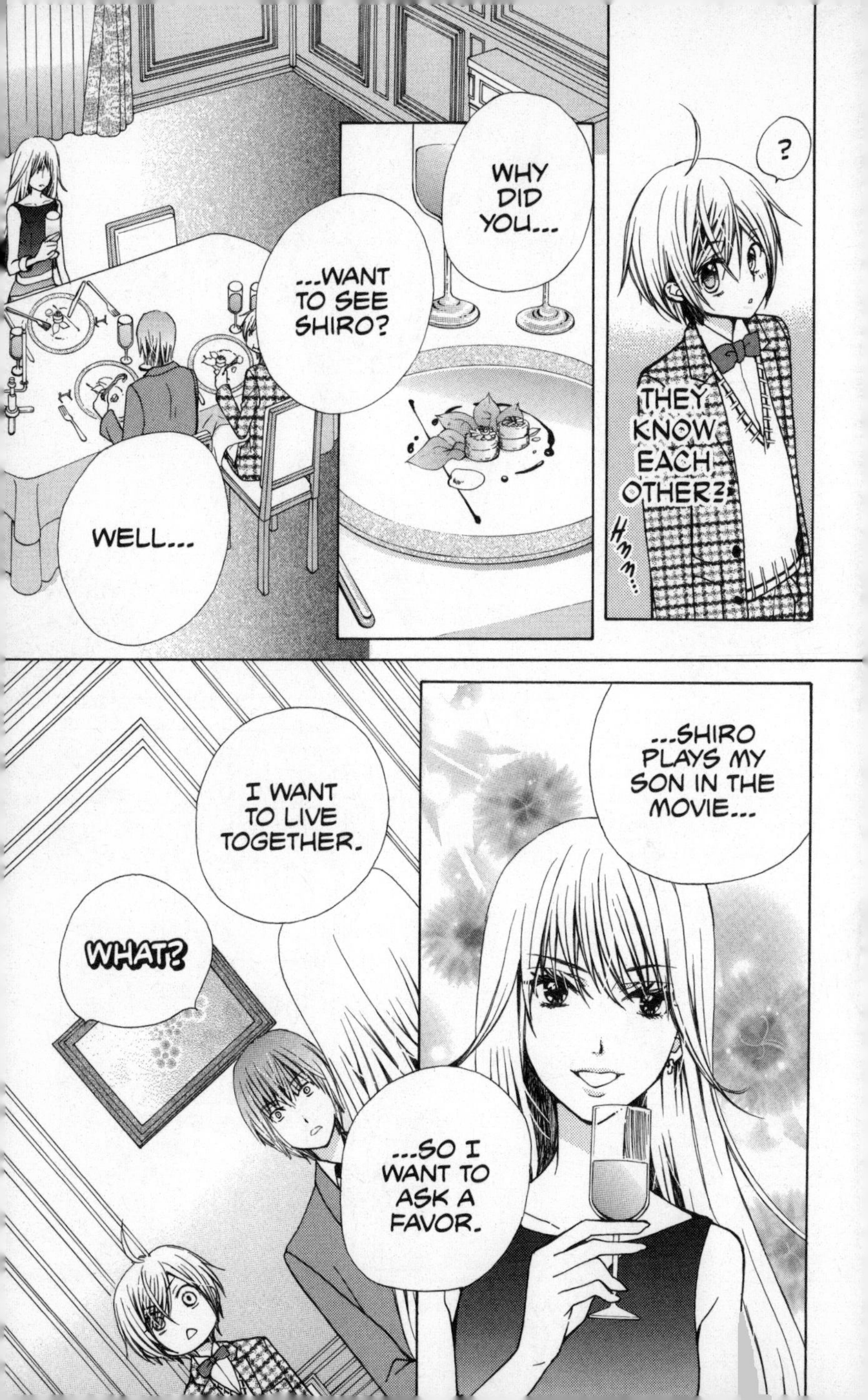
?
THEY KNOW EACH OTHER?
Hmm...
WHY DID YOU...
...WANT TO SEE SHIRO?
WELL...
...SHIRO PLAYS MY SON IN THE MOVIE...
...SO I WANT TO ASK A FAVOR.
I WANT TO LIVE TOGETHER.
WHAT?

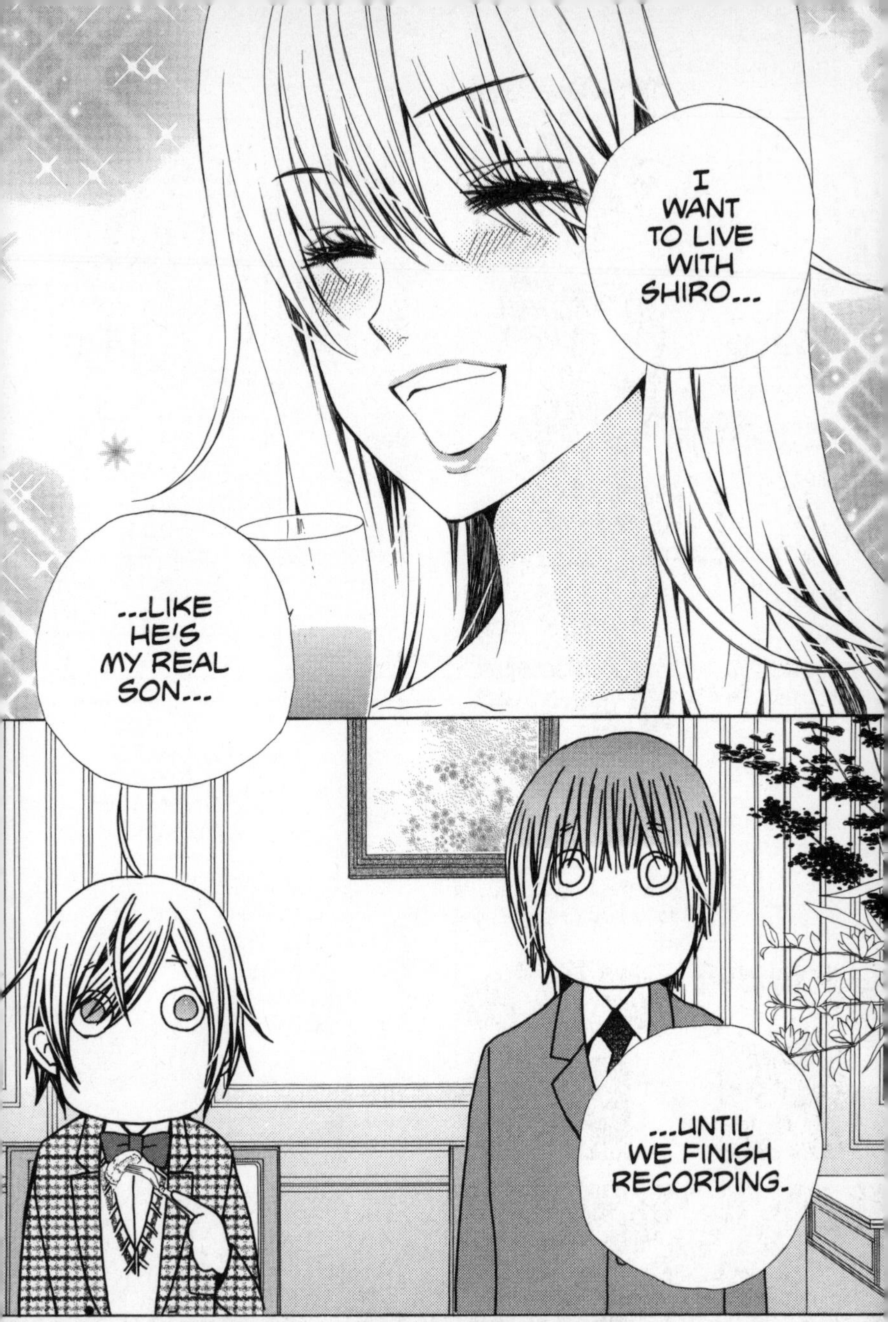
I WANT TO LIVE WITH SHIRO...
...LIKE HE'S MY REAL SON...
...UNTIL WE FINISH RECORDING.

Voice Over!: Seiyu Academy Volume 11 / End

♡ Sudden Bonus Materials Corner!! ♡

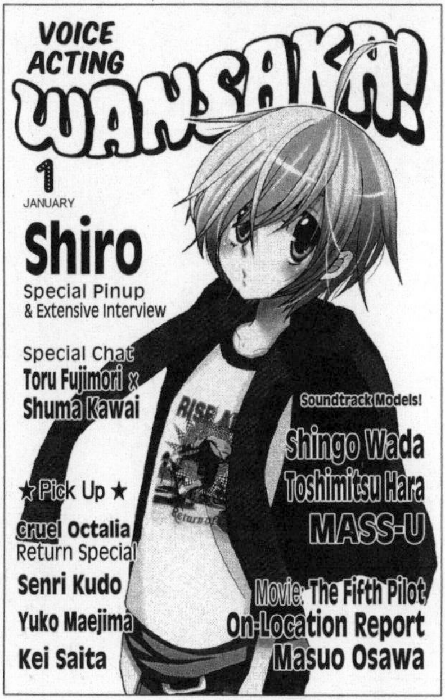
VOICE ACTING
WANSAKA!
1
JANUARY
Shiro
Special Pinup
& Extensive Interview
Special Chat
Toru Fujimori ×
Shuma Kawai
Soundtrack Models!
Shingo Wada
Toshimitsu Hara
MASS-U
★Pick Up★
Cruel Octalia
Return Special
Senri Kudo
Yuko Maejima
Kei Saita
Movie: The Fifth Pilot
On-Location Report
Masuo Osawa

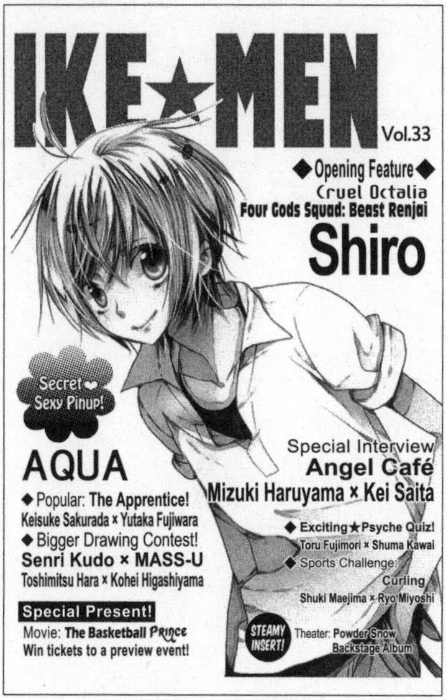
IKE★MEN
Vol.33
◆Opening Feature◆
Cruel Octalia
Four Gods Squad: Beast Renjai
Shiro
Secret♥
Sexy Pinup!
AQUA
Special Interview
Angel Café
Mizuki Haruyama × Kei Saita
◆Popular: The Apprentice!
Keisuke Sakurada × Yutaka Fujiwara
◆Bigger Drawing Contest!
Senri Kudo × MASS-U
Toshimitsu Hara × Kohei Higashiyama
◆Exciting★Psyche Quiz!
Toru Fujimori × Shuma Kawai
◆Sports Challenge:
Curling
Shuki Maejima × Ryo Miyoshi
Special Present!
Movie: The Basketball Prince
Win tickets to a preview event!
STEAMY INSERT!
Theater: Powder Snow
Backstage Album

↑ These are the magazines with Shiro on the cover that appear in the manga. My assistants I-san and M-yama-san made them! They're really detailed!! Wow!

This is the T-shirt AQUA wore at the concert. I-san designed it! Cool!! ↓

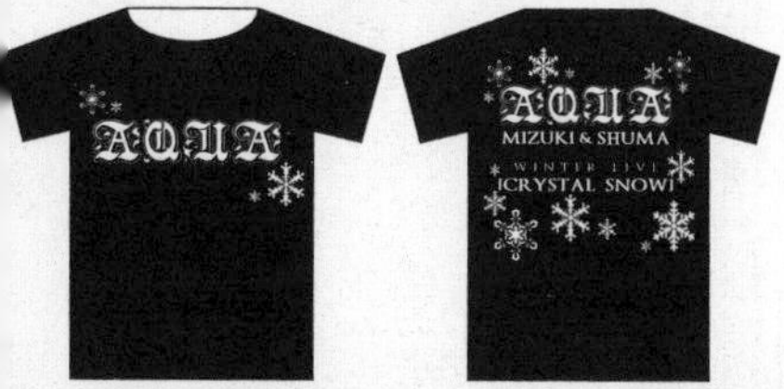
AQUA
AQUA
MIZUKI & SHUMA
WINTER LIVE
!CRYSTAL SNOW!

This is the T-shirt for the theater group Senri's parents were in. I-san again! ↓

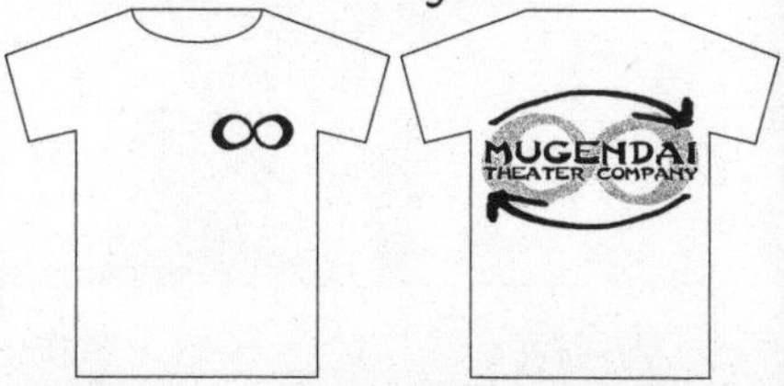
∞
MUGENDAI
THEATER COMPANY

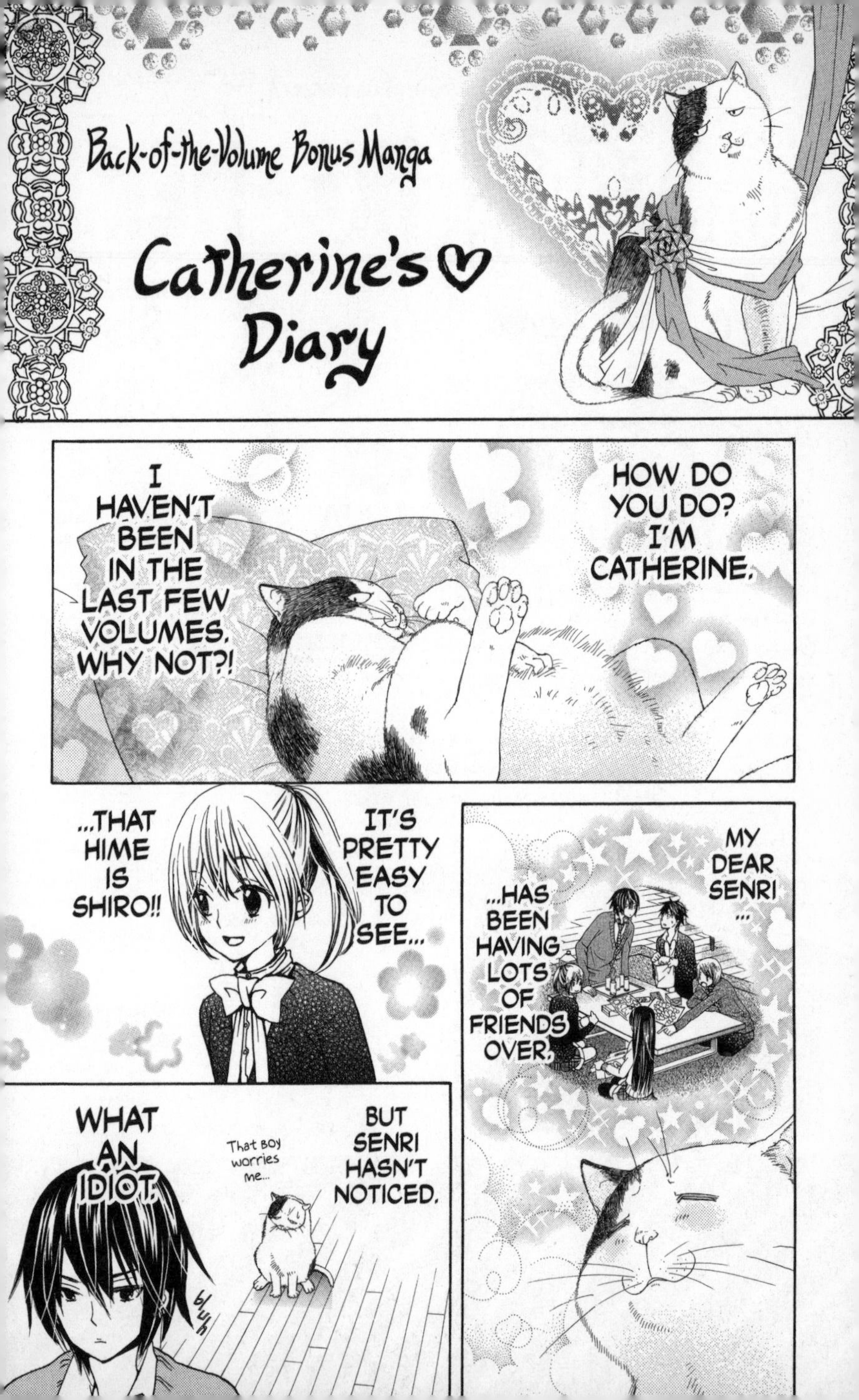

Back-of-the-Volume Bonus Manga
Catherine's ♡ Diary
HOW DO YOU DO? I'M CATHERINE.
I HAVEN'T BEEN IN THE LAST FEW VOLUMES. WHY NOT?!
MY DEAR SENRI ...
...HAS BEEN HAVING LOTS OF FRIENDS OVER.
IT'S PRETTY EASY TO SEE...
...THAT HIME IS SHIRO!!
BUT SENRI HASN'T NOTICED.
That boy worries me...
WHAT AN IDIOT.
blush

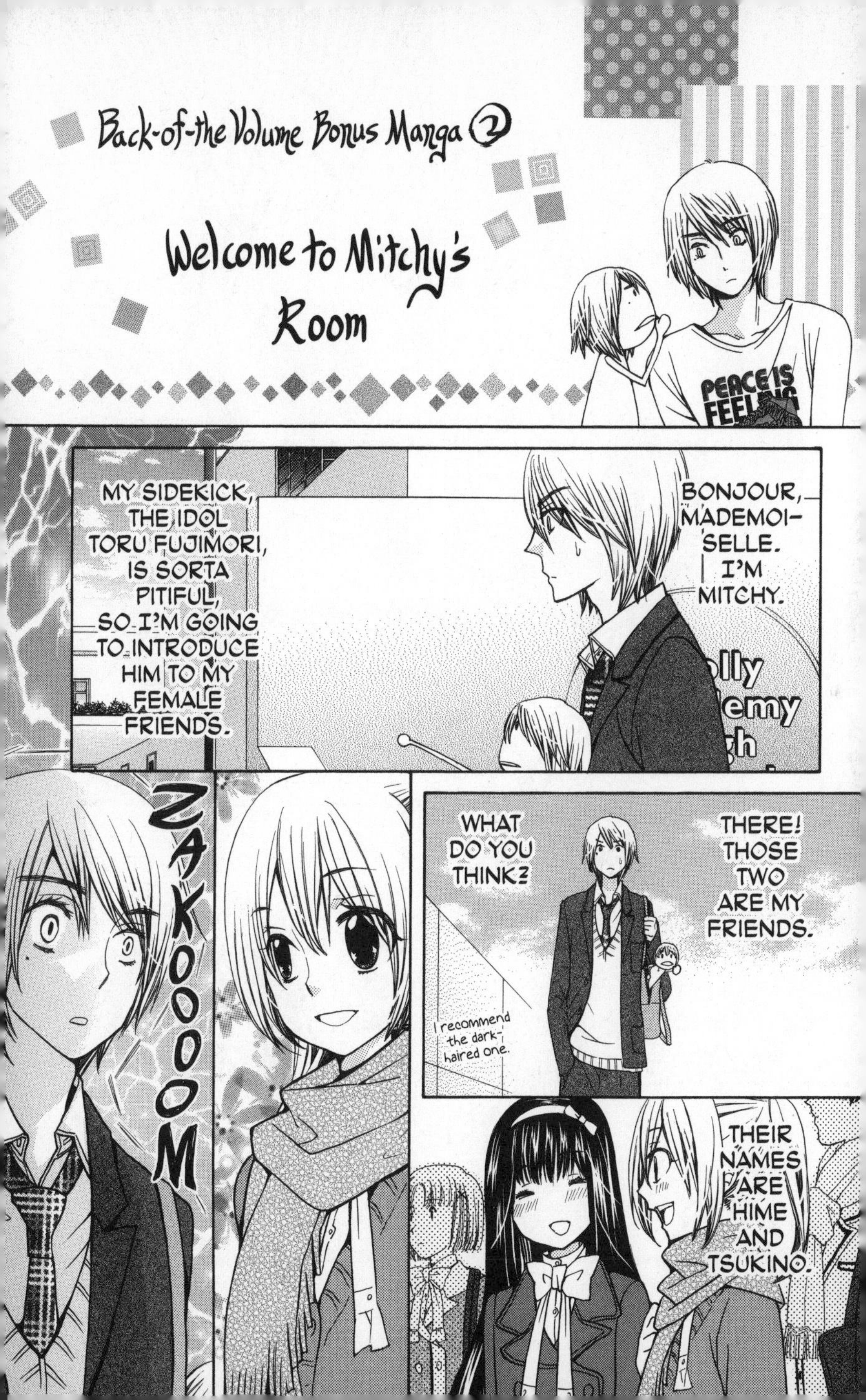
Back-of-the Volume Bonus Manga 2
Welcome to Mitchy's Room
PEACE IS FEELING
BONJOUR, MADEMOI-SELLE. I'M MITCHY.
MY SIDEKICK, THE IDOL TORU FUJIMORI, IS SORTA PITIFUL, SO I'M GOING TO INTRODUCE HIM TO MY FEMALE FRIENDS.
THERE! THOSE TWO ARE MY FRIENDS.
WHAT DO YOU THINK?
I recommend the dark-haired one.
THEIR NAMES ARE HIME AND TSUKINO.
ZAKOOOOOM

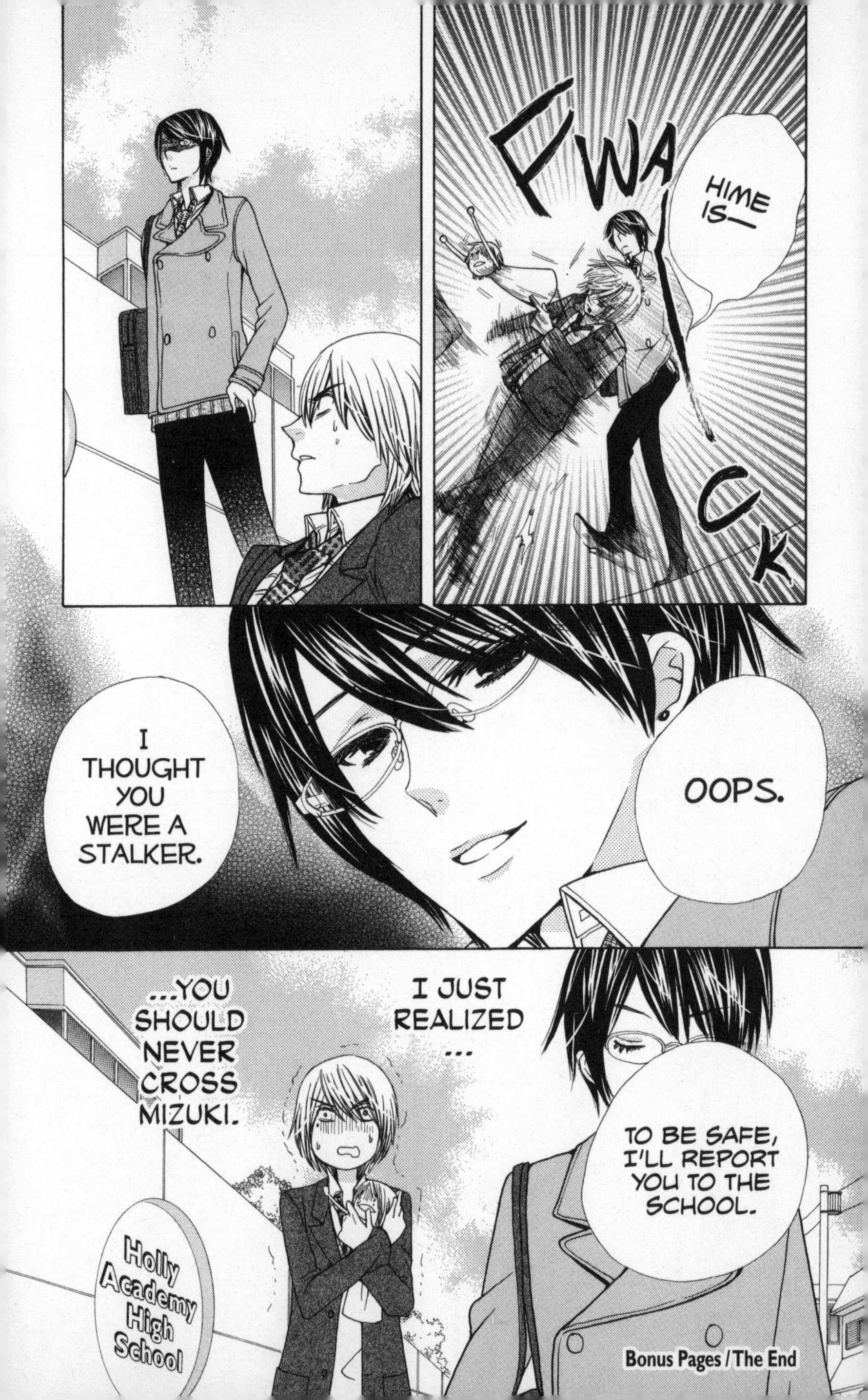
HIME IS—
FWA
CK
OOPS.
I THOUGHT YOU WERE A STALKER.
TO BE SAFE, I'LL REPORT YOU TO THE SCHOOL.
I JUST REALIZED...
...YOU SHOULD NEVER CROSS MIZUKI.
Holly Academy High School
Bonus Pages / The End

Maki Minami is from Saitama Prefecture in Japan. She debuted in 2001 with *Kanata no Ao* (Faraway Blue). Her other works include *Kimi wa Girlfriend* (You're My Girlfriend), *Mainichi ga Takaramono* (Every Day Is a Treasure), *Yuki Atataka* (Warm Winter) and *S•A*, which was published in English by VIZ Media.

# VOICE OVER! SEIYU ACADEMY
## VOL. 11
### Shojo Beat Edition

STORY AND ART BY
## MAKI MINAMI

Special Thanks
81produce
Tokyo Animator College
Tokyo Animation College

English Translation & Adaptation/John Werry
Touch-up Art & Lettering/Sabrina Heep
Design/Yukiko Whitley
Editor/Pancha Diaz



Printed in the U.S.A.

Published by VIZ Media, LLC
P.O. Box 77010
San Francisco, CA 94107

10 9 8 7 6 5 4 3 2 1
First printing, June 2015

www.viz.com
www.shojobeat.com